Android Application Development Cookbook

Second Edition

Over 100 recipes to help you solve the most common problems faced by Android Developers today

Rick Boyer

Kyle Mew

[PACKT] open source*
PUBLISHING   community experience distilled

BIRMINGHAM - MUMBAI

Android Application Development Cookbook
Second Edition

Copyright © 2016 Packt Publishing

All rights reserved. No part of this book may be reproduced, stored in a retrieval system, or transmitted in any form or by any means, without the prior written permission of the publisher, except in the case of brief quotations embedded in critical articles or reviews.

Every effort has been made in the preparation of this book to ensure the accuracy of the information presented. However, the information contained in this book is sold without warranty, either express or implied. Neither the authors, nor Packt Publishing, and its dealers and distributors will be held liable for any damages caused or alleged to be caused directly or indirectly by this book.

Packt Publishing has endeavored to provide trademark information about all of the companies and products mentioned in this book by the appropriate use of capitals. However, Packt Publishing cannot guarantee the accuracy of this information.

First published: March 2016

Production reference: 1220316

Published by Packt Publishing Ltd.
Livery Place
35 Livery Street
Birmingham B3 2PB, UK.

ISBN 978-1-78588-619-5

www.packtpub.com

Cover image by Karen Ann P. Boyer (karen@eboyer.net)

Credits

Authors
Rick Boyer
Kyle Mew

Reviewer
Emil Atanasov

Commissioning Editor
Edward Gordon

Content Development Editor
Parshva Sheth

Technical Editor
Menza Mathew

Copy Editors
Joanna McMahon
Merilyn Pereira

Project Coordinator
Nikhil Nair

Proofreader
Safis Editing

Indexer
Tejal Daruwale Soni

Production Coordinator
Aparna Bhagat

Cover Work
Aparna Bhagat

Disclaimer

The author is committed to updating the book, feel free to check out his site for updates to Android N.

About the Authors

Rick Boyer is a senior software engineer with over 20 years of experience, including desktop, web, and mobile development. His first PDA ignited a passion for mobile development, which has extended to Windows CE, Windows Phone, and now Android. In 2011, he left the corporate world to start his own consulting business, NightSky Development. He now focuses exclusively on Android and provides consulting and development for start-ups and small businesses. Feel free to contact him through his page, www.eBoyer.Net.

> I'd like to start by thanking Nadeem, the acquisition editor, for bringing me in to this project! I also want to thank Parshva, the content editor, for his kind words and support while writing these 15 chapters!
>
> Thanks to the friendly staff at my local Starbucks in Starmall, just outside Manila. If I wasn't writing code samples in my office, I was working on chapters at Starbucks. I was always greeted with a smile and questions on how the book was progressing.
>
> A special thanks to Niron for stepping up to the challenge of making the Android coffee design, used in the cover photo, and Leigh, the manager, for indulging us while we took pictures of our coffee.

Kyle Mew has been programming since the early eighties and has written for several technology websites. He has also written three radio plays and two other books on Android development.

About the Reviewer

Emil Atanasov is an IT consultant with broad experience in mobile technologies. He has been exploring the field of mobile development since 2006.

Emil has an MSc degree in media informatics from RWTH Aachen University, Germany, and an MSc in computer science from Sofia University, St. Kliment Ohridski, Bulgaria. He has worked for several huge USA-based companies and has been a freelancer for several years. Emil has experience in software design and development. He was involved in the process of redesigning, improving, and creating a number of mobile apps. Currently, he is focused on the rapidly growing mobile sector and manages a great team of developers that provide software solutions to clients around the world.

As an Android team leader and project manager, Emil led a team that developed a part of the Nook Color firmware, an e-magazine/e-book, which supports the proprietary Barnes & Nobel and some other e-book formats.

He is one of the people behind reviewing *Getting Started with Flurry Analytics*, *Packt Publishing*. He also contributed largely to *Objective C Memory Management*, *Packt Publishing*.

> I want to thank my family and friends for being so cool. Thank you for supporting me even though I'm such a bizarre geeky person, who spends most of his time in the digital world. Thank you, guys!

www.PacktPub.com

eBooks, discount offers, and more

Did you know that Packt offers eBook versions of every book published, with PDF and ePub files available? You can upgrade to the eBook version at `www.PacktPub.com` and as a print book customer, you are entitled to a discount on the eBook copy. Get in touch with us at `customercare@packtpub.com` for more details.

At `www.PacktPub.com`, you can also read a collection of free technical articles, sign up for a range of free newsletters and receive exclusive discounts and offers on Packt books and eBooks.

PACKTLiB

`https://www2.packtpub.com/books/subscription/packtlib`

Do you need instant solutions to your IT questions? PacktLib is Packt's online digital book library. Here, you can search, access, and read Packt's entire library of books.

Why Subscribe?

- Fully searchable across every book published by Packt
- Copy and paste, print, and bookmark content
- On demand and accessible via a web browser

Table of Contents

Preface — v

Chapter 1: Activities — 1
- Introduction — 1
- Declaring an activity — 2
- Starting a new activity with an intent object — 4
- Switching between activities — 6
- Passing data to another activity — 10
- Returning a result from an activity — 12
- Saving an activity's state — 14
- Storing persistent activity data — 18
- Understanding the activity lifecycle — 19

Chapter 2: Layouts — 25
- Introduction — 25
- Defining and inflating a layout — 26
- Using RelativeLayout — 28
- Using LinearLayout — 30
- Creating tables – TableLayout and GridLayout — 33
- Using ListView, GridView, and Adapters — 38
- Changing layout properties during runtime — 41
- Optimizing layouts with the Hierarchy Viewer — 42

Chapter 3: Views, Widgets, and Styles — 47
- Introduction — 47
- Inserting a widget into a layout — 49
- Using graphics to show button state — 52
- Creating a widget at runtime — 55
- Creating a custom component — 57
- Applying a style to a View — 59

Table of Contents

Turning a style into a theme — 62
Selecting theme based on the Android version — 63

Chapter 4: Menus — 69
Introduction — 69
Creating an Options menu — 70
Modifying menus and menu items during runtime — 75
Enabling Contextual Action Mode for a view — 78
Using Contextual Batch Mode with a ListView — 82
Creating a pop-up menu — 86

Chapter 5: Exploring Fragments, AppWidgets, and the System UI — 91
Introduction — 91
Creating and using a Fragment — 92
Adding and removing Fragments during runtime — 94
Passing data between Fragments — 98
Creating a shortcut on the Home screen — 108
Creating a Home screen widget — 110
Adding Search to the Action Bar — 118
Showing your app full screen — 123

Chapter 6: Working with Data — 129
Introduction — 129
Storing simple data — 130
Read and write a text file to internal storage — 134
Read and write a text file to external storage — 137
Including resource files in your project — 142
Creating and using an SQLite database — 147
Access data in the background using a Loader — 154

Chapter 7: Alerts and Notifications — 161
Introduction — 161
Lights, Action, and Sound – getting the user's attention! — 162
Creating a Toast using a custom layout — 166
Displaying a message box with AlertDialog — 170
Displaying a progress dialog — 173
Lights, Action, and Sound Redux using Notifications — 176
Creating a Media Player Notification — 182
Making a Flashlight with a Heads-Up Notification — 186

Chapter 8: Using the Touchscreen and Sensors — 191
Introduction — 191
Listening for click and long-press events — 192
Recognizing tap and other common gestures — 194

Pinch-to-zoom with multi-touch gestures	197
Swipe-to-Refresh	199
Listing available sensors – an introduction to the Android Sensor Framework	202
Reading sensor data – using the Android Sensor Framework events	206
Reading device orientation	210

Chapter 9: Graphics and Animation — 215

Introduction	215
Scaling down large images to avoid Out of Memory exceptions	217
A transition animation – defining scenes and applying a transition	222
Creating a Compass using sensor data and RotateAnimation	227
Creating a slideshow with ViewPager	232
Creating a Card Flip Animation with Fragments	236
Creating a Zoom Animation with a Custom Transition	243

Chapter 10: A First Look at OpenGL ES — 251

Introduction	251
Set up the OpenGL ES environment	252
Drawing shapes on GLSurfaceView	255
Applying Projection and Camera View while drawing	261
Moving the triangle with rotation	263
Rotating the triangle with user input	265

Chapter 11: Multimedia — 269

Introduction	269
Playing sound effects with SoundPool	270
Playing audio with MediaPlayer	274
Responding to hardware media controls in your app	278
Taking a photo with the default camera app	282
Taking a picture using the (old) Camera API	285
Taking a picture using the Camera2 (the new) API	290

Chapter 12: Telephony, Networks, and the Web — 299

Introduction	299
How to make a phone call	300
Monitoring phone call events	302
How to send SMS (text) messages	304
Receiving SMS messages	308
Displaying a web page in your application	312
Checking online status and connection type	315
Getting started with Volley for Internet requests	318
Canceling a Volley request	324

Table of Contents

Using Volley to request a JSON response	326
Using Volley to request an image	328
Using Volley's NetworkImageView and ImageLoader	331

Chapter 13: Getting Location and Using Geofencing — 333

Introduction	333
How to get the last location	335
Resolving problems reported with the GoogleApiClient OnConnectionFailedListener	340
How to receive location updates	343
Create and monitor a Geofence	346

Chapter 14: Getting Your App Ready for the Play Store — 353

Introduction	353
The new Android 6.0 Run-Time permission model	354
How to schedule an alarm	358
Receive notification of device boot	362
Using the AsyncTask for background work	364
Adding speech recognition to your app	368
Push Notification using GCM	371
How to add Google sign-in to your app	377

Chapter 15: The Backend as a Service Options — 383

Introduction	383
App42	384
Backendless	388
Buddy	391
Firebase	394
Kinvey	396

Index — 401

Preface

Android was first released in 2007 after being acquired by Google, Inc. Initially, Android was primarily used on a handset. Android 3.0 added features to take advantage of the growing tablet market.

In 2014, Google announced that Android had over 1 billion active users! With over 1 million applications available on Google Play, there's never been a more exciting time to join the Android community!

As we begin 2016, we have the recently released Android 6.0 with exciting new features for both users and developers.

What this book covers

Chapter 1, *Activities*, discusses Activities, which represent the fundamental building blocks for most applications. See examples of the most common tasks, such as creating an activity and passing control from one activity to another.

Chapter 2, *Layouts*, talks about Layout options; while Activities are fundamental to the UI, the layout actually defines what the user sees on the screen. Learn the main layout options available and best practices.

Chapter 3, *Views, Widgets, and Styles*, explores the basic UI object, from which all layouts are built. Widgets include everything from buttons and textboxes to more complicated NumberPicker and Calendar dialogs.

Chapter 4, *Menus*, teaches you how to use menus in Android. Learn how to create menus and how to control their behavior at runtime.

Chapter 5, *Exploring Fragments, AppWidgets, and the System UI*, shows how to create more flexible user interfaces by reusing UI components with Fragments. Take advantage of new OS features with translucent system bars or even make the System UI go away completely with Immersive Mode.

Preface

Chapter 6, Working with Data, helps you discover multiple methods that Android offers for persisting data, and know when it is the best to use each option. The Loader class example shows an efficient solution to present the data without tying up the UI Thread.

Chapter 7, Alerts and Notifications, shows multiple options for displaying notifications to your users. Options range from alerts in your application, using the system notification, and the Heads Up notification.

Chapter 8, Using the Touchscreen and Sensors, helps you learn the events for handling the standard user interactions, such as button clicks, long presses, and gestures. Access the device hardware sensors to determine orientation changes, device movement, and compass bearing.

Chapter 9, Graphics and Animation, helps you bring your app to life with animations! Take advantage of the many options Android offers for creating animations—from simple bitmaps to custom property animations.

Chapter 10, A First Look at OpenGL ES, discusses the OpenGL; when you need high-performance 2D and 3D graphics, turn to the Open Graphics library. Android supports OpenGL, a cross-platform Graphics API.

Chapter 11, Multimedia, takes advantage of the hardware features for playing audio. Use Android intents to call the default camera application or delve into the camera APIs to control the camera directly.

Chapter 12, Telephony, Networks, and the Web, uses the Telephony functions to initiate a phone call and to listen for incoming phone events. See how to send and receive SMS (text) messages. Use the WebView in your application to display web pages and learn how to use Volley to communicate directly with web services.

Chapter 13, Getting Location and Using Geofencing, shows you how to determine the user's location and the best practices so your app doesn't drain the battery. Use the new Location APIs to receive location updates and create Geofences.

Chapter 14, Getting Your App Ready for the Play Store, helps you polish your app for the Play Store and learn how to implement more advanced features, such as alarms and AsyncTask for background processing. See how to add Google Cloud Messaging (push notification) to your app and take advantage of Google Sign-in.

Chapter 15, The Backend as a Service Options, explores what a Backend as a Service provider can offer your app. Compare several top providers offering native Android support and free subscription options.

What you need for this book

Developing Android applications requires the Android SDK, available on multiple platforms, including Windows, Mac, and Linux.

Though not required, this book uses Android Studio, the official Android IDE. If you are new to Android development, visit the following link to review the current system requirements and download Android Studio with the SDK bundle for your platform:

`http://developer.android.com/sdk/index.html`

The Android SDK and Android Studio are both free of charge.

Who this book is for

This book assumes basic familiarity with programming concepts and Android fundamentals. Otherwise, if you are new to Android and learn best by jumping into the code, this book provides a wide range of the most common tasks.

As a "cookbook", it's easy to jump to your topic of interest and get the code working in your own application as quickly as possible.

Sections

In this book, you will find several headings that appear frequently (Getting ready, How to do it, How it works, There's more, and See also).

To give clear instructions on how to complete a recipe, we use these sections as follows:

Getting ready

This section tells you what to expect in the recipe, and describes how to set up any software or any preliminary settings required for the recipe.

How to do it...

This section contains the steps required to follow the recipe.

How it works...

This section usually consists of a detailed explanation of what happened in the previous section.

There's more...

This section consists of additional information about the recipe in order to make the reader more knowledgeable about the recipe.

See also

This section provides helpful links to other useful information for the recipe.

Conventions

In this book, you will find a number of text styles that distinguish between different kinds of information. Here are some examples of these styles and an explanation of their meaning.

Code words in text, database table names, folder names, filenames, file extensions, pathnames, dummy URLs, and user input are shown as follows: "Requesting a JSON response using `JsonObjectRequest()` basically works the same as `StringRequest()`."

A block of code is set as follows:

```
<activity
    android:name=".MainActivity"
    android:label="@string/app_name" >
    <intent-filter>
        <action android:name="android.intent.action.MAIN" />
        <category android:name=
            "android.intent.category.LAUNCHER"/>
    </intent-filter>
</activity>
```

New terms and important words are shown in bold. Words that you see on the screen, for example, in menus or dialog boxes, appear in the text like this: "Use the default **Phone & Tablet** option and select **Empty Activity** when prompted for **Activity Type**."

> Warnings or important notes appear in a box like this.

> Tips and tricks appear like this.

Reader feedback

Feedback from our readers is always welcome. Let us know what you think about this book—what you liked or disliked. Reader feedback is important for us as it helps us develop titles that you will really get the most out of.

To send us general feedback, simply e-mail `feedback@packtpub.com`, and mention the book's title in the subject of your message.

If there is a topic that you have expertise in and you are interested in either writing or contributing to a book, see our author guide at `www.packtpub.com/authors`.

Customer support

Now that you are the proud owner of a Packt book, we have a number of things to help you to get the most from your purchase.

Downloading the example code

You can download the example code files for this book from your account at `http://www.packtpub.com`. If you purchased this book elsewhere, you can visit `http://www.packtpub.com/support` and register to have the files e-mailed directly to you.

You can download the code files by following these steps:

1. Log in or register to our website using your e-mail address and password.
2. Hover the mouse pointer on the **SUPPORT** tab at the top.
3. Click on **Code Downloads & Errata**.
4. Enter the name of the book in the **Search** box.
5. Select the book for which you're looking to download the code files.
6. Choose from the drop-down menu where you purchased this book from.
7. Click on **Code Download**.

Preface

Once the file is downloaded, please make sure that you unzip or extract the folder using the latest version of:

- WinRAR / 7-Zip for Windows
- Zipeg / iZip / UnRarX for Mac
- 7-Zip / PeaZip for Linux

Errata

Although we have taken every care to ensure the accuracy of our content, mistakes do happen. If you find a mistake in one of our books—maybe a mistake in the text or the code—we would be grateful if you could report this to us. By doing so, you can save other readers from frustration and help us improve subsequent versions of this book. If you find any errata, please report them by visiting http://www.packtpub.com/submit-errata, selecting your book, clicking on the **Errata Submission Form** link, and entering the details of your errata. Once your errata are verified, your submission will be accepted and the errata will be uploaded to our website or added to any list of existing errata under the **Errata** section of that title.

To view the previously submitted errata, go to https://www.packtpub.com/books/content/support and enter the name of the book in the search field. The required information will appear under the **Errata** section.

Piracy

Piracy of copyrighted material on the Internet is an ongoing problem across all media. At Packt, we take the protection of our copyright and licenses very seriously. If you come across any illegal copies of our works in any form on the Internet, please provide us with the location address or website name immediately so that we can pursue a remedy.

Please contact us at copyright@packtpub.com with a link to the suspected pirated material.

We appreciate your help in protecting our authors and our ability to bring you valuable content.

Questions

If you have a problem with any aspect of this book, you can contact us at questions@packtpub.com, and we will do our best to address the problem.

1
Activities

This chapter covers the following recipes:

- ▶ Declaring an activity
- ▶ Starting a new activity with an intent object
- ▶ Switching between activities
- ▶ Passing data to another activity
- ▶ Returning a result from an activity
- ▶ Saving an activity's state
- ▶ Storing persistent activity data
- ▶ Understanding the activity lifecycle

Introduction

The Android SDK provides a powerful tool to program mobile devices, and the best way to master such a tool is to jump right in. Though you can read this book from beginning to end, as it is a cookbook, it is specifically designed to allow you to jump to specific tasks and get the results immediately.

Activities are the fundamental building block of most Android applications as the activity class provides the interface between the application and screen. Most Android applications will have at least one activity, if not several (but they are not required). A background service application will not necessarily require an activity if there is no user interface.

This chapter explains how to *declare* and *launch* activities within an application and how to manage several activities at once by sharing data between them, requesting results from them, and calling one activity from within another.

Activities

This chapter also briefly explores the **intent** object, which is often used in conjunction with activities. Intents can be used to transfer data between activities in your own application, as well as in external applications, such as those included with the Android operating system (a common example would be to use an intent to launch the default web browser).

> To begin developing Android applications, head over to the **Android Studio** page to download the new Android Studio IDE and the **Android SDK** bundle: `http://developer.android.com/sdk/index.html`

Declaring an activity

Activities and other application components, such as **services**, are declared in the `AndroidManifest` XML file. Declaring an activity is how we tell the system about our activity and how it can be requested. For example, an application will usually indicate that at least one activity should be visible as a desktop icon and serve as the main entry point to the application.

Getting ready

Android Studio is the new tool used to develop Android applications, replacing the now-deprecated **Eclipse ADT** solution. Android Studio will be used for all the recipes shown in this book, so if you have not already installed it, visit the Android Studio website (the link has been provided earlier) to install the IDE and the SDK bundle.

How to do it...

For this first example, we'll guide you through creating a new project. Android Studio provides a **Quick Start** wizard, which makes the process extremely easy. Follow these steps to get started:

1. Launch Android Studio, which brings up the **Welcome to Android Studio** dialog.
2. Click on the **Start a new Android Studio project** option.
3. Enter an application name; for this example, we have used `DeclareAnActivity`. Click on **Next**.
4. On the **Add an Activity to Mobile** dialog, click on the **Blank Activity** button, and then click on **Next**.
5. On the **Target Android Devices** dialog, chose **Android 6.0 (API 23)** as the minimum SDK (for this example, it really doesn't matter which API level you chose, as activities have existed since API level 1, but choosing the latest release is considered to be the best practice). Click on **Next**.

6. Since we chose the **Blank Activity** option earlier, the **Customize the Activity** dialog is shown. You can leave the defaults as provided, but note the default activity name is `MainActivity`. Click on **Finish**.

After finishing the wizard, Android Studio will create the project files. For this recipe, the two files that we will examine are `MainActivity.java` (which corresponds to the activity name mentioned in Step 6) and `AndroidManifest.xml`.

If you take a look at the `MainActivity.java` file, you will realize that it's pretty basic. This is because we chose the **Blank Activity** option (in Step 4). Now look at the `AndroidManifest.xml` file. This is where we actually declare the activity. Within the `<application>` element is the `<activity>` element:

```xml
<activity
    android:name=".MainActivity"
    android:label="@string/app_name">
    <intent-filter>
        <action android:name="android.intent.action.MAIN"/>

        <category android:name=
            "android.intent.category.LAUNCHER"/>
    </intent-filter>
</activity>
```

> When viewing this `xml` within Android Studio, you may notice that the label element shows the actual text as defined in the `strings.xml` resource file. This is just a small example of enhancements in the new IDE.

How it works...

Declaring an activity is a simple matter of declaring the `<activity>` element and specifying the name of the activity class with the `android:name` attribute. By adding the `<activity>` element to the **Android Manifest**, we are specifying our intention to include this component within our application. Any activities (or any other component for that matter) that are not declared in the manifest will not be included in the application. Attempting to access or utilize an undeclared component will result in an exception being thrown at runtime.

In the preceding code, there is another attribute—`android:label`. This attribute indicates the title shown on the screen as well as the icon label if this is the Launcher activity.

> For a complete list of available application attributes, take a look at this resource:
> `http://developer.android.com/guide/topics/manifest/activity-element.html`

Activities

Starting a new activity with an intent object

The Android application model can be seen as a service-oriented one, with activities as components and intents as the messages sent between them. Here, an intent is used to start an activity that displays the user's call log, but intents can be used to do many things and we will encounter them throughout this book.

Getting ready

To keep things simple, we are going to use an intent object to start one of Android's built-in applications rather than create a new one. This only requires a very basic application, so start a new Android project with Android Studio and call it `ActivityStarter`.

How to do it...

Again, to keep the example simple so that we can focus on the task at hand, we will create a function to show an intent in action and call this function from a button on our activity.

Once your new project is created in Android Studio, follow these steps:

1. Open the `MainActivity.java` class and add the following function:

   ```
   public void launchIntent(View view) {
       Intent intent = new Intent(Intent.ACTION_VIEW);
       intent.setData(Uri.parse("https://www.packtpub.com/"));
       startActivity(intent);
   }
   ```

   While you are typing this code, Android Studio will give this warning on View and intent: **Cannot resolve symbol 'Intent'**.

   This means that you need to add the library reference to the project. You can do this manually by entering the following code in the `import` section:

   ```
   import android.view.View;
   ```

   ```
   import android.content.Intent;
   ```

   Alternatively, just click on the words (in the red font), hit *Alt + Enter*, and let Android Studio add the library reference for you.

2. Open the `activity_main.xml` file and add the following XML:

   ```
   <Button
       android:layout_width="wrap_content"
       android:layout_height="wrap_content"
       android:text="Launch Browser"
   ```

```xml
        android:id="@+id/button"
        android:layout_centerVertical="true"
        android:layout_centerHorizontal="true"
        android:onClick="launchIntent"/>
```

```xml
<RelativeLayout xmlns:android="http://schemas.android.com/apk/res/android"
    xmlns:tools="http://schemas.android.com/tools" android:layout_width="match_parent"
    android:layout_height="match_parent" android:paddingLeft="16dp"
    android:paddingRight="16dp"
    android:paddingTop="16dp"
    android:paddingBottom="16dp" tools:context=".MainActivity">

    <TextView android:text="Hello world!" android:layout_width="wrap_content"
        android:layout_height="wrap_content" />

    <Button
        android:layout_width="wrap_content"
        android:layout_height="wrap_content"
        android:text="Launch Browser"
        android:id="@+id/button"
        android:layout_centerVertical="true"
        android:layout_centerHorizontal="true"
        android:onClick="launchIntent"/>

</RelativeLayout>
```

3. Now it's time to run the application and see the intent in action. You will need to either create an Android emulator (in Android Studio, go to **Tools | Android | AVD Manager**) or connect a physical device to your computer.

4. When you press the **Launch Browser** button, you will see the default web browser open with the URL specified.

How it works...

Though simple, this app demonstrates much of the power behind the Android OS. The intent object is just a message object. Intents can be used to communicate across your application's components (such as services and broadcast receivers) as well as with other applications on the device (as we did in this recipe).

> To test on a physical device, you may need to install drivers for your device (the drivers are specific to the hardware manufacturer). You will also need to enable Developer Mode on your device. Enabling Developer Mode varies according to the Android OS version. If you do not see the Developer Mode option in your device settings, open the **About Phone** option and begin tapping **Build Number**. After three taps, you should see a **Toast** message telling you that you are on your way to be a developer. Four more taps will enable the option.

Activities

In this recipe, we created an intent object by specifying `ACTION_VIEW` as what we want to do (our intention). You may have noticed that when you typed `Intent` and then the period, Android Studio provided a pop-up list of possibilities (this is the autocomplete feature), like this:

```
public void launchIntent(View view) {
    Log.i("MainActivity","launchIntent()");
    Intent intent = new Intent(Intent.ACTION_);
    intent.setData(Uri.parse("htt
    startActivity(intent);
}
```

ACTION_VIEW	String
ACTION_AIRPLANE_MODE_CHANGED	String
ACTION_ALL_APPS	String
ACTION_ANSWER	String
ACTION_APP_ERROR	String
ACTION_APPLICATION_RESTRICTIONS_CHANGED	String
ACTION_ASSIST	String
ACTION_ATTACH_DATA	String
ACTION_BATTERY_CHANGED	String
ACTION_BATTERY_LOW	String

`ACTION_VIEW`, along with a URL in the data, indicates that the intention is to view the website, so the default browser is launched (different data could launch different apps). In this example, our intent is just to view the URL, so we call the intent with just the `startActivity()` method. There are other ways to call the intent depending on our needs. In the *Returning a result from an activity* recipe, we will use the `startActivityForResult()` method.

There's more...

It's very common for Android users to download their favorite apps for web browsing, taking photos, text messaging, and so on. Using intents, you can let your app utilize your user's favorite apps instead of trying to reinvent all of this functionality.

See also

To start an activity from a menu selection, refer to the *Handling menu selections* recipe in *Chapter 4, Menus*.

Switching between activities

Often we will want to activate one activity from within another activity. Although this is not a difficult task, it will require a little more setting up to be done than the previous recipes as it requires two activities. We will create two activity classes and declare them both in the manifest. We'll also create a button, as we did in the previous recipe, to switch to the activity.

Chapter 1

Getting ready

We'll create a new project in Android Studio, just as we did in the previous recipes, and call this one `ActivitySwitcher`. Android Studio will create the first activity, `ActivityMain`, and automatically declare it in the manifest.

How to do it...

1. Since the Android Studio New Project wizard has already created the first activity, we just need to create the second activity. Open the **ActivitySwitcher** project and navigate to **File | New | Activity | Blank Activity**, as shown in this screenshot:

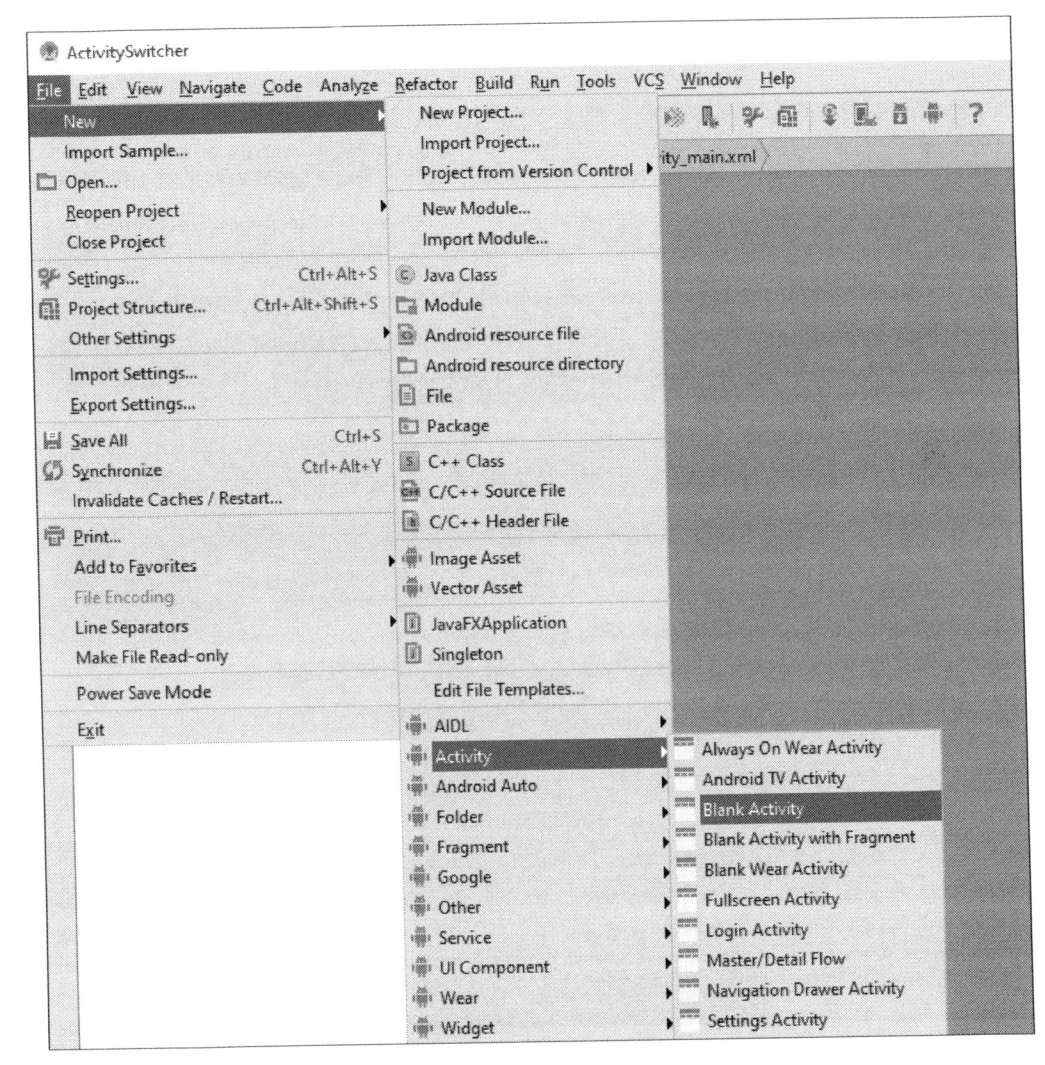

Activities

2. In the **Customize the Activity** dialog, you can leave the default **Activity Name** as it is, which is `Main2Activity`, or change it to `SecondActivity`, as shown here:

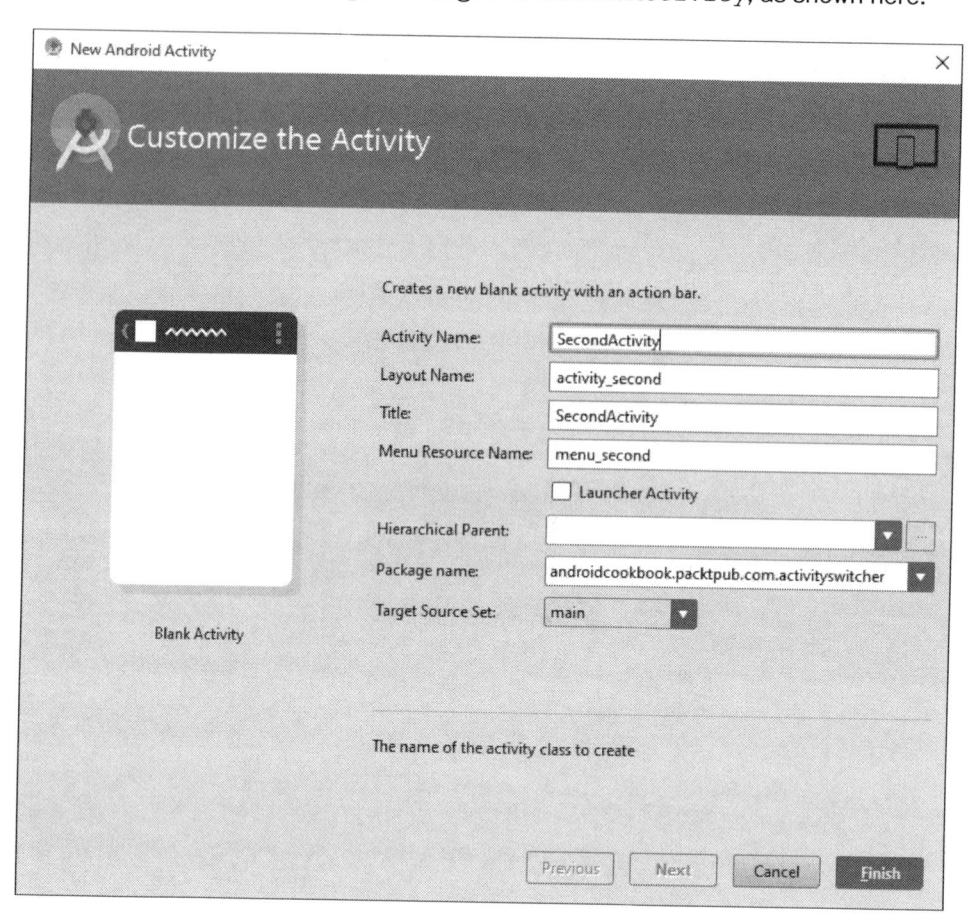

3. Open the `MainActivity.java` file and add the following function:

   ```
   public void onClickSwitchActivity(View view) {
       Intent intent = new Intent(this, SecondActivity.class);
       startActivity(intent);
   }
   ```

4. Now, open the `activity_main.xml` file located in the `\res\layout` folder and add the following XML to create the button:

   ```
   <Button
       android:id="@+id/button"
       android:layout_width="wrap_content"
       android:layout_height="wrap_content"
   ```

```
            android:layout_centerVertical="true"
            android:layout_centerHorizontal="true"
            android:text="Launch SecondActivity"
            android:onClick="onClickSwitchActivity"/>
```

5. You can actually run the code at this point and see the second activity come up. We're going to go further and add a button to `SecondActivity` to close it, which will bring us back to the first activity. Open the `SecondActivity.java` file and add this function:

    ```
    public void onClickClose(View view) {
        finish();
    }
    ```

6. Finally, add the **Close** button to the `SecondActivity` layout. Open the `activity_second.xml` file and add the following `<Button>` element just after the `<TextView>` element that was generated automatically:

    ```
    <Button
        android:id="@+id/buttonClose"
        android:layout_width="wrap_content"
        android:layout_height="wrap_content"
        android:text="Close"
        android:layout_centerVertical="true"
        android:layout_centerHorizontal="true"
        android:onClick="onClickClose"/>
    ```

7. Run the application on your device or emulator and see the buttons in action.

How it works...

The real work of this exercise is in the `onClickSwitchActivity()` method from Step 3. This is where we declare the second activity for the intent using `SecondActivity.class`. We went one step further by adding the close button to the second activity to show a common real-world situation—launching a new activity, then closing it, and returning to the original calling activity. This behavior is accomplished in the `onClickClose()` function. All it does is call `finish()`, but that tells the system that we're done with the activity. Finish doesn't actually return us to the calling activity or any specific activity for that matter; it just closes the current activity and relies on the **back stack**. If we want a specific activity, we can again use the intent object (we just change the class name while creating the intent).

This activity switching does not make a very exciting application. Our activity does nothing but demonstrate how to switch from one activity to another, which of course will form a fundamental aspect of almost any application that we develop.

Activities

If we had manually created the activities, we would need to add them to the manifest. By using these steps, Android Studio has already taken care of the XML. To see what Android Studio did, open the `AndroidManifest.xml` file and look at the `<application>` element:

```xml
<activity
    android:name=".MainActivity"
    android:label="@string/app_name">
    <intent-filter>
        <action android:name="android.intent.action.MAIN"/>
        <category android:name="android.intent.category.LAUNCHER/>
    </intent-filter>
</activity>
<activity
    android:name=".SecondActivity"
    android:label="@string/title_activity_second">
</activity>
```

One thing to note in the preceding autogenerated code is that the second activity does not have the `<intent-filter>` element. The main activity is generally the entry point when starting the application. That's why MAIN and LAUNCHER are defined—so that the system will know which activity to launch when the application starts.

See also

- To learn more about embedding widgets such as the Button, visit *Chapter 3, Views, Widgets, and Styles*.

Passing data to another activity

The intent object is defined as a messaging object. As a message object, its purpose is to communicate with other components of the application. In this recipe, we'll show you how to pass information with the intent and how to get it out again.

Getting ready

This recipe will pick up from where the previous one ended. We will call this project `SendData`.

How to do it...

Since this recipe is building on the previous recipe, most of the work is already done. We'll add an `EditText` element to the main activity so that we have something to send to `SecondActivity`. We'll use the (autogenerated) `TextView` view to display the message. Here are the complete steps:

Chapter 1

1. Open `activity_main.xml`, remove the existing `<TextView>` element, and add the following `<EditText>` element:

   ```xml
   <EditText
       android:id="@+id/editTextData"
       android:layout_width="match_parent"
       android:layout_height="wrap_content"/>
   ```

   The `<Button>` element that we created in the previous recipe doesn't change.

2. Now, open the `MainActivity.java` file and change the `onClickSwitchActivity()` method as follows:

   ```java
   public void onClickSwitchActivity(View view) {
       EditText editText = (EditText)findViewById(R.id.editTextData);
       String text = editText.getText().toString();
       Intent intent = new Intent(this, SecondActivity.class);
       intent.putExtra(Intent.EXTRA_TEXT, text);
       startActivity(intent);
   }
   ```

3. Next, open the `activity_second.xml` file and modify the `<TextView>` element to include the ID attribute:

   ```xml
   <TextView
       android:id="@+id/textViewText"
       android:text="@string/hello_world"
       android:layout_width="wrap_content"
       android:layout_height="wrap_content"/>
   ```

4. The last change is to edit the second activity to look for this new data and display it on the screen. Open `SecondActivity.java` and edit `onCreate()` as follows:

   ```java
   protected void onCreate(Bundle savedInstanceState) {
       super.onCreate(savedInstanceState);
       setContentView(R.layout.activity_second);
       TextView textView = (TextView)findViewById(
           R.id.textViewText);
       if (getIntent()!=null && getIntent().hasExtra(
           Intent.EXTRA_TEXT)) {
           textView.setText(getIntent().getStringExtra(
               Intent.EXTRA_TEXT));
       }
   }
   ```

5. Now run the project. Type some text on the main activity and press **Launch Second Activity** to see it send the data.

Activities

How it works...

As expected, the intent object is doing all the work. We created an intent just as in the previous recipe and then added some extra data. Did you notice the `putExtra()` method call? In our example, we used the already defined `Intent.EXTRA_TEXT` as the identifier, but we didn't have to. We can use any key we want (you've seen this concept before if you're familiar with name/value pairs).

The key point about using name/value pairs is that you have to use the same name to get the data back out. That's why we used the same key identifier when we read the extra data with `getStringExtra()`.

The second activity was launched with the intent that we created, so it's simply a matter of getting the intent and checking for the data sent along with it. We do this in `onCreate()`:

```
textView.setText(getIntent().getStringExtra(Intent.EXTRA_TEXT));
```

There's more...

We aren't limited to just sending `String` data. The intent object is very flexible and already supports basic data types. Go back to Android Studio and click on the `putExtra` method. Then hit *Ctrl* and the *Spacebar*. Android Studio will bring up the autocomplete list so that you can see the different data types that you can store.

Returning a result from an activity

Being able to start one activity from another is all well and good, but we will often need to know how the called activity has fared in its task or even which activity has been called. The `startActivityForResult()` method provides the solution.

Getting ready

Returning a result from an activity is not very different from the way we just called the activity in the previous recipes. You can either use the project from the previous recipe, or start a new project and call it `GettingResults`. Either way, once you have a project with two activities and the code needed to call the second activity, you're ready to begin.

How to do it...

There are only a few changes needed to get the results:

1. First of all, open `MainActivity.java` and add the following constant to the class:
   ```
   public static final String REQUEST_RESULT="REQUEST_RESULT";
   ```

2. Next, change the way the intent is called by modifying the `onClickSwitchActivity()` method to expect a result:

   ```
   public void onClickSwitchActivity(View view) {
       EditText editText = (EditText)findViewById(
           R.id.editTextData);
       String text = editText.getText().toString();
       Intent intent = new Intent(this, SecondActivity.class);
       intent.putExtra(Intent.EXTRA_TEXT,text);
       startActivityForResult(intent,1);
   }
   ```

3. Then, add this new method to receive the result:

   ```
   @Override
   protected void onActivityResult(int requestCode, int
       resultCode, Intent data) {
       super.onActivityResult(requestCode, resultCode, data);
       if (resultCode==RESULT_OK) {
           Toast.makeText(this, Integer.toString(
               data.getIntExtra(REQUEST_RESULT, 0)),
               Toast.LENGTH_LONG).show();
       }
   }
   ```

4. Finally, modify `onClickClose` in `SecondActivity.java` to set the return value as follows:

   ```
   public void onClickClose(View view) {
       Intent returnIntent = new Intent();
       returnIntent.putExtra(MainActivity.REQUEST_RESULT,42);
       setResult(RESULT_OK, returnIntent);
       finish();
   }
   ```

How it works...

As you can see, getting the results back is relatively straightforward. We just call the intent with `startActivityForResult`, so it knows that we want a result. We set up the `onActivityResult()` callback handler to receive the results. Finally, we make sure that the second activity returns a result with `setResult()` before closing the activity. In this example, we are just setting a result with a static value. We just display what we receive to demonstrate the concept.

Activities

It's good practice to check the result code to make sure that the user didn't cancel the action. It's technically an integer, but the system uses it as a boolean value. Check for either `RESULT_OK` or `RESULT_CANCEL` and proceed accordingly. In our example, the second activity doesn't have a cancel button, so why bother to check? What if the user hits the back button? The system will set the result code to `RESULT_CANCEL` and the intent to null, which will cause our code to throw an exception.

We made use of the **Toast** object, which is a convenient pop-up **message** that can be used to unobtrusively notify the user. It also functions as a handy method for debugging as it doesn't need a special layout or screen space.

There's more...

Besides the result code, `onActivityResults()` also includes a **Request Code**. Are you wondering where that came from? It is simply the integer value that was passed with the `startActivityForResult()` call, which takes this form:

```
startActivityForResult(Intent intent, int requestCode);
```

We didn't check the request code because we knew we had only one result to handle—but in trivial applications with several activities, this value can be used to identify where the request originated.

> If `startActivityForResult()` is called with a negative request code, it will behave exactly as if it were a call to `startActivity()`—that is, it will not return a result.

See also

- To learn more about creating new activity classes, refer to the *Switching between activities* recipe
- For more information about Toasts, check out the *Making a Toast* recipe in *Chapter 7, Alerts and Notifications*

Saving an activity's state

The mobile environment is very dynamic, with users changing tasks much more often than on desktops. With generally fewer resources on a mobile device, it should be expected that your application will be interrupted at some point. It's also very possible that the system will shut down your app completely to give additional resources to the task at hand. It's the nature of mobiles.

A user might start typing something in your app, be interrupted by a phone call, or switch over to another app to send a text message, and by the time they get back to your app, the system may have closed it down completely to free up the memory. To provide the best user experience, you need to expect such behavior and make it easier for your user to resume from where they left off. The good thing is that the Android OS makes this easier by providing callbacks to notify your app of state changes.

> Simply rotating your device will cause the OS to destroy and recreate your activity. This might seem a bit heavy-handed, but it's done for good reason—it's very common to have different layouts for portrait and landscape, so this ensures that your app is using the correct resources.

In this recipe, you'll see how to handle the `onSaveInstanceState()` and `onRestoreInstanceState()` callbacks to save your application's state. We will demonstrate this by creating a counter variable and increment it each time the **Count** button is pressed. We will also have an `EditText` and a `TextView` widget to see their default behavior.

Getting ready

Create a new project in Android Studio and name it `StateSaver`. We need only a single activity, so the autogenerated main activity is sufficient. However, we will need a few widgets, including `EditText`, `Button`, and `TextView`. Their layout (in `activity_main.xml`) will look like this:

```xml
<EditText
    android:id="@+id/editText"
    android:layout_width="match_parent"
    android:layout_height="wrap_content"
    android:layout_alignParentTop="true"
    android:layout_alignParentStart="true"/>

<Button
    android:id="@+id/button"
    android:layout_width="wrap_content"
    android:layout_height="wrap_content"
    android:layout_centerInParent="true"
    android:text="Count"
    android:onClick="onClickCounter"/>

<TextView
    android:id="@+id/textViewCounter"
```

Activities

```xml
android:layout_width="wrap_content"
android:layout_height="wrap_content"
android:layout_below="@id/button"/>
```

How to do it...

Perform the following set of steps:

1. To keep track of the counter, we need to add a global variable to the project, along with a key for saving and restoring. Add the following code to the `MainActivity.java` class:

   ```java
   static final String KEY_COUNTER = "COUNTER";
   private int mCounter=0;
   ```

2. Then add the code needed to handle the button press; it increments the counter and displays the result in the `TextView` widget:

   ```java
   public void onClickCounter(View view) {
       mCounter++;
       ((TextView)findViewById(R.id.textViewCounter)).setText(
       "Counter: " + Integer.toString(mCounter));
   }
   ```

3. To receive notifications of application state change, we need to add the `onSaveInstanceState()` and `onRestoreInstanceState()` methods to our application. Open `MainActivity.java` and add the following:

   ```java
   @Override
   protected void onSaveInstanceState(Bundle outState) {
       super.onSaveInstanceState(outState);
       outState.putInt(KEY_COUNTER,mCounter);
   }

   @Override
   protected void onRestoreInstanceState(Bundle savedInstanceState) {
       super.onRestoreInstanceState(savedInstanceState);
       mCounter=savedInstanceState.getInt(KEY_COUNTER);
   }
   ```

4. Run the program and try changing the orientation to see how it behaves (if you're using the emulator, *Ctrl + F11* will rotate the device).

How it works...

All activities go through multiple states during their lifetime. By setting up callbacks to handle the events, we can have our code save important information before the activity is destroyed.

Step 3 is where the actual saving and restoring occurs. The system sends a **Bundle** (a data object that also uses name/value pairs) to the methods. We use the `onSaveInstanceState()` callback to save the data and pull it out in the `onRestoreInstanceState()` callback.

But wait! Did you try typing text in the `EditText` view before rotating the device? If so, you'd have noticed that the text was also restored, but we don't have any code to handle that view. By default, the system will automatically save the state, provided it has a unique ID (not all views automatically have their state saved, such as the `TextView`, but we can manually save it if we want).

> Note that if you want Android to automatically save and restore the state of a view, it must have a unique ID (specified with the `android:id=` attribute in the layout). Beware; not all view types automatically save and restore the state of a view.

There's more...

The `onRestoreInstanceState()` callback is not the only place where the state can be restored. Look at the signature of `onCreate()`:

```
onCreate(Bundle savedInstanceState)
```

Both methods receive the same `Bundle` instance named `savedInstanceState`. You could move the restore code to the `onCreate()` method and it would work the same. But one catch is that the `savedInstanceState` bundle will be null if there is no data, such as during the initial creation of the activity. If you want to move the code from the `onRestoreInstanceState()` callback, just check to make sure that the data is not null, as follows:

```
if (savedInstanceState!=null) {
    mCounter = savedInstanceState.getInt(KEY_COUNTER);
}
```

See also

- The *Storing persistent activity data* recipe will introduce persistent storage.
- Take a look at *Chapter 6, Working with Data*, for more examples on Android activities.
- The *Understanding the activity lifecycle* recipe explains the Android Activity Lifecycle.

Storing persistent activity data

Being able to store information about our activities on a temporary basis is very useful, but more often than not, we will want our application to remember information across multiple sessions.

Android supports SQLite, but that could be a lot of overhead for simple data, such as the user's name or a high score. Fortunately, Android also provides a lightweight option for these scenarios, with `SharedPreferences`.

Getting ready

You can either use the project from the previous recipe or start a new project and call it `PersistentData` (in a real-world application, you'll likely be doing both anyway). In the previous recipe, we saved `mCounter` in the session state. In this recipe, we'll add a new method to handle `onPause()` and save `mCounter` to `SharedPreferences`. We'll restore the value in `onCreate()`.

How to do it...

We have only two changes to make, and both are in `MainActivity.java`:

1. Add the following `onPause()` method to save the data before the activity closes:

    ```
    @Override
    protected void onPause() {
        super.onPause();

        SharedPreferences settings = getPreferences(
            MODE_PRIVATE);
        SharedPreferences.Editor editor = settings.edit();
        editor.putInt(KEY_COUNTER, mCounter);
        editor.commit();
    }
    ```

2. Then add the following code at the end of `onCreate()` to restore the counter:

    ```
    SharedPreferences settings = getPreferences(MODE_PRIVATE);

    int defaultCounter = 0;
    mCounter = settings.getInt(KEY_COUNTER, defaultCounter);
    ```

3. Run the program and try it out.

How it works...

As you can see, this is very similar to saving state data, because it also uses name/value pairs. Here, we just stored an `int`, but we can just as easily store one of the other primitive data types. Each data type has equivalent getters and setters, for example, `SharedPreferences.getBoolean()` or `SharedPreferences.setString()`.

Saving our data requires the services of `SharedPreferences.Editor`. This is evoked with `edit()` and accepts `remove()` and `clear()` procedures as well as setters such as `putInt()`. Note that we must conclude any storing that we do here with the `commit()` statement.

There's more...

There is a slightly more sophisticated variant of the `getPreferences()` accessor: `getSharedPreferences()`. It can be used to store multiple preference sets.

Using more than one preference file

Using `getSharedPreferences()` is no different from using its counterpart, but it allows for more than one preference file. It takes the following form:

```
getSharedPreferences(String name, int mode)
```

Here, `name` is the file. The `mode` can be either `MODE_PRIVATE`, `MODE_WORLD_READABLE`, or `MODE_WORLD_WRITABLE` and describes the file's access levels.

See also

- *Chapter 6, Working with Data*, for more examples on data storage

Understanding the activity lifecycle

The Android OS is a dangerous place for an activity. The demand for resources on a battery-operated platform is managed quite ruthlessly by the system. Our activities can be dumped from memory when it's running low, without even a moment's notice and along with any data they contain. Therefore, it is essential to understand the activity lifecycle.

Activities

The following diagram shows the stages through which an activity passes during its lifetime:

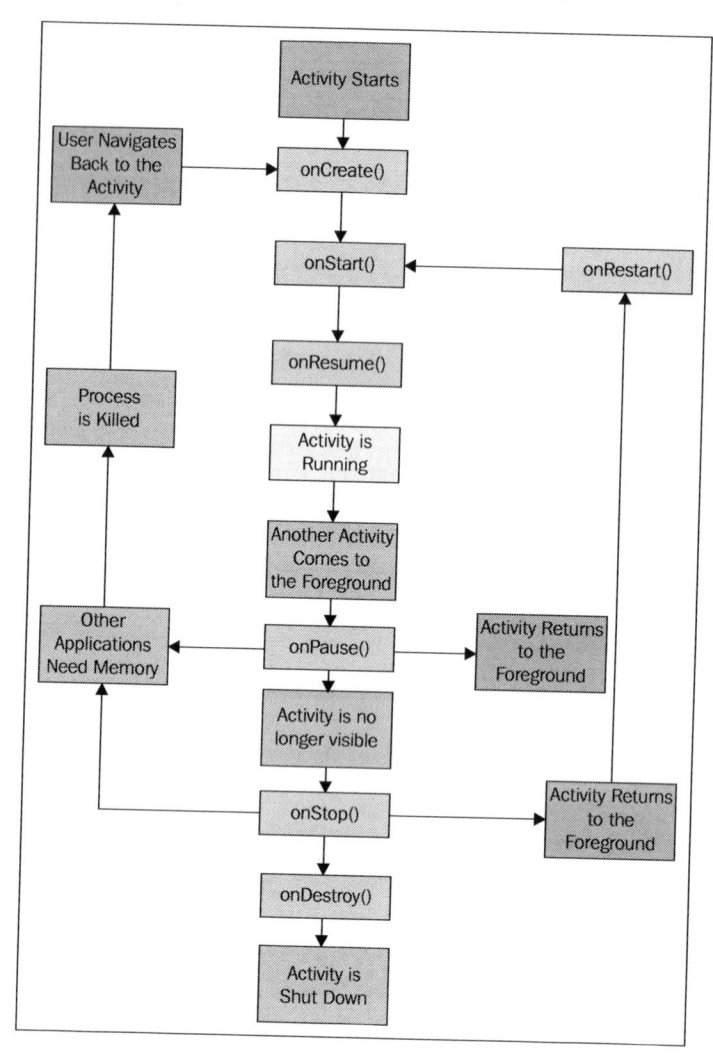

Along with the stages, the diagram also shows the methods that can be overridden. As you can see, we've already utilized most of these methods in the preceding recipes. Hopefully, getting the big picture will help in your understanding.

Chapter 1

Getting ready

Create a new project in Android Studio with a **Blank Activity**, and call it `ActivityLifecycle`. We will use the (autogenerated) `TextView` method to display the state information.

How to do it...

To see the application move through the various stages, we will create methods for all the stages:

1. Open `activity_main.xml` and add an ID to the autogenerated `TextView`:

   `android:id="@+id/textViewState"`

2. The remaining steps will be in `MainActivity.java`. Add the following global declaration:

   `private TextView mTextViewState;`

3. Modify the `onCreate()` method to save `TextView` and set the initial text:

   `mTextViewState = (TextView)findViewById(R.id.textViewState);`

   `mTextViewState.setText("onCreate()\n");`

4. Add the following methods to handle the remaining events:

   ```
   @Override
   protected void onStart() {
       super.onStart();
       mTextViewState.append("onStart()\n");
   }

   @Override
   protected void onResume() {
       super.onResume();
       mTextViewState.append("onResume()\n");
   }

   @Override
   protected void onPause() {
       super.onPause();
       mTextViewState.append("onPause()\n");
   }

   @Override
   ```

```
    protected void onStop() {
        super.onStop();
        mTextViewState.append("onStop()\n");
}

    @Override
    protected void onRestart() {
        super.onRestart();
        mTextViewState.append("onRestart()\n");
}

    @Override
    protected void onDestroy() {
        super.onDestroy();
        mTextViewState.append("onDestroy()\n");
}
```

5. Run the application and observe what happens when the activity is interrupted by pressing the Back and Home keys. Try other actions, such as task switching, to see how they impact your application.

How it works...

Our activity can exist in one of these three states: **active**, **paused**, or **stopped**. There is also a fourth state, **destroyed**, but we can safely ignore it:

- An activity is in the `active` state when its interface is available for the user. It persists from `onResume()` until `onPause()`, which is brought about when another activity comes to the foreground. If this new activity does not entirely obscure our activity, then ours will remain in the `paused` state until the new activity is finished or dismissed. It will then immediately call `onResume()` and continue.

- When a newly started activity fills the screen or makes our activity invisible, then our activity will enter the `stopped` state, and the resumption will always invoke a call to `onRestart()`.

- When an activity is in either the `paused` or `stopped` state, the operating system can (and will) remove it from the memory when the memory is low or when other applications demand it.

- It is worth noting that we never actually see the results of the `onDestroy()` method, as the activity is removed by this point. If you want to explore these methods further, then it is well worth employing `Activity.isFinishing()` to see whether the activity is really finishing before `onDestroy()` is executed, as seen in the following snippet:

```
@Override
  public void onPause() {
  super.onPause();
  mTextView.append("onPause()\n ");
  if (isFinishing()){
    mTextView.append(" ... finishing");
  }
}
```

> When implementing these methods, always call the superclass before doing any work.

There's more...

Shutting down an activity

To shut down an activity, directly call its `finish()` method, which in turn calls `onDestroy()`. To perform the same action from a child activity, use `finishFromChild(Activity child)`, where `child` is the calling subactivity.

It is often useful to know whether an activity is being shut down or merely paused, and the `isFinishing(boolean)` method returns a value that indicates which of these two states the activity is in.

2
Layouts

In this chapter, we will cover the following topics:

- Defining and inflating a layout
- Using RelativeLayout
- Using LinearLayout
- Creating tables – TableLayout and GridLayout
- Using ListView, GridView, and Adapters
- Changing layout properties during runtime
- Optimizing layouts with the Hierarchy Viewer

Introduction

In Android, the User Interface is defined in a **Layout**. A layout can be declared in XML or created dynamically in code. (It's recommended to declare the layout in XML rather than in code to keep the presentation layer separate from the implementation layer.) A layout can define an individual `ListItem`, a fragment, or even the entire Activity. Layout files are stored in the `/res/layout` folder and referenced in code with the following identifier: `R.layout.<filename_without_extension>`.

Android provides a useful variety of `Layout` classes that contain and organize individual elements of an activity (such as buttons, checkboxes, and other `Views`). The `ViewGroup` object is a container object that serves as the base class for Android's family of `Layout` classes. The Views placed in a layout form a hierarchy, with the topmost layout being the parent.

Layouts

Android provides several built-in layout types designed for specific purposes, such as the `RelativeLayout`, which allows Views to be positioned with respect to other elements. The `LinearLayout` can stack Views or align them horizontally, depending on the orientation specified. The `TableLayout` can be used for laying out a grid of Views. Within various layouts, we can also justify Views with `Gravity` and provide proportional size with `Weight` control. Layouts and `ViewGroups` can be nested within each other to create complex configurations. Over a dozen different Layout objects are provided for managing widgets, lists, tables, galleries, and other display formats, plus you can always derive from the base classes to create your own custom layouts.

Defining and inflating a layout

When using the Android Studio wizard to create a new project, it automatically creates the `res/layout/activity_main.xml` file (as shown in the following screenshot). It then inflates the XML file in the `onCreate()` callback with `setContentView(R.layout.activity_main)`.

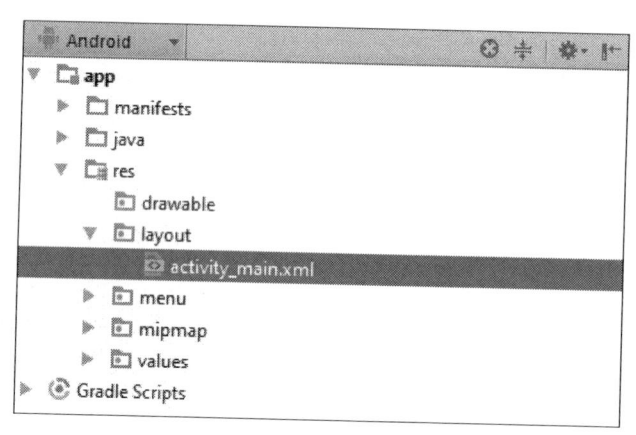

```
Android
▼ app
    ▶ manifests
    ▶ java
    ▼ res
        drawable
        ▼ layout
            activity_main.xml
        ▶ menu
        ▶ mipmap
        ▶ values
▶ Gradle Scripts
```

For this recipe, we will create two, slightly different layouts and switch between them with a button.

Getting ready

Create a new project in Android Studio and call it `InflateLayout`. Once the project is created, expand the `res/layout` folder so we can edit the `activity_main.xml` file.

How to do it...

1. Edit the `res/layout/activity_main.xml` file so it includes a button as defined here:

   ```
   <Button
       android:id="@+id/buttonLeft"
       android:layout_width="wrap_content"
       android:layout_height="wrap_content"
       android:text="Left Button"
       android:layout_centerVertical="true"
       android:layout_alignParentLeft="true"
       android:onClick="onClickLeft"/>
   ```

2. Now make a copy of `activity_main.xml` and call it `activity_main2.xml`. Change the button so it matches the following:

   ```
   <Button
       android:id="@+id/buttonRight"
       android:layout_width="wrap_content"
       android:layout_height="wrap_content"
       android:text="Right Button"
       android:layout_centerVertical="true"
       android:layout_alignParentRight="true"
       android:onClick="onClickRight"/>
   ```

3. Open `MainActivity.java` and add the following two methods to handle the button clicks:

   ```
   public void onClickLeft(View view) {
       setContentView(R.layout.activity_main2);
   }

   public void onClickRight(View view) {
       setContentView(R.layout.activity_main);
   }
   ```

4. Run this application on a device or emulator to see it in action.

How it works...

The key here is the call to `setContentView()`, which we have come across before in the autogenerated `onCreate()` code. Just pass a layout ID to `setContentView()` and it automatically inflates the layout.

Layouts

This code is meant to make the concept easy to understand but would be overkill for simply changing the property of a Button (in this example, we could just change the alignment on the button click). Inflating the layout is usually needed once, in the `onCreate()` method, but there are times when you may want to manually inflate a layout, as we did here. (If you were manually handling orientation changes, it would be a good example.)

There's more...

As well as identifying a layout using a resource ID, as we did here, `setContentView()` can also take a View as an argument, for example:

```
findViewById(R.id.myView)
setContentView(myView);
```

See also

- As mentioned previously, see the *Fragment* topic, in *Chapter 5, Exploring Fragments, AppWidgets, and the System UI*, for the alternative method to change the screen layout

Using RelativeLayout

As mentioned in the *Introduction*, the `RelativeLayout` allows Views to be position-relative to each other and the parent. `RelativeLayout` is particularly useful for reducing the number of nested layouts, which is very important for reducing memory and processing requirements.

Getting ready

Create a new project and call it `RelativeLayout`. The default layout uses a `RelativeLayout`, which we will use to align Views both horizontally and vertically.

How to do it...

1. Open the `res/layout/activity_main.xml` file and change it as follows:

    ```
    <TextView
        android:id="@+id/textView1"
        android:layout_width="wrap_content"
        android:layout_height="wrap_content"
        android:text="Centered"
        android:layout_centerVertical="true"
        android:layout_centerHorizontal="true" />
    <TextView
        android:id="@+id/textView2"
    ```

Layouts

```
        android:layout_width="wrap_content"
        android:layout_height="wrap_content"
        android:text="Below TextView1"
        android:layout_below="@+id/textView1"
        android:layout_toLeftOf="@id/textView1" />
    <TextView
        android:id="@+id/textView3"
        android:layout_width="wrap_content"
        android:layout_height="wrap_content"
        android:text="Bottom Right"
        android:layout_alignParentBottom="true"
        android:layout_alignParentEnd="true" />
```

2. Run the code, or view the layout in the **Design** tab

How it works...

This is a very straightforward exercise but it demonstrates several of the `RelativeLayout` options: `layout_centerVertical`, `layout_centerHorizontal`, `layout_below`, `layout_alignParentBottom`, and so on.

The most commonly used `RelativeLayout` layout attributes include:

- `layout_below`: This View should be below the View specified
- `layout_above`: This View should be above the View specified
- `layout_alignParentTop`: Align this View to the top edge of the parent
- `layout_alignParentBottom`: Align this View to the bottom edge of the parent
- `layout_alignParentLeft`: Align this View to the left edge of the parent
- `layout_alignParentRight`: Align this View to the right edge of the parent
- `layout_centerVertical`: Center this View vertically within the parent
- `layout_centerHorizontal`: Center this View horizontally within the parent
- `layout_center`: Center this View both horizontally and vertically within the parent

> For the complete list of `RelativeLayout` parameters, visit: http://developer.android.com/reference/android/widget/RelativeLayout.LayoutParams.html.

Layouts

There's more...

In contrast to what we saw earlier, here is an example using a `LinearLayout` just to center a `TextView` (creating the same effect as the `layout_center` parameter of `RelativeLayout`):

```xml
<?xml version="1.0" encoding="utf-8"?>
<LinearLayout xmlns:android="http://schemas.android.com/apk/res/android"
    android:orientation="horizontal"
    android:layout_width="match_parent"
    android:layout_height="match_parent"
    android:gravity="center">
    <LinearLayout
        android:layout_width="0dp"
        android:layout_height="wrap_content"
        android:layout_weight="1"
        android:gravity="center" >
        <TextView
            android:id="@+id/imageButton_speak"
            android:layout_width="wrap_content"
            android:layout_height="wrap_content"
            android:text="Centered" />
    </LinearLayout>
</LinearLayout>
```

Notice this layout is one level deeper than the equivalent `RelativeLayout` (which is a `LinearLayout` nested within the parent `LinearLayout`.) Though a simple example, it's a good idea to avoid unnecessary nesting as it can impact performance, especially when a layout is being repeatedly inflated (such as a `ListItem`).

See also

- The next recipe, *Using LinearLayout*, which will give you an alternative layout
- See the *Optimizing layouts with the Hierarchy Viewer* recipe for more information on efficient layout design

Using LinearLayout

Another common layout option is the `LinearLayout`, which arranges the child Views in a single column or single row, depending on the orientation specified. The default orientation (if not specified) is vertical, which aligns the Views in a single column.

Layouts

The `LinearLayout` has a key feature not offered in the `RelativeLayout`—the weight attribute. We can specify a `layout_weight` parameter when defining a View to allow the View to dynamically size based on the available space. Options include having a View fill all the remaining space (if a View has a higher weight), having multiple Views fit within the given space (if all have the same weight), or spacing the Views proportionally by their weight.

We will create a `LinearLayout` with three `EditText` Views to demonstrate how the weight attribute can be used. For this example, we will use three `EditText` Views—one to enter a `To Address` parameter, another to enter a `Subject`, and the third to enter a `Message`. The `To` and `Subject` Views will be a single line each, with the remaining space given to the Message View.

Getting ready

Create a new project and call it `LinearLayout`. We will replace the default `RelativeLayout` created in `activity_main.xml` with a `LinearLayout`.

How to do it...

1. Open the `res/layout/activity_main.xml` file and replace it as follows:

   ```xml
   <LinearLayout xmlns:android="http://schemas.android.com/apk/res/android"
       android:orientation="vertical"
       android:layout_width="match_parent"
       android:layout_height="match_parent">
       <EditText
           android:id="@+id/editTextTo"
           android:layout_width="match_parent"
           android:layout_height="wrap_content"
           android:hint="To" />
       <EditText
           android:id="@+id/editTextSubject"
           android:layout_width="match_parent"
           android:layout_height="wrap_content"
           android:hint="Subject" />
       <EditText
           android:id="@+id/editTextMessage"
           android:layout_width="match_parent"
           android:layout_height="0dp"
           android:layout_weight="1"
           android:gravity="top"
           android:hint="Message" />
   </LinearLayout>
   ```

2. Run the code, or view the layout in the **Design** tab.

Layouts

How it works...

When using vertical orientation with the `LinearLayout`, the child Views are created in a single column (stacked on top of each other). The first two Views use the `android:layout_height="wrap_content"` attribute, giving them a single line each. `editTextMessage` uses the following to specify the height:

```
android:layout_height="0dp"
android:layout_weight="1"
```

When using the `LinearLayout`, it tells Android to calculate the height based on the weight. A weight of 0 (the default if not specified) indicates the View should not expand. In this example, `editTextMessage` is the only View defined with a weight, so it alone will expand to fill any remaining space in the parent layout.

> When using the horizontal orientation, specify `android:layout_height="0dp"` (along with the weight) to have Android calculate the width.

It might be helpful to think of the weight attribute as a percentage. In this case, the total weight defined is 1, so this View gets 100 percent of the remaining space. If we assigned a weight of 1 to another View, the total would be 2, so this View would get 50 percent of the space. Try adding a weight to one of the other Views (make sure to change the height to `0dp` as well) to see it in action.

If you added a weight to one (or both) of the other Views, did you notice the text position? Without specifying a value for `gravity`, the text just remains in the center of the View space. The `editTextMessage` specifies: `android:gravity="top"`, which forces the text to the top of the View.

There's more...

Multiple attribute options can be combined using bitwise OR. (Java uses the pipe character (|) for OR). For example, we could combine two gravity options to both align along the top of the parent and center within the available space:

```
android:layout_gravity="top|center"
```

It should be noted that the `layout_gravity` and `gravity` tags are not the same thing. Where `layout_gravity` dictates where in its parent a View should lie, `gravity` controls the positioning of the contents within a View—for example, the alignment of text on a button.

See also

- The previous recipe, *Using the RelativeLayout*

Creating tables – TableLayout and GridLayout

When you need to create a table in your UI, Android provides two convenient layout options: the `TableLayout` (along with `TableRow`) and the `GridLayout` (added in API 14). Both layout options can create similar looking tables, but each using a different approach. With the `TableLayout`, rows and columns are added dynamically as you build the table. With the `GridLayout`, row and column sizes are defined in the layout definition.

Neither layout is better, it's just a matter of using the best layout for your needs. We'll create a 3 x 3 grid using each layout to give a comparison, as you could easily find yourself using both layouts, even within the same application.

Getting ready

To stay focused on the layouts and offer an easier comparison, we will create two separate applications for this recipe. Create two new Android projects, the first called `TableLayout` and the other called `GridLayout`.

How to do it...

1. Starting with the `TableLayout` project, open **activity_main.xml**. Change the root layout to `TableLayout`.
2. Add three `TableRows` with three sets of `TextViews` to each `TableRow` to create a 3 x 3 matrix. For demonstration purposes, the columns are labeled A-C and the rows 1-3, so the first row of `TextViews` will be A1, B1, and C1. The final result will look like this:

```
<TableLayout
    xmlns:android="http://schemas.android.com/apk/res/android"
    xmlns:tools="http://schemas.android.com/tools"
    android:layout_width="match_parent"
    android:layout_height="match_parent">
    <TableRow
        android:layout_width="match_parent"
        android:layout_height="match_parent">
        <TextView
```

```xml
            android:layout_width="wrap_content"
            android:layout_height="wrap_content"
            android:text="A1"
            android:id="@+id/textView1" />
        <TextView
            android:layout_width="wrap_content"
            android:layout_height="wrap_content"
            android:text="B1"
            android:id="@+id/textView2" />
        <TextView
            android:layout_width="wrap_content"
            android:layout_height="wrap_content"
            android:text="C1"
            android:id="@+id/textView3" />
    </TableRow>
    <TableRow
        android:layout_width="match_parent"
        android:layout_height="match_parent">
        <TextView
            android:layout_width="wrap_content"
            android:layout_height="wrap_content"
            android:text="A2"
            android:id="@+id/textView4" />
        <TextView
            android:layout_width="wrap_content"
            android:layout_height="wrap_content"
            android:text="B2"
            android:id="@+id/textView5" />
        <TextView
            android:layout_width="wrap_content"
            android:layout_height="wrap_content"
            android:text="C2"
            android:id="@+id/textView6" />
    </TableRow>
    <TableRow
        android:layout_width="match_parent"
        android:layout_height="match_parent">
        <TextView
            android:layout_width="wrap_content"
            android:layout_height="wrap_content"
            android:text="A3"
            android:id="@+id/textView7" />
```

```xml
            <TextView
                android:layout_width="wrap_content"
                android:layout_height="wrap_content"
                android:text="B3"
                android:id="@+id/textView8" />
            <TextView
                android:layout_width="wrap_content"
                android:layout_height="wrap_content"
                android:text="C3"
                android:id="@+id/textView9" />
        </TableRow>
</TableLayout>
```

3. Now, open the `GridLayout` project to edit `activity_main.xml`. Change the root layout to `GridLayout`. Add the `columnCount=3` and `rowCount=3` attributes to the `GridLayout` element.

4. Now, add nine `TextViews` to `GridLayout`. We will use the same text as the preceding `TableLayout` for a consistent comparison. Since the `GridView` does not use `TableRows`, the first three `TextViews` are in Row 1, the next three are in Row 2, and so on. The final result will look like this:

```xml
<GridLayout
    xmlns:android="http://schemas.android.com/apk/res/android"
    android:layout_width="match_parent"
    android:layout_height="match_parent"
    android:columnCount="3"
    android:rowCount="3" >
    <TextView
        android:layout_width="wrap_content"
        android:layout_height="wrap_content"
        android:text="A1"
        android:id="@+id/textView1" />
    <TextView
        android:layout_width="wrap_content"
        android:layout_height="wrap_content"
        android:text="B1"
        android:id="@+id/textView2" />
    <TextView
        android:layout_width="wrap_content"
        android:layout_height="wrap_content"
        android:text="C1"
        android:id="@+id/textView3" />
    <TextView
        android:layout_width="wrap_content"
        android:layout_height="wrap_content"
```

Layouts

```xml
            android:text="A2"
            android:id="@+id/textView4" />
        <TextView
            android:layout_width="wrap_content"
            android:layout_height="wrap_content"
            android:text="B2"
            android:id="@+id/textView5" />
        <TextView
            android:layout_width="wrap_content"
            android:layout_height="wrap_content"
            android:text="C2"
            android:id="@+id/textView6" />
        <TextView
            android:layout_width="wrap_content"
            android:layout_height="wrap_content"
            android:text="A3"
            android:id="@+id/textView7" />
        <TextView
            android:layout_width="wrap_content"
            android:layout_height="wrap_content"
            android:text="B3"
            android:id="@+id/textView8" />
        <TextView
            android:layout_width="wrap_content"
            android:layout_height="wrap_content"
            android:text="C3"
            android:id="@+id/textView9" />
</GridLayout>
```

5. You can either run the application or use the **Design** tab to see the results.

How it works...

As you can see when viewing the tables created, the tables basically look the same on screen. The main difference is the code to create them.

In the `TableLayout` XML, each row is added to the table using a `TableRow`. Each View becomes a column. This is not a requirement as cells can be skipped or left empty. (See how to specify the cell location in a `TableRow` in the following section.)

The `GridLayout` uses the opposite approach. The number of rows and columns are specified when creating the table. We don't have to specify the row or column information (though we can, discussed as follows). Android will automatically add each View to the cells in order.

There's more...

First, let's see more similarities between the layouts. Both layouts have the ability to stretch columns to use the remaining screen space. For the `TableLayout`, add the following attribute to the xml declaration:

    android:stretchColumns="1"

`stretchColumns` specifies the (zero based) index of the columns to stretch. (`android:shrinkColumns` is a zero-based index of columns that can shrink, so the table can fit the screen.)

To achieve the same effect with the `GridLayout`, add the following attribute to all the Views in the B column (`textView2`, `textView5`, and `textView8`):

    android:layout_columnWeight="1"

> All cells in a given column must define the weight or it will not stretch.

Now, let's look at some of the differences, as this is really the key to determine which layout to use for a given task. The first thing to note is how the columns and rows are actually defined. In the `TableLayout`, the rows are specifically defined, using a `TableRow`. (Android will determine the number of columns in the table based on the row with the most cells.) Use the `android:layoutColumn` attribute when defining the View to specify the column.

In contrast, with the `GridLayout`, the row and column counts are specified when defining the table (using the `columnCount` and `rowCount` as shown previously.)

In the preceding example, we just added `TextViews` to the `GridLayout` and let the system position them automatically. We can alter this behavior by specifying the row and column position when defining the View, such as:

    android:layout_row="2"
    android:layout_column="2"

> Android automatically increments the cell counter after adding each View, so the *next* View should also specify the row and column, otherwise, you may not get the intended result.

Like the `LinearLayout` shown in the *LinearLayout* recipe, the `GridLayout` also offers the orientation attribute of supporting both horizontal (the default) and vertical. The orientation determines how the cells are placed. (Horizontal fills the columns first, then moves down to the next row. Vertical fills the first column on each row, then moves to the next column.)

Layouts

Using ListView, GridView, and Adapters

The `ListView` and `GridView` are both descendants of `ViewGroup`, but they are used more like a View since they are data driven. In other words, rather than defining all the possible Views that might fill a `ListView` (or `GridView`) at design time, the contents are created dynamically from the data passed to the View. (The layout of the `ListItem` might be created at design time to control the look of the data during runtime.)

As an example, if you needed to present a list of countries to a user, you could create a `LinearLayout` and add a button for each country. There are several problems with this approach: determining the countries available, keeping the list of buttons up to date, having enough screen space to fit all the countries, and so on. Otherwise, you could create a list of countries to populate a `ListView`, which will then create a button for each entry.

We will create an example, using the second approach, to populate a `ListView` from an array of country names.

Getting ready

Create a new project in Android Studio and call it `ListView`. The default `ActivityMain` class extends the `Activity` class. We will change it to extend the `ListActivity` class instead. We will then create a simple string list and bind it to the `ListView`, to derivate the buttons at runtime.

How to do it...

1. Open the **MainActivity.java** file and change the base declaration so it will extend `ListActivity` instead of the `Activity` class:

   ```
   public class MainActivity extends ListActivity {
   ```

2. Change `onCreate()` so it matches the following:

   ```
   protected void onCreate(Bundle savedInstanceState) {
     super.onCreate(savedInstanceState);
     String[] countries = new String[]{"China", "France",
     "Germany", "India", "Russia", "United Kingdom",
     "United States"};

     ListAdapter countryAdapter = new
         ArrayAdapter<String>(this, android.R.layout.
         simple_list_item_1, countries);
     setListAdapter(countryAdapter);
   ```

```
            getListView().setOnItemClickListener(
                new AdapterView.OnItemClickListener() {
                @Override
                public void onItemClick(AdapterView<?> parent, View
                    view, int position, long id) {
                    String s = ((TextView) view).getText() + " " +
                        position;
                    Toast.makeText(getApplicationContext(), s,
                        Toast.LENGTH_SHORT).show();
                }
            });
        }
```

3. Now run the application on an emulator or device to see the populated `ListView`.

How it works...

We start by creating a simple array of country names, then use that to populate a `ListAdapter`. In this example, we used an `ArrayAdapter` when constructing the `ListAdapter`, but Android has several other adapter types available as well. Such as, if your data is stored in a database, you could use the `CursorAdapter`. If one of the built-in types doesn't meet your needs, you can always use the `CustomAdapter`.

We create the adapter with this line of code:

```
ListAdapter countryAdapter = new ArrayAdapter<String>(this,
    android.R.layout.simple_list_item_1, countries);
```

Here, we instantiate the `ArrayAdapter` using our string array (the last parameter). Notice the `android.R.layout.simple_list_item_1` parameter? This defines the layout for the button. Here, we are using one of the layouts as provided by Android, but we could create our own layout and pass our ID instead.

Once we have the adapter ready, we just pass it to the underlying `ListView` with the `setListAdapter()` call. (The underlying `ListView` comes from extending the `ListViewActivity`.) Finally, we implement the `setOnItemClickListener` to display a Toast when the user presses a button (which represents a country) in the list.

`ListViews` are very common in Android as they make efficient use of screen space with a scrolling View, which can be very handy on small screens. The `ScrollView` layout offers an alternative approach to create a similar scrolling effect. The main difference between the two approaches is that the `ScrollView` layout is fully inflated before being shown to the user, whereas the `ListView` only inflates the Views that will be visible. For limited data, this may not be an issue, but for larger data sets, the application could run out of memory before the list is even shown.

Layouts

Also, since the `ListView` is driven by a data adapter, the data can easily be changed. Even in our limited example, adding a new country to the screen is as simple as adding the name to the country list. More importantly, the list can be updated during runtime while the user is using the app (for example, downloading an updated list from a website to show real-time options).

There's more...

The `ListView` also supports a multiple selection mode using the `setChoiceMode()` method. To see it in action, add the following line of code after `setListAdapter()`:

```
getListView().setChoiceMode(ListView.CHOICE_MODE_MULTIPLE);
```

Then, change the `ListItem` layout from `android.R.layout.simple_list_item_1` to `android.R.layout.simple_list_item_checked`.

While most applications requiring a scrolling list turn to the `ListView`, Android also offers the `GridView`. They are very similar in functionality, even using the same data adapters. The main difference is visual which allows multiple columns. For a better understanding, let's change the `ListView` example to a `GridView`.

To start, we need to change `MainActivity` to extend from `Activity` again, instead of `ListActivity`. (This will undo the preceding Step 1.) Then, replace `onCreate()` with the following code:

```
protected void onCreate(Bundle savedInstanceState) {
    super.onCreate(savedInstanceState);
    GridView gridView = new GridView(this);
    setContentView(gridView);
    String[] countries = new String[]{"China", "France",
        "Germany", "India", "Russia", "United Kingdom",
        "United States"};
    ListAdapter countryAdapter = new ArrayAdapter<String>(this,
        android.R.layout.simple_list_item_1, countries);
    gridView.setAdapter(countryAdapter);
    gridView.setNumColumns(2);
    gridView.setOnItemClickListener(new
    AdapterView.OnItemClickListener() {
        @Override
        public void onItemClick(AdapterView<?> parent, View view,
            int position, long id) {
                String s = ((TextView) view).getText() + " " +
                    position;
                Toast.makeText(getApplicationContext(), s,
                    Toast.LENGTH_SHORT).show();
        }
    });
}
```

As you can see, there's more setup code for the `GridView` than there was for the `ListView`. The `onCreate()` method creates a new `GridView` and passes it in the `setContentView()` call. (We used this variation of `setContentView`, as was mentioned in *Defining and inflating a layout*, instead of creating a layout with just a `GridView`, but the end result is the same.)

The `ListViewActivity` base class handles much of this, but the `GridView` does not have a corresponding activity class to extend.

Changing layout properties during runtime

In Android development, it's generally the preferred practice to define the UI with XML and the application code in Java, keeping the User Interface code separate from the application code. There are times where it is much easier or more efficient, to alter (or even build) the UI from the Java code. Fortunately, this is easily supported in Android.

We saw a small example of modifying the layout from code in the previous recipe, where we set the number of `GridView` column to display in the code. In this recipe, we will obtain a reference to the `LayoutParams` object to change the margin during runtime.

Getting ready

Here we will set up a simple layout with XML and use a `LinearLayout.LayoutParams` object to change the margins of a View during runtime.

How to do it....

1. Open the `activity_main.xml` file and change the layout from `RelativeLayout` to `LinearLayout`. It will look as follows:

   ```
   <LinearLayout xmlns:android="http://schemas.android.com/apk/res/android"
       xmlns:tools="http://schemas.android.com/tools"
       android:layout_width="match_parent"
       android:layout_height="match_parent">
   </LinearLayout>
   ```

2. Add a TextView and include an ID as follows:

   `android:id="@+id/textView"`

3. Add `Button` and include an ID as follows:

   `android:id="@+id/button"`

Layouts

4. Open `MainActivity.java` and add the following code to the `onCreate()` method to set up an `onClick` event listener:

   ```
   Button button = (Button)findViewById(R.id.button);
   button.setOnClickListener(new View.OnClickListener() {
       @Override
       public void onClick(View view) {
           ((TextView)findViewById(
               R.id.textView)).setText("Changed at runtime!");
           LinearLayout.LayoutParams params = (LinearLayout.
               LayoutParams)view.getLayoutParams();
           params.leftMargin += 5;
       }
   });
   ```

5. Run the program on a device or emulator.

How it works...

Every View (and therefore `ViewGroup`) has a set of layout parameters associated with it. In particular, all Views have parameters to inform their parent of their desired height and width. These are defined with the `layout_height` and `layout_width` parameters. We can access this layout information from the code with the `getLayoutParams()` method. The layout information includes the layout height, width, margins, and any class-specific parameters. In this example, we moved the button on each click by obtaining the button `LayoutParams` and changing the margin.

Optimizing layouts with the Hierarchy Viewer

Before you can start optimizing your layouts, it helps to understand the Android layout process. Inflating a layout, begins when the activity first comes into display. Three steps occur:

- **Measure**: This is where the Views determine their size, starting with the parent and working through all the children. The parent may have to call its children multiple times to work out the final size.
- **Layout**: This is where the parent determines the position of its children
- **Draw**: This is where the Views are actually rendered

This process starts with the parent, which then iterates through all its children. Those children iterate through their children. This creates the Layout Tree, with the parent becoming the root node in the tree.

Layouts

Hierarchy Viewer is a tool included with the **Android SDK** for inspecting layouts. It graphically shows the Layout Tree along with timing results for each view/node. By examining the tree layout and the timing; you can look for inefficient design and bottlenecks. Armed with this information, you're in position to optimize your layouts.

For this recipe, we will use Hierarchy Viewer to inspect the example layout given in the *Using RelativeLayout* recipe.

Getting ready

In the *There's more...* section of the *Using RelativeLayout* recipe, a `LinearLayout` example was shown to highlight the difference between the layouts. The comment was made stating the `LinearLayout` required a nested layout. We're going to create a new project called `OptimizingLayouts` using the example `LinearLayout`. We will then use Hierarchy Viewer to inspect the layout. We will need a rooted Android device or the emulator for this Recipe.

> Hierarchy Viewer will only connect to rooted devices, such as an emulator.

How to do it...

1. Open the `OptimizingLayouts` project in Android Studio. Run the project on your rooted device (or emulator) and make sure the screen is visible (unlock if needed).
2. In Android Studio, start the Android Device Monitor by going to the following menu option: **Tools | Android | Android Device Monitor**.
3. In Android Device Monitor, change to the Hierarchy View perspective, by going to **Window | Open Perspective...** this will bring up the following dialog:

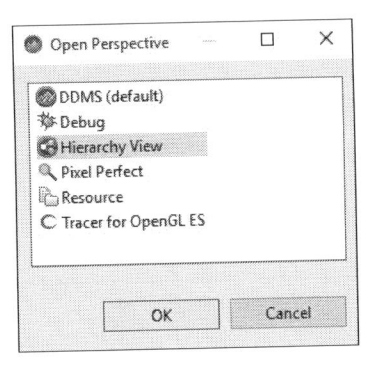

4. Now click on **Hierarchy Viewer** and on **OK**.

Layouts

5. In the **Windows** section on the left is the list of devices with the running processes. Click on the `OptimizingLayouts` process to inspect the layout.

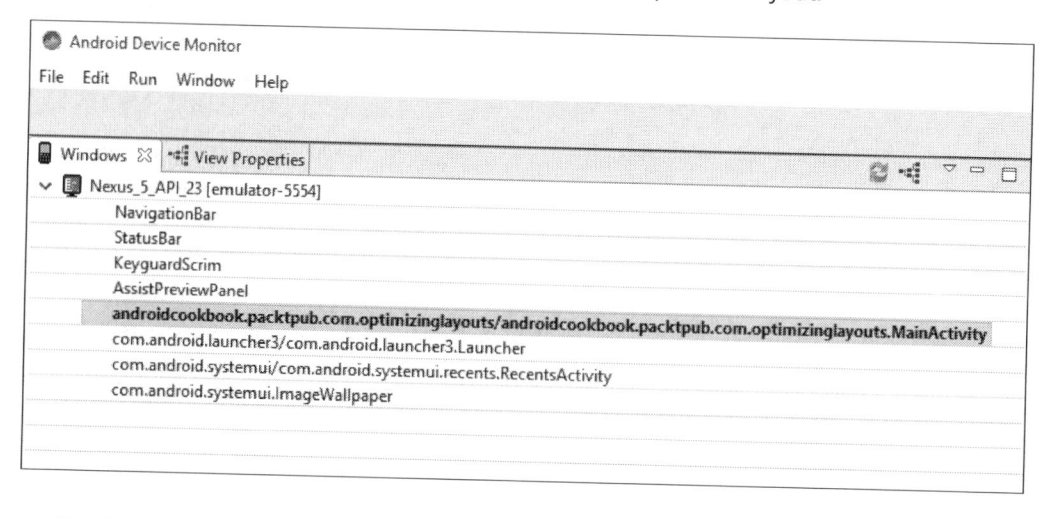

6. See the graphical representation of this activity in the **TreeView** section (in the center pane, which occupies most of the Hierarch Viewer perspective).

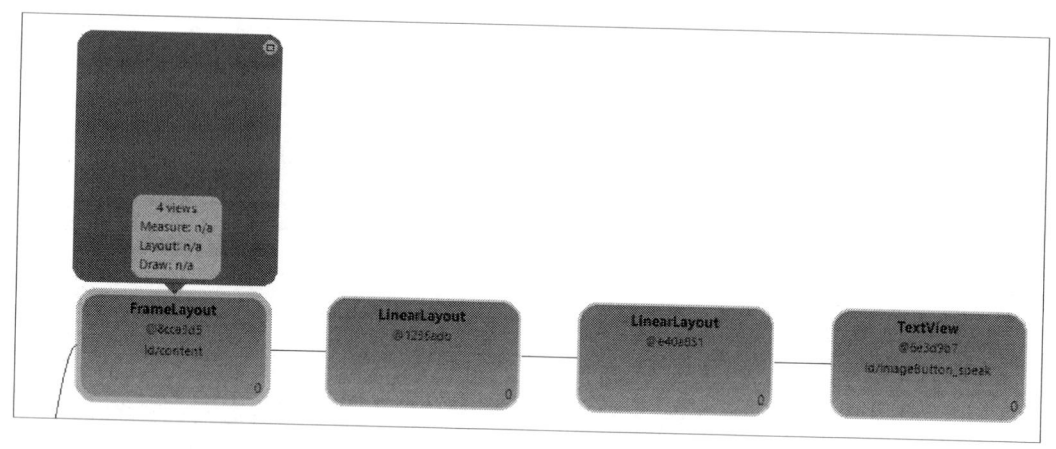

How it works...

The Tree Layout section shows a graphical hierarchy of the Views that comprise this layout, along with the layout times. (Unfortunately for this demonstration, the render times are too fast for visual color-coding references.) What's important for this example is the nested `LinearLayouts` as shown previously. (It's worth taking some time to explore the other Views that make up this layout so you can see what Android is doing for us behind the scenes.)

As already mentioned in the `RelativeLayout` example, the solution is to redesign this layout using the `RelativeLayout`. Ideally, we want a wider, flatter layout, rather than deeply nested layouts to reduce the number of iterations required during the sizing step. For timing purposes, this is obviously a trivial example, but even this example can have an impact. Imagine the user flicking through a `ListView` with thousands of items based on this inefficient layout. If you experience stuttering while scrolling, your optimizing steps could start by examining the layout in Hierarchy Viewer.

There's more...

Lint is another tool included with the Android SDK with built-in support by Android Studio. By default, you're already using Lint to check your code for issues such as deprecated API calls, unsupported API calls for the target API level, security issues, and so on. For our Optimizing Layout concerns, some of the conditions that Lint will automatically check include the following:

- Deep layouts — the default maximum is 10 levels
- Nested weights, which are bad for performance
- Useless parent
- Useless leaf

If you check the Lint warning in Android Studio for this layout, you will see the following warning on the second `LinearLayout` element:

```xml
<?xml version="1.0" encoding="utf-8"?>
<LinearLayout xmlns:android="http://schemas.android.com/apk/res/android"
    android:orientation="horizontal"
    android:layout_width="match_parent"
    android:layout_height="match_parent"
    android:gravity="center">

    <LinearLayout
        android:la  <LinearLayout
        android:layout_height="wrap_content"
        android:layout_weight="1"
        android:gravity="center" >
        <TextView
            android:id="@+id/imageButton_speak"
            android:layout_width="wrap_content"
            android:layout_height="wrap_content"
            android:text="Centered" />
    </LinearLayout>

</LinearLayout>
```

This LinearLayout layout or its LinearLayout parent is useless more... (Ctrl+F1)

Layouts

The `ViewStub` can also be used to optimize a layout. Think of the `ViewStub` as a "lazy load" for your layout. The layout in the `ViewStub` will not inflate until it's needed, which reduces the Views needed to inflate. The layout will render faster and use less memory. This is a great way to have functionality that is seldom used, such as a `Print` feature, available when needed, but that does not take up memory when not needed. Here's an example of a `ViewStub`:

```
<ViewStub
    android:id="@+id/viewStubPrint"
    android:inflatedId="@id/print"
    android:layout="@layout/print"
    android:layout_width="wrap_content"
    android:layout_height="wrap_content"/>
```

There are two ways to actually inflate the `ViewStub`:

- Set the visibility parameter of `ViewStub` to `VISIBLE`:

```
((ViewStub) findViewById(R.id.viewStubPrint)).
    setVisibility(View.VISIBLE);
```

- Call the `inflate()` method on the `ViewStub`:

```
View view = ((ViewStub) findViewById(
    R.id.viewStubPrint)).inflate();
```

Once the `ViewStub` is inflated, the `ViewStub` ID will be removed from the layout and replaced with the inflated ID.

3
Views, Widgets, and Styles

In this chapter, we will cover the following topics:

- Inserting a widget into a layout
- Using graphics to show the button state
- Creating a widget at runtime
- Creating a custom component
- Applying a style to a View
- Turning a style into a theme
- Selecting a theme based on the Android OS version

Introduction

The term **widgets** can refer to several different concepts in Android. When most people talk about widgets, they are referring to **app widgets**, which are typically seen on the home screen. App widgets are like mini applications by themselves as they usually provide a subset of functionality, based on their main application. (Usually, most app widgets are installed along with an application, but that is not a requirement. They can be standalone apps in a widget format.) A common app widget example is a weather application that offers several different app widgets for the home screen. *Chapter 5, Exploring Fragments, AppWidgets, and the System UI,* will discuss home screen app widgets and provide recipes to create your own.

When developing for Android, the term widgets generally refers to specialized Views placed in the layout files, such as a Button, TextView, CheckBox, and so on. In this chapter, we will focus on widgets for app development.

Views, Widgets, and Styles

To see the list of widgets provided in the **Android SDK**, open a layout file in Android Studio, and click on the **Design** tab. Along the left side of the Design view, you will see the **Widget** section below the **Layout** section, as in the following screenshot:

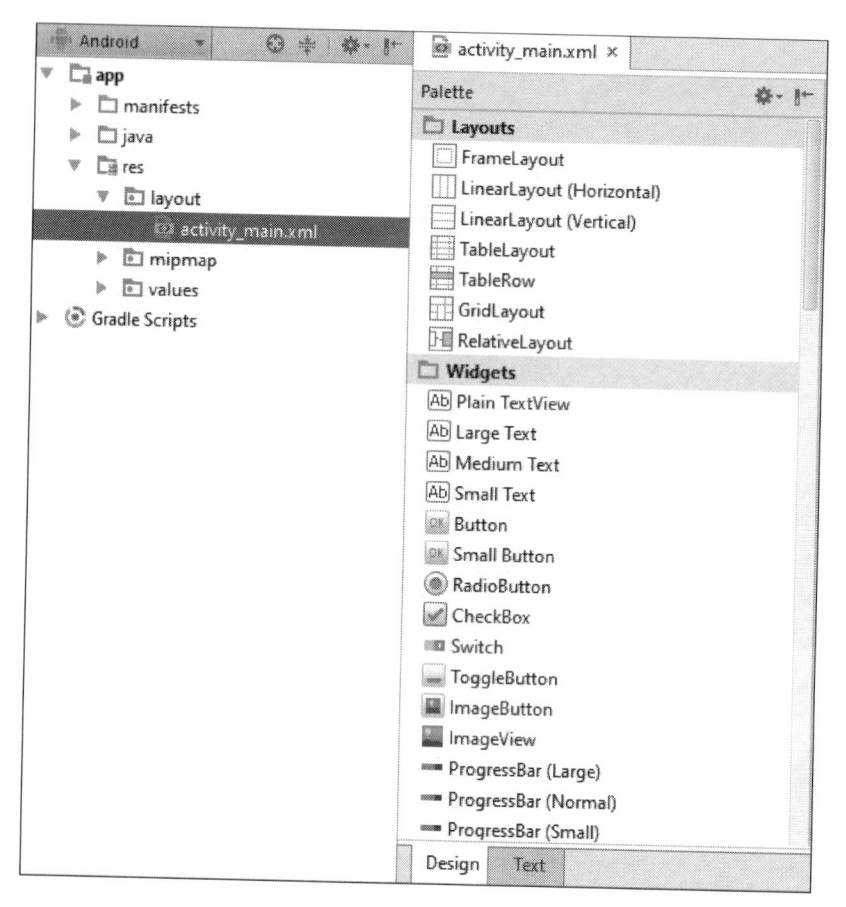

As you can see from the list, the **Android SDK** provides many useful widgets—from a simple TextView, Button, or Checkbox to the much more complex widgets such as the Clock, DatePicker, and Calendar. As useful as the built-in widgets are, it's also very easy to expand on what's provided in the SDK. We can extend an existing widget to customize its functionality, or we can create our own widget from scratch by extending the base View class. (We will provide an example of this in the *Creating a custom component* recipe later.)

The visual look of widgets can also be customized. These settings can be used to create **styles**, which in turn can be used to create **themes**. Just like with other development environments, creating a theme offers the benefit of easily changing the appearance throughout our entire application with minimal effort. Lastly, the Android SDK also provides many built-in themes and variations, such as the Holo theme from Android 3/4 and the Material theme from Android 5. (Android 6.0 did not release a new theme.)

Inserting a widget into a layout

As you may have seen from previous recipes, **widgets** are declared in a layout file, or created in code. For this recipe, we will go step-by-step to add a button with the Android Studio Designer. (For later recipes, we will just show the layout XML from the TextView.) After creating the button, we will create an `onClickListener()`.

Getting ready

Start a new project in Android Studio and call it `InsertWidget`. Use the default options for creating a Phone and Tablet project and select **Empty Activity** when prompted for the Activity Type. You can delete the default TextView (or leave it) as it will not be needed for this recipe.

How to do it...

To insert a widget into a layout, follow these steps:

1. Open the **activity_main.xml** file in Android Studio and click on the **Design** tab.

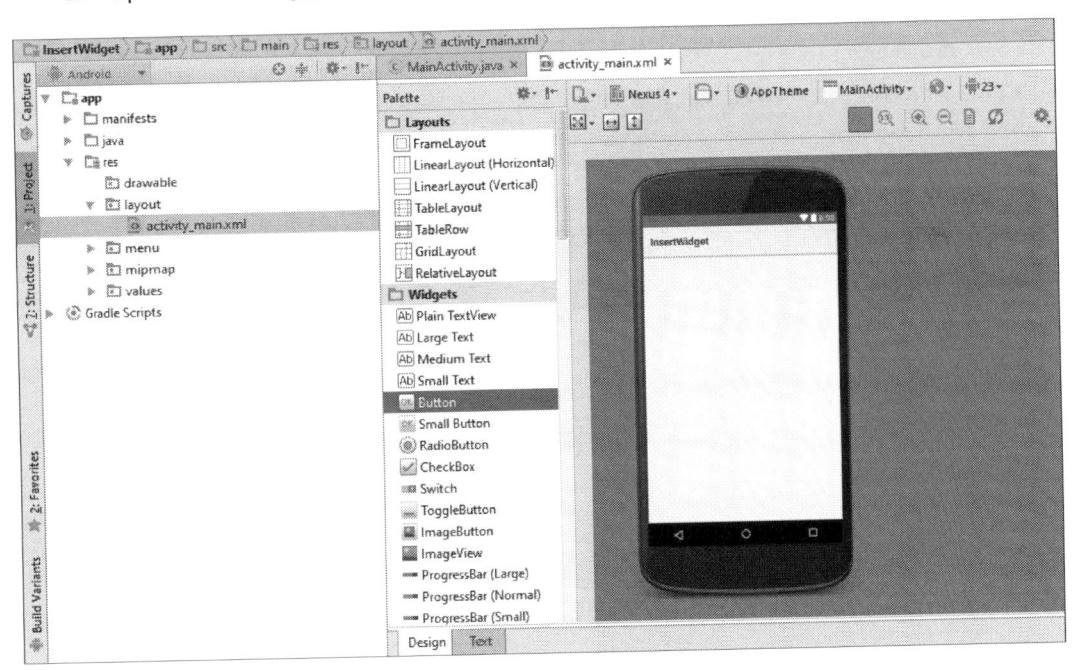

Views, Widgets, and Styles

2. Find **Button** in the widget list and drag it to the center of the activity screen on the right. Android will automatically set the layout parameters based on where the button is dropped. If you center the button as shown in the screenshot, Android Studio will set those parameters in the XML.

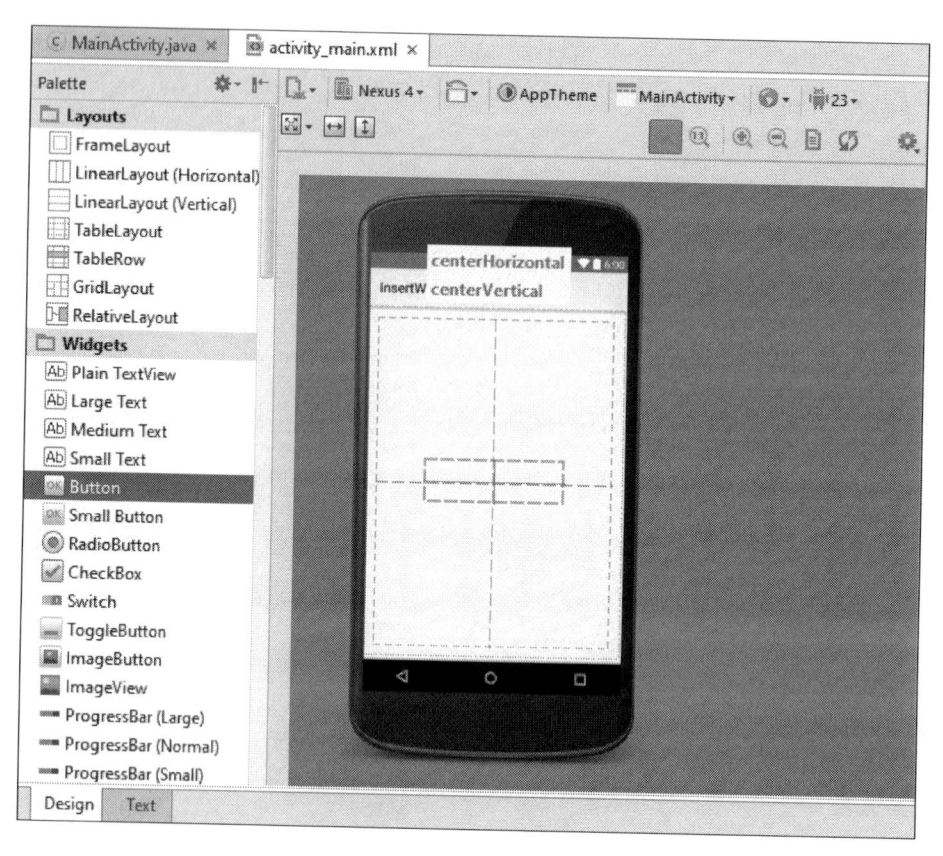

3. To view the `xml` created, click on the **Text** tab as shown in the following screenshot. See how the button is centered using the `RelativeLayout` parameters. Also, take note of the default ID as we will need it for the next step.

```xml
activity_main.xml ×
<RelativeLayout xmlns:android="http://schemas.android.com/apk/res/android"
    xmlns:tools="http://schemas.android.com/tools"
    android:layout_width="match_parent"
    android:layout_height="match_parent"
    tools:context=".MainActivity">
<Button
    android:layout_width="wrap_content"
    android:layout_height="wrap_content"
    android:text="New Button"
    android:id="@+id/button"
    android:layout_centerVertical="true"
    android:layout_centerHorizontal="true"
    tools:ignore="HardcodedText" />
</RelativeLayout>
```
Design   Text

4. Now, open the `MainActivity.java` file to edit the code. Add the following code to the `onCreate()` method to set up the `onClickListener()`:

```java
Button button = (Button)findViewById(R.id.button);
button.setOnClickListener(new View.OnClickListener() {
    @Override
    public void onClick(View view) {
        Toast.makeText(MainActivity.this,"Clicked",
            Toast.LENGTH_SHORT).show();
    }
});
```

5. Run the application on a device or emulator.

How it works...

Creating the UI with the Android Studio is as simple as dragging and dropping Views. You can also edit the properties of the Views directly in the **Design** tab. Switching to the XML code is as simple as hitting the **Text** tab.

What we did here is very common in Android development—creating the UI in XML, then hooking up the UI components (Views) in the Java code. To reference a View from code, it must have a resource identifier associated with it. This is done using the `id` parameter:

```
android:id="@+id/button"
```

Our `onClickListener` function displays a pop-up message on the screen called **Toast**, when the button is pressed.

Views, Widgets, and Styles

There's more...

Take a look again at the format of the identifier we created previously, `@+id/button`. The `@` specifies this is going to be a resource and the `+` sign indicates a new resource. (If we failed to include the plus sign, we would get a compile time error stating **No resource matched the indicated name**).

See also

- Butter Knife (Open Source Project)—Field and method binding for Android Views: `http://jakewharton.github.io/butterknife/`

Using graphics to show button state

We've talked about the versatility of Android Views and how behavior and visual appearance can be customized. In this recipe, we will create a drawable **state selector**, which is a resource defined in XML that specifies the drawable to use based on the View's state. The most commonly used states, along with the possible values, include:

- `state_pressed=["true" | "false"]`
- `state_focused=["true" | "false"]`
- `state_selected=["true" | "false"]`
- `state_checked=["true" | "false"]`
- `state_enabled=["true" | "false"]`

To define a state selector, create an XML file with the `<selector>` element, as shown:

```
<?xml version="1.0" encoding="utf-8"?>
<selector xmlns:android="http://schemas.android.com/apk/res/android" >
</selector>
```

Within the `<selector>` element, we define an `<item>` to identify the drawable to be used based on the specified state(s). Here's an example `<item>` element using multiple states:

```
<item
    android:drawable="@android:color/darker_gray"
    android:state_checked="true"
    android:state_selected="false"/>
```

> It's important to remember the file is read from top to bottom so the first item that meets the state requirements will be used. A default drawable, one with no states included, would need to go last.

Chapter 3

For this recipe, we will use a state selector to change the background color based on the `ToggleButton` state.

Getting ready

Create a new project in Android Studio and call it `StateSelector` using the default **Phone & Tablet** options. When prompted for the **Activity Type**, select **Empty Activity**. To make it easier to type the code for this recipe, we will use a color as the graphic to represent the button state.

How to do it...

We will start by creating the state selector, which is a resource file defined with XML code. We will then set up the button to use our new state selector. Here are the steps:

1. Create a new XML file in the `res/drawable` folder and call it: `state_selector.xml`. The file should consist of the following XML code:

    ```xml
    <?xml version="1.0" encoding="utf-8"?>
    <selector xmlns:android="http://schemas.android.com/apk/res/android">
        <item
            android:drawable="@android:color/darker_gray"
            android:state_checked="true"/>
        <item
            android:drawable="@android:color/white"
            android:state_checked="false"/>
    </selector>
    ```

2. Now open the **activity_main.xml** file and drop in a `ToggleButton` as follows:

    ```xml
    <ToggleButton
        android:layout_width="wrap_content"
        android:layout_height="wrap_content"
        android:text="New ToggleButton"
        android:id="@+id/toggleButton"
        android:layout_centerVertical="true"
        android:layout_centerHorizontal="true"
        android:background="@drawable/state_selector" />
    ```

3. Run the application on a device or emulator.

Views, Widgets, and Styles

How it works...

The main concept to understand here is the Android State Selector. As shown in Step 2, we created a resource file which specified a **drawable** (a color in this case) based on `state_checked`.

Android supports many other state conditions besides checked. While typing in `android:state`, look at the autocomplete dropdown to see the list of other options.

Once we have the drawable resource created (the XML from step 1), we just have to tell the view to use it. Since we wanted the background color to change based on the state, we use the `android:background` property.

`state_selector.xml` is a drawable resource that can be passed to any property that accepts a drawable. We could, for example, replace the button in a checkbox with the following XML:

```
android:button="@drawable/state_selector"
```

There's more...

What if we wanted actual images for the graphics instead of just a color change? This is as easy as changing the drawable referenced in the item state.

The source code available for download uses two graphic images, downloaded from: `https://pixabay.com/` (this was chosen because the images are free to use and didn't require a login.)

Once you have your desired images, place them in the `res/drawable` folder. Then, change the state item line in the XML to reference your images. Here's an example:

```
<item
    android:drawable="@drawable/checked_on"
    android:state_checked="true"/>
```

(Change `check_on` to match your image resource name.)

Using designated folders for screen-specific resources

When Android encounters a `@drawable` reference, it expects to find the target in one of the `res/drawable` folders. These are designed for different screen densities: `ldpi` (low dots per inch), `mdpi` (medium), `hdpi` (high), and `xhdpi` (extra-high) and they allow us to create resources for specific target devices. When an application is running on a specific device, Android will load resources from the designated folder that most closely matches the actual screen density.

If it finds this folder empty, it will try the next nearest match and so on until it finds the named resource. For tutorial purposes, a separate set of files for each possible density is not required, and so placing our images in the `drawable` folder is a simple way to run the exercise on any device.

> For a complete list of resource identifiers available, visit `http://developer.android.com/guide/topics/resources/providing-resources.html`.

See also

For another example on Android resource selection, see the recipe on *Selecting theme based on the OS version* later.

Creating a widget at runtime

As mentioned before, generally, the UI is declared in XML files and then modified during runtime through the Java code. It is possible to create the UI completely in Java code, though for a complex layout, it would generally not be considered best practice.

The GridView example from the previous chapter was created in code. But unlike the GridView recipe, in this recipe, we are going to add a view to the existing layout defined in `activity_main.xml`.

Getting ready

Create a new project in Android Studio and call it `RuntimeWidget`. Select the **Empty Activity** option when prompted for the **Activity type**.

How to do it...

We will start by adding an ID attribute to the existing layout so we can access the layout in code. Once we have a reference to the layout in code, we can add new views to the existing layout. Here are the steps:

1. Open the `res/layout/activity_main.xml` and add an ID attribute to the main `RelativeLayout`, as follows:

   ```
   android:id="@+id/layout"
   ```

2. Completely remove the default `<TextView>` element.

Views, Widgets, and Styles

3. Open the `MainActivity.java` file so we can add code to the `onCreate()` method. Add the following code (after `setContentView()`) to get a reference to the `RelativeLayout`:

    ```
    RelativeLayout layout = (RelativeLayout)findViewById(R.id.layout);
    ```

4. Create a DatePicker and add it to the layout with the following code:

    ```
    DatePicker datePicker = new DatePicker(this);
    layout.addView(datePicker);
    ```

5. Run the program on a device or emulator.

How it works...

This is hopefully very straightforward code. First, we get a reference to the parent layout using `findViewById`. We added the ID to the existing RelativeLayout (in step 1) to make it easier to reference. We create a DatePicker in code and add it to the layout with the `addView()` method.

There's more...

What if we wanted to create the entire layout from code? Though it may not be considered best practice, there are times when it is certainly easier (and less complex) to create a layout from code. Let's see how this example would look if we didn't use the layout from `activity_main.xml`. Here's how the onCreate() would look:

```
@Override
protected void onCreate(Bundle savedInstanceState) {
    super.onCreate(savedInstanceState);
    RelativeLayout layout = new RelativeLayout(this);
    DatePicker datePicker = new DatePicker(this);
    layout.addView(datePicker);
    setContentView(layout);
}
```

In this example, it's really not that different. If you create a view in code and want to reference it later, you either need to keep a reference to the object, or assign the view an ID to use `findViewByID()`. To give a view an ID, use the **setID()** method by passing in **View.generateViewId()** (to generate a unique ID) or define the ID using **<resources>** in xml.

Creating a custom component

As we have seen in previous recipes, the Android SDK provides a wide range of components. But what happens when you can't find a prebuilt component that fits your unique needs? You can always create your own!

In this recipe, we will walk through creating a custom component that derives from the View class, just like the built-in widgets. Here's a high-level overview:

1. Create a new class that extends View.
2. Create custom constructor(s).
3. Override onMeasure(), and the default implementation returns a size of 100 x 100.
4. Override onDraw(), and the default implementation draws nothing.
5. Define custom methods and listeners (such as on<Event>()).
6. Implement custom functionality.

> While overriding onMeasure() and onDraw() is not strictly required, the default behavior is likely not what you would want.

Getting ready

Start a new project in Android Studio and call it CustomView. Use the default wizard options, including the **Phone & Tablet SDK** and select **Empty Activity** when prompted for the Activity type. Once the project files are created and open in Android Studio, you are ready to begin.

How to do it...

We will create a new class for our custom component to derive from the Android View class. Our custom component could be a subclass of an existing class, such as the Activity, but we will create it in a separate file to make it easier to maintain. Here are the steps:

1. Start by creating a new Java class and also call it CustomView. This is where we will implement our custom component, as described in the introduction.
2. Change the class constructor so it extends View. It should look as follows:

    ```
    public class CustomView extends View {
    ```

3. Define a Paint object for the class, which will be used in the onDraw():

    ```
    final Paint mPaint = new Paint();
    ```

Views, Widgets, and Styles

4. Create a default constructor, which requires the activity `Context`, so we can inflate the view. We will set the paint properties here as well. The constructor should look as follows:

```java
public CustomView(Context context) {
    super(context);
    mPaint.setColor(Color.BLACK);
    mPaint.setTextSize(30);
}
```

5. Override the onDraw() method as follows:

```java
@Override
protected void onDraw(Canvas canvas) {
    super.onDraw(canvas);
    setBackgroundColor(Color.CYAN);
    canvas.drawText("Custom Text", 100, 100, mPaint);
    invalidate();
}
```

6. Finally, inflate our custom view in `MainActivity.java` by replacing the `setContentView()` with our view, as shown:

```java
setContentView(new CustomView(this));
```

7. Run the application on a device or emulator to see it in action.

How it works...

We start by extending the View class, just as the built-in components do. Next, we create the default constructor. This is important as we need the context to pass down to the super class, which we do with the call:

```java
super(context);
```

We need to override `onDraw()`, otherwise, as mentioned in the introduction, our custom view won't display anything. When `onDraw()` is called, the system passes in a **Canvas** object. The canvas is the area of the screen for our view. (Since we didn't override `onMeasure()`, our view would be 100 x 100, but since our entire activity consists of just this view, we get the whole screen as our canvas.)

We created the `Paint` object at the class level, and as `final`, to be more efficient with memory allocation. (`onDraw()` should be as efficient as possible since it can be called multiple times per second.) As you see from running the program, our onDraw() implementation just sets the background color to cyan and prints text to the screen (using `drawText()`).

There's more...

Actually, there's a lot more. We've just touched the surface of what you can do with a custom component. Fortunately, as you see from this example, it doesn't take a lot of code to get basic functionality. We could easily spend an entire chapter on topics such as passing layout parameters to the view, adding listener callbacks, overriding `onMeasure()`, using our view in the IDE, and so on. These are all features you can add as your needs dictate.

While a custom component should be able to handle any solution, there are other options that might require less coding. Extending an existing widget is often sufficient without the overhead of a custom component from scratch. If what you need is a solution with multiple widgets, there's also the **compound control**. A compound control, such as a combo box, is just two or more controls grouped together as a single widget.

A compound control would generally extend from a layout, not a View, since you will be adding multiple widgets. You probably wouldn't need to override onDraw() and onMeasure(), as each widget would handle the drawing in their respective methods.

See also

- For more information on drawing, look at *Chapter 9, Graphics and Animation*. For full details on the View object, refer to the Android Developer resource at: `http://developer.android.com/reference/android/view/View.html`

Applying a style to a View

A **style** is a collection of property settings to define the look of a View. As you have already seen while defining layouts, a view offers many settings to determine how it looks, as well as functions. We have already set a view height, width, background color, and padding, plus there are many more settings such as text color, font, text size, margin, and so on. Creating a style is as simple as pulling these settings from the layout and putting them in a style resource.

In this recipe, we will go through the steps of creating a style and hooking it up to a view.

Similar to Cascading Style Sheets, Android Styles allow you to specify your design settings separate from the UI code.

Getting ready

Create a new Android Studio project and call it `Styles`. Use the default wizard options to create a Phone & Tablet project and select Empty Activity when prompted for the Activity. By default, the wizard also creates a `styles.xml` file, which we will use for this recipe.

Views, Widgets, and Styles

How to do it...

We will create our own style resource to change the appearance of a `TextView`. We can add our new style to the `styles.xml` resource created by Android Studio using the following steps:

1. Open the default `styles.xml` file located in `res/values`, as shown here:

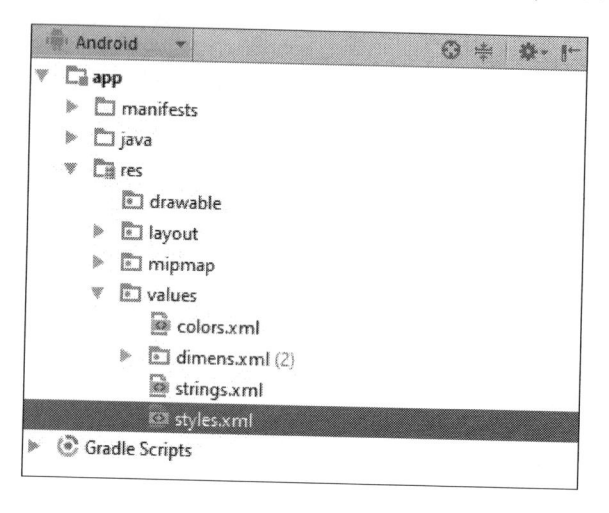

2. We will create a new style called `MyStyle` by adding the following XML below the existing `AppTheme` style:

   ```
   <style name="MyStyle">
       <item name="android:layout_width">match_parent</item>
       <item name="android:layout_height">wrap_content</item>
       <item name="android:background">#000000</item>
       <item name="android:textColor">#AF0000</item>
       <item name="android:textSize">20sp</item>
       <item name="android:padding">8dp</item>
       <item name="android:gravity">center</item>
   </style>
   ```

3. Now tell the view to use this style. Open the `activity_main.xml` file and add the following attribute to the existing `<TextView>` element:

   ```
   style="@style/MyStyle"
   ```

4. Either run the application or view the results in the **Design** tab.

Chapter 3

How it works...

A **style** is a resource, defined by using the `<style>` element nested in a `<resources>` element of an xml file. We used the existing `styles.xml` file, but that is not a requirement, as we can use whatever filename we want. As seen in this recipe, multiple `<style>` elements can be included in one xml file.

Once the style is created, you can easily apply it to any number of other views as well. What if you wanted to have a button with the same style? Just drop a button in the layout and assign the same style.

What if we created a new button, but wanted the button to expand the full width of the view? How do we override the style for just that view? Simple, specify the attribute in the layout as you've always done. The local attribute will take priority over the attribute in the **style**.

There's more...

There is another feature of styles: **inheritance**. By specifying a parent when defining the style, we can have styles build on each other, creating a hierarchy of styles. If you look at the default style in `styles.xml`: `AppTheme`, you will see the following line:

```
<style name="AppTheme" parent="Theme.AppCompat.Light.DarkActionBar">
```

`AppTheme` inherits from a theme defined in the Android SDK.

> If you want to inherit from a style you have created yourself, there is a shortcut method. Instead of using the parent attribute, you can specify the parent name first, followed by a period, then the new name, such as:
>
> `<style name="MyParent.MyStyle" >`

You saw how to specify a style for a view, but what if we wanted all the TextViews in our application to use a specific style? We'd have to go back to each TextView and specify the style. But there's another way. We can include a `textViewStyle` item in a style to automatically assign a style to all TextViews. (There's a style for each of the widget types so you can do this for Buttons, ToggleButtons, TextViews, and so on.)

To set the style for all TextViews, add the following line to the `AppTheme` style:

```
<item name="android:textViewStyle">@style/MyStyle</item>
```

Since the theme for our application already uses `AppThem`, we only have to add that single line to `AppTheme` to have all our TextViews styled with our custom `MyStyle`.

Views, Widgets, and Styles

See also

The Android Design Support Library at:

```
http://android-developers.blogspot.de/2015/05/android-design-support-library.html
```

Turning a style into a theme

A **theme** is a style applied to an Activity or the whole application. To set a theme, use the `android:theme` attribute in the `AndroidManifest.xml` file. The `theme` attribute applies to the `<Application>` element as well as the `<Activity>` elements. All views within that element will be styled with the theme specified.

It's common to set the Application theme, but then override a specific Activity with a different theme.

In the previous recipe, we set the `textViewStyle` using the AppTheme style (which the wizard created automatically.) In this recipe, you will learn how to set both the Application and Activity themes.

Along with the style settings we have already explored, there are additional style options we didn't discuss because they don't apply to a View, they apply to the window as a whole. Settings such as hiding the application title or Action Bar and setting the window background, just to name a few, apply to the window and therefore must be set as a theme.

For this recipe, we are going to create a new theme based on the auto-generated `AppTheme`. Our new theme will modify the window appearance to make it a **dialog**. We will also look at the `theme` settings in the `AndroidManifest.xml`.

Getting ready

Start a new project in Android Studio and call it `Themes`. Use the default wizard options and select the **Empty Activity** when prompted for the Activity type.

How to do it...

We start by adding a new theme to the existing `styles.xml` file to make our activity look like a dialog. Here are the steps to create the new theme and set activity to use the new theme:

1. Since **themes** are defined in the same resource as **styles**, open the `styles.xml` file located in `res/values` and create a new style. We will create a new style based on the AppTheme already provided, and set `windowIsFloating`. The XML will be as follows:

   ```
   <style name="AppTheme.MyDialog">
       <item name="android:windowIsFloating">true</item>
   </style>
   ```

2. Next, set the Activity to use this new dialog theme. Open the `AndroidManifest.xml` file and add a `theme` attribute to the Activity element, as shown:

   ```
   <activity android:name=".MainActivity"
       android:theme="@style/AppTheme.MyDialog">
   ```

   Note that both Application and Activity will now have a theme specified.

3. Now run the application on a device or emulator to see the dialog theme in action.

How it works...

Our new theme `MyDialog` inherits the base `AppTheme` using the alternative parent declaration, since `AppTheme` is defined in our code (and not a system theme). As mentioned in the introduction, some settings apply to the window as a whole, which is what we see with the `windowIsFloating` setting. Once our new theme is declared, we assign our theme to the activity in the `AndroidManifest` file.

There's more...

You might have noticed we could have just added the `windowIsFloating` to the existing `AppTheme` and been done. Since this application only has one Activity, the end result would be the same, but then, any new activities would also appear as a dialog.

Selecting theme based on the Android version

Most users prefer to see apps using the latest themes provided by Android. **Now supports Material Theme** is common for apps upgrading to Android Lollipop. To be competitive with the many other apps in the market, you'll probably want to upgrade your app as well, but what about your users who are still running older versions of Android? By setting up our resources properly, we can use **resource selection** in Android to automatically define the parent theme based on the Android OS version the user is running.

First, let's explore the three main themes available in Android:

- Theme – Gingerbread and earlier
- Theme.Holo – Honeycomb (API 11)
- Theme.Material – Lollipop (API 21)

(As of writing this, there does not appear to be a new theme in Android 6.0.)

This recipe will show how to properly set up the resource directories for Android to use the most appropriate theme based on the API version the app is running on.

Views, Widgets, and Styles

Getting ready

Start a new project in Android Studio and call it `AutomaticThemeSelector`. Use the default wizard option to make a Phone & Tablet project. Select the **Empty Activity** when prompted for the Activity Type.

How to do it...

Depending on the API version selected, Android Studio may use the App Compatability libraries. We don't want to use these libraries for this project since we want to explicitly set which theme to use. We will start by making sure we are extending from the generic Activity class, then we can add our new style resources to select the theme based on the API. Here are the steps:

1. We need to make sure `MainActivity` extends from `Activity` and not `AppCompatActivity`. Open `ActivityMain.java` and if necessary, change it to read as follows:

   ```
   public class MainActivity extends Activity {
   ```

2. Open `activity_main.xml` and drop in two views: a Button and a Checkbox.

3. Open `styles.xml` and remove `AppTheme` as it will not be used. Add our new theme so the file reads as follows:

   ```xml
   <resources>
       <style name="AutomaticTheme" parent="android:Theme.Light">
       </style>
   </resources>
   ```

4. We need to create two new values folders for API 11 and 21. To do this, we need to change Android Studio to use the Project view rather than the Android view. (Otherwise, we won't see the new folders in the next step.) At the top of the **Project** window, it shows **Android**, change this to **Project** for the Project View. See the following screenshot:

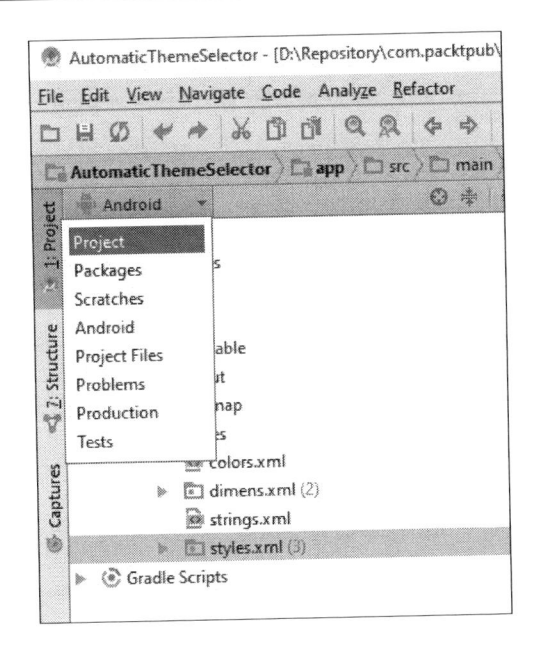

5. Create a new directory by right-clicking on the `res` folder and navigating to **New | Directory**, as shown in this screenshot:

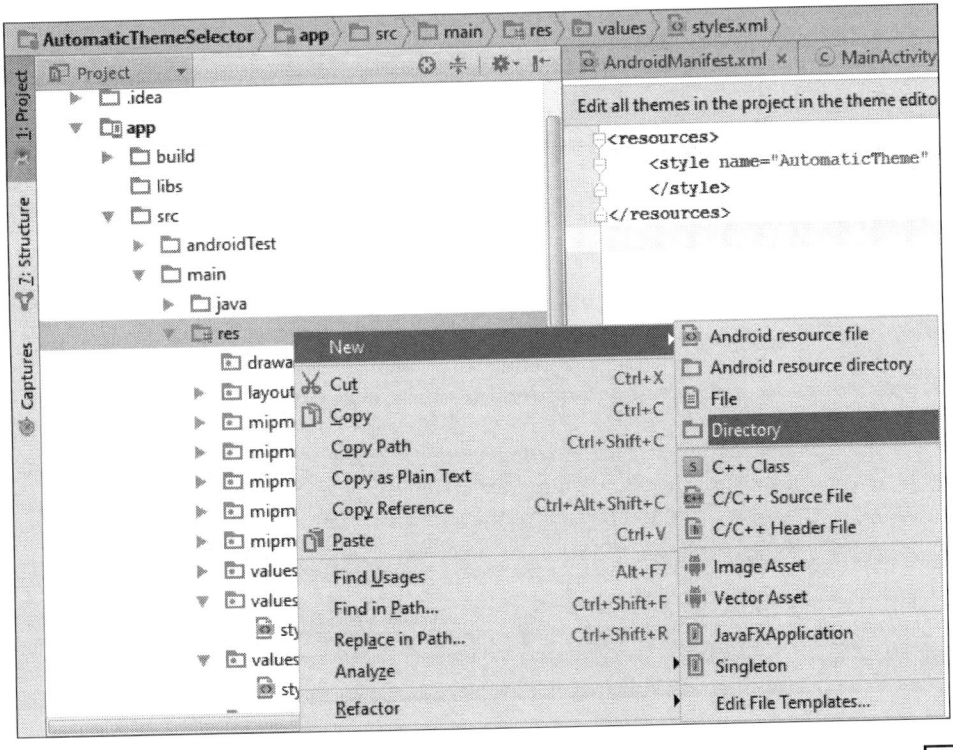

Views, Widgets, and Styles

Use the following name for the first directory: `values-v11`

Repeat this for the second directory using `values-v21`

6. Now create a `styles.xml` file in each of the new directories. (Right-click on the `values-v11` directory and go to the **New | File** option.) For `values-v11`, use the following style to define the Holo theme:

```
<resources>
    <style name="AutomaticTheme"
        parent="android:Theme.Holo.Light">
    </style>
</resources>
```

For the values-v21, use the following code to define the Material theme:

```
<resources>
    <style name="AutomaticTheme"
        parent="android:Theme.Material.Light">
    </style>
</resources>
```

7. The last step is to tell the application to use our new theme. To do this, open `AndroidManifest.xml` and change the `android:theme` attribute to `AutomaticTheme`. It should read as follows:

`android:theme="@style/AutomaticTheme"`

8. Now run the application on a physical device or emulator. If you want to see the three different themes, you will need to have a device or emulator running the different versions of Android.

How it works...

In this recipe, we are using the Android resource selection process to assign the appropriate theme (which is a resource) based on the API version. Since we need to choose the theme based on the OS version in which it was released, we created two new values folders specifying the API version. This gives us a total of three `styles.xml` files: the default style, one in the `values-v11` directory, and the last in the `values-v21` directory.

Notice the same theme name is defined in all three `styles.xml` files. This is how the resource selection works. Android will use the resource from the directory that best fits our values. Here we are using the API level, but other criteria are available as well. It is very common to define separate resources based on other criteria, such as screen size, screen density, and even orientation.

The last step was to specify our new theme as the application theme, which we did in the Android Manifest.

There's more...

For more information on resource selection, see the *Using designated folders for screen-specific resources* topic in the previous recipe, *Using graphics to show button state*.

4
Menus

In this chapter, we will cover the following topics:

- Creating an Options menu
- Modifying menus and menu items during runtime
- Enabling Contextual Action Mode for a view
- Using Contextual Batch Mode with a ListView
- Creating a pop-up menu

Introduction

The Android OS is an ever-changing environment. The earliest Android devices (prior to Android 3.0), were required to have a hardware menu button. Though a hardware button is no longer required, menus are no less important. In fact, the **Menu** API has expanded to now support three different types of menus:

- **Options Menu and Action Bar**: This is the standard menu, which is used for global options of your application. Use this for additional features such as search, settings, and so on.
- **Contextual Mode** (**Contextual Action Mode**): This is generally activated by long press. (Think of this as similar to a right-click on the desktop.) This is used to take an action on the pressed item, such as replying to an e-mail or deleting a file.
- **Pop-up Menu**: This provides a pop-up selection (like a spinner) for an additional action. The menu options are not meant to affect the item pressed, instead use Contextual Mode as described previously. An example would be hitting the share button and getting an additional list of share options.

Menus

Menu resources are similar to other Android UI components; they are generally created in XML, but can be created in code as well. Our first recipe, as shown in the following section, will show the XML menu format and how to inflate it.

Creating an Options menu

Before we actually create and display a menu, let's look at a menu to see the end result. The following is a screenshot showing the menu section of Chrome:

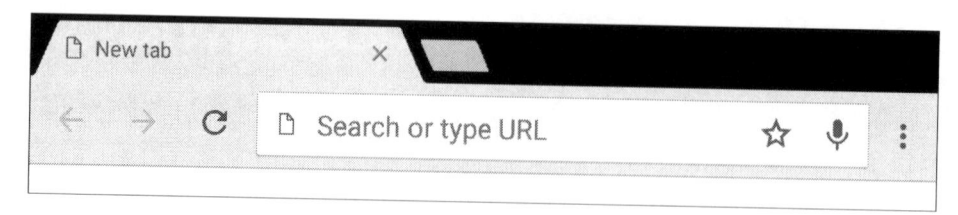

The most obvious feature to note is that the menu will look different based on the screen size. By default, menu items will be added to the Overflow menu—that's the menu you see when you press the three dots at the far right edge.

Menus are typically created in resource files using `XML` (like many other Android resources) but they are stored in the `res/menu` directory though they can also be created in code. To create a menu resource, use the `<menu>` element as shown:

```xml
<menu xmlns:android="http://schemas.android.com/apk/res/android">
</menu>
```

The `<item>` element defines each individual menu item and is enclosed in the `<menu>` element. A basic menu item looks as follows:

```xml
<item
    android:id="@+id/settings"
    android:title="@string/settings" />
```

The most common `<item>` attributes are the following:

- `id`: This is the standard resource identifier
- `title`: This indicates the text to display
- `icon`: This is a draw-able resource
- `showAsAction`: This has been explained as follows (*see the following paragraph*)
- `enabled`: This is enabled by default

Let's look at `showAsAction` in more detail.

The `showAsAction` attribute controls how the menu item is shown. The options include the following:

- `ifRoom`: This menu item should be included in the Action Bar if there's enough space
- `withText`: This indicates that both the title and the icon should be shown
- `never`: This indicates that the menu item should never be included in the Action Bar; always show in the overflow menu
- `always`: This indicates that the menu item should be always included in the Action Bar (use sparingly as space is limited)

> Multiple options can be combined using the pipe (|) separator, such as `showAsAction="ifRoom|withText"`.

With the fundamentals of the menu resource covered, we are now ready to create a standard Options menu and inflate it.

Getting ready

Use Android Studio to create a new project called `OptionsMenu`. Use the default **Phone & Tablet** option and select the **Empty Activity** option when prompted for the Activity Type. Since the wizard does not create the `res/menu` folder by default, navigate to **File | New | Directory** to create it before continuing.

How to do it...

With the new project created as described in the preceding section, you are ready to create a menu. However, first, we will add a string resource to the `strings.xml` file for the menu title. We will use the new string for the menu title when we create the XML for the menu. Here are the steps:

1. Start by opening the `strings.xml` file and add the following `<string>` element to the `<resources>` element:

   ```
   <string name="menu_settings">Settings</string>
   ```

2. Create a new file in the `res/menu` directory and call it `menu_main.xml`.

3. Open the `menu_main.xml` file and add the following XML to define the menu:

   ```
   <?xml version="1.0" encoding="utf-8"?>
   <menu
       xmlns:android="http://schemas.android.com/apk/
           res/android"
       xmlns:app="http://schemas.android.com/apk/res-auto">
       <item android:id="@+id/menu_settings"
   ```

Menus

```
            android:title="@string/menu_settings"
            app:showAsAction="never">
        </item>
    </menu>
```

4. With the menu now created, we just have to override the `onCreateOptionsMenu()` method in `ActivityMain.java` to inflate the menu:

    ```
    @Override
    public boolean onCreateOptionsMenu(Menu menu) {
        getMenuInflater().inflate(R.menu.menu_main, menu);
        return true;
    }
    ```

5. Run the program on a device or emulator to see the menu in the Action Bar.

How it works...

There are two basic steps here:

1. Define the menu in XML.
2. Inflate the menu when the activity is created.

As a good programming habit, we define the string in the `strings.xml` file rather than hardcoding it in the XML. We then use the standard Android string identifier to set the title for the menu in Step 3. Since this is a "Settings" menu item, we don't want this to be shown in the Action Bar. To make sure it is never shown, use `showAsAction="never"`.

With the menu defined, we will use the menu inflater in Step 4 to load the menu during the Activity creation. Notice the `R.menu.menu_main` menu resource syntax? This is why we create the XML in the `res/menu` directory — so the system will know this is a menu resource.

In Step 4, we used `app:showAsAction` rather than Android: `android:showAsAction`. This is because we are using the `AppCompat` library (also referred to as the Android Support Library). By default, the Android Studio new project wizard includes the support library in the project.

There's more...

If you ran the program in Step 5, then you must have seen the **Settings** menu item when you pressed the menu overflow button. But that was it. Nothing else happened. Obviously, menu items aren't very useful if the application doesn't respond to them. Responding to the **Options** menu is done through the `onOptionsItemSelected()` callback.

Add the following method to the application to see a Toast when the Settings menu is selected:

```java
@Override
public boolean onOptionsItemSelected(MenuItem item) {
    if (item.getItemId() == R.id.menu_settings) {
        Toast.makeText(this, "Settings",
            Toast.LENGTH_LONG).show();
    } else {
        return super.onContextItemSelected(item);
    }
    return true;
}
```

That's it. You now have a working menu!

> As shown in the preceding example, return `true` when you've handled the callback; otherwise, call the super class as shown in the `else` statement.

Using a menu item to launch an activity

In this example, we show a Toast so we can see a working example; however, we could just as easily launch a new activity if needed. As you did in the *Starting a new activity with an Intent object* recipe of *Chapter 1, Activities*, create an Intent and call it with `startActivity()`.

Creating sub menus

Sub menus are created and accessed in almost exactly the same manner as other menu elements and can be placed in any of the provided menus, although they cannot be placed within other sub menus. To define a sub menu, include a `<menu>` element within an `<item>` element. Here is the XML form this recipe with two sub menu items added:

```xml
<?xml version="1.0" encoding="utf-8"?>
<menu
    xmlns:android="http://schemas.android.com/apk/res/android"
    xmlns:app="http://schemas.android.com/apk/res-auto">
    <item android:id="@+id/menu_settings
        android:title="@string/menu_settings"
        app:showAsAction="never">
        <menu>
            <item android:id="@+id/menu_sub1"
                android:title="Storage Settings" />
            <item android:id="@+id/menu_sub2"
                android:title="Screen Settings" />
        </menu>
    </item>
</menu>
```

Menus

Grouping menu items

Another menu feature that Android supports is grouping menu items. Android provides several methods for groups, including the following:

- `setGroupVisible()`: Show or hide all items
- `setGroupEnabled()`: Enable or disable all items
- `setGroupCheckable()`: Set the checkable behavior

> Android will keep all grouped items with `showAsAction="ifRoom"` together. This means all items in the group with `showAsAction="ifRoom"` will be in the Action Bar or all items will be in the overflow.

To create a group, add the `<item>` menu elements to a `<group>` element. Here is an example using the menu XML from this recipe with two additional items in a group:

```xml
<?xml version="1.0" encoding="utf-8"?>
<menu
    xmlns:android="http://schemas.android.com/apk/res/android"
    xmlns:app="http://schemas.android.com/apk/res-auto">

    <group android:id="@+id/group_one" >
        <item android:id="@+id/menu_item1"
            android:title="Item 1"
            app:showAsAction="ifRoom"/>
        <item android:id="@+id/menu_item2"
            android:title="Item 2"
            app:showAsAction="ifRoom"/>
    </group>
    <item android:id="@+id/menu_settings"
        android:title="@string/menu_settings"
        app:showAsAction="never"/>
</menu>
```

See also

- For complete details on the menu, visit the Android Developer Menu Resources site at `http://developer.android.com/guide/topics/resources/menu-resource.html`

Modifying menus and menu items during runtime

Though it's been stated many times, it's considered the "best" programming practice to create UI in XML rather than in Java. There are still times when you may need to do it in code. This is especially true if you wanted a menu item to be visible (or enabled) based on some external criteria. Menus can also be included in resource folders, but there are times when you need code to perform the logic. One example might be if you wanted to offer an upload menu item only if the user is logged in to your app.

In this recipe, we will create and modify the menu only through code.

Getting ready

Create a new project in Android Studio and call it `RuntimeMenu` using the default **Phone & Tablet** option. Select the **Empty Activity** option when prompted to add an Activity. Since we will create and modify the menu completely in code, we will not need to create a `res/menu` directory.

How to do it...

To start, we will add string resources for our menu items and a button to toggle the menu visibility. Open the `res/strings.xml` file and follow these steps:

1. Add the following two strings to the existing `<resources>` element:

    ```xml
    <string name="menu_download">Download</string>
    <string name="menu_settings">Settings</string>
    ```

2. Add a button to `activity_main.xml` with `onClick()` set to `toggleMenu` as shown here:

    ```xml
    <Button
        android:id="@+id/buttonToggleMenu"
        android:layout_width="wrap_content"
        android:layout_height="wrap_content"
        android:text="Toggle Menu"
        android:layout_centerVertical="true"
        android:layout_centerHorizontal="true"
        android:onClick="toggleMenu"/>
    ```

Menus

3. Open `ActivityMain.java` and add the following three lines of code just below the class declaration:

   ```
   private final int MENU_DOWNLOAD = 1;
   private final int MENU_SETTINGS = 2;
   private boolean showDownloadMenu = false;
   ```

4. Add the following method for the button to call:

   ```
   public void toggleMenu(View view) {
       showDownloadMenu=!showDownloadMenu;
   }
   ```

5. When the activity is first created, Android calls `onCreateOptionsMenu()` to create the menu. Here is the code to dynamically build the menu:

   ```
   @Override
   public boolean onCreateOptionsMenu(Menu menu) {
       menu.add(0, MENU_DOWNLOAD, 0, R.string.menu_download);
       menu.add(0, MENU_SETTINGS, 0, R.string.menu_settings);
       return true;
   }
   ```

6. For best programming practice, don't use `onCreateOptionsMenu()` to update or change your menu; instead, use `onPrepareOptionsMenu()`. Here is the code to change the visibility of the **Download** menu item based on our flag:

   ```
   @Override
   public boolean onPrepareOptionsMenu(Menu menu) {
       MenuItem menuItem = menu.findItem(MENU_DOWNLOAD);
       menuItem.setVisible(showDownloadMenu);
       return true;
   }
   ```

7. Though not technically required for this recipe, this `onOptionsItemSelected()` code shows how to respond to each menu item:

   ```
   @Override
   public boolean onOptionsItemSelected(MenuItem item) {
       switch (item.getItemId()) {
           case MENU_DOWNLOAD:
               Toast.makeText(this, R.string.menu_download,
                   Toast.LENGTH_LONG).show();
               break;
           case MENU_SETTINGS:
               Toast.makeText(this, R.string.menu_settings,
                   Toast.LENGTH_LONG).show();
               break;
   ```

```
            default:
                return super.onContextItemSelected(item);
    }
        return true;
}
```

8. Run the program on a device or emulator to see the menu changes.

How it works...

We created an override for `onCreateOptionsMenu()`, just like we did in the previous recipe, *Creating an Options Menu*. But instead of inflating an existing menu resource, we created the menu using the `Menu.add()` method. Since we want to modify the menu items later as well as respond to the menu item events, we have defined our own menu IDs and passed them to the `add()` method.

`onOptionsItemSelected()` is called for all the menu items, so we get the menu ID and use a `switch` statement based on the IDs we created. We return `true` if we are handling the menu event, otherwise we pass the event to the super class.

Changing the menu occurs in the `onPrepareOptionsMenu()` method. To simulate an external event, we created a button to toggle a Boolean flag. The visibility of the **Download** menu is determined by the flag. This is where you would want to create your custom code based on whatever criteria you set. Your flag could be set using the current player level or maybe when a new level is ready for release; you send a Push message, which enables the menu item.

There's more...

What if we wanted this **Download** option to be easily noticed to indicate whether it's available? We could tell Android we want the menu in the Action Bar by adding the following code to `onPrepareOptionsMenu()` (before the return statement):

```
menuItem.setShowAsAction(MenuItem.SHOW_AS_ACTION_ALWAYS);
```

Now if you run the code, you will see the **Download** menu item in the Action Bar, but the behavior isn't correct.

Earlier, when we didn't have a menu item in the Action Bar, Android called `onPrepareOptionsMenu()` each time we opened the overflow menu so the visibility was always updated. To correct this behavior, add the following line of code to the `toggleMenu()` method called by the button:

```
invalidateOptionsMenu();
```

The `invalidateOptionsMenu()` call tells Android that our option menu is no longer valid, which then forces a call to `onPrepareOptionsMenu()` giving us the behavior we expect.

> Android considers the menu as always open if a menu item is displayed in the Action Bar.

Enabling Contextual Action Mode for a view

A Context Menu provides additional options related to a specific view—the same concept as a right-click on the desktop. Android currently supports two different approaches: the floating Context Menu and Contextual Mode. Contextual Action Mode was introduced in Android 3.0. The older floating Context Menu could lead to confusion since there was no indication of the currently selected item and it didn't support actions on multiple items—such as selecting multiple emails to delete in one action.

Creating a Floating Context Menu

If you need to use the old style Context Menu, for example, to support preAndroid 3.0 devices, it's very similar to the Option Menu API, just different method names. To create the menu, use `onCreateContextMenu()` instead of `onCreateOptionsMenu()`. To handle the menu item selection, use `onContextItemSelected()` instead of `onOptionsItemSelected()`. Finally, call `registerForContextMenu()` to let the system know you want Context Menu events for the view.

Since Contextual Mode is considered the preferred way to display context options, this recipe will focus on the newer API. Contextual Mode offers the same features as the floating Context Menu, but also adds additional functionality by allowing multiple item selection when using batch mode.

This recipe will demonstrate the setup of Contextual Mode for a single view. Once activated, with a long press, a **Contextual Action Bar** (**CAB**) will replace the Action Bar until Contextual Mode is finished.

> The Contextual Action Bar is not the same as the Action Bar and your activity does not need to include an Action Bar.

Chapter 4

Getting ready

Use Android Studio to create a new project and call it `ContextualMode`. Use the default **Phone & Tablet** option and select **Empty Activity** when prompted to add an Activity. Create a menu directory (`res/menu`) as we did in the first recipe, *Creating an Options menu*, to store the XML for the contextual menu.

How to do it...

We will create an **ImageView** to serve as the host view to initialize Contextual Mode. Since Contextual Mode is usually triggered with a long press, we will set up a long click listener in `onCreate()` for the `ImageView`. When called, we will start Contextual Mode and pass an `ActionMode` callback to handle the Contextual Mode events. Here are the steps:

1. We will start by adding two new string resources. Open the `strings.xml` file and add the following:

    ```
    <string name="menu_cast">Cast</string>
    <string name="menu_print">Print</string>
    ```

2. With the strings created, we can now create the menu by creating a new file in `res/menu` called `context_menu.xml` using the following XML:

    ```
    <?xml version="1.0" encoding="utf-8"?>
    <menu
        xmlns:android="http://schemas.android.com/apk/res/android"
        xmlns:app="http://schemas.android.com/apk/res-auto">
    <item android:id="@+id/menu_cast"
        android:title="@string/menu_cast" />
    <item android:id="@+id/menu_print"
        android:title="@string/menu_print" /> </menu>
    ```

3. Now add an `ImageView` to `activity_main.xml` to serve as the source for initiating Contextual Mode. Here is the XML for the ImageView:

    ```
    <ImageView
        android:id="@+id/imageView"
        android:layout_width="wrap_content"
        android:layout_height="wrap_content"
        android:layout_centerVertical="true"
        android:layout_centerHorizontal="true"
        android:src="@mipmap/ic_launcher"/>
    ```

Menus

4. With the UI now set up, we can add the code for Contextual Mode. First, we need a global variable to store the `ActionMode` instance returned when we call `startActionMode()`. Add the following line of code to `MainActivity.java` below the class constructor:

```
ActionMode mActionMode;
```

5. Next, create an `ActionMode` callback to pass to `startActionMode()`. Add the following code to the `MainActivity` class below the code in the previous step:

```
private ActionMode.Callback mActionModeCallback = new ActionMode.Callback() {
    @Override
    public boolean onCreateActionMode(ActionMode mode,
        Menu menu) {
        mode.getMenuInflater().inflate(R.menu.context_menu,
            menu);
        return true;
    }
    @Override
    public boolean onPrepareActionMode(ActionMode mode,
        Menu menu) {
        return false;
    }
    @Override
    public boolean onActionItemClicked(ActionMode mode,
        MenuItem item) {
        switch (item.getItemId()) {
            case R.id. menu_cast:
                Toast.makeText(MainActivity.this, "Cast",
                    Toast.LENGTH_SHORT).show();
                mode.finish();
                return true;
            case R.id. menu_print:
                Toast.makeText(MainActivity.this, "Print",
                    Toast.LENGTH_SHORT).show();
                mode.finish();
                return true;
            default:
                return false;
        }
    }
    @Override
    public void onDestroyActionMode(ActionMode mode) {
        mActionMode = null;
    }
};
```

6. With the `ActionMode` callback created, we just need to call `startActionMode()` to begin Contextual Mode. Add the following code to the `onCreate()` method to set up the long click listener:

```
ImageView imageView = (ImageView)findViewById(
    R.id.imageView);
imageView.setOnLongClickListener(new
    View.OnLongClickListener() {
    public boolean onLongClick(View view) {
        if (mActionMode != null) return false;
        mActionMode = startActionMode(mActionModeCallback);
        return true;
    }
});
```

7. Run the program on a device or emulator to see the CAB in action.

How it works...

As you saw in Step 2, we have used the same menu XML to define the contextual menu as the other menus.

The main piece of code to understand is the `ActionMode` callback. This is where we handle the Contextual Mode events: initializing the menu, handling menu item selections, and cleaning up. We start Contextual Mode in the long press event with a call to `startActionMode()` by passing in the `ActionMode` callback created in Step 5.

When action mode is triggered, the system calls the `onCreateActionMode()` callback, which inflates the menu and displays it in the Contextual Action Bar. The user can dismiss the Contextual Action Bar by pressing the back arrow or the back key. The CAB is also dismissed when the user makes a menu selection. We show a Toast to give a visual feedback for this recipe but this is where you would implement your functionality.

There's more...

In this example, we store the `ActionMode` returned from the `startActionMode()` call. We use it to prevent a new instance from being created when the Action Mode is already active. We could also use this instance to make changes to the Contextual Action Bar itself, such as changing the title with the following:

```
mActionMode.setTitle("New Title");
```

This is particularly useful when working with multiple item selections as we'll see in the next recipe.

Menus

See also

- See the next recipe, *Using Contextual Batch Mode with a ListView*, to work with multiple items selection

Using Contextual Batch Mode with a ListView

As discussed in the previous recipe, Contextual Mode supports two forms of use: single View mode (as demonstrated) and multiple selection (or batch) mode. Batch mode is where Contextual Mode outperforms the old style Context Menu as multiple selections were not supported.

If you've ever used an e-mail app such as Gmail or a file browser, you've probably seen Contextual Mode when selecting multiple items. Here is a screenshot from Solid Explorer, which shows an excellent implementation of Material Theme and Contextual Mode:

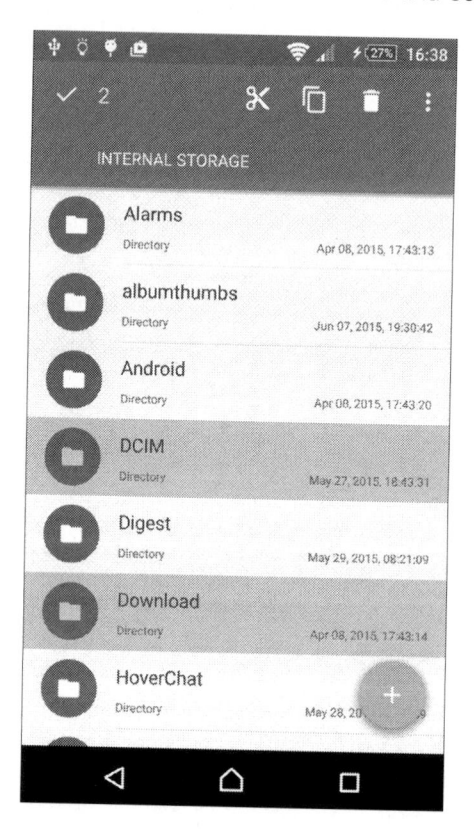

In this recipe, we will create a `ListView` populated with multiple country names to demonstrate multiple selections or batch mode. This example will use the normal long press event and also the item click event to start Contextual Mode.

Getting ready

Create a new project in Android Studio and call it `ContextualBatchMode`. Use the default **Phone & Tablet** option and select **Empty Activity** when prompted to add an Activity. Create a menu directory (`res/menu`) for the contextual menu.

How to do it...

Similar to the previous recipe, we start by creating a menu in XML to inflate when Contextual Mode begins. We need to define `MultiChoiceModeListener` to handle batch mode with the `ListView`. We then set up the `ListView` to allow multiple selections and pass in the `MultiChoiceModeListener`. Here are the steps:

1. Open the `strings.xml` file and add two new string resources for the menu items as follows:

    ```xml
    <string name="menu_move">Move</string>
    <string name="menu_delete">Delete</string>
    ```

2. Create a new file called `contextual_menu.xml` in the `res/menu` folder with the following XML:

    ```xml
    <?xml version="1.0" encoding="utf-8"?>
    <menu
        xmlns:android="http://schemas.android.com/apk/res/android"
        xmlns:app="http://schemas.android.com/apk/res-auto">
        <item android:id="@+id/menu_move"
            android:title="@string/menu_move" />
        <item android:id="@+id/menu_delete"
            android:title="@string/menu_delete" />
    </menu>
    ```

3. Since we need a `ListView`, we will change `MainActivity` to extend from `ListActivity` as follows:

    ```
    public class MainActivity extends ListActivity
    ```

Menus

4. Create a `MultiChoiceModeListener` to handle the Contextual Action Bar events. Add the following code to `MainActivity.java` below the class constructor:

```java
AbsListView.MultiChoiceModeListener
    mMultiChoiceModeListener = new
        AbsListView.MultiChoiceModeListener() {
    @Override
    public void onItemCheckedStateChanged(ActionMode mode,
        int position, long id, boolean checked) {
    }

    @Override
    public boolean onCreateActionMode(ActionMode mode, Menu
        menu) {
        // Inflate the menu for the CAB
        MenuInflater inflater = mode.getMenuInflater();
        inflater.inflate(R.menu.contextual_menu, menu);
        return true;
    }

    @Override
    public boolean onPrepareActionMode(ActionMode mode,
        Menu menu) {
        return false;
    }

    @Override
    public boolean onActionItemClicked(ActionMode mode,
        MenuItem item) {
        // Handle menu selections
        switch (item.getItemId()) {
            case R.id.menu_move:
                Toast.makeText(MainActivity.this, "Move",
                    Toast.LENGTH_SHORT).show();
                mode.finish();
                return true;
            case R.id.menu_delete:
                Toast.makeText(MainActivity.this, "Delete",
                    Toast.LENGTH_SHORT).show();
                mode.finish();
                return true;
            default:
                return false;
        }
    }
}
```

```
        @Override
        public void onDestroyActionMode(ActionMode mode) {
        }
    };
```

5. Next, we will change the `onCreate()` to set up the `ListView` and populate a `ListAdapter` using a string array of country names, as follows:

```
@Override
protected void onCreate(Bundle savedInstanceState) {
    super.onCreate(savedInstanceState);

    String[] countries = new String[]{"China", "France",
        "Germany", "India", "Russia", "United Kingdom",
            "United States"};
    ListAdapter countryAdapter = new ArrayAdapter<String>(
        this, android.R.layout.simple_list_item_checked,
            countries);
    setListAdapter(countryAdapter);
    getListView().setChoiceMode(
        ListView.CHOICE_MODE_MULTIPLE_MODAL);
    getListView().setMultiChoiceModeListener(
        mMultiChoiceModeListener);

    getListView().setOnItemClickListener(new
        AdapterView.OnItemClickListener() {
            @Override
            public void onItemClick(AdapterView<?> parent, View
                view, int position, long id) {
                ((ListView)parent).setItemChecked(position,
                    true);
            }
        });
}
```

6. Run the program on a device or emulator to see the CAB in action.

How it works...

The three key elements to make Action Mode work in batch mode are:

1. Creating a Contextual Menu to inflate
2. Defining `MultiChoiceModeListener` to pass to `setMultiChoiceModeListener()`
3. Set `ChoiceMode` of the `ListView` to CHOICE_MODE_MULTIPLE_MODAL.

Menus

`MultiChoiceModeListener` serves the same purpose as the `ActionMode` callback used in single-view Contextual Mode, and in fact, implements `ActionMode.Callback`. As with `ActionMode.Callback`, the menu is inflated when `MultiChoiceModeListener` calls `onCreateActionMode()`.

By default, Context Mode is initiated with a long press on an item in the `ListView`. We will go a step further by starting Contextual Mode when the item is checked using the `onItemClick()` event. If we don't do this, the only way to initiate the Contextual Mode would be with a long click, which may leave many users unaware of the additional functionality.

There's more...

As mentioned in the introduction to this chapter, your activity does not need to include an Action Bar to use a Contextual Action Bar. If you do have an Action Bar and it's visible, it will be overlaid with the CAB. If you do not have an Action Bar as the default with this recipe, the layout will be redrawn to include the CAB (and redrawn again when the CAB is dismissed). If you want the Action Bar to be visible, either change the theme for the Activity or change the base class and set up the `ListView` manually.

See also

- For more information on the `ListView`, refer to *Chapter 2, Layouts*

Creating a pop-up menu

A pop-up menu is attached to a view similar to the dropdown on a spinner. The idea of a pop-up menu is to provide additional options to complete an action. A common example might be a **Reply** button in an e-mail app. When pressed, several reply options are shown, such as: **Reply**, **Reply All**, and **Forward**.

Here is an example of the pop-up menu from the recipe:

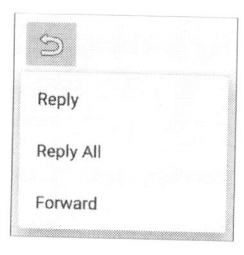

Chapter 4

Android will show the menu options below the anchor view if there is room; otherwise, it will show them above the view.

> A pop-up menu is *not* meant to affect the view itself. That is the purpose of a Context Menu. Instead refer to the Floating Menu/Context Mode described in the *Enabling Contextual Action Mode for a view* recipe.

In this recipe, we will create the pop-up menu shown previously, using an `ImageButton` as the anchor view.

Getting ready

Create a new project in Android Studio and call it `PopupMenu`. Use the default **Phone & Tablet** option and select **Empty Activity** when prompted to add an Activity. As before, create a menu directory (`res/menu`) to store the menu XML.

How to do it...

We start by creating the XML menu to inflate on the button press. After inflating the pop-up menu, we call `setOnMenuItemClickListener()` by passing in the callback to handle the menu item selection. Here are the steps:

1. Add the following strings to `strings.xml`:

    ```xml
    <string name="menu_reply">Reply</string>
    <string name="menu_reply_all">Reply All</string>
    <string name="menu_forward">Forward</string>
    ```

2. Create a new file in the `res/menu` directory called `menu_popup.xml` using the following XML:

    ```xml
    <?xml version="1.0" encoding="utf-8"?>
    <menu
        xmlns:android="http://schemas.android.com/
            apk/res/android"
        xmlns:app="http://schemas.android.com/apk/res-auto">
        <item android:id="@+id/menu_reply"
            android:title="@string/menu_reply" />
        <item android:id="@+id/menu_reply_all"
            android:title="@string/menu_reply_all" />
        <item android:id="@+id/menu_forward"
            android:title="@string/menu_forward" />
    </menu>
    ```

Menus

3. Create an `ImageButton` in `activity_main.xml` to provide the anchor view for the pop-up menu. Create it as shown in the following XML code:

```xml
<ImageButton
    android:id="@+id/imageButtonReply"
    android:layout_width="wrap_content"
    android:layout_height="wrap_content"
    android:layout_centerVertical="true"
    android:layout_centerHorizontal="true"
    android:src="@android:drawable/ic_menu_revert"
    android:onClick="showPopupMenu"/>
```

4. Open `MainActivity.java` and add the following `OnMenuItemClickListener` below the class constructor:

```java
private PopupMenu.OnMenuItemClickListener
    mOnMenuItemClickListener = new
        PopupMenu.OnMenuItemClickListener() {
    @Override
    public boolean onMenuItemClick(MenuItem item) {
        // Handle menu selections
        switch (item.getItemId()) {
            case R.id.menu_reply:
                Toast.makeText(MainActivity.this, "Reply",
                    Toast.LENGTH_SHORT).show();
                return true;
            case R.id.menu_reply_all:
                Toast.makeText(MainActivity.this,"Reply
                    All",Toast.LENGTH_SHORT).show();
                return true;
            case R.id.menu_forward:
                Toast.makeText(MainActivity.this,
                    "Forward", Toast.LENGTH_SHORT).show();
                return true;
            default:
                return false;
        }
    }
};
```

5. The final code is to handle the button `onClick()` event, as follows:

```java
public void showPopupMenu(View view) {
    PopupMenu popupMenu = new PopupMenu(
        MainActivity.this,view);
    popupMenu.inflate(R.menu.menu_popup);
    popupMenu.setOnMenuItemClickListener(
        mOnMenuItemClickListener);
    popupMenu.show();
}
```

6. Run the program on a device or emulator to see the pop-up menu.

How it works...

If you have read the previous menu recipes, this will probably look very familiar. Basically, we just inflate a pop-up menu when the `ImageButton` is pressed. We set up a menu item listener to respond to the menu selection.

The key is to understand each of the menu options available in Android so you can use the correct menu type for a given scenario. This will help your application by providing a consistent user experience and reducing the learning curve.

5
Exploring Fragments, AppWidgets, and the System UI

In this chapter, we will cover the following topics:

- Creating and using a Fragment
- Adding and removing Fragments during runtime
- Passing data between Fragments
- Creating a shortcut on the Home screen
- Creating a Home screen widget
- Adding Search to the Action Bar
- Showing your app full screen

Introduction

With a firm understanding of layouts from *Chapter 2, Layouts*, we'll dig deeper into UI development with Fragments. Fragments are a way to separate your UI into smaller sections that can easily be reused. Think of Fragments as mini-activities, complete with their own classes, layouts, and lifecycle. Instead of designing your screen in one Activity Layout, possibly duplicating functionality across multiple layouts, you can break the screen into smaller, logical sections and turn them in to Fragments. Your Activity Layout can then reference one or multiple Fragments, as needed. The first three recipes will explore Fragments in-depth.

Exploring Fragments, AppWidgets, and the System UI

With an understanding of Fragments, we're ready to expand on our discussion of Widgets. In *Chapter 3, Views, Widgets, and Styles*, we discussed how to add widgets to your own app. Now, we'll look at how to create an App Widget so users can put their app on their Home screen.

The last recipes of the chapter will explore System UI options. We have a recipe for adding a `Search` option to the Action Bar using the Android `SearchManager` API. The last recipe shows Full Screen mode and several additional variations of altering the System UI.

Creating and using a Fragment

Android didn't always support Fragments. The early versions of Android were designed for phones, when screens had relatively small displays. It wasn't until Android started being used on tablets that there was a need to split the screen into smaller sections. Android 3.0 introduced the `Fragments` class and the Fragment Manager.

Along with a new class, also came the Fragment Lifecycle. The Fragment Lifecycle is similar to the Activity Lifecycle introduced in *Chapter 1, Activities*, as most events parallel the Activity Lifecycle.

Here's a brief overview of the main callbacks:

- `onAttach()`: It's called when the Fragment is associated with an Activity.
- `onCreate()`: It's called when the Fragment is first created.
- `onCreateView()`: It's called when the Fragment is about to be displayed for the first time.
- `onActivityCreated()`: It's called when the associated Activity is created.
- `onStart()`: It's called when the Fragment will become visible to the user.
- `onResume()`: It's called just before a Fragment is displayed.
- `onPause()`: It's called when the Fragment is first suspended. The user may return to the Fragment, but this is where you should persist any user data.
- `onStop()`: It's called when the Fragment is no longer visible to the user.
- `onDestroyView()`: It's called to allow final cleanup.
- `onDetach()`: It's called when the Fragment is no longer associated with the Activity.

For our first exercise, we will create a new Fragment derived from the standard `Fragment` class. But there are several other `Fragment` classes we could derive from, including:

- `DialogFragment`: It's used for creating a floating dialog
- `ListFragment`: It's creates a `ListView` in a Fragment, similar to the `ListActivity`
- `PreferenceFragment`: It's creates a list of Preference objects, commonly used for a Settings page

Chapter 5

In this recipe, we will walk through creating a basic Fragment derived from the `Fragment` class and include it in an Activity Layout.

Getting ready

Create a new project in Android Studio and call it: `CreateFragment`. Use the default **Phone & Tablet** options and select the **Empty Activity** option when prompted for the Activity Type.

How to do it...

In this recipe, we will create a new `Fragment` class with an accompanying layout file. We will then add the Fragment to the Activity Layout so it will be visible when the Activity starts. Here are the steps to create and display a new Fragment:

1. Create a new layout called `fragment_one.xml` using the following XML:

    ```xml
    <RelativeLayout xmlns:android="http://schemas.android.com/apk/res/android"
        android:layout_height="match_parent"
        android:layout_width="match_parent">
        <TextView
            android:layout_width="wrap_content"
            android:layout_height="wrap_content"
            android:text="Fragment One"
            android:id="@+id/textView"
            android:layout_centerVertical="true"
            android:layout_centerHorizontal="true" />
    </RelativeLayout>
    ```

2. Create a new Java file called `FragmentOne` with the following code:

    ```java
    public class FragmentOne extends Fragment {
        @Override
        public View onCreateView(LayoutInflater inflater,
            ViewGroup container, Bundle savedInstanceState) {
                return inflater.inflate(R.layout.fragment_one,
                    container, false);
        }
    }
    ```

3. Open the `main_activity.xml` file and replace the existing `<TextView>` element with the following `<fragment>` element:

    ```xml
    <fragment
        android:name="com.packtpub.androidcookbook.createfragment.FragmentOne"
        android:id="@+id/fragment"
    ```

Exploring Fragments, AppWidgets, and the System UI

```
android:layout_width="wrap_content"
android:layout_height="wrap_content"
android:layout_centerVertical="true"
android:layout_centerHorizontal="true"
tools:layout="@layout/fragment_one" />
```

4. Run the program on a device or emulator.

How it works...

We start by creating a new class, the same as we do for an Activity. In this recipe, we only create an overwrite for the `onCreateView()` method to load our Fragment layout. But, just like with the Activity events, we can override the other events as we need them. Once the new Fragment is created, we then add it to the Activity Layout. Since the `Activity` class was created before `Fragments` existed, they do not support `Fragments`. If we were using pure framework classes, we would want to use `FragmentActivity` instead. If you used the Android Studio New Project Wizard, then by default the `MainActivity` extends `AppCompatActivity`, which already includes support for Fragments.

There's more...

We're only creating a single, simple Fragment in this recipe to teach the fundamentals of Fragments. But this is a good time to point out the power of Fragments. If we are creating multiple Fragments (and usually we are, as that's the point of using Fragments), when creating the Activity Layouts as we did in Step 4, we could create different layout configurations using the Android Resource Folders. The portrait layout may have only a single Fragment while the landscape may have two or more.

Adding and removing Fragments during runtime

Defining a Fragment in the layout, as we did in the previous recipe, is known as a static Fragment and cannot be changed during runtime. Rather than using the `<fragment>` element, we will create a container to hold the Fragment, then create the Fragment dynamically in the Activity's `onCreate()` method.

The `FragmentManager` provides the APIs for adding, removing, and changing Fragments during runtime using a `FragmentTransaction`. A Fragment transaction consists of:

- Starting a transaction
- Performing one or multiple actions
- Committing the transaction

Chapter 5

This recipe will demonstrate the `FragmentManager` by adding and removing Fragments during runtime.

Getting ready

Create a new project in Android Studio and call it: `RuntimeFragments`. Use the default **Phone & Tablet** options and select the **Empty Activity** option when prompted for the **Activity Type**.

How to do it...

To demonstrate adding and removing Fragments, we first need to create the Fragments, which we will do be extending the `Fragment` class. After creating the new Fragments, we need to alter the layout for the Main Activity to include the `Fragment` container. From there, we just add the code to handle the Fragment transactions. Here are the steps:

1. Create a new layout file called `fragment_one.xml` and include the following XML:

    ```xml
    <RelativeLayout xmlns:android="http://schemas.android.com/
      apk/res/android"
        android:layout_height="match_parent"
        android:layout_width="match_parent">
        <TextView
            android:layout_width="wrap_content"
            android:layout_height="wrap_content"
            android:text="Fragment One"
            android:id="@+id/textView"
            android:layout_centerVertical="true"
            android:layout_centerHorizontal="true" />
    </RelativeLayout>
    ```

2. The second layout file called `fragment_two.xml` is almost identical, with the only difference being the text:

    ```
    android:text="Fragment Two"
    ```

3. Create a new Java file called `FragmentOne` with the following code:

    ```java
    public class FragmentOne extends Fragment {
        @Override
        public View onCreateView(LayoutInflater inflater,
          ViewGroup container, Bundle savedInstanceState) {
            return inflater.inflate(R.layout.fragment_one,
              container, false);
        }
    }
    ```

    Import from the following library:

    ```
    android.support.v4.app.Fragment
    ```

4. Create the second Java file called `FragmentTwo` with the following code:

   ```
   public class FragmentTwo extends Fragment {
       @Override
       public View onCreateView(LayoutInflater inflater,
         ViewGroup container, Bundle savedInstanceState) {
           return inflater.inflate(R.layout.fragment_two,
             container, false);
       }
   }
   ```

   Import from the following library:

   ```
   android.support.v4.app.Fragment
   ```

5. Now we need to add a container and a button to the Main Activity layout. Change `main_activity.xml` as follows:

   ```
   <?xml version="1.0" encoding="utf-8"?>
   <RelativeLayout xmlns:android="http://schemas.android.com/
     apk/res/android"
       xmlns:tools="http://schemas.android.com/tools"
       android:layout_width="match_parent"
       android:layout_height="match_parent">
       <FrameLayout
           android:id="@+id/frameLayout"
           android:layout_width="match_parent"
           android:layout_height="wrap_content"
           android:layout_above="@+id/buttonSwitch"
           android:layout_alignParentTop="true">
       </FrameLayout>
       <Button
           android:id="@+id/buttonSwitch"
           android:layout_width="wrap_content"
           android:layout_height="wrap_content"
           android:text="Switch"
           android:layout_alignParentBottom="true"
           android:layout_centerInParent="true"
           android:onClick="switchFragment"/>
   </RelativeLayout>
   ```

6. With the Fragments created and the container added to the layout, we are now ready to write the code to manipulate the Fragments. Open `MainActivity.java` and add the following code below the class constructor:

   ```
   FragmentOne mFragmentOne;
   FragmentTwo mFragmentTwo;
   int showingFragment=0;
   ```

7. Add the following code to the existing `onCreate()` method, below `setContentView()`:

   ```
   mFragmentOne = new FragmentOne();
   mFragmentTwo = new FragmentTwo();
   FragmentManager fragmentManager =
       getSupportFragmentManager();
   FragmentTransaction fragmentTransaction =
       fragmentManager.beginTransaction();
   fragmentTransaction.add(R.id.frameLayout, mFragmentOne);
   fragmentTransaction.commit();
   showingFragment=1;
   ```

   Import from the following libraries:

   ```
   android.support.v4.app.FragmentManager
   android.support.v4.app.FragmentTransaction
   ```

8. The last code we need to add handles the Fragment switching, called by the button:

   ```
   public void switchFragment(View view) {
       FragmentManager fragmentManager =
           getSupportFragmentManager();
       FragmentTransaction fragmentTransaction =
           fragmentManager.beginTransaction();
       if (showingFragment==1) {
           fragmentTransaction.replace(R.id.frameLayout,
               mFragmentTwo);
           showingFragment = 2;
       } else {
           fragmentTransaction.replace(R.id.frameLayout,
               mFragmentOne);
           showingFragment=1;
       }
       fragmentTransaction.commit();
   }
   ```

9. Run the program on a device or emulator.

How it works...

Most of the steps for this recipe involve setting up the Fragments. Once the Fragments are declared, we create them in the `onCreate()` method. Though the code can be condensed to a single line, it's shown in the long form as it makes it easier to read and understand.

Exploring Fragments, AppWidgets, and the System UI

First, we get the `FragmentManager` so we can begin a `FragmentTransaction`. Once we have a `FragmentTransaction`, we start the transaction with `beginTransaction()`. Multiple actions can occur within the transaction, but all we need here is to `add()` our initial Fragment. We call the `commit()` method to finalize the transaction.

Now that you understand the Fragment transaction, here is the succinct version for `onCreate()`:

```
getFragmentManager().beginTransaction().add(R.id.framLayout,
    mFragmentOne).commit();
```

`switchFragment` does basically the same type of Fragment transaction. Instead of calling the `add()` method, we call the `replace()` method with the existing Fragment. We keep track of the current Fragment with the `showingFragment` variable so we know which Fragment to show next. We are not limited to switching between two Fragments either. If we needed additional Fragments, we just need to create them.

There's more...

In the *Switching between activities* recipe from *Chapter 1, Activities*, we discussed the back stack. Most users would expect the back key to move backward through the "screens" and they don't know or care if those screens are activities or Fragments. Fortunately, Android makes it very easy to add Fragments to the back stack just by adding a call to `addToBackStack()` before calling `commit()`.

> When a Fragment is removed or replaced without adding it to the back stack, it is immediately destroyed. If it is added to the back stack, it is stopped and, if the user returns to the Fragment, it is restarted, instead of recreated.

Passing data between Fragments

Often, the need arises to pass information between the Fragments. An email application serves as a classic example. It's common to have the list of emails in one Fragment, and show the email details in another Fragment (this is commonly referred to as a Master/Detail pattern). Fragments make creating this pattern easier because we only have to code each Fragment once, then we can include them in different layouts. We can easily have a single Fragment in a portrait layout with the ability to swap out the master Fragment with the detail Fragment when an email is selected. We can also create a two-panel layout where both the list and detail Fragments are side-by-side. Either way, when the user clicks the email in the list, the email opens up in the detail panel. This is when we need to communicate between two Fragments.

Since one of the primary goals of Fragments is that they be completely self-contained, direct communication between Fragments is discouraged, and for good reason. If Fragments had to rely on other Fragments, your code would likely break when the layouts changed and only one Fragment was available. Fortunately, direct communication is not required for this scenario either. All Fragment communication should pass through the host Activity. The host activity is responsible for managing the Fragments and can properly route the messages.

Now the question becomes: How do Fragments communicate with the activity? The answer is with an `interface`. You're probably already familiar with an interface, as that's how a view communicates an event back to an activity. A button click is a common example.

In this recipe, we will create two Fragments to demonstrate passing data from one Fragment to another via the host activity. We'll also build on what we learned from the previous recipe by including two different Activity Layouts—one for portrait and one for landscape. When in portrait mode, the activity will swap the Fragments as needed. Here is a screenshot of when the application first runs in portrait mode:

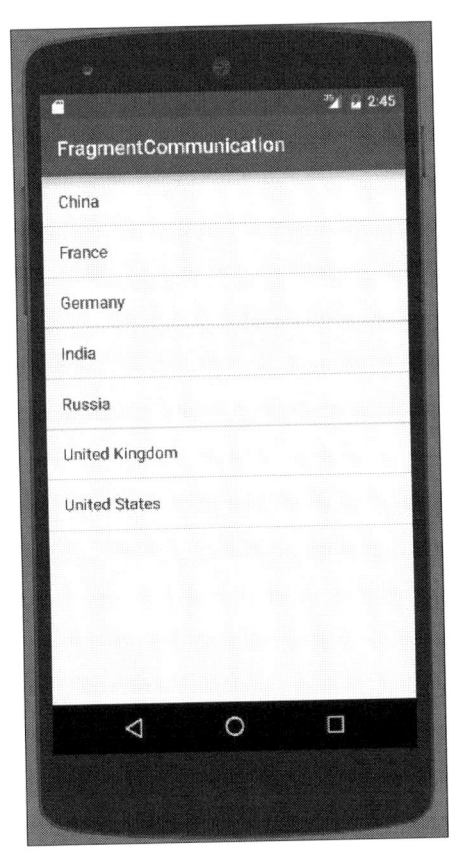

Exploring Fragments, AppWidgets, and the System UI

This is the screen showing the detail Fragment when you click on a country name:

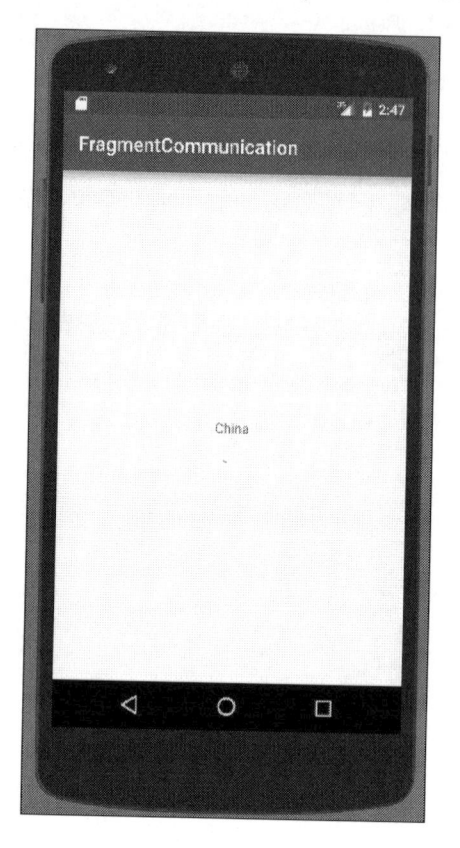

When in landscape, both Fragments will be side-by-side, as shown in the landscape screenshot:

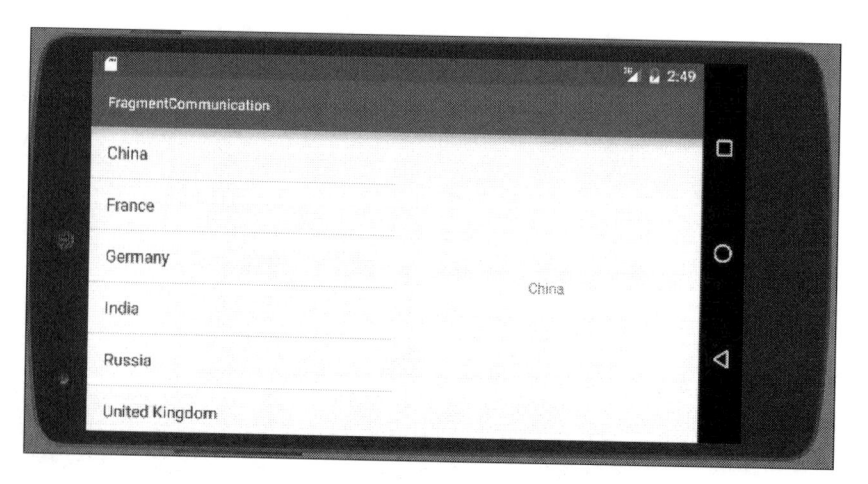

Since the Master/Detail pattern generally involves a list for the master, we'll take advantage of the `ListFragment` (mentioned in the *Creating and using a Fragment* introduction.) When an item in the list is selected, the item text (country name in our example) will be sent to the detail Fragment via the host Activity.

Getting ready

Create a new project in Android Studio and call it: `Fragmentcommunication`. Use the default **Phone & Tablet** options and select **Empty Activity** when prompted for the **Activity Type**.

How to do it...

To fully demonstrate working Fragments, we'll need to create two Fragments. The first Fragment will extend from the `ListFragment` so it will not need a layout. We're going to go one step further by creating both portrait and landscape layouts for our Activity. For portrait mode, we'll swap Fragments and for landscape mode, we'll show both Fragments side-by-side.

> When typing this code, Android Studio will offer two different library import options. Since the New Project Wizard automatically references the `AppCompat` library, we need to use the support library APIs instead of the framework APIs. Though very similar, the following code uses the support Fragment APIs.

Here are the steps, starting with the first Fragment:

1. Create a new Java class called `MasterFragment` and change it so it extends `ListFragment` as shown:

    ```
    public class MasterFragment extends ListFragment
    ```

    Import from the following library:

    ```
    android.support.v4.app.ListFragment
    ```

2. Create the following `interface` inside the `MasterFragment` class:

    ```
    public interface OnMasterSelectedListener {
        public void onItemSelected(String countryName);
    }
    ```

3. Set up the interface callback listener with the following code:

    ```
    private OnMasterSelectedListener
      mOnMasterSelectedListener=null;

    public void setOnMasterSelectedListener(
      OnMasterSelectedListener listener) {
        mOnMasterSelectedListener=listener;
    }
    ```

Exploring Fragments, AppWidgets, and the System UI

4. The last step for the `MasterFragment` is to create a `ListAdapter` to populate the `ListView`, which we do in the `onViewCreated()` method. We'll use the `setOnItemClickListener()` to call our `OnMasterSelectedListener` interface when a country name is selected with the following code:

```
public void onViewCreated(View view, Bundle
  savedInstanceState) {
    super.onViewCreated(view, savedInstanceState);
    String[] countries = new String[]{"China", "France",
      "Germany", "India", "Russia", "United Kingdom",
        "United States"};
    ListAdapter countryAdapter = new ArrayAdapter<String>(
      getActivity(), android.R.layout.simple_list_item_1,
        countries);
    setListAdapter(countryAdapter);
    getListView().setChoiceMode(
      ListView.CHOICE_MODE_SINGLE);
    getListView().setOnItemClickListener(new
      AdapterView.OnItemClickListener() {
        @Override
        public void onItemClick(AdapterView<?> parent, View
          view, int position, long id) {
            if (mOnMasterSelectedListener != null) {
                mOnMasterSelectedListener.onItemSelected(((
                  TextView) view).getText().toString());
            }
        }
    });
}
```

5. Next we need to create the `DetailFragment`, starting with the Layout. Create a new layout file called: `fragment_detail.xml` with the following XML:

```
<?xml version="1.0" encoding="utf-8"?>
<RelativeLayout
    xmlns:android="http://schemas.android.com/apk/
      res/android"
    android:layout_width="match_parent"
    android:layout_height="match_parent">
    <TextView
        android:id="@+id/textViewCountryName"
        android:layout_width="wrap_content"
        android:layout_height="wrap_content"
        android:layout_centerVertical="true"
        android:layout_centerHorizontal="true" />
</RelativeLayout>
```

6. Create a new Java class called `DetailFragment` extending from `Fragment` as follows:

   ```
   public class DetailFragment extends Fragment
   ```

   Import from the following library:

   ```
   android.support.v4.app.Fragment
   ```

7. Add the following constant to the class:

   ```
   public static String KEY_COUNTRY_NAME="KEY_COUNTRY_NAME";
   ```

8. Override `onCreateView()` as follows:

   ```
   public View onCreateView(LayoutInflater inflater, ViewGroup
     container, Bundle savedInstanceState) {
       return inflater.inflate(R.layout.fragment_detail,
         container, false);
   }
   ```

9. Code the `onViewCreated()` as follows:

   ```
   public void onViewCreated(View view, Bundle
     savedInstanceState) {
       super.onViewCreated(view, savedInstanceState);

       Bundle bundle = getArguments();
       if (bundle != null &&
         bundle.containsKey(KEY_COUNTRY_NAME)) {
           showSelectedCountry(bundle.getString(
             KEY_COUNTRY_NAME));
       }
   }
   ```

10. The last step for this Fragment is to update the TextView when we receive the selected country name. Add the following method to the class:

    ```
    public void showSelectedCountry(String countryName) {
        ((TextView)getView().findViewById(
          R.id.textViewCountryName)).setText(countryName);
    }
    ```

11. The existing `activity_main.xml` layout will handle the portrait mode layout. Remove the existing `<TextView>` and replace with the following `<FrameLayout>`:

    ```
    <FrameLayout
        android:id="@+id/frameLayout"
        android:layout_width="match_parent"
        android:layout_height="match_parent"/>
    ```

Exploring Fragments, AppWidgets, and the System UI

12. Create a new directory in the **res** folder for the landscape layout as: `res/layout-land`.

> If you do not see the new res/layout-land directory, change from **Android view** to **Project view**.

13. Create a new `activity_main.xml` layout in `res/layout-land` as follows:

    ```
    <?xml version="1.0" encoding="utf-8"?>
    <LinearLayout xmlns:android="http://schemas.android.com/
       apk/res/android"
        xmlns:tools="http://schemas.android.com/tools"
        android:layout_width="match_parent"
        android:layout_height="match_parent"
        android:orientation="horizontal">
        <FrameLayout
            android:id="@+id/frameLayoutMaster"
            android:layout_width="0dp"
            android:layout_weight="1"
            android:layout_height="match_parent"/>
        <FrameLayout
            android:id="@+id/frameLayoutDetail"
            android:layout_width="0dp"
            android:layout_weight="1"
            android:layout_height="match_parent"/>
    </LinearLayout>
    ```

14. The final steps are to set up the `MainActivity` to handle the Fragments. Open the `MainActivity.java` file and add the following class variable to track single/dual pane:

    ```
    boolean dualPane;
    ```

15. Next, change `onCreate()` as follows:

    ```
    protected void onCreate(Bundle savedInstanceState) {
        super.onCreate(savedInstanceState);
        setContentView(R.layout.activity_main);

        MasterFragment masterFragment=null;
        FrameLayout frameLayout =
          (FrameLayout)findViewById(R.id.frameLayout);
        if (frameLayout != null) {
           dualPane=false;
           FragmentTransaction fragmentTransaction =
              getSupportFragmentManager().beginTransaction();
    ```

```java
            masterFragment=(MasterFragment)
              getSupportFragmentManager().
                findFragmentByTag("MASTER");
            if (masterFragment == null) {
                masterFragment = new MasterFragment();
                fragmentTransaction.add(R.id.frameLayout,
                   masterFragment, "MASTER");
            }
            DetailFragment detailFragment = (DetailFragment)
              getSupportFragmentManager().findFragmentById(
                 R.id.frameLayoutDetail);
            if (detailFragment != null) {
                fragmentTransaction.remove(detailFragment);
            }
            fragmentTransaction.commit();
        } else {
            dualPane=true;
            FragmentTransaction fragmentTransaction =
               getSupportFragmentManager().beginTransaction();
            masterFragment=(MasterFragment)
              getSupportFragmentManager().findFragmentById(
                 R.id.frameLayoutMaster);
            if (masterFragment==null) {
                masterFragment = new MasterFragment();
                fragmentTransaction.add(R.id.frameLayoutMaster,
                   masterFragment);
            }
            DetailFragment detailFragment=(DetailFragment)
              getSupportFragmentManager().findFragmentById(
                 R.id.frameLayoutDetail);
            if (detailFragment==null) {
                detailFragment = new DetailFragment();
                fragmentTransaction.add(R.id.frameLayoutDetail,
                   detailFragment);
            }
            fragmentTransaction.commit();
      }
      masterFragment.setOnMasterSelectedListener(new
        MasterFragment.OnMasterSelectedListener() {
            @Override
            public void onItemSelected(String countryName) {
                sendCountryName(countryName);
            }
        });
  }
```

Exploring Fragments, AppWidgets, and the System UI

16. The last code to add is the `sendCountryName()` method, which handles sending the country name to `DetailFragment`:

    ```
    private void sendCountryName(String countryName) {
        DetailFragment detailFragment;
        if (dualPane) {
            //Two pane layout
            detailFragment = (DetailFragment)
                getSupportFragmentManager().findFragmentById(
                    R.id.frameLayoutDetail);
            detailFragment.showSelectedCountry(countryName);
        } else {
            // Single pane layout
            detailFragment = new DetailFragment();
            Bundle bundle = new Bundle();
            bundle.putString(DetailFragment.KEY_COUNTRY_NAME,
                countryName);
            detailFragment.setArguments(bundle);
            FragmentTransaction fragmentTransaction =
                getSupportFragmentManager().beginTransaction();
            fragmentTransaction.replace(R.id.frameLayout,
                detailFragment);
            fragmentTransaction.addToBackStack(null);
            fragmentTransaction.commit();
        }
    }
    ```

17. Run the program on a device or emulator.

How it works...

We start by creating the `MasterFragment`. In the Master/Detail pattern we are using, this usually represents a list, so we create a list by extending the `ListFragment`. The `ListFragment` is the Fragment equivalent of the `ListActivity`. Other than extending from a Fragment, it's basically the same.

As stated in the recipe introduction, we shouldn't attempt to communicate directly with other Fragments.

To provide a means to communicate the list item selection, we expose the interface: `OnMasterSelectedListener`. We call `onItemSelected()` every time an item is selected in the list.

Most of the work for passing data between Fragments is done in the host activity but, ultimately, the receiving Fragment needs a way to receive the data. `DetailFragment` supports this in two ways:

- Passing the country name in the argument bundle, available at creation time.
- A public method for the activity to call directly.

When the activity creates the Fragment, it also creates a `bundle` to hold the data we want to send. Here we add the country name using `KEY_COUNTRY_NAME` defined in Step 7. We retrieve this bundle with `getArguments()` in `onViewCreated()`. If the key is found in the bundle, it is extracted and displayed using the `showSelectedCountry()` method. This is the same method the activity will call directly if the Fragment is already visible (in the two-panel layout).

Most of the work for this recipe is in the activity. We created two layouts: one for portrait and one for landscape. Android will choose the landscape layout using the `res/layout-land` directory created in *Step 12*. Both layouts use a `<FrameLayout>` placeholder, similar to the previous exercise. We manage the Fragments in both `onCreate()` and `sendCountryName()`.

In `onCreate()`, we set the `dualPane` flag by checking whether the current layout includes the `frameLayout` view. If `frameLayout` is found (it won't be null), then we have only a single panel because the `frameLayout` ID is only in the portrait layout. If frameLayout is not found, then we have two `<FrameLayout>` elements instead: one for the `MasterFragment` and another for the `DetailFragment`.

The last thing we do in the `onCreate()` is to set up the `MasterFragment` listener by creating an anonymous callback, which passes the country name to `sendCountryName()`.

`sendCountryName()` is where the data is actually passed to the `DetailFragment`. If we are in portrait (or single pane) mode, we need to create a `DetailFragment` and replace the existing `MasterFragment`. This is where we create the bundle with the country name and call `setArguments()`. Notice how we call `addToBackStack()` before committing the transaction? This allows the back key to bring the user back to the list (`MasterFragment`). If we are in landscape mode, the `DetailFragment` is already visible so we call the `showSelectedCountry()` public method directly.

There's more...

In the `MasterFragment`, before sending the `onItemSelected()` event, we check to make sure the listener is not null with this code:

```
if (mOnMasterSelectedListener != null)
```

Exploring Fragments, AppWidgets, and the System UI

Though it's the job of the activity to set up the callback to receive the events, we don't want this code to crash if there's no listener. An alternative approach would be to verify the activity extends our interface in the Fragment's `onAttach()` callback.

See also

- For more information on ListViews, see *Using ListView, GridView and Adapters* in Chapter 2, *Layouts*.
- For more information on resource directories, see *Selecting themes based on the Android version* in Chapter 3, *Views, Widgets, and Styles*.

Creating a shortcut on the Home screen

This recipe explains how to create a link or create a shortcut for your app on the user's Home screen. So as not to be too obtrusive, it's generally best to make this an option for the user to initiate, such as in the settings.

Here is a screenshot showing our shortcut on the Home screen:

As you can see, this is just a shortcut, but we will explore creating a Home screen (AppWidget) in the next recipe.

Getting ready

Create a new project in Android Studio and call it: `HomescreenShortcut`. Use the default **Phone & Tablet** options and select the **Empty Activity** option when prompted for the **Activity Type**.

How to do it...

The first step is to add the appropriate permission. Here are the steps:

1. Open the `AndroidManifest` file and add the following permission:

   ```
   <uses-permission android:name="com.android.launcher.
     permission.INSTALL_SHORTCUT" />
   ```

2. Next, open `activity_main.xml` and replace the existing TextView with the following button:

   ```
   <Button
       android:layout_width="wrap_content"
       android:layout_height="wrap_content"
       android:text="Create Shortcut"
       android:id="@+id/button"
       android:layout_centerVertical="true"
       android:layout_centerHorizontal="true"
       android:onClick="createShortcut"/>
   ```

3. Add the following method to `ActivityMain.java`:

   ```
   public void createShortcut(View view) {
       Intent shortcutIntent = new Intent(this,
         MainActivity.class);
       shortcutIntent.setAction(Intent.ACTION_MAIN);
       Intent intent = new Intent();
       intent.putExtra(Intent.EXTRA_SHORTCUT_INTENT,
         shortcutIntent);
       intent.putExtra(Intent.EXTRA_SHORTCUT_NAME,
         getString(R.string.app_name));
       intent.putExtra(Intent.EXTRA_SHORTCUT_ICON_RESOURCE,
         Intent.ShortcutIconResource.fromContext(this,
           R.mipmap.ic_launcher));
       intent.setAction(
         "com.android.launcher.action.INSTALL_SHORTCUT");
       sendBroadcast(intent);
   }
   ```

4. Run the program on a device or emulator. Notice, each time you press the button, the app will make a shortcut on the Home screen.

How it works...

Once you set up the proper permission, this is a rather straightforward task. When the button is clicked, the code creates a new intent called: `shortcutIntent`. This is the intent that will be called when the icon is pressed on the Home screen. The next intent created, `installIntent`, is responsible for actually creating the shortcut.

There's more...

If you also wanted to remove the shortcut, you would need the following permission:

```
<uses-permission android:name="com.android.launcher.
   permission.UNINSTALL_SHORTCUT" />
```

Instead of using the INSTALL_SHORTCUT action, you would set the following action instead:

```
com.android.launcher.action.UNINSTALL_SHORTCUT
```

Creating a Home screen widget

Before we dig in to the code for creating an App Widget, let's cover the basics. There are three required and one optional component:

- The `AppWidgetProviderInfo` file: It's an XML resource described later on
- The `AppWidgetProvider` class: This is a Java class
- The View layout file: It's a standard layout XML file, with some restrictions listed later on
- The App Widget configuration Activity (optional): This Activity launches when placing the widget to set configuration options

The `AppWidgetProvider` must also be declared in the `AndroidManifest` file. Since the `AppWidgetProvider` is a helper class based on the Broadcast Receiver, it is declared in the manifest with the `<receiver>` element. Here is an example manifest entry:

```
<receiver android:name="AppWidgetProvider" >
    <intent-filter>
        <action android:name=
           "android.appwidget.action.APPWIDGET_UPDATE" />
    </intent-filter>
    <meta-data android:name="android.appwidget.provider"
        android:resource="@xml/appwidget_info" />
</receiver>
```

The meta-data points to the `AppWidgetProviderInfo` file, which is placed in the `res/xml` directory. Here is a sample `AppWidgetProviderInfo.xml` file:

```xml
<appwidget-provider xmlns:android="http://schemas.android.com/
  apk/res/android"
    android:minWidth="40dp"
    android:minHeight="40dp"
    android:updatePeriodMillis="1800000"
    android:previewImage="@drawable/preview_image"
    android:initialLayout="@layout/appwidget"
    android:configure="com.packtpub.androidcookbook.
      AppWidgetConfiguration"
    android:resizeMode="horizontal|vertical"
    android:widgetCategory="home_screen">
</appwidget-provider>
```

Here's a brief overview of the available attributes:

- `minWidth`: The default width when placed on the Home screen
- `minHeight`: The default height when placed on the Home screen
- `updatePeriodMillis`: It's part of `onUpdate()` polling interval (in milliseconds)
- `initialLayout`: The AppWidget layout
- `previewImage` (optional): The image shown when browsing App Widgets
- `configure` (optional): The activity to launch for configuration settings
- `resizeMode` (optional): The flags indicate resizing options — `horizontal`, `vertical`, `none`
- `minResizeWidth` (optional): The minimum width allowed when resizing
- `minResizeHeight` (optional): The minimum height allowed when resizing
- `widgetCategory` (optional): Android 5+ only supports Home screen widgets

The `AppWidgetProvider` extends the `BroadcastReceiver` class, which is why `<receiver>` is used when declaring the `AppWidget` in the Manifest. As it's `BroadcastReceiver`, the class still receives the OS broadcast events, but the helper class filters those events down to those applicable for an App Widget. The `AppWidgetProvider` class exposes the following methods:

- `onUpdate()`: It's called when initially created and at the interval specified.
- `onAppWidgetOptionsChanged()`: It's called when initially created and any time the size changes.
- `onDeleted()`: It's called any time a widget is removed.

Exploring Fragments, AppWidgets, and the System UI

- `onEnabled()`: It's called the first time a widget is placed (is not called when adding a second and subsequent widgets).
- `onDisabled()`: It's called when the last widget is removed.
- `onReceive()`: It's called on every event received, including the preceding event. Usually not overridden as the default implementation only sends the applicable events.

The last required component is the layout. Remote Views only support a subset of the available layouts. As an App Widget is a Remote View, only the following layouts are supported:

- `FrameLayout`
- `LinearLayout`
- `RelativeLayout`
- `GridLayout`

And the following widgets:

- `AnalogClock`
- `Button`
- `Chronometer`
- `ImageButton`
- `ImageView`
- `ProgressBar`
- `TextView`
- `ViewFlipper`
- `ListView`
- `GridView`
- `StackView`
- `AdapterViewFlipper`

Chapter 5

With the App Widget basics covered, it's now time to start coding. Our example will cover the basics so you can expand the functionality as needed. This recipe uses a View with a clock, which, when pressed, opens our activity.

This screenshot shows the widget in the widget list when adding to the Home screen:

> The widget list appearance varies by launcher.

Here's a screenshot showing the widget after it is added to the Home screen:

Getting ready

Create a new project in Android Studio and call it: `AppWidget`. Use the default **Phone & Tablet** options and select the **Empty Activity** option when prompted for the **Activity Type**.

How to do it...

We'll start by creating the widget layout, which resides in the standard layout resource directory. Then we'll create the xml resource directory to store the `AppWidgetProviderInfo` file. We'll add a new Java class and extend `AppWidgetProvider`, which handles the `onUpdate()` call for the widget. With the receiver created, we can then add it to the Android Manifest.

Chapter 5

Here are the detailed steps:

1. Create a new file in `res/layout` called `widget.xml` using the following XML:

   ```xml
   <?xml version="1.0" encoding="utf-8"?>
   <RelativeLayout xmlns:android="http://schemas.android.com/
     apk/res/android"
       android:layout_width="match_parent"
       android:layout_height="match_parent">
       <AnalogClock
           android:layout_width="wrap_content"
           android:layout_height="wrap_content"
           android:id="@+id/analogClock"
           android:layout_centerVertical="true"
           android:layout_centerHorizontal="true" />
   </RelativeLayout>
   ```

2. Create a new directory called `xml` in the resource directory. The final result will be: `res/xml`.

3. Create a new file in `res/xml` called `appwidget_info,xml` using the following xml:

   ```xml
   <appwidget-provider xmlns:android="http://schemas.android.com/apk/
   res/android"
       android:minWidth="40dp"
       android:minHeight="40dp"
       android:updatePeriodMillis="0"
       android:initialLayout="@layout/widget"
       android:resizeMode="none"
       android:widgetCategory="home_screen">
   </appwidget-provider>
   ```

   > If you cannot see the new xml directory, switch from **Android** view to **Project** view in the **Project** panel dropdown.

4. Create a new Java class called `HomescreenWidgetProvider` extending `AppWidgetProvider`.

5. Add the following `onUpdate()` method to the `HomescreenWidgetProvider` class:

   ```java
   public void onUpdate(Context context, AppWidgetManager
       appWidgetManager, int[] appWidgetIds) {
       super.onUpdate(context, appWidgetManager,
         appWidgetIds);
       for (int count=0; count<appWidgetIds.length; count++) {
           RemoteViews appWidgetLayout = new
             RemoteViews(context.getPackageName(),
               R.layout.widget);
   ```

Exploring Fragments, AppWidgets, and the System UI

```
            Intent intent = new Intent(context,
                MainActivity.class);
            PendingIntent pendingIntent =
                PendingIntent.getActivity(context, 0, intent, 0);
            appWidgetLayout.setOnClickPendingIntent(
                R.id.analogClock, pendingIntent);
            appWidgetManager.updateAppWidget(
                appWidgetIds[count], appWidgetLayout);
        }
    }
```

6. Add `HomescreenWidgetProvider` to `AndroidManifest` using the following XML declaration within the `<application>` element:

```xml
<receiver android:name=".HomescreenWidgetProvider" >
    <intent-filter>
        <action android:name="android.appwidget.
            action.APPWIDGET_UPDATE" />
    </intent-filter>
    <meta-data android:name="android.appwidget.provider"
        android:resource="@xml/appwidget_info" />
</receiver>
```

7. Run the program on a device or emulator. After first running the application, the widget will then be available to add to the Home screen.

How it works...

Our first step is to create the layout file for the widget. This is a standard layout resource with the restrictions based on the App Widget being a Remote View, as discussed in the recipe introduction. Though our example uses an Analog Clock widget, this is where you'd want to expand the functionality based on your application needs.

The xml resource directory serves to store the `AppWidgetProviderInfo`, which defines the default widget settings. The configuration settings determine how the widget is displayed when initially browsing the available widgets. We use very basic settings for this recipe, but they can easily be expanded to include additional features such as a preview image to show a functioning widget and sizing options. The `updatePeriodMillis` attribute sets the update frequency. Since the update will wake up the device, it's a trade-off between having up-to-date data and battery life. (This is where the optional Settings Activity is useful to let the user decide.)

The `AppWidgetProvider` class is where we handle the `onUpdate()` event triggered by the `updatePeriodMillis` polling. Our example doesn't need any updating so we set the polling to zero. The update is still called when initially placing the widget. The `onUpdate()` is where we set the pending intent to open our app when the clock is pressed.

Since the `onUpdate()` method is probably the most complicated aspect of AppWidgets, we'll explain this is some detail. First, it's worth noting that `onUpdate()` will occur only once each polling interval for all the widgets is created by this provider. (Widgets created after the first will be on the cycle of the first widget.) This explains the `for` loop, as we need it to iterate through all the existing widgets. This is where we create a pending intent to call our app when the clock is pressed. As discussed earlier, an AppWidget is a Remote View. Therefore, to get the layout, we call `RemoteViews()` with our fully qualified package name and the layout ID. Once we have the layout, we can attach the pending intent to the clock view using `setOnClickPendingIntent()`. We call the `AppWidgetManager` named `updateAppWidget()` to initiate the changes we made.

The last step to make all this work is to declare the widget in the Android Manifest. We identify the action we want to handle with the `<intent-filter>`. Most App Widgets will likely want to handle the Update event, as ours does. The other item to note in the declaration is this line:

```xml
<meta-data android:name="android.appwidget.provider"
    android:resource="@xml/appwidget_info" />
```

This tells the system where to find our configuration file.

There's more...

Adding an App Widget configuration Activity allows greater flexibility with your widget. Not only can you offer polling options, but you could offer different layouts, click behaviors, and so on. Users tend to really appreciate flexible App Widgets.

Adding a configuration Activity requires a few additional steps. The Activity needs to be declared in the Manifest as usual, but needs to include the `APPWIDGET_CONFIGURE` action, as shown in this example:

```xml
<activity android:name=".AppWidgetConfigureActivity">
    <intent-filter>
        <action android:name=
            "android.appwidget.action.APPWIDGET_CONFIGURE"/>
    </intent-filter>
</activity>
```

The Activity also needs to be specified in the `AppWidgetProviderInfo` file using the configure attribute, as shown in this example:

```
android:configure="com.packtpub.androidcookbook.appwidget.
AppWidgetConfigureActivity"
```

The `configure` attribute requires the fully qualified package name as this Activity will be called from outside of your application.

Exploring Fragments, AppWidgets, and the System UI

> Remember, the `onUpdate()` method will not be called when using a configuration Activity. The configuration Activity is responsible for handling any initial setup, if required.

See also

- For App Widget Design Guidelines, visit Google's page at: `http://developer.android.com/design/patterns/widgets.html`

Adding Search to the Action Bar

Along with the Action Bar, Android 3.0 introduced the `SearchView` widget, which can be included as a menu item when creating a menu. This is now the recommended UI pattern to provide a consistent user experience.

The following screenshot shows the initial appearance of the Search icon in the Action Bar:

This screenshot shows how the Search option expands when pressed:

If you want to add a Search functionality to your application, this recipe will walk you through the steps to set up your User Interface and properly configure the Search Manager API.

Getting ready

Create a new project in Android Studio and call it: `SearchView`. Use the default **Phone & Tablet** options and select **Empty Activity** when prompted for the Activity Type.

Chapter 5

How to do it...

To set up the Search UI pattern, we need to create the Search menu item and a resource called `searchable`. We'll create a second activity to receive the search query. Then we'll hook it all up in the `AndroidManifest` file. To get started, open the `strings.xml` file in `res/values` and follow these steps:

1. Add the following string resources:

    ```xml
    <string name="search_title">Search</string>
    <string name="search_hint">Enter text to search</string>
    ```

2. Create the menu directory: `res/menu`.

3. Create a new menu resource called `menu_options.xml` in `res/menu` using the following xml:

    ```xml
    <?xml version="1.0" encoding="utf-8"?>
    <menu
        xmlns:android="http://schemas.android.com/apk/
          res/android"
        xmlns:app="http://schemas.android.com/apk/res-auto">
        <item android:id="@+id/menu_search"
            android:title="@string/search_title"
            android:icon="@android:drawable/ic_menu_search"
            app:showAsAction="collapseActionView|ifRoom"
            app:actionViewClass=
              "android.support.v7.widget.SearchView" />
    </menu>
    ```

4. Override `onCreateOptionsMenu()` to inflate the menu and set up the Search Manager as follows:

    ```java
    public boolean onCreateOptionsMenu(Menu menu) {
        MenuInflater inflater = getMenuInflater();
        inflater.inflate(R.menu.menu_options, menu);
        SearchManager searchManager = (SearchManager)
          getSystemService(Context.SEARCH_SERVICE);
        SearchView searchView = (SearchView)
          MenuItemCompat.getActionView(
            menu.findItem(R.id.menu_search));
        searchView.setSearchableInfo(
          searchManager.getSearchableInfo(getComponentName()));
        return true;
    }
    ```

5. Create a new xml resource directory: `res/xml`.

Exploring Fragments, AppWidgets, and the System UI

6. Create a new file in the `res/xml` called `searchable.xml` using the following xml:

    ```xml
    <?xml version="1.0" encoding="utf-8"?>
    <searchable xmlns:android="http://schemas.android.com/
       apk/res/android"
        android:label="@string/app_name"
        android:hint="@string/search_hint" />
    ```

7. Crate a new layout called `activity_search_result.xml` using this xml:

    ```xml
    <?xml version="1.0" encoding="utf-8"?>
    <RelativeLayout xmlns:android="http://schemas.android.com/apk/res/
       android"
        xmlns:tools="http://schemas.android.com/tools"
        android:layout_width="match_parent"
        android:layout_height="match_parent" >
        <TextView
            android:id="@+id/textViewSearchResult"
            android:layout_width="wrap_content"
            android:layout_height="wrap_content"
            android:layout_centerInParent="true" />
    </RelativeLayout>
    ```

8. Create a new Activity called `SearchResultActivity`.

9. Add the following variable to the class:

    ```
    TextView mTextViewSearchResult;
    ```

10. Change the `onCreate()` to load our layout, set the TextView and check for the QUERY action:

    ```java
    protected void onCreate(Bundle savedInstanceState) {
        super.onCreate(savedInstanceState);
        setContentView(R.layout.activity_search_result);
        mTextViewSearchResult = (TextView)findViewById(
           R.id.textViewSearchResult);

        if (Intent.ACTION_SEARCH.equals(
          getIntent().getAction())) {
            handleSearch(getIntent().getStringExtra(
              SearchManager.QUERY));
       }
    }
    ```

11. Add the following method to handle the search:

    ```java
    private void handleSearch(String searchQuery) {
        mTextViewSearchResult.setText(searchQuery);
    }
    ```

―― Chapter 5

12. With the User Interface and code now complete, we just need to hook everything up correctly in the `AndroidManifest`. Here is the complete manifest including both activities:

```xml
<?xml version="1.0" encoding="utf-8"?>
<manifest xmlns:android="http://schemas.android.com/apk/res/android"
    package="com.packtpub.androidcookbook.searchview" >
    <application
        android:allowBackup="true"
        android:icon="@mipmap/ic_launcher"
        android:label="@string/app_name"
        android:supportsRtl="true"
        android:theme="@style/AppTheme" >
        <meta-data
            android:name="android.app.default_searchable"
            android:value=".SearchResultActivity" />
        <activity android:name=".MainActivity" >
            <intent-filter>
                <action android:name=
                    "android.intent.action.MAIN" />
                <category android:name=
                    "android.intent.category.LAUNCHER" />
            </intent-filter>
        </activity>
        <activity android:name=".SearchResultActivity" >
            <intent-filter>
                <action android:name=
                    "android.intent.action.SEARCH" />
            </intent-filter>
            <meta-data android:name=
                "android.app.searchable" android:resource=
                "@xml/searchable" />
        </activity>
    </application>
</manifest>
```

13. Run the application on a device or emulator. Type in a search query and hit the **Search** button (or press enter). The `SearchResultActivity` will display showing the search query entered.

Exploring Fragments, AppWidgets, and the System UI

How it works...

Since the New Project Wizard uses the `AppCompat` library, our example uses the support library API. Using the support library provides the greatest device compatibility as it allows the use of modern features (such as the Action Bar) on older versions of the Android OS. This can sometimes provide an extra challenge as often the official documentation focuses on the framework API. Though usually the support library closely follows the framework API, they are not always interchangeable. The Search UI pattern is one of those situations, so it's worth paying extra attention to the steps outlined previously.

We start by creating string resources for the `searchable`, as declared in Step 6.

In Step 3, we create the menu resource, as we've done many times. One difference is that we use the `app` namespace for the `showAsAction` and `actionViewClass` attributes. The earlier versions of the Android OS don't include these attributes in their Android namespace. This serves as a way to bring new functionality to older versions of the Android OS

In Step 4, we set up the `SearchManager`, again using the support library APIs.

Step 6 is where we define the `searchable`, which is an xml resource used by the `SearchManager`. The only required attribute is the `label`, but the `hint` is recommended so the user will have an idea of what they should type in the field.

> The `android:label` must match the application name or the activity name and must use a string resource (as it does not work with a hard-coded string).

Steps 7-11 are for the `SearchResultActivity`. Calling a second activity is not a requirement of the `SearchManager`, but is commonly done to provide a single activity for all searches initiated in your application.

If you ran the application at this point, you would see the search icon, but nothing would work. Step 12 is where we put it all together in the `AndroidManifest` file. The first item to note is the following:

```
<meta-data
android:name="android.app.default_searchable"
android:value=".SearchResultActivity" />
```

Notice this is in the application element and not in either of the `<activity>` elements.

We specify the searchable resource in the `SearchResultActivity` `<meta-data>` element:

```
<meta-data android:name="android.app.searchable" android:resource="@xml/searchable" />
```

We also need to set the intent filter for `SearchResultActivity` as we do here:

```
<intent-filter>
    <action android:name="android.intent.action.SEARCH" />
</intent-filter>
```

The `SearchManager` broadcasts the `SEARCH` intent when the user initiates the search. This declaration directs the intent to the `SearchResultActivity` activity. Once the search is triggered, the query text is sent to the `SearchResultActivity` using the `SEARCH` intent. We check for the `SEARCH` intent in the `onCreate()` and extract the query string using the following code:

```
if (Intent.ACTION_SEARCH.equals(getIntent().getAction())) {
    handleSearch(getIntent().getStringExtra(SearchManager.QUERY));
}
```

You now have the Search UI pattern fully implemented. With the UI pattern complete, how you handle the search is specific to your application needs. Depending on your application, you might search a local database or maybe a web service.

See also

To take your search to the Internet, see *Internet queries* in *Chapter 12, Telephony, Networks, and the Web*.

Showing your app full screen

Android 4.4 (API 19) introduced a UI feature called Immersive Mode. Unlike the previous full screen flag, your app receives all the touch events while in Immersive Mode. This mode is ideal for certain activities, such as reading books and news, full-screen drawing, gaming, or watching a video. There are several different approaches to full screen, and each have a best use case:

- Reading books/articles, and so on: Immersive Mode with easy access to the system UI
- Game/Drawing app: Immersive Mode for full screen use but minimal system UI
- Watching video: Full screen and normal system UI

The key difference between the modes is how the System UI responds. In the first two scenarios, your app is expecting user interaction, so the System UI is hidden to make it easier for your user (such as not hitting the back button while playing a game). While using full screen with a normal system UI, such as watching a video, you wouldn't expect your user to use the screen at all, so when they do, the system UI should respond normally. In all modes, the user can bring back the System UI with a swipe inward across the hidden System Bar.

Exploring Fragments, AppWidgets, and the System UI

Since watching a video doesn't require the new **Immersive Mode**, full-screen mode can be achieved using the two flags: SYSTEM_UI_FLAG_FULLSCREEN and SYSTEM_UI_FLAG_HIDE_NAVIGATION, available since Android 4.0 (API 14).

Our recipe will demonstrate setting up Immersive Mode. We're also going to add the ability to toggle the System UI with a tap on the screen.

Getting ready

Create a new project in Android Studio and call it: ImmersiveMode. Use the default **Phone & Tablet** options and select **Empty Activity** when prompted for the **Activity Type**. When selecting the **Minimum API Level**, choose **API 19** or higher.

How to do it...

We'll create two functions for handling the system UI visibility, then we'll create a gesture listener to detect the screen tap. All the steps for this recipe are adding code to MainActivity.java, so open the file and let's begin:

1. Add the following method to hide the System UI:

   ```
   private void hideSystemUi() {
       getWindow().getDecorView().setSystemUiVisibility(
           View.SYSTEM_UI_FLAG_IMMERSIVE |
           View.SYSTEM_UI_FLAG_FULLSCREEN |
           View.SYSTEM_UI_FLAG_LAYOUT_STABLE |
           View.SYSTEM_UI_FLAG_LAYOUT_HIDE_NAVIGATION |
           View.SYSTEM_UI_FLAG_LAYOUT_FULLSCREEN |
           View.SYSTEM_UI_FLAG_HIDE_NAVIGATION);
   }
   ```

2. Add the following method to show the System UI:

   ```
   private void showSystemUI() {
       getWindow().getDecorView().setSystemUiVisibility(
           View.SYSTEM_UI_FLAG_LAYOUT_STABLE |
           View.SYSTEM_UI_FLAG_LAYOUT_HIDE_NAVIGATION |
           View.SYSTEM_UI_FLAG_LAYOUT_FULLSCREEN);
   }
   ```

3. Add the following class variable:

   ```
   private GestureDetectorCompat mGestureDetector;
   ```

4. Add the following `GestureListener` class at the class level, below the previous class variable:

```
private class GestureListener extends
   GestureDetector.SimpleOnGestureListener {
     @Override
     public boolean onDown(MotionEvent event) {
         return true;
     }

     @Override
     public boolean onFling(MotionEvent event1, MotionEvent
         event2, float velocityX, float velocityY) {
         return true;
     }

     @Override
     public boolean onSingleTapUp(MotionEvent e) {
         if (getSupportActionBar() != null &&
            getSupportActionBar().isShowing()) {
               hideSystemUi();
         } else {
               showSystemUI();
         }
         return true;
     }
}
```

5. Override the `onTouchEvent()` callback with the following:

```
public boolean onTouchEvent(MotionEvent event){
    mGestureDetector.onTouchEvent(event);
    return super.onTouchEvent(event);
}
```

6. Add the following code to the `onCreate()` method to set the `GestureListener` and hide the System UI:

```
mGestureDetector = new GestureDetectorCompat(this, new
   GestureListener());
hideSystemUi();
```

7. Run the application on a device or emulator. Swiping inward across a hidden System Bar will show the System UI. Tapping the screen will toggle the System UI.

How it works...

We create the `showSystemUI()` and `hideSystemUI()` methods by using `setSystemUiVisibility()` on the application window. The flags we set (and don't set) control what is visible and what is hidden. When we set the visibility without the `SYSTEM_UI_FLAG_IMMERSIVE` flag, we in effect, disable Immersive Mode.

If all we wanted to do was hide the System UI, we could just add `hideSystemUI()` to `onCreate()` and we'd be done. The problem is it wouldn't stay hidden. Once the user exited Immersive Mode, it would stay in the regular display mode. That's why we created the `GestureListener`. (We'll discuss gestures again in *Chapter 8, Using the Touchscreen and Sensors*.) Since we only want to respond to the `onSingleTapUp()` gesture, we don't implement the full range of gestures. When `onSingleTapUp` is detected, we toggle the System UI.

There's more...

Let's look at some of the other important tasks that can be performed:

Sticky Immersion

There's another option we can use if we want the System UI to stay hidden automatically. Instead of using `SYSTEM_UI_FLAG_IMMERSIVE` to hide the UI, we can use `SYSTEM_UI_FLAG_IMMERSIVE_STICKY`.

Dimming the System UI

If all you need is to reduce the visibility of the Navigation bar, there's also `SYSTEM_UI_FLAG_LOW_PROFILE` to dim the UI.

Use this flag with the same `setSystemUiVisibility()` call as the Immersive Mode flag:

```
getWindow().getDecorView().setSystemUiVisibility(View.SYSTEM_UI_FLAG_LOW_PROFILE);
```

Call `setSystemUiVisibility()` with 0 to clear all flags:

```
getWindow().getDecorView().setSystemUiVisibility(0);
```

Setting the Action Bar as an Overlay

If you just need to hide or show the Action Bar, use these methods:

```
getActionBar().hide();
getActionBar().show();
```

One problem with this approach is that the system resizes the layout each time either method is called. Instead, you might want to consider using a theme option to make the System UI behave as an overlay. To enable overlay mode, add the following to the theme:

```
<item name="android:windowActionBarOverlay">true</item>
```

Translucent system bars

These two themes enable the translucent settings:

```
Theme.Holo.NoActionBar.TranslucentDecor
Theme.Holo.Light.NoActionBar.TranslucentDecor
```

If you are creating your own theme, use the following theme settings:

```
<item name="android:windowTranslucentNavigation">true</item>
<item name="android:windowTranslucentStatus">true</item>
```

See also

The *Recognizing a gesture* recipe in *Chapter 8, Using the Touchscreen and Sensors*.

6
Working with Data

In this chapter, we will cover the following topics:

- Storing simple data
- Read and write a text file to internal storage
- Read and write a text file to external storage
- Including resource files in your project
- Creating and using an SQLite database
- Access data in the background using a Loader

Introduction

Since almost any application, big or small, requires saving some kind of data, Android offers many options. From saving a simple value to creating full databases using SQLite, storage options include the following:

- Shared preferences: simple name/value pairs
- Internal storage: data files in private storage
- External storage: data files in private or public storage
- SQLite database: private data can expose the data through a Content Provider
- Cloud storage: Private server or Service Provider

Working with Data

There are benefits and tradeoffs to using internal and external storage. We will list some of the differences here to help you decide whether to use internal or external storage:

- **Internal storage**:
    - Unlike external storage, internal storage is always available, but generally has less free space
    - Files are not accessible to the user (unless the device has root access)
    - Files are automatically deleted when your app is uninstalled (or with the Clear Cache/Cleanup File option in the App Manager)

- **External storage**:
    - The device may not have external storage or it may be inaccessible (such as when it's connected to a computer)
    - Files are accessible to the user (and other apps) without requiring root access
    - Files are not deleted when your app is uninstalled (unless you use `getExternalFilesDir()` to get app-specific public storage)

In this chapter, we will demonstrate working with shared preferences, internal and external storage, and SQLite databases. For cloud storage, take a look at the Internet recipes in *Chapter 12, Telephony, Networks, and the Web* and Online Service Providers in *Chapter 15, Backend as a Service Options*.

Storing simple data

It's a common requirement to store simple data, and Android makes it simple using the Preferences API. It's not limited to just user preferences either; you can store any of the primitive data types using a name/value pair.

We'll demonstrate saving a name from an `EditText` and displaying it when the application starts. The following screenshot shows how the application looks the first time with no saved name, and then on startup, after a name is saved:

Working with Data

Getting ready

Create a new project in Android Studio and call it: `Preferences`. Use the default **Phone & Tablet** options and select **Empty Activity** when prompted for the **Activity Type**.

How to do it...

We'll use the existing **TextView** to display a **Welcome back** message and create a new `EditText` button to save the name. Start by opening `activity_main.xml`:

1. Replace the existing **TextView** and add the following new views:

   ```
   <TextView
       android:id="@+id/textView"
       android:text="Hello World!"
       android:layout_width="wrap_content"
       android:layout_height="wrap_content" />

   <EditText
       android:id="@+id/editTextName"
       android:layout_width="wrap_content"
       android:layout_height="wrap_content"
       android:layout_centerVertical="true"
       android:layout_centerHorizontal="true"
       android:hint="Enter your name" />

   <Button
       android:id="@+id/button"
       android:layout_width="wrap_content"
       android:layout_height="wrap_content"
       android:text="Save"
       android:layout_centerHorizontal="true"
       android:layout_below="@id/editTextName"
       android:onClick="saveName"/>
   ```

2. Open `ActivityMain.java` and add the following global declarations:

   ```
   private final String NAME="NAME";
   private EditText mEditTextName;
   ```

3. Add the following code to `onCreate()` to save a reference to the `EditText` and to load any saved name:
   ```
   TextView textView = (TextView)findViewById(R.id.textView);
   SharedPreferences sharedPreferences = getPreferences(
     MODE_PRIVATE);
   String name = sharedPreferences.getString(NAME,null);
   if (name==null) {
       textView.setText("Hello");
   } else {
       textView.setText("Welcome back " + name + "!");
   }
   mEditTextName = (EditText)findViewById(R.id.editTextName);
   ```

4. Add the following `saveName()` method:
   ```
   public void saveName(View view) {
       SharedPreferences.Editor editor =
         getPreferences(MODE_PRIVATE).edit();
       editor.putString(NAME, mEditTextName.getText().
         toString());
       editor.commit();
   }
   ```

5. Run the program on a device or emulator. Since we are demonstrating persisting data, it loads the name during the `onCreate()`, so save a name and restart the program to see it load.

How it works...

To load the name, we first get a reference to `SharedPreference` so we can call the `getString()` method. We pass in the key for our name/value pair and the default value to return if the key is not found.

To save the preference, we first need to get a reference to the Preference Editor. We use `putString()` and follow it with `commit()`. Without `commit()`, the change will not be saved.

There's more...

Our example stores all the preferences in a single file. We can also store preferences in different files using `getSharedPreferences()` and passing in the name. This option can be used if you want to have separate profiles for multiple users.

Working with Data

Read and write a text file to internal storage

When simple name/value pairs are not sufficient, Android also supports regular file operations including working with text and binary data.

The following recipe demonstrates how to read and write a file to internal or private storage.

Getting ready

Create a new project in Android Studio and call it: `InternalStorageFile`. Use the default **Phone & Tablet** options and select **Empty Activity** when prompted for the **Activity Type**.

How to do it...

To demonstrate both reading and writing text, we'll need a layout with an `EditText` and two buttons. Start by opening `main_activity.xml` and follow these steps:

1. Replace the existing `<TextView>` element with the following views:
   ```xml
   <EditText
       android:id="@+id/editText"
       android:layout_width="wrap_content"
       android:layout_height="wrap_content"
       android:inputType="textMultiLine"
       android:ems="10"
       android:layout_above="@+id/buttonRead"
       android:layout_alignParentTop="true"
       android:layout_centerHorizontal="true" />
   <Button
       android:layout_width="wrap_content"
       android:layout_height="wrap_content"
       android:text="Read"
       android:id="@+id/buttonRead"
       android:layout_centerVertical="true"
       android:layout_centerHorizontal="true"
       android:onClick="readFile"/>
   <Button
       android:layout_width="wrap_content"
       android:layout_height="wrap_content"
       android:text="Write"
       android:id="@+id/buttonWrite"
       android:layout_below="@+id/buttonRead"
       android:layout_centerHorizontal="true"
       android:onClick="writeFile"/>
   ```

Chapter 6

2. Now open `ActivityMain.java` and add the following global variables:

   ```
   private final String FILENAME="testfile.txt";
   EditText mEditText;
   ```

3. Add the following to the `onCreate()` method, after `setContentView ()`:

   ```
   mEditText = (EditText)findViewById(R.id.editText);
   ```

4. Add the following `writeFile()` method:

   ```
   public void writeFile(View view) {
       try {
           FileOutputStream fileOutputStream =
               openFileOutput(FILENAME, Context.MODE_PRIVATE);
           fileOutputStream.write(
               mEditText.getText().toString().getBytes());
           fileOutputStream.close();
       } catch (java.io.IOException e) {
           e.printStackTrace();
       }
   }
   ```

5. Now add the `readFile()` method:

   ```
   public void readFile(View view) {
       StringBuilder stringBuilder = new StringBuilder();
       try {
           InputStream inputStream = openFileInput(FILENAME);
           if ( inputStream != null ) {
               InputStreamReader inputStreamReader = new
                   InputStreamReader(inputStream);
               BufferedReader bufferedReader = new
                   BufferedReader(inputStreamReader);
               String newLine = null;
               while ((newLine = bufferedReader.readLine()) !=
                   null ) {
                   stringBuilder.append(newLine+"\n");
               }
               inputStream.close();
           }
       } catch (java.io.IOException e) {
           e.printStackTrace();
       }
       mEditText.setText(stringBuilder);
   }
   ```

6. Run the program on a device or emulator.

Working with Data

How it works...

We use the `InputStream` and `FileOutputStream` classes to read and write, respectively. Writing to the file is as simple as getting the text from the `EditText` and calling the `write()` method.

Reading back the contents is a little more involved. We could use the `FileInputStream` class for reading, but when working with text, the helper classes make it easier. In our example, we open the file with `openFileInput()`, which returns an `InputStream` object. We then use the `InputStream` to get a `BufferedReader`, which offers the `ReadLine()` method. We loop through each line in the file and append it to our `StringBuilder`. When we're finished reading the file, we assign the text to the `EditText`.

> Our previous file was created in the app's private data folder. To view the contents of the file, you can use the Android Device Monitor to pull the file to your computer. The full file path is: /data/data/com.packtpub.androidcookbook.internalstoragetile/files/testfile.txt.

The following screenshot shows how the file appears when viewed through the **Android Device Monitor**:

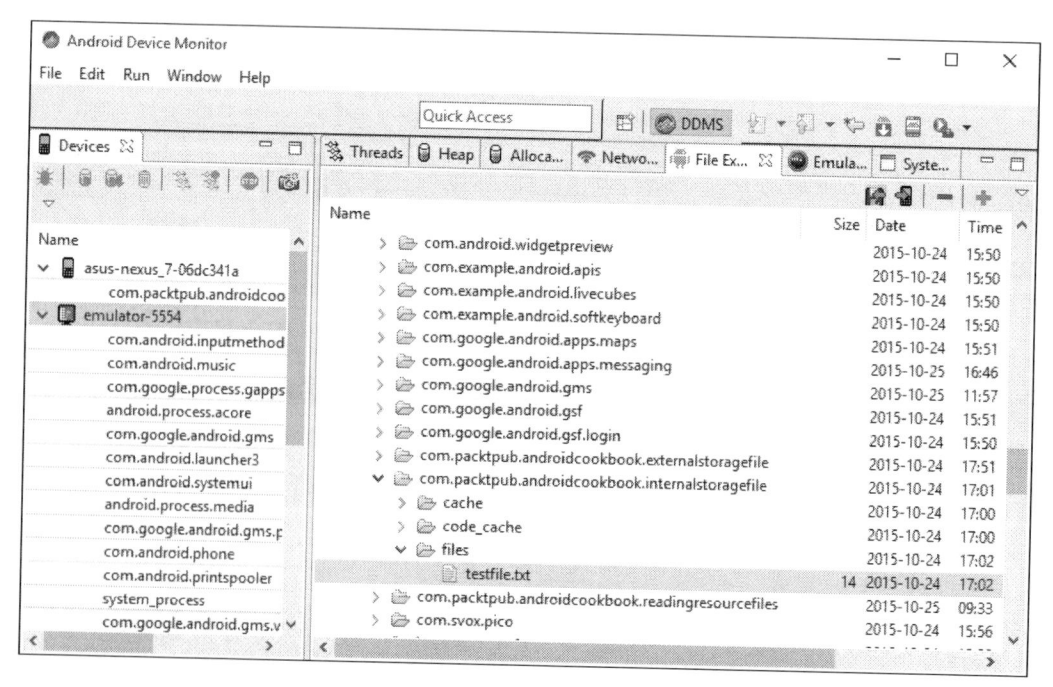

Chapter 6

> You will need a device with root access to view the private folder shown previously.

There's more...

Let's see some additional information that can be helpful.

Cache Files

If all you need is to temporarily store data, you can also use the cache folder. The following method returns the cache folder as a `File` object (the next recipe demonstrates working with the `File` object):

```
getCacheDir()
```

The main benefit of the cache folder is that the system can clear the cache if running low on storage space. (The user can also clear the cache folder from Apps Management in Settings.)

For example, if your app downloads news articles, you could store those in the cache. When your app starts, you can display the news already downloaded. These are files that are not required to make your app work. If the system is low on resources, the cache can be cleared without adversely affecting your app. (Even though the system may clear the cache, it's still a good idea for your app to remove old files as well.)

See also

- The next recipe, *Read and write a text file to external storage*.

Read and write a text file to external storage

The process of reading and writing files to external storage is basically the same as using internal storage. The difference is in obtaining a reference to the storage location. Also, as mentioned in the *Introduction*, external storage may not be available, so it's best to check availability before attempting to access it.

This recipe will read and write a text file, as we did in the previous recipe. We'll also demonstrate how to check the external storage state before we access it.

Working with Data

Getting ready

Create a new project in Android Studio and call it: `ExternalStorageFile`. Use the default **Phone & Tablet** options and select **Empty Activity** when prompted for the **Activity Type**. We will use the same layout as the previous recipe, so you can just copy and paste if you typed it in already. Otherwise, use the layout from Step 1 in the previous recipe, *Read and write a text file to internal storage*.

How to do it...

As mentioned previously in the *Getting ready* section, we'll use the layout from the previous recipe. With the layout file done, the first step will be to add permission to access the write to external storage. Here are the steps:

1. Open the Android Manifest and add the following permission:

    ```
    <uses-permission android:name=
       "android.permission.WRITE_EXTERNAL_STORAGE" />
    ```

2. Next, open `ActivityMain.java` and add the following global variables:

    ```
    private final String FILENAME="testfile.txt";
    EditText mEditText;
    ```

3. Add the following to the `onCreate()` method, after `setContentView()`:

    ```
    mEditText = (EditText)findViewById(R.id.editText);
    ```

4. Add the following two methods to check the storage state:

    ```
    public boolean isExternalStorageWritable() {
        if (Environment.MEDIA_MOUNTED.equals(
          Environment.getExternalStorageState())) {
            return true;
        }
        return false;
    }

    public boolean isExternalStorageReadable() {
        if (Environment.MEDIA_MOUNTED.equals(
          Environment.getExternalStorageState()) ||
              Environment.MEDIA_MOUNTED_READ_ONLY.
    equals(Environment.getExternalStorageState())) {
            return true;
        }
        return false;
    }
    ```

Chapter 6

5. Add the following `writeFile()` method:

```java
public void writeFile(View view) {
    if (isExternalStorageWritable()) {
        try {
            File textFile = new File(
                Environment.getExternalStorageDirectory(),
                    FILENAME);
            FileOutputStream fileOutputStream = new
                FileOutputStream(textFile);
            fileOutputStream.write(mEditText.getText().
                toString().getBytes());
            fileOutputStream.close();
        } catch (java.io.IOException e) {
            e.printStackTrace();
            Toast.makeText(this, "Error writing file",
                Toast.LENGTH_LONG).show();
        }
    } else {
        Toast.makeText(this, "Cannot write to External
            Storage", Toast.LENGTH_LONG).show();
    }
}
```

6. Add the following `readFile()` method:

```java
public void readFile(View view) {
    if (isExternalStorageReadable()) {
        StringBuilder stringBuilder = new StringBuilder();
        try {
            File textFile = new File(
                Environment.getExternalStorageDirectory(),
                    FILENAME);
            FileInputStream fileInputStream = new
                FileInputStream(textFile);
            if (fileInputStream != null ) {
                InputStreamReader inputStreamReader = new
                    InputStreamReader(fileInputStream);
                BufferedReader bufferedReader = new
                    BufferedReader(inputStreamReader);
                String newLine = null;
                while ( (newLine =
                    bufferedReader.readLine()) != null ) {
                        stringBuilder.append(newLine+"\n");
                }
```

139

Working with Data

```
                    fileInputStream.close();
                }
                mEditText.setText(stringBuilder);
            } catch (java.io.IOException e) {
                e.printStackTrace();
                Toast.makeText(this, "Error reading
                    file", Toast.LENGTH_LONG).show();
            }
        } else {
            Toast.makeText(this, "Cannot read External
                Storage", Toast.LENGTH_LONG).show();
        }
    }
```

7. Run the program on a device or emulator with external storage.

How it works...

Reading and writing files are basically the same for both internal and external storage. The main difference is that we should check for the availability of the external storage before attempting to access it, which we do with the `isExternalStorageWritable()` and `isExternalStorageReadable()` methods. When checking the storage state, `MEDIA_MOUNTED` means we can read and write to it.

Unlike the internal storage example, we request the working path as we do in this line of code:

```
File textFile = new File(
    Environment.getExternalStorageDirectory(), FILENAME);
```

The actual reading and writing is done with the same classes, as it is just the location that is different.

> It is not safe to hard code an external folder path. The path can vary between versions of the OS and especially between hardware manufacturers. It is always best to call `getExternalStorageDirectory()`, as shown.

There's more...

Some additional information are discussed as follows.

Getting public folders

The `getExternalStorageDirectory()` method returns the root folder of the external storage. If you want to obtain specific public folders, such as the `Music` or `Ringtone` folder, use `getExternalStoragePublicDirectory()` and pass in the desired folder type, for example:

```
getExternalStoragePublicDirectory(Environment.DIRECTORY_MUSIC)
```

Checking available space

One issue consistent between internal and external storage is limited space. If you know how much space you will need ahead of time, you can call the `getFreeSpace()` method on the `File` object. (`getTotalSpace()` will return the total space.) Here is a simple example to using the call to `getFreeSpace()`:

```
if (Environment.getExternalStorageDirectory().getFreeSpace() <
RQUIRED_FILE_SPACE) {
    //Not enough space
} else {
    //We have enough space
}
```

Deleting a file

There are many helper methods available through the `File` object, including deleting a file. If we wanted to delete the text file we created in the example, we could call `delete()` as follows:

```
textFile.delete()
```

Working with directories

Though it's called a `File` object, it supports directory commands as well, such as making and removing directories. If you want to make or remove a directory, build the `File` object, then call the respective methods: `mkdir()` and `delete()`. (There's also a method called `mkdirs()` (plural) that will create parent folders as well.) See the following link for a complete list.

Preventing files from being included in galleries

Android employs a **media scanner** that automatically includes sound, video, and image files in the system collections, such as the Image Gallery. To exclude your directory, create an empty file called `.nomedia` (note the preceding period) in the same directory as the files you wish to exclude.

Working with Data

See also

- For a complete list of methods available in the `File` class, visit `http://developer.android.com/reference/java/io/File.html`

Including resource files in your project

Android provides two options for including files in your project: the `raw` folder and the `Assets` folder. Which option you use depends on your requirements. To start, we'll give a brief overview of each option to help you decide when to use each option:

- **Raw files**
    - Included in the resource directory: `/res/raw`
    - As a resource, accessed through the raw identifier: `R.raw.<resource>`
    - A good place for storing media files such as MP3, MP4, and OOG files

- **Asset files**
    - Creates a filesystem compiled in your APK (does *NOT* provide a resource ID)
    - Access files using their file names, generally making them easier to use with dynamically created names
    - Some APIs do not support a Resource Identifier and therefore require including as an Asset

Generally, `raw` files are easier to work with since they are accessed through the resource identifier. As we'll demonstrate in this recipe, the main difference is how you access the file. In this example, we will load both a `raw` text file and an `asset` text file and display the contents.

Getting ready

Create a new project in Android Studio and call it: `ReadingResourceFiles`. Use the default **Phone & Tablet** options and select **Empty Activity** when prompted for the **Activity Type**.

How to do it...

To demonstrate reading content from both resource locations, we'll create a split layout. We also need to create both resource folders as they are not included in the default Android project. Here are the steps:

1. Open `activity_main.xml` and replace the contents with the following layout:

    ```xml
    <?xml version="1.0" encoding="utf-8"?>
    <LinearLayout xmlns:android="http://schemas.android.com/apk/res/android"
        xmlns:tools="http://schemas.android.com/tools"
        android:layout_width="match_parent"
        android:layout_height="match_parent"
        android:orientation="vertical">
        <TextView
            android:id="@+id/textViewRaw"
            android:layout_width="match_parent"
            android:layout_height="0dp"
            android:layout_weight="1"
            android:gravity=
                "center_horizontal|center_vertical"/>
        <TextView
            android:id="@+id/textViewAsset"
            android:layout_width="match_parent"
            android:layout_height="0dp"
            android:layout_weight="1"
            android:gravity=
                "center_horizontal|center_vertical"/>
    </LinearLayout>
    ```

2. Create the `raw` resource folder in the res folder. It will read as: `res/raw`.

3. Create a new text file by right-clicking on the `raw` folder and select **New | File**. Name the file `raw_text.txt` and type some text in the file. (This text will display when you run the application.)

Working with Data

4. Create the `asset` folder. The `asset` folder is trickier because of the location. Fortunately, Android Studio provides a menu option that makes creating it very easy. Go to the **File** menu (or right-click on the **app** node) and select **New | Folder | Assets Folder** as shown in this screenshot:

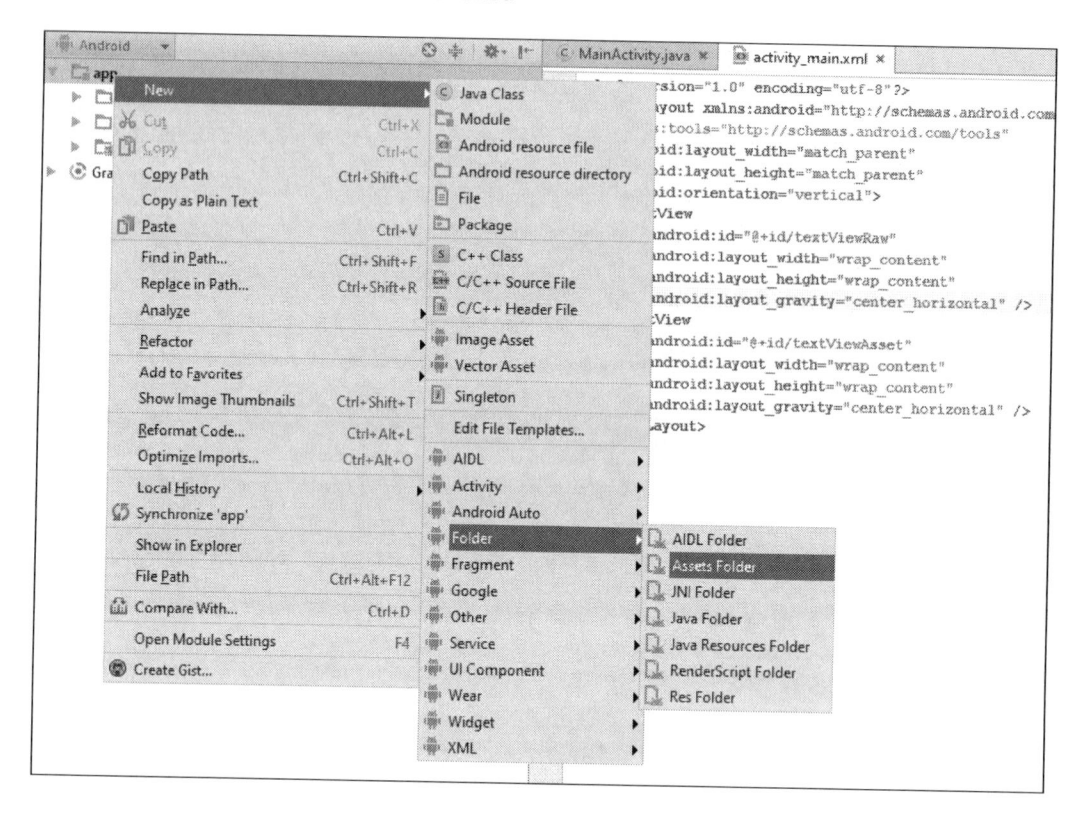

5. Create another text file in the asset folder called `asset_text.txt`. Again, whatever text you type here will be shown when you run the app. Here's how the final result should look after both text files are created:

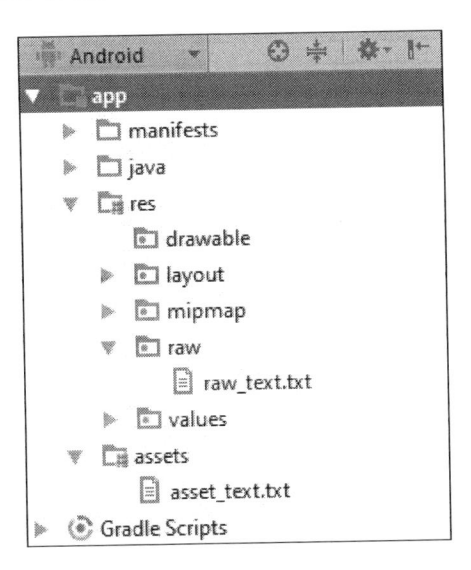

6. Now it's time for the code. Open `MainActivity.java` and add the following method to read the text file (which is passed into the method):

```
private String getText(InputStream inputStream) {
    StringBuilder stringBuilder = new StringBuilder();
    try {;
        if ( inputStream != null ) {
            InputStreamReader inputStreamReader = new
              InputStreamReader(inputStream);
            BufferedReader bufferedReader = new
              BufferedReader(inputStreamReader);
            String newLine = null;
            while ((newLine = bufferedReader.readLine()) !=
              null ) {
                stringBuilder.append(newLine+"\n");
            }
            inputStream.close();
        }
    } catch (java.io.IOException e) {
        e.printStackTrace();
    }
    return stringBuilder.toString();
}
```

Working with Data

7. Finally, add the following code to the `onCreate()` method:

```
TextView textViewRaw =
   (TextView)findViewById(R.id.textViewRaw);
textViewRaw.setText(getText(this.getResources().
   openRawResource(R.raw.raw_text)));

TextView textViewAsset =
   (TextView)findViewById(R.id.textViewAsset);
try {
    textViewAsset.setText(getText(this.getAssets().open(
       "asset_text.txt")));
} catch (IOException e) {
    e.printStackTrace();
}
```

8. Run the program on a device or emulator.

How it works...

To summarize, the only difference is in how we get a reference to each file. This line of code reads the `raw` resource:

```
this.getResources().openRawResource(R.raw.raw_text)
```

And this code reads the `asset` file:

```
this.getAssets().open("asset_text.txt")
```

Both calls return an `InputStream`, which the `getText()` method uses to read the file contents. It is worth noting, though, that the call to open the `asset` text file requires an additional `try/catch`. As noted in the recipe introduction, resources are indexed so we have compile time verification, which the `asset` folder does not have.

There's more...

A common approach is to include resources in your APK, but download new resources as they become available. (See the network communication in *Chapter 12, Telephony, Networks, and the Web*.) If new resources aren't available, you can always fall back on the resources in your APK.

See also

- Network communication recipes in *Chapter 12, Telephony, Networks, and the Web.*

Creating and using an SQLite database

In this recipe, we're going to demonstrate working with an SQLite database. If you are already familiar with SQL databases from other platforms, then much of what you know will apply. If you are new to SQLite, take a look at the reference links in the "See also" section as this recipe assumes a basic understanding of database concepts including schemas, tables, cursors, and raw SQL.

To get you up and running with an SQLite database quickly, our example implements the basic CRUD operations. Generally, when creating a database in Android, you create a class that extends `SQLiteOpenHelper`, which is where your database functionality is implemented. Here is a list of the functions to provide each of the basic operations:

- Create: `insert()`
- Read: `query()` and `rawQuery()`
- Update: `update()`
- Delete: `delete()`

To demonstrate a fully working database, we will create a simple `Dictionary` database, so we can store words and their definitions. We'll demonstrate the CRUD operations by allowing adding new words (with their definitions) and updating existing word definitions. We'll show words in a `ListView` using a cursor. Pressing a word in the `ListView` will read the definition from the database and display it in a Toast message. A long press will delete the word.

Getting ready

Create a new project in Android Studio and call it: `SQLiteDatabase`. Use the default **Phone & Tablet** options and select **Empty Activity** when prompted for the **Activity Type**.

Working with Data

How to do it...

First, we'll create the UI, which will consist of two `EditText` fields, a button, and a `ListView`. As we add words to the database, they will populate the `ListView`. To start, open `activity_main.xml` and follow these steps:

1. Replace the existing `<TextView>` with these new views:

   ```
   <EditText
       android:id="@+id/et_word"
       android:layout_width="wrap_content"
       android:layout_height="wrap_content"
       android:layout_alignParentTop="true"
       android:layout_alignParentLeft="true"
       android:layout_alignParentStart="true"
       android:hint="Word"/>
   <EditText
       android:id="@+id/et_definition"
       android:layout_width="match_parent"
       android:layout_height="wrap_content"
       android:layout_below="@+id/editTextWord"
       android:layout_alignParentLeft="true"
       android:layout_alignParentStart="true"
       android:hint="Definition"/>
   <Button
       android:layout_width="wrap_content"
       android:layout_height="wrap_content"
       android:text="Save"
       android:id="@+id/button_add_update"
       android:layout_alignParentRight="true"
       android:layout_alignParentTop="true" />
   <ListView
       android:layout_width="wrap_content"
       android:layout_height="wrap_content"
       android:id="@+id/listView"
       android:layout_below="@+id/et_definition"
       android:layout_alignParentLeft="true"
       android:layout_alignParentBottom="true" />
   ```

Chapter 6

2. Add a new Java class to the project named `DictionaryDatabase`. This class extends from `SQLiteOpenHelper` and handles all the SQLite functions. Here is the class declaration:

   ```
   public class DictionaryDatabase extends SQLiteOpenHelper {
   ```

3. Below the declaration, add the following constants:

   ```
   private static final String DATABASE_NAME =
       "dictionary.db";
   private static final String TABLE_DICTIONARY =
       "dictionary";

   private static final String FIELD_WORD = "word";
   private static final String FIELD_DEFINITION =
       "definition";
   private static final int DATABASE_VERSION = 1;
   ```

4. Add the following constructor, `OnCreate()` and `onUpgrade()` methods:

   ```
   DictionaryDatabase(Context context) {
        super(context, DATABASE_NAME, null, DATABASE_VERSION);
   }

   @Override
   public void onCreate(SQLiteDatabase db) {
        db.execSQL("CREATE TABLE " + TABLE_DICTIONARY +
                "(_id integer PRIMARY KEY," +
                FIELD_WORD + " TEXT, " +
                FIELD_DEFINITION + " TEXT);");
   }

   @Override
   public void onUpgrade(SQLiteDatabase db, int oldVersion,
      int newVersion) {
        //Handle database upgrade as needed
   }
   ```

5. The following methods are responsible for creating, updating, and deleting the records:

   ```
   public void saveRecord(String word, String definition) {
        long id = findWordID(word);
        if (id>0) {
            updateRecord(id, word, definition);
        } else {
   ```

149

Working with Data

```
            addRecord(word,definition);
        }
    }

    public long addRecord(String word, String definition) {
        SQLiteDatabase db = getWritableDatabase();

        ContentValues values = new ContentValues();
        values.put(FIELD_WORD, word);
        values.put(FIELD_DEFINITION, definition);
        return db.insert(TABLE_DICTIONARY, null, values);
    }

    public int updateRecord(long id, String word, String definition) {
        SQLiteDatabase db = getWritableDatabase();
        ContentValues values = new ContentValues();
        values.put("_id", id);
        values.put(FIELD_WORD, word);
        values.put(FIELD_DEFINITION, definition);
        return db.update(TABLE_DICTIONARY, values, "_id = ?",
          new String[]{String.valueOf(id)});
    }
    public int deleteRecord(long id) {
        SQLiteDatabase db = getWritableDatabase();
        return db.delete(TABLE_DICTIONARY, "_id = ?", new
          String[]{String.valueOf(id)});
    }
```

6. And these methods handle reading the information from the database:

```
    public long findWordID(String word) {
        long returnVal = -1;
        SQLiteDatabase db = getReadableDatabase();
        Cursor cursor = db.rawQuery(
            "SELECT _id FROM " + TABLE_ DICTIONARY +
                " WHERE " + FIELD_WORD + " = ?", new String[]{word});
        Log.i("findWordID","getCount()="+cursor.getCount());
        if (cursor.getCount() == 1) {
            cursor.moveToFirst();
            returnVal = cursor.getInt(0);
        }
        return returnVal;
    }
```

```java
public String getDefinition(long id) {
    String returnVal = "";
    SQLiteDatabase db = getReadableDatabase();
    Cursor cursor = db.rawQuery(
        "SELECT definition FROM " + TABLE_DICTIONARY +
            " WHERE _id = ?", new String[]{String.valueOf(id)});
    if (cursor.getCount() == 1) {
        cursor.moveToFirst();
        returnVal = cursor.getString(0);
    }
    return returnVal;
}

public Cursor getWordList() {
    SQLiteDatabase db = getReadableDatabase();
    String query = "SELECT _id, " + FIELD_WORD +
        " FROM " + TABLE_DICTIONARY + " ORDER BY " + FIELD_WORD +
            " ASC";
    return db.rawQuery(query, null);
}
```

7. With the database class finished, open `MainActivity.java`. Add the following global variables below the class declaration:

```java
EditText mEditTextWord;
EditText mEditTextDefinition;
DictionaryDatabase mDB;
ListView mListView;
```

8. Add the following method to save the fields when the button is clicked:

```java
private void saveRecord() {
    mDB.saveRecord(mEditTextWord.getText().toString(),
        mEditTextDefinition.getText().toString());
    mEditTextWord.setText("");
    mEditTextDefinition.setText("");
    updateWordList();
}
```

9. Add this method to populate the `ListView`:

```java
private void updateWordList() {
    SimpleCursorAdapter simpleCursorAdapter = new
        SimpleCursorAdapter(
            this,
            android.R.layout.simple_list_item_1,
            mDB.getWordList(),
```

Working with Data

```java
            new String[]{"word"},
            new int[]{android.R.id.text1},
            0);
        mListView.setAdapter(simpleCursorAdapter);
}
```

10. Finally, add the following code to `onCreate()`:

```java
mDB = new DictionaryDatabase(this);

mEditTextWord = (EditText)findViewById(R.id.editTextWord);
mEditTextDefinition =
   (EditText)findViewById(R.id.editTextDefinition);

Button buttonAddUpdate =
   (Button)findViewById(R.id.buttonAddUpdate);
buttonAddUpdate.setOnClickListener(new
   View.OnClickListener() {
     @Override
     public void onClick(View v) {
        saveRecord();
     }
});

mListView = (ListView)findViewById(R.id.listView);
mListView.setOnItemClickListener(new
   AdapterView.OnItemClickListener() {
     @Override
     public void onItemClick(AdapterView<?> parent, View
        view, int position, long id) {
          Toast.makeText(MainActivity.this,
             mDB.getDefinition(id),Toast.LENGTH_SHORT).show();
     }
});
mListView.setOnItemLongClickListener(new
   AdapterView.OnItemLongClickListener() {
     @Override
     public boolean onItemLongClick(AdapterView<?> parent,
        View view, int position, long id) {
          Toast.makeText(MainActivity.this,
             "Records deleted = " + mDB.deleteRecord(id),
                Toast.LENGTH_SHORT).show();
          updateWordList();
          return true;
     }
});
updateWordList();
```

11. Run the program on a device or emulator and try it out.

How it works...

We'll start by explaining the `DictionaryDatabase` class as that's the heart of an SQLite database. The first item to note is the constructor:

```
DictionaryDatabase(Context context) {
    super(context, DATABASE_NAME, null, DATABASE_VERSION);
}
```

Notice `DATABASE_VERSION`? Only when you make changes to your database schema do you need to increment this value.

Next is `onCreate()`, where the database is actually created. This is only called the first time the database is created, not each time the class is created. It's also worth noting the `_id` field. Android does not require tables to have a primary field, except for some classes such as `SimpleCursorAdapter`, require `_id`.

We're required to implement the `onUpgrade()` callback, but as this is a new database, there's nothing to do. This method will be called when the database version is incremented.

The `saveRecord()` method handles calling `addRecord()` or `updateRecord()`, as appropriate. Since we are going to modify the database, both methods call `getWritableDatabase()` so we can make changes. A writeable database requires more resources so if you don't need to make changes, get a read-only database instead.

The last method to note is `getWordList()`, which returns all the words in the database using a cursor object. We use this cursor to populate the `ListView`, which brings us to `ActivityMain.java`. The `onCreate()` method does the standard initialization we've seen before and also creates an instance of the database with the following line of code:

```
mDB = new DictionaryDatabase(this);
```

The `onCreate()` method is also where we set up the events to show the word definition (with a Toast) when an item is pressed and to delete the word on a long press. Probably the most complicated code is in `updateWordList()`.

This isn't the first time we've used an adapter, but this is the first cursor adapter, so we'll explain. We use the `SimpleCursorAdapter` to create a mapping between our field in the cursor and the `ListView` item. We use the `layout.simple_list_item_1` layout, which only includes a single text field with ID `android.R.id.text1`. In a real application, we'd probably create a custom layout and include the definition in the `ListView` item, but we wanted to demonstrate a method to read the definition from the database.

We call `updateWordList()` in three places—during `onCreate()` to create the initial list, then again after we add/update a list, and lastly when deleting a list.

Working with Data

There's more...

Though this is a fully functioning example of SQLite, it is still just the basics. A whole book can, and has, been written on SQLite for Android.

Upgrading a database

As we mentioned previously, when we increment the database version, the `onUpgrade()` method will be called. What you do here is dependent on the change(s). If you changed an existing table, ideally you'll want to migrate the user data to the new format by querying the existing data and inserting it into the new format. Keep in mind, there is no guarantee the user will upgrade in consecutive order—so they could jump from version 1 to version 4, for example.

See also

- SQLite Home Page: `https://www.sqlite.org/`
- SQLite Database Android Reference: `http://developer.android.com/reference/android/database/sqlite/SQLiteDatabase.html`

Access data in the background using a Loader

Any potentially long-running operations should not be done on the UI thread, as this can cause your application to be slow or become non-responsive. The Android OS will bring up the **Application Not Responding** (**ANR**) dialog when apps become non-responsive.

Since querying databases can be time-consuming, Android introduced the Loader API in Android 3.0. A Loader processes the query on a background thread and notifies the UI thread when it finishes.

The two primary benefits to Loaders include:

- Querying the database is (automatically) handled on a background thread
- The Query auto-updates (when using a Content Provider data source)

To demonstrate a Loader, we will modify the previous SQLite database example to use a `CursorLoader` to populate the `ListView`.

Getting ready

We will use the project from the previous example, *Creating and using an SQLite database*, as the base for this recipe. Create a new project in Android Studio and call it: Loader. Use the default **Phone & Tablet** options and select **Empty Activity** when prompted for the **Activity Type**. Copy the `DictionaryDatabase` class and the layout from the previous recipe. Though we will use parts of the previous `ActivityMain.java` code, we will start at the beginning in this recipe to make it easier to follow.

How to do it...

With the project set up as described previously, we will start by creating two new Java classes, and then tie it all together in `ActivityMain.java`. Here are the steps:

1. Create a new Java class called `DictionaryAdapter` that extends `CursorAdapter`. This class replaces the `SimpleCursorAdapter` we used in the previous recipe. Here is the full code:

```java
public class DictionaryAdapter extends CursorAdapter {
    public DictionaryAdapter(Context context, Cursor c,
      int flags) {
        super(context, c, flags);
    }

    @Override
    public View newView(Context context, Cursor cursor,
      ViewGroup parent) {
        return LayoutInflater.from(context).inflate(
          android.R.layout.simple_list_item_1,parent,
            false);
    }

    @Override
    public void bindView(View view, Context context, Cursor
      cursor) {
        TextView textView = (TextView)view.findViewById(
          android.R.id.text1);
        textView.setText(cursor.getString(
          getCursor().getColumnIndex("word")));
    }
}
```

Working with Data

2. Next, create another new Java class and call this one `DictionaryLoader`. Though this is the class that handles the data loading on the background thread, it's actually very simple:

   ```
   public class DictionaryLoader extends CursorLoader {
       Context mContext;
       public DictionaryLoader(Context context) {
           super(context);
           mContext = context;
       }

       @Override
       public Cursor loadInBackground() {
           DictionaryDatabase db = new
               DictionaryDatabase(mContext);
           return db.getWordList();
       }
   }
   ```

3. Next, open `ActivityMain.java`. We need to change the declaration to implement the `LoaderManager.LoaderCallbacks<Cursor>` interface as follows:

   ```
   public class MainActivity extends AppCompatActivity
       implements {
   ```

4. Add the adapter to the global declarations. The complete list is as follows:

   ```
   EditText mEditTextWord;
   EditText mEditTextDefinition;
   DictionaryDatabase mDB;
   ListView mListView;
   DictionaryAdapter mAdapter;
   ```

5. Change `onCreate()` to use the new adapter and add a call to update the Loader after deleting a record. The final `onCreate()` method should look as follows:

   ```
   protected void onCreate(Bundle savedInstanceState) {
       super.onCreate(savedInstanceState);
       setContentView(R.layout.activity_main);

       mDB = new DictionaryDatabase(this);

       mEditTextWord = (EditText) findViewById(R.id.editTextWord);
       mEditTextDefinition = (EditText) findViewById(
           R.id.editTextDefinition);
   ```

```java
        Button buttonAddUpdate = (Button) findViewById(
            R.id.buttonAddUpdate);
        buttonAddUpdate.setOnClickListener(new View.OnClickListener()
{
            @Override
            public void onClick(View v) {
                saveRecord();
            }
        });

        mListView = (ListView) findViewById(R.id.listView);
        mListView.setOnItemClickListener(new AdapterView.
OnItemClickListener() {
            @Override
            public void onItemClick(AdapterView<?> parent, View
              view, int position, long id) {
                Toast.makeText(MainActivity.this,
                    mDB.getDefinition(id),
                       Toast.LENGTH_SHORT).show();
            }
        });
        mListView.setOnItemLongClickListener(new
          AdapterView.OnItemLongClickListener() {
            @Override
            public boolean onItemLongClick(AdapterView<?>
              parent, View view, int position, long id) {
                Toast.makeText(MainActivity.this, "Records
                    deleted = " + mDB.deleteRecord(id),
                       Toast.LENGTH_SHORT).show();
                getSupportLoaderManager().restartLoader(0,
                    null, MainActivity.this);
                return true;
            }
        });
        getSupportLoaderManager().initLoader(0, null, this);
        mAdapter = new
          DictionaryAdapter(this,mDB.getWordList(),0);
        mListView.setAdapter(mAdapter);
    }
```

Working with Data

6. We no longer have the `updateWordList()` method, so change `saveRecord()` as follows:

   ```
   private void saveRecord() {
       mDB.saveRecord(mEditTextWord.getText().toString(),
           mEditTextDefinition.getText().toString());
       mEditTextWord.setText("");
       mEditTextDefinition.setText("");
       getSupportLoaderManager().restartLoader(0, null,
           MainActivity.this);
   }
   ```

7. Finally, implement these three methods for the Loader interface:

   ```
   @Override
   public Loader<Cursor> onCreateLoader(int id, Bundle args) {
       return new DictionaryLoader(this);
   }

   @Override
   public void onLoadFinished(Loader<Cursor> loader, Cursor data) {
       mAdapter.swapCursor(data);
   }

   @Override
   public void onLoaderReset(Loader<Cursor> loader) {
       mAdapter.swapCursor(null);
   }
   ```

8. Run the program on a device or emulator.

How it works...

The default `CursorAdapter` requires a Content Provider URI. Since we are accessing the SQLite database directly (and not through a Content Provider), we don't have a URI to pass, so instead we created a custom adapter by extending the `CursorAdapter` class. `DictionaryAdapter` still performs the same functionality as the previous `SimpleCursorAdapter` from the previous recipe, namely mapping the data from the cursor to the item layout.

Chapter 6

The next class we added was `DictionaryLoader`, which is the actual Loader. As you can see, it's actually very simple. All it does is return the cursor from `getWordList()`. The key here is that this query is being handled in a background thread and will call the `onLoadFinished()` callback (in `MainActivity.java`) when it finishes. Fortunately, most of the heavy lifting is handled in the base class.

This takes us to `ActivityMain.java`, where we implemented the following three callbacks from the `LoaderManager.LoaderCallbacks` interface:

- `onCreateLoader()`: It's initially called in `onCreate()` with the `initLoader()` call. It's called again with the `restartLoader()` call, after we make changes to the database.
- `onLoadFinished()`: It's called when the Loader `loadInBackground()` finishes.
- `onLoaderReset()`: It's called when the Loader is being recreated (such as with the `restart()` method). We set the old cursor to `null` because it will be invalidated and we don't want a reference kept around.

There's more...

As you saw in the previous example, we need to manually notify the Loader to requery the database using `restartLoader()`. One of the benefits of using a Loader is that it can auto-update, but it requires a Content Provider as the data source. A Content Provider supports using an SQLite database as the data source, and for a serious application, would be recommended. See the following Content Provider link to get started.

See also

- The *AsyncTask* recipe in *Chapter 14, Getting Your App Ready for the Play Store.*
- Creating a Content Provider: `http://developer.android.com/guide/topics/providers/content-provider-creating.html`

7
Alerts and Notifications

In this chapter, we will cover the following topics:

- Lights, Action, and Sound – getting the user's attention!
- Creating a Toast using a custom layout
- Displaying a message box with AlertDialog
- Displaying a progress dialog
- Lights, Action, and Sound Redux using Notifications
- Creating a Media Player Notification
- Making a Flashlight with a Heads-Up Notification

Introduction

Android provides many ways to notify your user—from non-visual methods, including sounds, lights, and vibration, to visual methods including Toasts, Dialogs, and Status Bar notifications.

Keep in mind, notifications distract your user, so it's a good idea to be very judicious when using any notification. Users like to be in control of their device (it is theirs, after all) so give them the option to enable and disable notifications as they desire. Otherwise, your user might get annoyed and uninstall your app altogether.

We'll start by reviewing the following non-UI based notification options:

- Flash LED
- Vibrate phone
- Play ringtone

Alerts and Notifications

Then we'll move on to visual notifications, including:

- Toasts
- `AlertDialog`
- `ProgressDialog`
- Status Bar Notifications

The recipes that follow will show you how to implement these features in your own applications. It's worth reading the following link to understand "best practices" when using notifications:

> Refer to **Android Notification Design Guidelines** at `http://developer.android.com/design/patterns/notifications.html`

Lights, Action, and Sound – getting the user's attention!

Most of the recipes in this chapter use the Notification object to alert your users, so this recipe will show an alternative approach for when you don't actually need a notification.

As the recipe title implies, we're going to use lights, action, and sound:

- **Lights**: Normally, you'd use the LED device, but that is only available through the Notification object, which we'll demonstrate later in the chapter. Instead we'll take this opportunity to use `setTorchMode()` (added in API 23—Android 6.0), to use the camera flash as a flashlight. (Note: as you'll see in the code, this feature will only work on an Android 6.0 device with a camera flash.)
- **Action**: We'll vibrate the phone.
- **Sound**: We'll use the `RingtoneManager` to play the default notification sound.

As you'll see, the code for each of these is quite simple.

As demonstrated in the following *Lights, Action, and Sound Redux using Notifications* recipe, all three options: LED, vibrate, and sounds, are available through the Notification object. The Notification object would certainly be the most appropriate method to provide alerts and reminders when the user is not actively engaged in your app. But for those times when you want to provide feedback while they are using your app, these options are available. The vibrate option is a good example; if you want to provide haptic feedback to a button press (common with keyboard apps), call the vibrate method directly.

Chapter 7

Getting ready

Create a new project in Android Studio and call it: `LightsActionSound`. When prompted for the API level, we need API 21 or above to compile the project. Select **Empty Activity** when prompted for the **Activity Type**.

How to do it...

We'll use three buttons to initiate each action, so start by opening `activity_main.xml` and follow these steps:

1. Replace the existing `<TextView>` element with the following three buttons:

    ```xml
    <ToggleButton
        android:id="@+id/buttonLights"
        android:layout_width="wrap_content"
        android:layout_height="wrap_content"
        android:text="Lights"
        android:layout_centerHorizontal="true"
        android:layout_above="@+id/buttonAction"
        android:onClick="clickLights" />
    <Button
        android:id="@+id/buttonAction"
        android:layout_width="wrap_content"
        android:layout_height="wrap_content"
        android:text="Action"
        android:layout_centerVertical="true"
        android:layout_centerHorizontal="true"
        android:onClick="clickVibrate"/>
    <Button
        android:id="@+id/buttonSound"
        android:layout_width="wrap_content"
        android:layout_height="wrap_content"
        android:text="Sound"
        android:layout_below="@+id/buttonAction"
        android:layout_centerHorizontal="true"
        android:onClick="clickSound"/>
    ```

2. Add the following permission to the Android Manifest:

    ```xml
    <uses-permission android:name="android.permission.VIBRATE"></uses-permission>
    ```

Alerts and Notifications

3. Open `ActivityMain.java` and add the following global variables:

   ```
   private CameraManager mCameraManager;
   private String mCameraId=null;
   private ToggleButton mButtonLights;
   ```

4. Add the following method to get the Camera ID:

   ```
   private String getCameraId() {
       try {
           String[] ids = mCameraManager.getCameraIdList();
           for (String id : ids) {
               CameraCharacteristics c =
                   mCameraManager.getCameraCharacteristics(id);
               Boolean flashAvailable = c.get(
                   CameraCharacteristics.FLASH_INFO_AVAILABLE);
               Integer facingDirection = c.get(
                   CameraCharacteristics.LENS_FACING);
               if (flashAvailable != null && flashAvailable
                   && facingDirection != null
                   && facingDirection ==
                   CameraCharacteristics.
                   LENS_FACING_BACK) {
                   return id;
               }
           }
       } catch (CameraAccessException e) {
           e.printStackTrace();
       }
       return null;
   }
   ```

5. Add the following code to the `onCreate()` method:

   ```
   mButtonLights = (ToggleButton)findViewById(R.id.buttonLights);
   if (Build.VERSION.SDK_INT >= Build.VERSION_CODES.M) {
       mCameraManager = (CameraManager)
           this.getSystemService(Context.CAMERA_SERVICE);
       mCameraId = getCameraId();
       if (mCameraId==null) {
           mButtonLights.setEnabled(false);
       } else {
           mButtonLights.setEnabled(true);
       }
   } else {
       mButtonLights.setEnabled(false);
   }
   ```

Chapter 7

6. Now add the code to handle each of the button clicks:

```
public void clickLights(View view) {
    if (Build.VERSION.SDK_INT >= Build.VERSION_CODES.M) {
        try {
            mCameraManager.setTorchMode(mCameraId,
                mButtonLights.isChecked());
        } catch (CameraAccessException e) {
            e.printStackTrace();
        }
    }
}

public void clickVibrate(View view) {
    ((Vibrator)getSystemService(
        VIBRATOR_SERVICE)).vibrate(1000);
}

public void clickSound(View view) {
    Uri notificationSoundUri = RingtoneManager
        .getDefaultUri(RingtoneManager.TYPE_NOTIFICATION);
    Ringtone ringtone = RingtoneManager
        .getRingtone(getApplicationContext(),
            notificationSoundUri);
    ringtone.play();
}
```

7. You're ready to run the application on a physical device. The code presented here will need Android 6.0 (or higher) to use the flashlight option.

How it works...

As you can see from the previous paragraphs, most of the code is related to finding and opening the camera to use the flash feature. `setTorchMode()` was introduced in API 23, which is why we have the API version check:

```
if (Build.VERSION.SDK_INT >= Build.VERSION_CODES.M) {}
```

This app demonstrates using the new `camera2` libraries, which were introduced in Lollipop (API 21). The `vibrate` and `ringtone` methods have both been available since API 1.

The `getCameraId()` method is where we check for the camera. We want an outward-facing camera with a flash. If one is found, the ID is returned, otherwise it is null. If the camera id is null, we disable the button.

Alerts and Notifications

For playing the sound, we use the `Ringtone` object from the `RingtoneManager`. Besides it being relatively easy to implement, another benefit to this method is that we can use the default notification sound, which we get with this code:

```
Uri notificationSoundUri = RingtoneManager.
    getDefaultUri(RingtoneManager.TYPE_NOTIFICATION);
```

This way, if the user changes their preferred notification sound, we use it automatically.

Last is the call to vibrate the phone. This was the simplest code to use, but it does require permission, which we added to the Manifest:

```
<uses-permission android:name="android.permission.VIBRATE">
    </uses-permission>
```

There's more...

In a production-level application, you wouldn't want to simply disable the button if you didn't have to. In this case, there are other means to use the camera flash as a flashlight. Take a look at the multi-media chapter for additional examples on using the camera, where we'll see `getCameraId()` used again.

See also

- Refer to the *Lights, Action, and Sound Redux with Notifications* recipe later in this chapter to see the equivalent features using the Notification object
- Refer to *Chapter 11, Multimedia,* for examples using the new camera API and other sound options

Creating a Toast using a custom layout

We've used Toasts quite a bit already in previous chapters as they provide a quick and easy way to display information—both for the user and for ourselves when debugging.

The previous examples have all used the simple one-line syntax, but the Toast isn't limited to this. Toasts, like most components in Android, can be customized, as we'll demonstrate in this recipe.

Chapter 7

Android Studio offers a shortcut for making the simple Toast statement. As you start to type the Toast command, press *Ctrl + Spacebar* and you'll see the following:

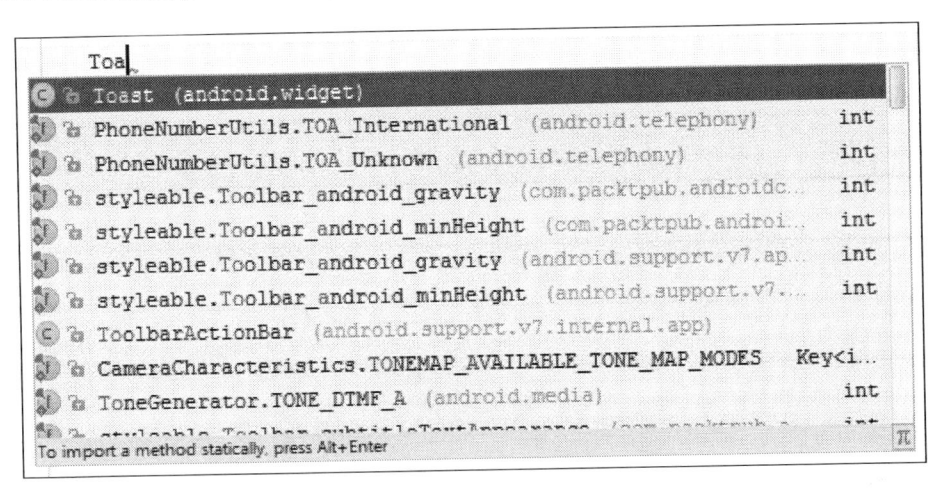

Press *Enter* to auto-complete. Then, press *Ctrl + Spacebar* again and you'll see the following:

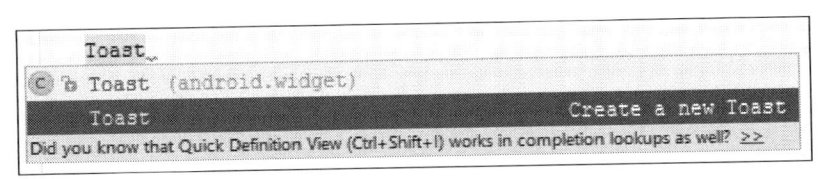

When you press *Enter* again, it will auto-complete with the following:

```
Toast.makeText(MainActivity.this, "", Toast.LENGTH_SHORT).show();
```

Alerts and Notifications

In this recipe, we'll use the Toast Builder to change the default layout, and gravity to create a custom Toast as shown in this screenshot:

Getting ready

Create a new project in Android Studio and call it: `CustomToast`. Use the default **Phone & Tablet** options and select **Empty Activity** when prompted for the **Activity Type**.

How to do it...

We're going to change the shape of the Toast to a square and create a custom layout to display an image and text message. Start by opening `activity_main.xml` and follow these steps:

1. Replace the existing `<TextView>` element with a `<Button>` as follows:
    ```
    <Button
        android:layout_width="wrap_content"
        android:layout_height="wrap_content"
        android:text="Show Toast"
    ```

```xml
        android:id="@+id/button"
        android:layout_alignParentTop="true"
        android:layout_centerHorizontal="true"
        android:onClick="showToast"/>
```

2. Create a new resource file in the `res/drawable` folder named: `border_square.xml` and type the following code:

```xml
<?xml version="1.0" encoding="utf-8"?>
<layer-list xmlns:android="http://schemas.android.com/apk/
    res/android">
    <item
        android:left="4px"
        android:top="4px"
        android:right="4px"
        android:bottom="4px">
        <shape android:shape="rectangle" >
            <solid android:color="@android:color/black" />
            <stroke android:width="5px" android:color=
                "@android:color/white"/>
        </shape>
    </item>
</layer-list>
```

3. Create a new resource file in the `res/layout` folder named: `toast_custom.xml` and type the following code:

```xml
<?xml version="1.0" encoding="utf-8"?>
<LinearLayout xmlns:android="http://schemas.android.com/apk/res/
android"
    android:id="@+id/toast_layout_root"
    android:layout_width="match_parent"
    android:layout_height="match_parent"
    android:orientation="horizontal"
    android:background="@drawable/border_square">
    <ImageView
        android:layout_width="wrap_content"
        android:layout_height="wrap_content"
        android:id="@+id/imageView"
        android:layout_weight="1"
        android:src="@mipmap/ic_launcher" />
    <TextView
        android:id="@android:id/message"
        android:layout_width="0dp"
        android:layout_height="match_parent"
        android:layout_weight="1"
```

Alerts and Notifications

```
            android:textColor="@android:color/white"
            android:padding="10dp" />
</LinearLayout>
```

4. Now open `ActivityMain.java` and type the following method:

```java
public void showToast(View view) {
    LayoutInflater inflater = (LayoutInflater)this
        .getSystemService(Context.LAYOUT_INFLATER_SERVICE);
    View layout = inflater.inflate(R.layout.toast_custom,
        null);
    ((TextView) layout.findViewById(android.R.id.message))
        .setText("Custom Toast");
    Toast toast = new Toast(this);
    toast.setGravity(Gravity.CENTER, 0, 0);
    toast.setDuration(Toast.LENGTH_LONG);
    toast.setView(layout);
    toast.show();
}
```

5. Run the program on a device or emulator.

How it works...

This custom Toast changes the default gravity, shape, and adds an image just to show that "it can be done".

The first step is to create a new Toast layout, which we do by inflating our `custom_toast` layout. Once we have the new layout, we need to get the `TextView` so we can set our message, which we do with the standard `setText()` method. With this done, we create a Toast object and set the individual properties. We set the Toast gravity with the `setGravity()` method. The gravity determines where on the screen our Toast will display. We specify our custom layout with the `setView()` method call. And just like in the single line variation, we display the Toast with the `show()` method.

Displaying a message box with AlertDialog

In *Chapter 4, Menus*, we created a theme to make an Activity look like a dialog. In this recipe, we'll demonstrate how to create a dialog using the `AlertDialog` class. The `AlertDialog` offers a Title, up to three buttons, and a list or custom layout area, as shown in this example:

Chapter 7

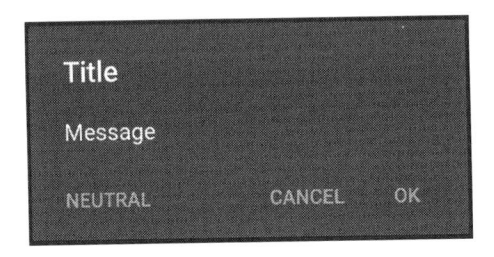

> The button placement can vary depending on the OS version.

Getting ready

Create a new project in Android Studio and call it: `AlertDialog`. Use the default **Phone & Tablet** options and select the **Empty Activity** option when prompted for the **Activity Type**.

How to do it...

To demonstrate, we'll create a **Confirm Delete** dialog to prompt the user for confirmation after pressing the *Delete* button. Start by opening the `main_activity.xml` layout file and follow these steps:

1. Add the following `<Button>`:

   ```xml
   <Button
       android:id="@+id/buttonClose"
       android:layout_width="wrap_content"
       android:layout_height="wrap_content"
       android:text="Delete"
       android:layout_centerVertical="true"
       android:layout_centerHorizontal="true"
       android:onClick="confirmDelete"/>
   ```

2. Add the `confirmDelete()` method called by the button:

   ```java
   public void confirmDelete(View view) {
       AlertDialog.Builder builder = new
           AlertDialog.Builder(this);
       builder.setTitle("Delete")
           .setMessage("Are you sure you?")
           .setPositiveButton(android.R.string.ok,
               new DialogInterface.OnClickListener() {
                   public void onClick(DialogInterface dialog,
                       int id) {
   ```

Alerts and Notifications

```
                Toast.makeText(MainActivity.this, "OK 
                    Pressed", Toast.LENGTH_SHORT).show();
        }})
        .setNegativeButton(android.R.string.cancel,
            new DialogInterface.OnClickListener() {
                public void onClick(DialogInterface dialog, 
                    int id) {
                Toast.makeText(MainActivity.this, "Cancel 
                    Pressed", Toast.LENGTH_SHORT).show();
        }});
    builder.create().show();
}
```

3. Run the application on a device or emulator.

How it works...

This dialog is meant to serve as a simple confirmation dialog—such as confirming a delete action. Basically, just create an `AlertDialog.Builder` object and set the properties as needed. We use a Toast message to indicate the user selection and we don't even have to close the dialog; it's taken care of by the base class.

There's more...

As shown in the recipe introduction screenshot, the `AlertDialog` also has a third button, called the Neutral button, and can be set using the following method:

```
builder.setNeutralButton()
```

Add an icon

To add an icon to the dialog, use the `setIcon()` method. Here is an example:

```
.setIcon(R.mipmap.ic_launcher)
```

Using a list

We can also create a list of items to select with various list-setting methods, including:

```
.setItems()
.setAdapter()
.setSingleChoiceItems()
.setMultiChoiceItems()
```

As you can see, there are also methods for single-choice (using a radio button) and multi-choice lists (using a checkbox).

> You can't use both the Message and the Lists, as `setMessage()` will take priority.

Custom Layout

Finally, we can also create a custom layout, and set it using:

```
.setView()
```

If you use a custom layout and replace the standard buttons, you are also responsible for closing the dialog. Use `hide()` if you plan to reuse the dialog and `dismiss()` when finished to release the resources.

Displaying a progress dialog

The `ProgressDialog` has been available since API 1, and is widely used. As we'll demonstrate in this recipe, it's simple to use, but keep this statement in mind (from the Android Dialog Guidelines site):

> *Avoid ProgressDialog*
>
> *Android includes another dialog class called ProgressDialog that shows a dialog with a progress bar. However, if you need to indicate loading or indeterminate progress, you should instead follow the design guidelines for Progress & Activity and use a ProgressBar in your layout.*

`http://developer.android.com/guide/topics/ui/dialogs.html`

This message doesn't mean the `ProgressDialog` is deprecated or is bad code. It's suggesting that the use of the `ProgressDialog` should be avoided, since the user cannot interact with your app while the dialog is displayed. If possible, use a layout that includes a progress bar, instead of using a `ProgressDialog`.

The Google Play app provides a good example. When adding items to download, Google Play shows a progress bar, but it's not a dialog, so the user can continue interacting with the app, even adding more items to download. If possible, use that approach instead.

Alerts and Notifications

There are times when you may not have that luxury, such as after placing an order, the user is going to expect an order confirmation. (Even with Google Play, you still see a confirmation dialog when actually purchasing apps.) So, remember, avoid the progress dialog if possible. But, for those times when something must complete before continuing, this recipe provides an example of how to use the `ProgressDialog`. The following screenshot shows the `ProgressDialog` from the recipe:

Getting ready

Create a new project in Android Studio and call it: `ProgressDialog`. Use the default **Phone & Tablet** options and select **Empty Activity** when prompted for the **Activity Type**.

Chapter 7

How to do it...

1. Since this is just a demonstration on using the ProgressDialog, we will create a button to show the dialog. To simulate waiting for a server response, we will use a delayed message to dismiss the dialog. To start, open `activity_main.xml` and follow these steps:

2. Replace the `<TextView>` with the following `<Button>`:

   ```
   <Button
       android:layout_width="wrap_content"
       android:layout_height="wrap_content"
       android:text="Show Dialog"
       android:id="@+id/button"
       android:layout_centerVertical="true"
       android:layout_centerHorizontal="true"
       android:onClick="startProgress"/>
   ```

3. Open `MainActivity.java` and add the following two global variables:

   ```
   private ProgressDialog mDialog;
   final int THIRTY_SECONDS=30*1000;
   ```

4. Add the `showDialog()` method referenced by the button click:

   ```
   public void startProgress(View view) {
       mDialog= new ProgressDialog(this);
       mDialog.setMessage("Doing something...");
       mDialog.setCancelable(false);
       mDialog.show();
       new Handler().postDelayed(new Runnable() {
           public void run() {
               mDialog.dismiss();
           }}, THIRTY_SECONDS);
   ```

5. Run the program on a device or emulator. When you press the **Show Dialog** button, you'll see the dialog as shown in the screen from the Intro.

How it works...

We use the `ProgressDialog` class to display our dialog. The options should be self-explanatory, but this setting is worth noting:

```
mDialog.setCancelable(false);
```

Alerts and Notifications

Normally, a dialog can be cancelled using the *back* key, but when this is set to false, the user is stuck on the dialog until it is hidden/dismissed from the code. To simulate a delayed response from a server, we use a `Handler` and the `postDelayed()` method. After the specified milliseconds (30,000 in this case, to represent 30 seconds), the `run()` method will be called, which dismisses our dialog.

There's more...

We used the default `ProgressDialog` settings for this recipe, which creates an indeterminate dialog indicator, for example, the continuously spinning circle. If you can measure the task at hand, such as loading files, you can use a determinate style instead. Add and run this line of code:

```
mDialog.setProgressStyle(ProgressDialog.STYLE_HORIZONTAL);
```

You will get the following dialog style as an output to the preceding line of code:

Lights, Action, and Sound Redux using Notifications

You're probably already familiar with Notifications as they've become a prominent feature (even making their way to the desktop environment) and for good reason. They provide an excellent means to send information to your user. They provide the least intrusive option of all the alerts and notification options available.

As we saw in the first recipe, *Lights, Action, and Sound – getting the user's attention!*, lights, vibration, and sound are all very useful for getting the user's attention. That's why the Notification object includes support for all three methods, as we'll demonstrate in this recipe. Given this ability to get your user's attention, care should still be taken not to abuse your user. Otherwise, they'll likely uninstall your app. It's generally a good idea to give your users the option to enable/disable notifications and even how to present the notification—with sound or without, and so on.

Getting ready

Create a new project in Android Studio and call it: `LightsActionSoundRedux`. Use the default **Phone & Tablet** options and select **Empty Activity** when prompted for the **Activity Type**.

─── Chapter 7

How to do it...

We'll need permission to use the vibrate option, so start by opening the Android Manifest file, and follow these steps:

1. Add the following permission:

    ```
    <uses-permission android:name=
        "android.permission.VIBRATE"/>
    ```

2. Open `activity_main.xml` and replace the existing `<TextView>` with the following buttons:

    ```
    <Button
        android:id="@+id/buttonSound"
        android:layout_width="wrap_content"
        android:layout_height="wrap_content"
        android:text="Lights, Action, and Sound"
        android:layout_centerVertical="true"
        android:layout_centerHorizontal="true"
        android:onClick="clickLightsActionSound"/>
    ```

3. Now open `MainActivity.java` and add the following methods to handle the button click:

    ```
    public void clickLightsActionSound(View view) {
        Uri notificationSoundUri =
            RingtoneManager.getDefaultUri(
                RingtoneManager.TYPE_NOTIFICATION);
        NotificationCompat.Builder notificationBuilder = new
            NotificationCompat.Builder(this)
            .setSmallIcon(R.mipmap.ic_launcher)
            .setContentTitle("LightsActionSoundRedux")
            .setContentText("Lights, Action & Sound")
            .setSound(notificationSoundUri)
            .setLights(Color.BLUE, 500, 500)
            .setVibrate(new long[]{250,500,250,500,250,500});
        NotificationManager notificationManager =
            (NotificationManager) this.getSystemService(
                Context.NOTIFICATION_SERVICE);
        notificationManager.notify(0,
            notificationBuilder.build());
    }
    ```

4. Run the program on a device or emulator.

177

Alerts and Notifications

How it works...

First, we combined all three actions into a single notification, simply because we could. You don't have to use all three extra notification options, or even any. Only the following are required:

```
.setSmallIcon()
.setContentText()
```

If you don't set both the icon and text, the notification will not show.

Second, we used the `NotificationCompat` to build our notification. This comes from the support library and makes it easier to be backward compatible with older OS versions. If we request a notification feature that is not available on the user's version of OS, it will simply be ignored.

The three lines of code that produce our extra notification options include the following:

```
.setSound(notificationSoundUri)
.setLights(Color.BLUE, 500, 500)
.setVibrate(new long[]{250,500,250,500,250,500});
```

It's worth noting that we use the same sound URI with the notification as we did with the `RingtoneManager` from the earlier *Lights, Action, and Sound* recipe. The vibrate feature also required the same vibrate permission as the previous recipe, but notice the value we send is different. Instead of sending just a duration for the vibration, we are sending a vibrate pattern. The first value represents the `off` duration (in milliseconds), the next value represents the vibration `on` duration, and repeats.

> On devices with LED notification, you won't see the LED notification while the screen is active.

There's more...

This recipe shows the basics of a notification, but like many features on Android, options have expanded with later OS releases.

Adding a button to the notification using addAction()

There are several design considerations you should keep in mind when adding action buttons, as listed in the Notification Guidelines linked in the chapter introduction. You can add a button (up to three) using the `addAction()` method on the notification builder. Here's an example of a notification with one action button:

Here's the code to create this notification:

```
NotificationCompat.Builder notificationBuilder = new
    NotificationCompat.Builder(this)
        .setSmallIcon(R.mipmap.ic_launcher)
        .setContentTitle("LightsActionSoundRedux")
        .setContentText("Lights, Action & Sound");
Intent activityIntent = new Intent(this,MainActivity.class);
PendingIntent pendingIntent = PendingIntent.getActivity(
    this,0,activityIntent,0);
notificationBuilder.addAction(
    android.R.drawable.ic_dialog_email, "Email",
        pendingIntent);
notificationManager.notify(0, notificationBuilder.build());
```

An `Action` requires three parameters—the image, the text, and a `PendingIntent`. The first two items are for the visual display, while the third item, the `PendingIntent`, is called when the user presses the button.

The previous code creates a very simple `PendingIntent`; it just launches the app. This is probably the most common intent for notifications, and is often used for when the user presses the notification. To set the notification intent, use the following code:

```
.setContentIntent(pendingIntent)
```

A button action would probably require more information as it should take the user to the specific item in your app. You should also create an application back-stack for the best user experience. Take a look at the topic "**Preserving Navigation when Starting an Activity**" at the following link:

http://developer.android.com/guide/topics/ui/notifiers/notifications.html#NotificationResponse

Alerts and Notifications

Expanded notifications

Expanded notifications were introduced in Android 4.1 (API 16) and are available by using the `setStyle()` method on the Notification Builder. If the user's OS does not support expanded notifications, the notification will appear as a normal notification.

The three expanded styles currently available in the `NotificationCompat` library include:

- InboxStyle
- BigPictureStyle
- BigTextStyle

Here's an example of each notification style, and the code used to create the example:

> InboxStyle - Big Content Title 7:51 PM
> Line 1
> Line 2

- InboxStyle:

```
NotificationCompat.Builder notificationBuilderInboxStyle =
    new NotificationCompat.Builder(this)
        .setSmallIcon(R.mipmap.ic_launcher);
NotificationCompat.InboxStyle inboxStyle = new
    NotificationCompat.InboxStyle();
inboxStyle.setBigContentTitle("InboxStyle - Big Content Title")
    .addLine("Line 1")
    .addLine("Line 2");
notificationBuilderInboxStyle.setStyle(inboxStyle);
notificationManager.notify(0,
    notificationBuilderInboxStyle.build());
```

> LightsActionSoundRedux 7:57 PM

- BigPictureStyle:

  ```
  NotificationCompat.Builder
      notificationBuilderBigPictureStyle = new
          NotificationCompat.Builder(this)
              .setSmallIcon(R.mipmap.ic_launcher)
              .setContentTitle("LightsActionSoundRedux")
              .setContentText("BigPictureStyle");
  NotificationCompat.BigPictureStyle bigPictureStyle = new
      NotificationCompat.BigPictureStyle();
  bigPictureStyle.bigPicture(BitmapFactory.decodeResource(
      getResources(), R.mipmap.ic_launcher));
  notificationBuilderBigPictureStyle.setStyle(
      bigPictureStyle);
  notificationManager.notify(0,
      notificationBuilderBigPictureStyle.build());
  ```

  > **LightsActionSoundRedux** 7:58 PM
  > This is an example of the BigTextStyle
  > expanded notification.

- BigTextStyle

  ```
  NotificationCompat.Builder notificationBuilderBigTextStyle
      = new NotificationCompat.Builder(this)
          .setSmallIcon(R.mipmap.ic_launcher)
          .setContentTitle("LightsActionSoundRedux");
  NotificationCompat.BigTextStyle BigTextStyle = new
      NotificationCompat.BigTextStyle();
  BigTextStyle.bigText("This is an example of the
      BigTextStyle expanded notification.");
  notificationBuilderBigTextStyle.setStyle(BigTextStyle);
  notificationManager.notify(0,
      notificationBuilderBigTextStyle.build());
  ```

Lock screen notifications

Android 5.0 (API 21) and above can show notifications on the lock screen, based on the user's lock screen visibility. Use `setVisibility()` to specify the notification visibility using the following values:

- `VISIBILITY_PUBLIC`: All content can be displayed
- `VISIBILITY_SECRET`: No content should be displayed
- `VISIBILITY_PRIVATE`: Display the basic content (title and icon) but the rest is hidden

Alerts and Notifications

See also

- See the *Creating a Media Player Notification* and *Making a Flashlight with a Heads-Up Notification* recipes for additional notification options with Android 5.0 (API 21) and greater

Creating a Media Player Notification

This recipe is going to take a look at the new Media Player style introduced in Android 5.0 (API 21). Unlike the previous recipe, *Lights, Action, and Sound Redux using Notifications*, which used `NotificationCompat`, this recipe does not, as this style is not available in the support library.

Here's a screenshot showing how the notification will appear:

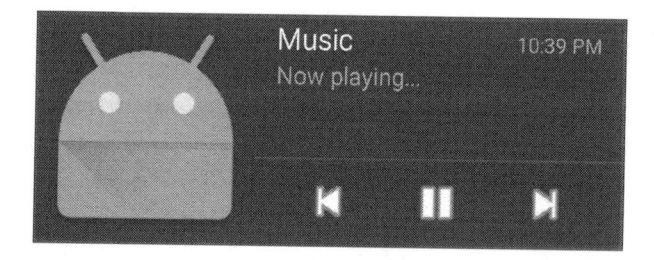

This screenshot shows an example of the Media Player Notification on a lock screen:

Getting ready

Create a new project in Android Studio and call it: `MediaPlayerNotification`. When prompted for the API level, we need API 21 (or higher) for this project. Select **Empty Activity** when prompted for the **Activity Type**.

How to do it...

We just need a single button to call our code to send the notification. Open `activity_main.xml` and follow these steps:

1. Replace the existing `<TextView>` with the following button code:

   ```
   <Button
       android:layout_width="wrap_content"
       android:layout_height="wrap_content"
       android:text="Show Notification"
       android:id="@+id/button"
       android:layout_centerVertical="true"
       android:layout_centerHorizontal="true"
       android:onClick="showNotification"/>
   ```

2. Open `MainActivity.java` and add the `showNotification()` method:

   ```
   @Deprecated
   public void showNotification(View view) {
       Intent activityIntent = new Intent(
           this,MainActivity.class);
       PendingIntent pendingIntent =
           PendingIntent.getActivity(this, 0, activityIntent,
               0);

       Notification notification;
       if (Build.VERSION.SDK_INT >= Build.VERSION_CODES.M) {
           notification = new Notification.Builder(this)
               .setVisibility(Notification.VISIBILITY_PUBLIC)
               .setSmallIcon(Icon.createWithResource(this,
                   R.mipmap.ic_launcher))
               .addAction(new Notification.Action.Builder(
                   Icon.createWithResource(this,
                       android.R.drawable.ic_media_previous),
                           "Previous", pendingIntent).build())
               .addAction(new Notification.Action.Builder(
                   Icon.createWithResource(this,
                       android.R.drawable.ic_media_pause),
                           "Pause", pendingIntent).build())
               .addAction(new Notification.Action.Builder(
                   Icon.createWithResource(this,
                       android.R.drawable.ic_media_next),
                           "Next", pendingIntent).build())
               .setContentTitle("Music")
               .setContentText("Now playing...")
   ```

Alerts and Notifications

```java
                    .setLargeIcon(Icon.createWithResource(this,
                        R.mipmap.ic_launcher))
                    .setStyle(new Notification.MediaStyle()
                        .setShowActionsInCompactView(1))
                        .build();
            } else {
                notification = new Notification.Builder(this)
                    .setVisibility(Notification.VISIBILITY_PUBLIC)
                    .setSmallIcon(R.mipmap.ic_launcher)
                    .addAction(new Notification.Action.Builder(
                        android.R.drawable.ic_media_previous,
                        "Previous", pendingIntent).build())
                    .addAction(new Notification.Action.Builder(
                        android.R.drawable.ic_media_pause, "Pause",
                        pendingIntent).build())
                    .addAction(new Notification.Action.Builder(
                        android.R.drawable.ic_media_next, "Next",
                        pendingIntent).build())
                    .setContentTitle("Music")
                    .setContentText("Now playing...")
                    .setLargeIcon(BitmapFactory.decodeResource(
                        getResources(), R.mipmap.ic_launcher))
                    .setStyle(new Notification.MediaStyle()
                    .setShowActionsInCompactView(1))
                    .build();
            }
            NotificationManager notificationManager =
                (NotificationManager) this.getSystemService(
                Context.NOTIFICATION_SERVICE);
            notificationManager.notify(0, notification);
        }
```

3. Run the program on a device or emulator.

How it works...

The first detail to note is that we decorate our `showNotification()` method with:

```
@Deprecated
```

This tells the compiler we know we are using deprecated calls. (Without this, the compiler will flag the code.) We follow this with an API check, using this call:

```
if (Build.VERSION.SDK_INT >= Build.VERSION_CODES.M)
```

Chapter 7

The icon resource was changed in API 23, but we want this application to run on API 21 (Android 5.0) and later, so we still need to call the old methods when running on API 21 and API 22.

If the user is running on Android 6.0 (or higher), we use the new `Icon` class to create our icons, otherwise we use the old constructor. (You'll notice the IDE will show the deprecated calls with a strikethrough.) Checking the current OS version during runtime is a common strategy for remaining backward compatible.

We create three actions using `addAction()` to handle the media player functionality. Since we don't really have a media player going, we use the same intent for all the actions, but you'll want to create separate intents in your application.

To make the notification visible on the lock screen, we need to set the visibility level to `VISIBILITY_PUBLIC`, which we do with the following call:

```
.setVisibility(Notification.VISIBILITY_PUBLIC)
```

This call is worth noting:

```
.setShowActionsInCompactView(1)
```

Just as the method name implies, this sets the actions to show when the notification is shown with a reduced layout. (See the lock screen image in the recipe introduction.)

There's more...

We only created the visual notification in this recipe. If we were creating an actual media player, we could instantiate a `MediaSession` class and pass in the session token with this call:

```
.setMediaSession(mMediaSession.getSessionToken())
```

This will allow the system to recognize the media content and react accordingly, such as updating the lock screen with the current album artwork.

See also

- Refer to **Developer doc – MediaSession** at https://developer.android.com/reference/android/media/session/MediaSession.html
- The *Lock Screen Visibility* section in the *Lights, Action, and Sound Redux using Notifications* recipe discusses the visibility options.

Alerts and Notifications

Making a Flashlight with a Heads-Up Notification

Android 5.0—Lollipop (API 21) introduced a new type of notification called the Heads-Up Notification. Many people do not care for this new notification as it can be extremely intrusive, as it forces its way on top of other apps. (See the following screenshot.) Keep this in mind when using this type of notification. We're going to demonstrate the Heads-Up Notification with a Flashlight as this demonstrates a good use-case scenario.

Here's a screenshot showing the Heads-Up Notification we'll create further on:

If you have a device running Android 6.0, you may have noticed the new Flashlight settings option. As a demonstration, we're going to create something similar in this recipe.

Getting ready

Create a new project in Android Studio and call it: `FlashlightWithHeadsUp`. When prompted for the API level, we need API 23 (or higher) for this project. Select **Empty Activity** when prompted for the **Activity Type**.

How to do it...

Our activity layout will consist of just a `ToggleButton` to control the flashlight mode. We'll be using the same `setTorchMode()` code as the *Lights, Action, and Sound – getting the user's attention!* recipe presented earlier, and add a Heads-Up Notification. We'll need permission to use the vibrate option, so start by opening the Android Manifest and following these steps:

1. Add the following permission:

    ```
    <uses-permission android:name=
        "android.permission.VIBRATE"/>
    ```

2. Specify that we only want a single instance of `MainActivity` by adding `android:launchMode="singleInstance"` to the `<MainActivity>` element. It will look as follows:

    ```
    <activity android:name=".MainActivity"
        android:launchMode="singleInstance">
    ```

3. With the changes to `AndroidManifest` done, open the `activity_main.xml` layout and replace the existing `<TextView>` element with this `<ToggleButton>` code:

```xml
<ToggleButton
    android:id="@+id/buttonLight"
    android:layout_width="wrap_content"
    android:layout_height="wrap_content"
    android:text="Flashlight"
    android:layout_centerVertical="true"
    android:layout_centerHorizontal="true"
    android:onClick="clickLight"/>
```

4. Now open `ActivityMain.java` and add the following global variables:

```java
private static final String ACTION_STOP="STOP";
private CameraManager mCameraManager;
private String mCameraId=null;
private ToggleButton mButtonLight;
```

5. Add the following code to the `onCreate()` to set up the camera:

```java
mButtonLight = (ToggleButton)findViewById(
    R.id.buttonLight);

mCameraManager = (CameraManager) this.getSystemService(
    Context.CAMERA_SERVICE);
mCameraId = getCameraId();
if (mCameraId==null) {
    mButtonLight.setEnabled(false);
} else {
    mButtonLight.setEnabled(true);
}
```

6. Add the following method to handle the response when the user presses the notification:

```java
@Override
protected void onNewIntent(Intent intent) {
    super.onNewIntent(intent);
    if (ACTION_STOP.equals(intent.getAction())) {
        setFlashlight(false);
    }
}
```

Alerts and Notifications

7. Add the method to get the camera id:

```
private String getCameraId() {
    try {
        String[] ids = mCameraManager.getCameraIdList();
        for (String id : ids) {
            CameraCharacteristics c =
                mCameraManager.getCameraCharacteristics(id);
            Boolean flashAvailable = c.get(
                CameraCharacteristics.FLASH_INFO_AVAILABLE);
            Integer facingDirection = c.get(
                CameraCharacteristics.LENS_FACING);
            if (flashAvailable != null && flashAvailable
                && facingDirection != null
                && facingDirection ==
                CameraCharacteristics
                .LENS_FACING_BACK) {
                return id;
            }
        }
    } catch (CameraAccessException e) {
        e.printStackTrace();
    }
    return null;
}
```

8. Add these two methods to handle the flashlight mode:

```
public void clickLight(View view) {
    setFlashlight(mButtonLight.isChecked());
    if (mButtonLight.isChecked()) {
        showNotification();
    }
}

private void setFlashlight(boolean enabled) {
    mButtonLight.setChecked(enabled);
    try {
        mCameraManager.setTorchMode(mCameraId, enabled);
    } catch (CameraAccessException e) {
        e.printStackTrace();
    }
}
```

9. Finally, add this method to create the notification:

```
private void showNotification() {
    Intent activityIntent = new Intent(
        this,MainActivity.class);
    activityIntent.setAction(ACTION_STOP);
    PendingIntent pendingIntent =
        PendingIntent.getActivity(this,0,activityIntent,0);
    final Builder notificationBuilder = new Builder(this)
        .setContentTitle("Flashlight")
        .setContentText("Press to turn off the
            flashlight")
        .setSmallIcon(R.mipmap.ic_launcher)
        .setLargeIcon(BitmapFactory.decodeResource(
            getResources(), R.mipmap.ic_launcher))
        .setContentIntent(pendingIntent)
        .setVibrate(new long[]{DEFAULT_VIBRATE})
        .setPriority(PRIORITY_MAX);
    NotificationManager notificationManager =
        (NotificationManager) this.getSystemService(
            Context.NOTIFICATION_SERVICE);
    notificationManager.notify(0,
        notificationBuilder.build());
}
```

10. You're ready to run the application on a physical device. As noted previously, you'll need an Android 6.0 (or higher) device, with an outward-facing camera flash.

How it works...

Since this recipe uses the same flashlight code as *Lights, Action, and Sound – getting the user's attention!*, we'll jump to the `showNotification()` method. Most of the notification builder calls are the same as previous examples, but there are two significant differences:

```
.setVibrate()
.setPriority(PRIORITY_MAX)
```

> Notifications will not be escalated to Heads-Up Notifications unless the priority is set to HIGH (or above) and uses either vibrate or sound.
>
> Note this from the Developer documentation given at: http://developer.android.com/reference/android/app/Notification.html#headsUpContentView:
>
> "At its discretion, the system UI may choose to show this as a heads-up notification."

Alerts and Notifications

We create a `PendingIntent` as we've done previously, but here we set the action with:

```
activityIntent.setAction(ACTION_STOP);
```

We set the app to only allow a single instance in the `AndroidManifest` file, as we don't want to start a new instance of the app when the user presses the notification. The `PendingIntent` we created sets the action, which we check in the `onNewIntent()` callback. If the user opens the app without pressing the notification, they can still disable the flashlight with the `ToggleButton`.

There's more...

Just like in the *Creating a Toast using a custom layout* recipe earlier, we can use a custom layout with notifications. Use the following method on the builder to specify the layout:

```
headsupContentView()
```

See also

- Refer to the *Lights, Action, and Sound – getting the user's attention!* recipe

8
Using the Touchscreen and Sensors

In this chapter, we will cover the following topics:

- Listening for click and long-press events
- Recognizing tap and other common gestures
- Pinch-to-zoom with multi-touch gestures
- Swipe-to-Refresh
- Listing available sensors – an introduction to the Android Sensor Framework
- Reading sensor data – using the Android Sensor Framework events
- Reading device orientation

Introduction

These days, mobile devices are packed with sensors, often including a gyroscope, magnetic, gravity, pressure, and/or temperature sensors, not to mention the touchscreen. This provides many new and exciting options to interact with your user. Through the sensors, you can determine three-dimensional device location and how the device itself is being used, such as shaking, rotation, tilt, and so on. Even the touchscreen offers many new input methods from just the simple click to gestures and multi-touch.

We'll start this chapter by exploring touchscreen interactions, starting with a simple click and long-press, then move on to detecting common gestures using the `SimpleOnGestureListener` class. Next we'll look at a multi-touch using the pinch-to-zoom gesture with `ScaleGestureDetector`.

Using the Touchscreen and Sensors

This book is meant to offer a quick guide to adding features and functionality to your own applications. As such, it focuses on the code needed. It's highly recommended that you spend some time reading the Design Guidelines as well.

> Google Gesture Design Guidelines at `https://www.google.com/design/spec/patterns/gestures.html`

In the later part of this chapter we'll look at the sensor abilities in Android, using the Android Sensor Framework. We'll demonstrate how to obtain a list of all the available sensors, plus how to check for a specific sensor. Once we obtain a sensor, we'll demonstrate setting up a listener to read the sensor data. Finally, we'll end the chapter with a demonstration on how to determine the device orientation.

Listening for click and long-press events

Almost every application needs to recognize and respond to basic events such as clicks and long-presses. It's so basic, in most of the recipes, we use the XML `onClick` attribute, but the more advanced listeners require setting up through code.

Android provides an Event Listener interface for receiving a single notification when certain actions occur, as shown in the following list:

- `onClick()`: It's called when a View is pressed
- `onLongClick()`: It's called when the View is long-pressed
- `onFocusChange()`: It's called when the user navigates to or from the View
- `onKey()`: It's called when a hardware key is pressed or released
- `onTouch()`: It's called when a touch event occurs

This recipe will demonstrate responding to the click event, as well as the long-press event.

Getting ready

Create a new project in Android Studio and call it: `PressEvents`. Use the default **Phone & Tablet** options and select **Empty Activity** when prompted for the **Activity Type**.

How to do it...

Setting up to receive basic View events is very simple. First we will create a View; we'll use a button for our example, then set the Event Listener in the Activity's `onCreate()` method. Here are the steps:

1. Open `activity_main.xml` and replace the existing `TextView` with the following `Button`:

   ```
   <Button
       android:id="@+id/button"
       android:layout_width="wrap_content"
       android:layout_height="wrap_content"
       android:text="Button"
       android:layout_centerVertical="true"
       android:layout_centerHorizontal="true" />
   ```

2. Now open `MainActivy.java` and add the following code to the existing `onCreate()` method:

   ```
   Button button = (Button)findViewById(R.id.button);
   button.setOnClickListener(new View.OnClickListener() {
       @Override
       public void onClick(View v) {
           Toast.makeText(MainActivity.this, "Click",
               Toast.LENGTH_SHORT).show();
       }
   });
   button.setOnLongClickListener(new
           View.OnLongClickListener() {
       @Override
       public boolean onLongClick(View v) {
           Toast.makeText(MainActivity.this, "Long Press",
               Toast.LENGTH_SHORT).show();
           return true;
       }
   });
   ```

3. Run the application on a device or emulator and try a regular click and long-press.

Using the Touchscreen and Sensors

How it works...

In most of the examples used in this book, we set up the `onClick` listener in XML using the following attribute:

```
android:onClick=""
```

You may notice the XML `onClick()` method callback requires the same method signature as the `setOnClickListener.onClick()` callback:

```
public void onClick(View v) {}
```

That's because Android automatically sets up the callback for us when we use the XML `onClick` attribute. This example also demonstrates that we can have multiple listeners on a single View.

The last point to note is that the `onLongClick()` method returns a Boolean, as do most of the other event listeners. Return `true` to indicate the event has been handled.

There's more...

Although a button is typically used to indicate where a user should "press", we could have used both the `setOnClickListener()` and `setOnLongClickListener()` with any View, even a `TextView`.

As mentioned in the introduction, there are other Event Listeners. You can use Android Studio's auto-complete feature. Start by typing the following command:

```
button.setOn
```

Then press *Ctrl + Spacebar* to see the list.

Recognizing tap and other common gestures

Unlike the Event Listeners described in the previous recipe, gestures require a two-step process:

- Gather the movement data
- Analyze the data to determine whether it matches a known gesture

Chapter 8

Step 1 begins when the user touches the screen, which fires the `onTouchEvent()` callback with the movement data sent in a `MotionEvent` object. Fortunately, Android makes Step 2, analyzing the data, easier with the `GestureDetector` class, which detects the following gestures:

- `onTouchEvent()`
- `onDown()`
- `onFling()`
- `onLongPress()`
- `onScroll()`
- `onShowPress()`
- `onDoubleTap()`
- `onDoubleTapEvent()`
- `onSingleTapConfirmed()`

This recipe will demonstrate using the `GestureDetector.SimpleOnGestureListener` to recognize the touch and double tap gestures.

Getting ready

Create a new project in Android Studio and call it: `CommonGestureDetector`. Use the default **Phone & Tablet** options and select **Empty Activity** when prompted for the **Activity Type**.

How to do it...

We will be using the activity itself for detecting gestures, so we don't need to add any Views to the layout. Open `MainActivity.java` and follow these steps:

1. Add the following global variable:

   ```
   private GestureDetectorCompat mGestureDetector;
   ```

2. Add the following `GestureListener` class within the `MainActivity` class:

   ```
   private class GestureListener extends
           GestureDetector.SimpleOnGestureListener {
       @Override
       public boolean onSingleTapConfirmed(MotionEvent e) {
           Toast.makeText(MainActivity.this,
               "onSingleTapConfirmed",
               Toast.LENGTH_SHORT).show();
           return super.onSingleTapConfirmed(e);
       }
       @Override
   ```

Using the Touchscreen and Sensors

```
        public boolean onDoubleTap(MotionEvent e) {
            Toast.makeText(MainActivity.this, "onDoubleTap",
                Toast.LENGTH_SHORT).show();
            return super.onDoubleTap(e);
        }
    }
```

3. Override the `onTouchEvent()` as follows:

   ```
   public boolean onTouchEvent(MotionEvent event) {
       mGestureDetector.onTouchEvent(event);
       return super.onTouchEvent(event);
   }
   ```

4. Last, add the following line of code to `onCreate()`:

   ```
   mGestureDetector = new GestureDetectorCompat(this, new
       GestureListener());
   ```

5. Run this application on a device or emulator.

How it works...

We're using `GestureDetectorCompat`, which is from the Support Library allowing gesture support on devices running Android 1.6 and later.

As mentioned in the recipe introduction, detecting gestures is a two-step process. To gather the movement, or gesture, data, we start tracking the movement with the touch event. Every time the `onTouchEvent()` is called, we send that data to the `GestureDetector`. The `GestureDetector` handles the second step, analyzing the data. Once a gesture has been detected, the appropriate callback is made. Our example handles both the single and double tap gestures.

There's more...

Your application can easily add support for the remaining gestures detected by the `GestureDetector` simply by overriding the appropriate callback.

See also

- See the next recipe, *Pinch-to-zoom with multi-touch gestures*, for multi-touch gestures

Pinch-to-zoom with multi-touch gestures

The previous recipe used the `SimpleOnGestureListener` to provide detection of simple, one-finger, gestures. In this recipe, we will demonstrate multi-touch with the common pinch-to-zoom gesture using the `SimpleOnScaleGestureListener` class.

The following screenshot shows the icon zoomed out using the application created in the following recipe:

The following screenshot shows the icon zoomed in:

Using the Touchscreen and Sensors

Getting ready

Create a new project in Android Studio and call it: `MultiTouchZoom`. Use the default **Phone & Tablet** options and select **Empty Activity** when prompted for the **Activity Type**.

How to do it...

To provide a visual indication of the pinch-to-zoom, we'll use an `ImageView` with the application icon. Open `activity_main.xml` and follow these steps:

1. Replace the existing `TextView` with the following `ImageView`:

    ```xml
    <ImageView
        android:id="@+id/imageView"
        android:layout_width="wrap_content"
        android:layout_height="wrap_content"
        android:src="@mipmap/ic_launcher"
        android:layout_centerVertical="true"
        android:layout_centerHorizontal="true" />
    ```

2. Now open `MainActivity.java` and add the following global variables to the class:

    ```java
    private ScaleGestureDetector mScaleGestureDetector;
    private float mScaleFactor = 1.0f;
    private ImageView mImageView;
    ```

3. Override `onTouchEvent()` as follows:

    ```java
    public boolean onTouchEvent(MotionEvent motionEvent) {
        mScaleGestureDetector.onTouchEvent(motionEvent);
        return true;
    }
    ```

4. Add the following `ScaleListener` class to the `MainActivity` class:

    ```java
    private class ScaleListener extends ScaleGestureDetector.SimpleOnScaleGestureListener {
        @Override
        public boolean onScale(ScaleGestureDetector
            scaleGestureDetector) {
            mScaleFactor *=
                scaleGestureDetector.getScaleFactor();
            mScaleFactor = Math.max(0.1f,
                Math.min(mScaleFactor, 10.0f));
            mImageView.setScaleX(mScaleFactor);
    ```

```
            mImageView.setScaleY(mScaleFactor);
            return true;
        }
    }
```

5. Add the following code to the existing `onCreate()` method:
   ```
   mImageView=(ImageView)findViewById(R.id.imageView);
   mScaleGestureDetector = new ScaleGestureDetector(this, new
       ScaleListener());
   ```

6. To experiment with the pinch-to-zoom functionality, run the application on a device with a touchscreen.

How it works...

The `ScaleGestureDetector` does all the work by analyzing the gesture data and reporting the final scale factor through the `onScale()` callback. We get the actual scale factor by calling `getScaleFactor()` on `ScaleGestureDetector`.

We use an `ImageView` with the application icon to provide a visual representation of the scaling by setting the `ImageView` scale using the scale factor returned from `ScaleGestureDetector`. To prevent the scaling from becoming too large or too small, we add the following check:

```
mScaleFactor = Math.max(0.1f, Math.min(mScaleFactor, 10.0f));
```

Swipe-to-Refresh

Pulling down a list to indicate a manual refresh is known as the Swipe-to-Refresh gesture. It's such a common feature that this functionality has been encapsulated in a single widget called `SwipeRefreshLayout`.

Using the Touchscreen and Sensors

This recipe will show how to use the widget to add Swipe-to-Refresh functionality with a `ListView`. The following screenshot shows the refresh in action:

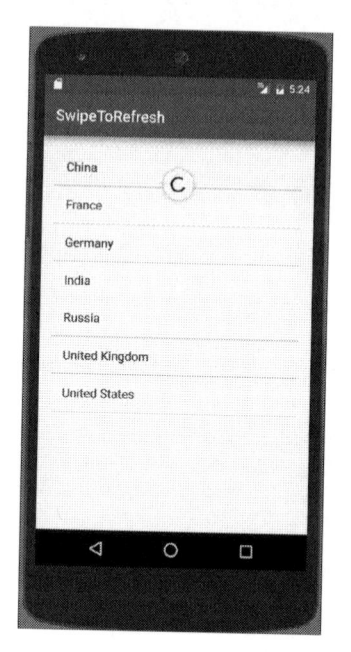

Getting ready

Create a new project in Android Studio and call it: `SwipeToRefresh`. Use the default **Phone & Tablet** options and select **Empty Activity** when prompted for the **Activity Type**.

How to do it...

First, we need to add the `SwipeRefreshLayout` widget and `ListView` to the activity layout, then we will implement the refresh listener in the java code. Here are the detailed steps:

1. Open `activity_main.xml` and replace the existing `<TextView>` with the following:

    ```
    <android.support.v4.widget.SwipeRefreshLayout
        xmlns:android="http://schemas.android.com/apk/
            res/android"
        android:id="@+id/swipeRefresh"
        android:layout_width="match_parent"
        android:layout_height="match_parent">
        <ListView
            android:id="@android:id/list"
    ```

```
            android:layout_width="match_parent"
            android:layout_height="match_parent" />
    </android.support.v4.widget.SwipeRefreshLayout>
```

2. Now open `MainActivity.java` and add the following global variables to the class:

   ```
   SwipeRefreshLayout mSwipeRefreshLayout;
   ListView mListView;
   List mArrayList = new ArrayList<>();
   private int mRefreshCount=0;
   ```

3. Add the following method to handle the refresh:

   ```
   private void refreshList() {
       mRefreshCount++;
       mArrayList.add("Refresh: " + mRefreshCount);
       ListAdapter countryAdapter = new ArrayAdapter<String>(
           this, android.R.layout.simple_list_item_1,
               mArrayList);
       mListView.setAdapter(countryAdapter);
       mSwipeRefreshLayout.setRefreshing(false);
   }
   ```

4. Add the following code to the existing `onCreate()` method:

   ```
   mSwipeRefreshLayout = (SwipeRefreshLayout)findViewById(
       R.id.swipeRefresh);
   mSwipeRefreshLayout.setOnRefreshListener(
       new SwipeRefreshLayout.OnRefreshListener() {
       @Override
       public void onRefresh() {
           refreshList();
       }
   });

   mListView = (ListView)findViewById(android.R.id.list);
   final String[] countries = new String[]{"China", "France",
       "Germany", "India", "Russia", "United Kingdom",
           "United States"};
   mArrayList = new ArrayList<String>(
       Arrays.asList(countries));
   ListAdapter countryAdapter = new ArrayAdapter<String>(
       this, android.R.layout.simple_list_item_1, mArrayList);
   mListView.setAdapter(countryAdapter);
   ```

5. Run the application on a device or emulator.

Using the Touchscreen and Sensors

How it works...

Most of the code for this recipe is to simulate a refresh by adding items to the `ListView` each time the refresh method is called. The main steps for implementing the Swipe-to-Refresh include:

1. Add the `SwipeRefreshLayout` widget.
2. Include the `ListView` within the `SwipeRefreshLayout`.
3. Add the `OnRefreshListener` to call your refresh method.
4. Call `setRefreshing(false)` after completing your update.

That's it. The widget makes adding Swipe-to-Refresh very easy!

There's more...

Although the Swipe-to-Refresh gesture is a common feature of applications these days, it's still good practice to include a menu item (especially for accessibility reasons). Here is a snippet of XML for the menu layout:

```xml
<menu xmlns:android="http://schemas.android.com/apk/res/android" >
    <item
        android:id="@+id/menu_refresh"
        android:showAsAction="never"
        android:title="@string/menu_refresh"/>
</menu>
```

Call your refresh method in the `onOptionsItemSelected()` callback. When performing a refresh from code, such as from the menu item event, you want to notify `SwipeRefreshLayout` of the refresh so it can update the UI. Do this with the following code:

```
SwipeRefreshLayout.setRefreshing(true);
```

This tells the `SwipeRefreshLayout` that a refresh is starting so it can display the in-progress indicator.

Listing available sensors – an introduction to the Android Sensor Framework

Android includes support for hardware sensors using the Android Sensor Framework. The framework includes the following classes and interfaces:

- SensorManager
- Sensor

- `SensorEventListener`
- `SensorEvent`

Most Android devices include hardware sensors, but they vary greatly between different manufacturers and models. If your application utilizes sensors, you have two choices:

- Specify the sensor in the Android Manifest
- Check for the sensor at runtime

To specify your application uses a sensor, include the `<uses-feature>` declaration in the Android Manifest. Here is an example requiring a compass to be available:

```
<uses-feature android:name="android.hardware.sensor.compass"
    android:required="true"/>
```

If your application utilizes the compass, but does not require it to function, you should set `android:required="false"` instead, otherwise the application will not be available through Google Play.

Sensors are grouped into the following three categories:

- Motion sensors
- Environmental sensors
- Position sensors

The Android SDK provides support for the following sensor types:

Sensor	Detects	Use
TYPE_ACCELEROMETER	Motion detection including gravity	Used to determine shake, tilt, and so on
TYPE_AMBIENT_TEMPERATURE	Measures ambient room temperature	Used for determining local temperature
TYPE_GRAVITY	Measures the force of gravity on all three axes	Used for motion detection
TYPE_GYROSCOPE	Measures rotation on all three axes	Used to determine turn, spin, and so on
TYPE_LIGHT	Measures light level	Used for setting screen brightness
TYPE_LINEAR_ACCELERATION	Motion detection excluding gravity	Used to determine acceleration
TYPE_MAGNETIC_FIELD	Measures geomagnetic field	Used to create a compass or determine bearing
TYPE_PRESSURE	Measures air pressure	Used for barometer

Using the Touchscreen and Sensors

Sensor	Detects	Use
TYPE_PROXIMITY	Measures object relative to the screen	Used to determine whether the device is being held against the ear during a phone call
TYPE_RELATIVE_HUMIDITY	Measures relative humidity	Used to determine dew point and humidity
TYPE_ROTATION_VECTOR	Measures device orientation	Used to detect motion and rotation

There are two additional sensors: TYPE_ORIENTATION and TYPE_TEMPERATURE, that have been deprecated as they have been replaced by newer sensors.

This recipe will demonstrate retrieving a list of available sensors. Here is a screenshot from a physical device:

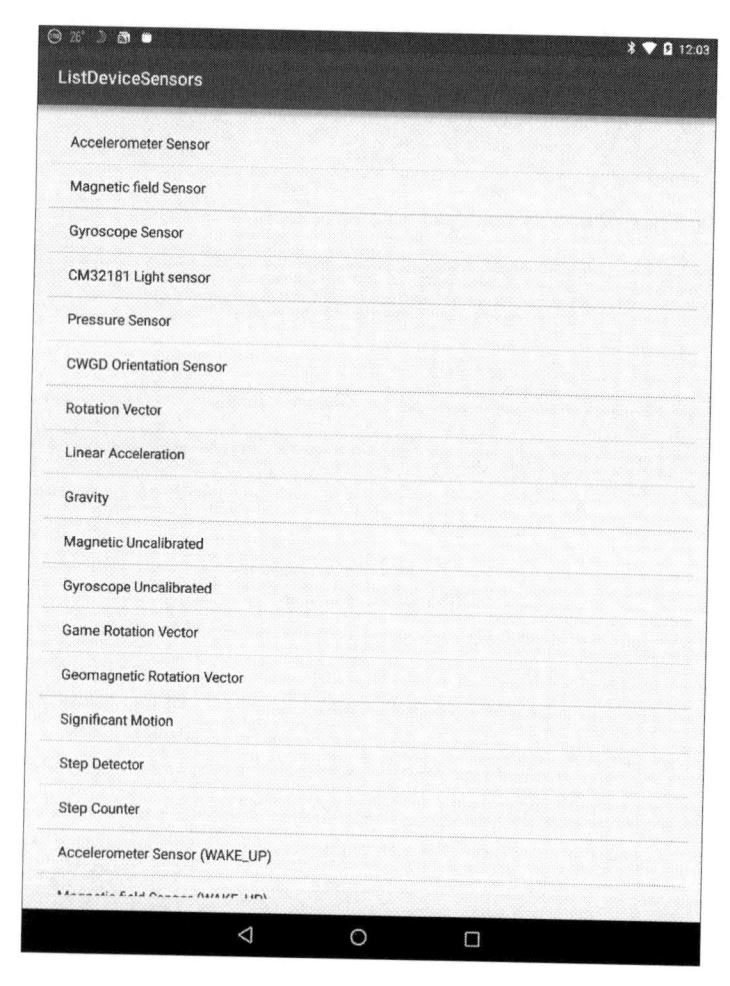

Getting ready

Create a new project in Android Studio and call it: `ListDeviceSensors`. Use the default **Phone & Tablet** options and select **Empty Activity** when prompted for the **Activity Type**.

How to do it...

First, we'll query the list of sensors available, then display the results in a `ListView`. Here are the detailed steps:

1. Open `activity_main.xml` and replace the existing `TextView` with the following:

   ```xml
   <ListView
       android:id="@+id/list"
       android:layout_width="match_parent"
       android:layout_height="match_parent" />
   ```

2. Next, open `ActivityMain.java` and add the following code to the existing `onCreate()` method:

   ```java
   ListView listView = (ListView)findViewById(R.id.list);
   List sensorList = new ArrayList<String>();

   List<Sensor> sensors = ((SensorManager) getSystemService(
           Context.SENSOR_SERVICE)).getSensorList(Sensor.TYPE_ALL);
   for (Sensor sensor : sensors ) {
       sensorList.add(sensor.getName());
   }
   ListAdapter sensorAdapter = new ArrayAdapter<String>(this,
           android.R.layout.simple_list_item_1, sensorList);
   listView.setAdapter(sensorAdapter);
   ```

3. Run the program on a device or emulator.

How it works...

The following line of code is responsible for getting the list of available sensors; the rest of the code is to populate the `ListView`:

```java
List<Sensor> sensors = ((SensorManager) getSystemService(
        Context.SENSOR_SERVICE)).getSensorList(Sensor.TYPE_ALL);
```

Notice that we get back a list of `Sensor` objects. We only get the sensor name to display in the `ListView`, but there are other properties available as well. See the link provided in the *See also* section for a complete list.

Using the Touchscreen and Sensors

There's more...

As shown in the introduction screenshot from a Nexus 9, a device can have multiple sensors of the same type. If you are looking for a specific sensor, you can pass in one of the constants from the table shown in the introduction. In this case, if you wanted to see all the Accelerometer sensors available, you could use this call:

```
List<Sensor> sensors = sensorManager.getSensorList(Sensor.TYPE_ACCELEROMETER);
```

If you're not looking for a list of sensors, but need to work with a specific sensor, you can check for a default sensor using this code:

```
if (sensorManager.getDefaultSensor(Sensor.TYPE_ACCELEROMETER) != null){
    //Sensor is available - do something here
}
```

See also

- **Android Developer Sensor** website at http://developer.android.com/reference/android/hardware/Sensor.html

Reading sensor data – using the Android Sensor Framework events

The previous recipe, *Listing available sensors – an introduction to the Android Sensor Framework*, provided an introduction to the Android Sensor Framework. Now we'll look at reading the sensor data using the `SensorEventListener`. The `SensorEventListener` interface only has two callbacks:

- onSensorChanged()
- onAccuracyChanged()

When the sensor has new data to report, it calls the `onSensorChanged()` with a `SensorEvent` object. This recipe will demonstrate reading the Light sensor, but since all the sensors use the same framework, it's very easy to adapt this example to any of the other sensors. (See the list of sensor types available in the previous recipe's introduction.)

Getting ready

Create a new project in Android Studio and call it: `ReadingSensorData`. Use the default **Phone & Tablet** options and select **Empty Activity** when prompted for the **Activity Type**.

How to do it...

We'll add a `TextView` to the activity layout to display the sensor data, then we'll add the `SensorEventListener` to the java code. We'll use the `onResume()` and `onPause()` events to start and stop our Event Listener. To get started, open `activity_main.xml` and follow these steps:

1. Modify the existing `TextView` as follows:

    ```xml
    <TextView
        android:id="@+id/textView"
        android:layout_width="wrap_content"
        android:layout_height="wrap_content"
        android:layout_centerHorizontal="true"
        android:layout_centerVertical="true"
        android:text="0"/>
    ```

2. Now open `MainActivity.java` and add the following global variable declarations:

    ```java
    private SensorManager mSensorManager;
    private Sensor mSensor;
    private TextView mTextView;
    ```

3. Add the `SensorListener` class to the `MainActivity` class as follows:

    ```java
    private SensorEventListener mSensorListener = new
    SensorEventListener() {
        @Override
        public void onSensorChanged(SensorEvent event) {
            mTextView.setText(String.valueOf(event.values[0]));
        }
        @Override
        public void onAccuracyChanged(Sensor sensor, int
            accuracy) {
            //Nothing to do
        }
    };
    ```

4. We'll register and unregister the sensor events in the `onResume()` and `onPause()` as follows:

    ```java
    @Override
    protected void onResume() {
        super.onResume();
        mSensorManager.registerListener(mSensorListener, mSensor,
        SensorManager.SENSOR_DELAY_NORMAL);
    }
    ```

Using the Touchscreen and Sensors

```
@Override
protected void onPause() {
    super.onPause();
    mSensorManager.unregisterListener(mSensorListener);
}
```

5. Add the following code to the `onCreate()`:

    ```
    mTextView = (TextView)findViewById(R.id.textView);
    mSensorManager = (SensorManager)
        getSystemService(Context.SENSOR_SERVICE);
    mSensor = mSensorManager.getDefaultSensor(
        Sensor.TYPE_LIGHT);
    ```

6. You can now run the application on a physical device to see the raw data from the light sensor.

How it works...

Using the Android Sensor Framework starts with obtaining the Sensor, which we do in `onCreate()`. Here, we call `getDefaultSensor()`, requesting `TYPE_LIGHT`. We register the listener in `onResume()` and unregister again in `onPause()` to reduce battery consumption. We pass in our `mSensorListener` object when we call `registerListener()`.

In our case, we are only looking for the sensor data, which is sent in the `onSensorChanged()` callback. When the sensor changes, we update the `TextView` with the sensor data.

There's more...

Now that you've worked with one sensor, you know how to work with all the sensors, as they all use the same framework. Of course, what you do with the data will vary greatly, depending on the type of data you're reading. The Environment sensors, as shown here, return a single value, but the Position and Motion sensors can also return additional elements, indicated as follows.

Environment sensors

Android supports the following four environment sensors:

- Humidity
- Light
- Pressure
- Temperature

Chapter 8

The environment sensors are generally easier to work with since the data returned is in a single element and doesn't usually require calibration or filtering. We used the Light sensor for this demonstration since most devices include a light sensor to control the screen brightness.

Position sensors

The Position sensors include:

- Geomagnetic Field
- Proximity

The following sensor types use the Geomagnetic field:

- `TYPE_GAME_ROTATION_VECTOR`
- `TYPE_GEOMAGNETIC_ROTATION_VECTOR`
- `TYPE_MAGNETIC_FIELD`
- `TYPE_MAGNETIC_FIELD_UNCALIBRATED`

These sensors return three values in the `onSensorChanged()` event, except for the `TYPE_MAGNETIC_FIELD_UNCALIBRATED`, which sends six values.

A third sensor, the Orientation sensor, has been deprecated, and it is now recommended to use `getRotation()` and `getRotationMatrix()` to calculate the orientation changes. (For device orientation, such as Portrait and Landscape modes, see the next recipe: *Reading device orientation*.)

Motion sensors

The Motion sensors include the following:

- Accelerometer
- Gyroscope
- Gravity
- Linear acceleration
- Rotation vector

These include the following sensor types:

- `TYPE_ACCELEROMETE`
- `TYPE_GRAVITY`
- `TYPE_GYROSCOPE`
- `TYPE_GYROSCOPE_UNCALIBRATED`
- `TYPE_LINEAR_ACCELERATION`

Using the Touchscreen and Sensors

- `TYPE_ROTATION_VECTOR`
- `TYPE_SIGNIFICANT_MOTION`
- `TYPE_STEP_COUNTER`
- `TYPE_STEP_DETECTOR`

These sensors also include three data elements, with the exception of the last three. The `TYPE_SIGNIFICANT_MOTION` and `TYPE_STEP_DETECTOR` indicate an event, while the `TYPE_STEP_COUNTER` returns the number of steps since last boot (while the sensor was active).

See also

- The *Listing available sensors – an introduction to the Android Sensor Framework* recipe
- The *Creating a Compass using sensor data and RotateAnimation* recipe in *Chapter 9, Graphics and Animation*
- For device orientation, see the *Reading device orientation* recipe
- *Chapter 13, Getting Location and Using Geofencing*, covers the *GPS and Location* recipe

Reading device orientation

Although the Android framework will automatically load a new resource (such as the layout) upon orientation changes, there are times when you may wish to disable this behavior. If you wish to be notified of the orientation change instead of Android handling it automatically, add the following attribute to the Activity in the Android Manifest:

```
android:configChanges="keyboardHidden|orientation|screenSize"
```

When any of the following configuration changes occur, the system will notify you through the `onConfigurationChanged()` method instead of handling it automatically:

- `keyboardHidden`
- `orientation`
- `screenSize`

The `onConfigurationChanged()` signature is as follows:

```
onConfigurationChanged (Configuration newConfig)
```

Chapter 8

You'll find the new orientation in `newConfig.orientation`.

> Disabling the automatic configuration change (which causes the layout to be reloaded and state information to be reset) should not be used as a replacement for properly saving state information. Your application can still be interrupted or stopped altogether at any time and killed by the system. (See *Saving an activity's state* in *Chapter 1, Activities*, for properly saving a state.)

This recipe will demonstrate how to determine the current device orientation.

Getting ready

Create a new project in Android Studio and call it: `GetDeviceOrientation`. Use the default **Phone & Tablet** options and select **Empty Activity** when prompted for the **Activity Type**.

How to do it...

We'll add a button to the layout to check the orientation on demand. Start by opening `activity_main.xml` and follow these steps:

1. Replace the existing `TextView` with the following `Button`:

    ```
    <Button
        android:layout_width="wrap_content"
        android:layout_height="wrap_content"
        android:text="Check Orientation"
        android:id="@+id/button"
        android:layout_centerVertical="true"
        android:layout_centerHorizontal="true"
        android:onClick="checkOrientation"/>
    ```

2. Add the following method to handle the button click:

    ```
    public void checkOrientation(View view) {
        int orientation = getResources()
            .getConfiguration().orientation;
        switch (orientation) {
            case Configuration.ORIENTATION_LANDSCAPE:
                Toast.makeText(MainActivity.this,
                    "ORIENTATION_LANDSCAPE",
                    Toast.LENGTH_SHORT).show();
                break;
            case Configuration.ORIENTATION_PORTRAIT:
                Toast.makeText(MainActivity.this,
                    "ORIENTATION_PORTRAIT",
                    Toast.LENGTH_SHORT).show();
    ```

Using the Touchscreen and Sensors

```
                break;
            case Configuration.ORIENTATION_UNDEFINED:
                Toast.makeText(MainActivity.this,
                    "ORIENTATION_UNDEFINED",
                    Toast.LENGTH_SHORT).show();
                break;
        }
    }
```

3. Run the application on a device or emulator.

> Use *Ctrl* + *F11* to rotate the emulator.

How it works...

All we need to do to get the current orientation is call this line of code:

```
getResources().getConfiguration().orientation
```

The orientation is returned as an `int`, which we compare to one of three possible values, as demonstrated.

There's more...

Getting current device rotation

Another scenario where you may need to know the current orientation is when working with camera data—pictures and/or videos. Often, the image may be rotated according to the device orientation or to compensate for the current orientation. In this scenario, there's another option available to get the rotation:

```
int rotation =
    getWindowManager().getDefaultDisplay().getRotation();
```

In the preceding line of code, `rotation` will be one of the following values:

- `Surface.ROTATION_0`
- `Surface.ROTATION_90`
- `Surface.ROTATION_180`
- `Surface.ROTATION_270`

> The rotation value will be from its normal orientation. For example, when using a table with a normal orientation of landscape, if a picture is taken in portrait orientation, the value will be ROTATION_90 or ROTATION_270.

See also

- The *Saving an activity's state* recipe in *Chapter 1, Activities*
- Refer to **Configuration Developer Link** at `http://developer.android.com/reference/android/content/res/Configuration.html`
- Refer to **Display Developer Link** at `http://developer.android.com/reference/android/view/Display.html#getRotation()`

9
Graphics and Animation

In this chapter, we will cover the following topics:

- Scaling down large images to avoid Out of Memory exceptions
- A transition animation – defining scenes and applying a transition
- Creating a Compass using sensor data and RotateAnimation
- Creating a slideshow with ViewPager
- Creating a Card Flip Animation with Fragments
- Creating a Zoom Animation with a Custom Transition

Introduction

Animations can be both visually appealing and functional, as demonstrated with the simple button press. The graphical representation of the button press brings the app alive, plus it provides a functional value by giving the user a visual response to the event.

The Android Framework provides several animation systems to make it easier to include animations in your own application. They include the following:

- **View Animation**: (The original animation system.) It usually requires less code but has limited animation options
- **Property Animation**: It's a more flexible system allowing animation of any property of any object
- **Drawable Animation**: It uses drawable resources to create frame-by-frame animations (like a movie)

Graphics and Animation

The Property Animation system was introduced in Android 3.0, and it is usually preferred over View Animation because of the flexibility. The main drawbacks to View Animation include:

- Limited aspects of what can be animated—such as scale and rotation
- Can only animate the contents of the view—it cannot change where on the screen the view is drawn (so it cannot animate moving a ball across the screen)
- Can only animate View objects

Here is a simple example demonstrating a View Animation to "blink" a view (a simple simulation of a button press):

```
Animation blink =AnimationUtils.loadAnimation(this,R.anim.blink);
view.startAnimation(blink);
```

Here are the contents for the `blink.xml` resource file, located in the `res/anim` folder:

```xml
<?xml version="1.0" encoding="utf-8"?>
<set xmlns:android="http://schemas.android.com/apk/res/android">
    <alpha android:fromAlpha="1.0"
        android:toAlpha="0.0"
        android:background="#000000"
        android:interpolator="@android:anim/linear_interpolator"
        android:duration="100"
        android:repeatMode="restart"
        android:repeatCount="0"/>
</set>
```

As you can see, it's very simple to create this animation, so if the View Animation accomplishes your goal, use it. When it doesn't meet your needs, turn to the Property Animation system. We'll demonstrate Property Animation using the new `objectAnimator` in the *Creating a Card Flip Animation with Fragments* and *Creating a Zoom Animation with a Custom Transition* recipes.

The *A transition animation – defining scenes and applying a transition* recipe will provide additional information on the Android Transition Framework, which we will use in many of the recipes.

> Interpolator is a function that defines the rate of change for an animation.

`Interpolators` will be mentioned in several recipes in this chapter and in the previous blink example. The Interpolator defines how the transition is calculated. A Linear Interpolator will calculate the change evenly over the set duration, whereas an `AccelerateInterpolator` function would create a faster movement through the duration. Here is the full list of Interpolators available, along with the XML Identifier:

- `AccelerateDecelerateInterpolator (`
    `@android:anim/accelerate_decelerate_interpolator)`
- `AccelerateInterpolator (`
    `@android:anim/accelerate_interpolator)`
- `AnticipateInterpolator (`
    `@android:anim/anticipate_interpolator)`
- `AnticipateOvershootInterpolator (`
    `@android:anim/anticipate_overshoot_interpolator)`
- `BounceInterpolator (@android:anim/bounce_interpolator)`
- `CycleInterpolator (@android:anim/cycle_interpolator)`
- `DecelerateInterpolator (@android:anim/decelerate_interpolator)`
- `LinearInterpolator (@android:anim/linear_interpolator)`
- `OvershootInterpolator (`
    `@android:anim/overshoot_interpolator)`

Although animations don't generally require much memory, the graphic resources often do. Many of the images you may want to work with often exceed the available device memory. In the first recipe of this chapter, *Scaling down large images to avoid Out of Memory exceptions*, we'll discuss how to subsample (or scale down) images.

Scaling down large images to avoid Out of Memory exceptions

Working with images can be very memory intensive, often resulting in your application crashing with an *Out of Memory* exception. This is especially true with pictures taken with the device camera, as they often have a much higher resolution than the device itself.

Since loading a higher resolution image than the UI supports doesn't provide any visual benefit in this example, this recipe will demonstrate how to take smaller samples of the image for display. We'll use the `BitmapFactory` to first check the image size then load a scaled-down image.

Graphics and Animation

Here's a screenshot from this recipe showing a thumbnail of a very large image:

Getting ready

Create a new project in Android Studio and call it: `LoadLargeImage`. Use the default **Phone & Tablet** options and select **Empty Activity** when prompted for the **Activity Type**.

We'll need a large image for this recipe; so we turned to `www.Pixabay.com` for an image. Since the image itself doesn't matter, we downloaded the first image shown at the time. (The full size image is 6000 x 4000 and 3.4MB.)

How to do it...

As stated previously in *Getting ready*, we need a large image to demonstrate the scaling. Once you have the image, follow these steps:

1. Copy the image to `res/drawable` as `image_large.jpg` (use the appropriate extension if you choose a different file type).

2. Open `activity_main.xml` and replace the existing `TextView` with the following `ImageView`:

   ```xml
   <ImageView
           android:id="@+id/imageViewThumbnail"
           android:layout_width="100dp"
           android:layout_height="100dp"
           android:layout_centerInParent="true" />
   ```

3. Now open `MainActivity.java` and add this method, which we'll explain shortly:

   ```java
   public Bitmap loadSampledResource(int imageID, int
           targetHeight, int targetWidth) {
       final BitmapFactory.Options options = new
           BitmapFactory.Options();
       options.inJustDecodeBounds = true;
       BitmapFactory.decodeResource(getResources(), imageID,
           options);
       final int originalHeight = options.outHeight;
       final int originalWidth = options.outWidth;
       int inSampleSize = 1;
       while ((originalHeight / (inSampleSize *2)) >
           targetHeight && (originalWidth / (inSampleSize *2))
           > targetWidth) {
           inSampleSize *= 2;
       }
       options.inSampleSize = inSampleSize;
       options.inJustDecodeBounds = false;
       return BitmapFactory.decodeResource(getResources(),
           imageID, options);
   }
   ```

4. Add the following code to the existing `onCreate()` method:

   ```java
   ImageView imageView = (ImageView)findViewById(
       R.id.imageViewThumbnail);
   imageView.setImageBitmap(loadSampledResource(
       R.drawable.image_large, 100, 100));
   ```

5. Run the application on a device or emulator.

Graphics and Animation

How it works...

The purpose of the `loadSampledResource()` method is to load a smaller image, to reduce the memory consumption of the image. If we attempted to load the full image chosen from www.Pixabay.Com (see the previous *Getting ready* section), the app would require over 3 MB of RAM to load. That's more memory than most devices can handle (at the moment anyway), and even if it could be loaded completely, would provide no visual benefit for our thumbnail view.

To avoid an `Out of Memory` situation, we use the `inSampleSize` property of the `BitmapFactory.Options` to reduce, or subsample, the image. (If we set the `inSampleSize=2`, it will reduce the image by half. If we use `inSampleSize=4`, it will reduce the image by one-fourth) To calculate the `inSampleSize`, first we need to know the image size. We can use the `inJustDecodeBounds` property as follows:

```
options.inJustDecodeBounds = true;
```

This tells the `BitmapFactory` to get the image dimensions without actually storing the image contents. Once we have the image size, we calculate the sample using this code:

```
while ((originalHeight / (inSampleSize *2)) > targetHeight &&
    (originalWidth / (inSampleSize *2)) > targetWidth) {
        inSampleSize *= 2;
}
```

The purpose of this code is to determine the largest sample size that does not reduce the image below the target dimensions. To do that, we double the sample size and check whether the size exceeds the target size dimensions. If it doesn't, we save the doubled sample size and repeat. Once the reduced size falls below the target dimensions, we use the last saved `inSampleSize`.

> From the `inSampleSize` documentation (link in the following *See also* section), note that the decoder uses a final value based on powers of 2, any other value will be rounded down to the nearest power of 2.

Once we have the sample size, we set the `inSampleSize` property and set `inJustDecodeBounds` to `false`, to load normally. Here is the code:

```
options.inSampleSize = inSampleSize;
options.inJustDecodeBounds = false;
```

It's important to note, this recipe illustrates the concept for applying the task in your own application. Loading and processing images can be a long operation, which could cause your application to stop responding. This is not a good thing and could cause Android to show the **Application Not Responding** (**ANR**) dialog. It is recommended to perform long tasks on a background thread to keep your UI thread responsive. The `AsyncTask` class is available for doing background network processing, but there are many other libraries available as well (links at the end of the recipe):

- **Volley**: Perform fast, scalable UI operations over the network (see *Chapter 12, Telephony, Networks, and the Web*)
- **Picasso**: A powerful image-downloading and caching library for Android
- **Android Universal Image Loader**: Powerful and flexible library for loading, caching, and displaying images

There's more...

It's important to note that the `targetHeight` and `targetWidth` parameters we pass to the `loadSampledResource()` method do not actually set the image size. If you run the application using the same size image we used, the sample size will be 32, resulting in a loaded image size of 187 x 125.

If your layout needs a specific size of image, either set the size in the layout file, or you can modify the image size directly using the Bitmap class.

See also

- **Developer Docs: BitmapFactory.inSampleSize()** at `https://developer.android.com/reference/android/graphics/BitmapFactory.Options.html#inSampleSize`
- Refer to the **Android Universal Image Loader** page at `https://github.com/nostra13/Android-Universal-Image-Loader`
- Refer to **Picasso** at `https://square.github.io/picasso/`
- Check the *AsyncTask* task in *Chapter 14, Getting Your App Ready for the Play Store*, for processing long-running operations on a background thread.

Graphics and Animation

A transition animation – defining scenes and applying a transition

The Android Transition Framework offers the following:

- **Group-level animations**: Animation applies to all views in a hierarchy
- **Transition-based animation**: Animation based on starting and ending property change
- **Built-in animations**: Some common transition effects, such as fade-in/out and movement
- **Resource file support**: Save animation values to a resource (XML) file to load during runtime
- **Lifecycle callbacks**: Receive callback notifications during the animation

A transition animation consists of the following:

- **Starting Scene**: The view (or `ViewGroup`) at the start of the animation
- **Transition**: The change type (see later on)
- **Ending Scene**: The ending view (or `ViewGroup`)
- **Transitions**: Android provides built-in support for the following three transitions:
    - **AutoTransition (default transition)**: Fade out, move, and resize, then fade in (in that order)
    - **Fade**: Fade in, fade out (default), or both (specify order)
    - **ChangeBounds**: Move and resize

The Transition Framework will automatically create the frames needed to animate from the start to end scenes.

The following are some known limitations of the Transition Framework when working with the following classes:

- **SurfaceView**: Animations may not appear correct since `SurfaceView` animations are performed on a non-UI thread, so they may be out of sync with the application
- **TextView**: Animating text size changes may not work correctly resulting in the text jumping to the final state
- **AdapterView**: Classes that extend the `AdapterView`, such as the `ListView` and `GridView`, may hang
- **TextureView**: Some transitions may not work

― Chapter 9

This recipe provides a quick tutorial on using the transition animation system. We'll start by defining the scenes and transition resources, then applying the transition, which creates the animation. The following steps will walk you through creating the resources in XML, as they are generally recommended. Resources can also be created through code, which we'll discuss in the *There's more* section.

Getting ready

Create a new project in Android Studio and call it: `TransitionAnimation`. On the **Target Android Devices** dialog, select the **Phone & Tablet** option and choose API 19 (or above) for the **Minimum SDK**. Select **Empty Activity** when prompted for the **Activity Type**.

How to do it...

Here are the steps to create the resource files and apply the transition animation:

1. Change the existing `activity.main.xml` layout file as follows:

   ```
   <?xml version="1.0" encoding="utf-8"?>
   <RelativeLayout xmlns:android="http://schemas.android.com/apk/res/android"
       xmlns:tools="http://schemas.android.com/tools"
       android:id="@+id/layout"
       android:layout_width="match_parent"
       android:layout_height="match_parent">
       <TextView
           android:layout_width="wrap_content"
           android:layout_height="wrap_content"
           android:text="Top"
           android:id="@+id/textViewTop"
           android:layout_alignParentTop="true"
           android:layout_centerHorizontal="true" />
       <TextView
           android:layout_width="wrap_content"
           android:layout_height="wrap_content"
           android:text="Bottom"
           android:id="@+id/textViewBottom"
           android:layout_alignParentBottom="true"
           android:layout_centerHorizontal="true" />
       <Button
           android:layout_width="wrap_content"
           android:layout_height="wrap_content"
           android:text="Go"
           android:id="@+id/button"
   ```

Graphics and Animation

```xml
            android:layout_centerInParent="true"
            android:onClick="goAnimate"/>
    </RelativeLayout>
```

2. Create a new layout file called `activity_main_end.xml` using the following XML:

```xml
    <?xml version="1.0" encoding="utf-8"?>
    <RelativeLayout xmlns:android="http://schemas.android.com/apk/res/
    android"
        xmlns:tools="http://schemas.android.com/tools"
        android:id="@+id/layout"
        android:layout_width="match_parent"
        android:layout_height="match_parent">
        <TextView
            android:layout_width="wrap_content"
            android:layout_height="wrap_content"
            android:text="Bottom"
            android:id="@+id/textViewBottom"
            android:layout_alignParentTop="true"
            android:layout_centerHorizontal="true" />
        <TextView
            android:layout_width="wrap_content"
            android:layout_height="wrap_content"
            android:text="Top"
            android:id="@+id/textViewTop"
            android:layout_alignParentBottom="true"
            android:layout_centerHorizontal="true" />
        <Button
            android:layout_width="wrap_content"
            android:layout_height="wrap_content"
            android:text="Go"
            android:id="@+id/button"
            android:layout_centerInParent="true"/>
    </RelativeLayout>
```

3. Make a new transition resource directory (**File | New | Android resource directory** and choose **Transition** as the **Resource type**).

4. Create a new file in the `res/transition` folder called `transition_move.xml` using the following XML:

```xml
    <?xml version="1.0" encoding="utf-8"?>
    <changeBounds xmlns:android=
        "http://schemas.android.com/apk/res/android" />
```

5. Add the `goAnimate()` method using the following code:

   ```
   public void goAnimate(View view) {
       ViewGroup root = (ViewGroup) findViewById(R.id.layout);
       Scene scene = Scene.getSceneForLayout(root,
           R.layout.activity_main_end, this);
       Transition transition = TransitionInflater.from(this)
           .inflateTransition(R.transition.transition_move);
       TransitionManager.go(scene, transition);
   }
   ```

6. You're ready to run the application on a device or emulator.

How it works...

You probably find the code itself rather simple. As outlined in the recipe introduction, we just need to create the starting and ending scenes and set the transition type. Here's a detailed breakdown of the code.

Creating the start scene

Running the following line of code will create the start scene:

```
ViewGroup root = (ViewGroup) findViewById(R.id.layout);
```

Creating the transition:

Running the following line of code will create the transition:

```
Transition transition = TransitionInflater.from(this)
    .inflateTransition(R.transition.transition_move);
```

Defining the ending scene:

Running the following line of code will define the ending scene:

```
Scene scene = Scene.getSceneForLayout(root,
    R.layout.activity_main_end, this);
```

Starting the transition:

Running the following line of code will start the transition:

```
TransitionManager.go(scene, transition);
```

Though simple, most of the work for this recipe was in creating the necessary resource files.

Graphics and Animation

There's more...

Now we'll take a look at creating this same transition animation with a code-only solution (although we'll still use the initial `activity_main.xml` layout file):

```
ViewGroup root = (ViewGroup) findViewById(R.id.layout);
Scene scene = new Scene(root);

Transition transition = new ChangeBounds();
TransitionManager.beginDelayedTransition(root,transition);

TextView textViewTop = (TextView)findViewById(R.id.textViewTop);
RelativeLayout.LayoutParams params =
    (RelativeLayout.LayoutParams)textViewTop.getLayoutParams();
params.addRule(RelativeLayout.ALIGN_PARENT_BOTTOM,1);
params.addRule(RelativeLayout.ALIGN_PARENT_TOP, 0);
textViewTop.setLayoutParams(params);

TextView textViewBottom = (TextView)findViewById(
    R.id.textViewBottom);
params = (RelativeLayout.LayoutParams)
    textViewBottom.getLayoutParams();
params.addRule(RelativeLayout.ALIGN_PARENT_BOTTOM,0);
params.addRule(RelativeLayout.ALIGN_PARENT_TOP, 1);
textViewBottom.setLayoutParams(params);

TransitionManager.go(scene);
```

We still need the starting and ending scene along with the transition; the only difference is how we create the resources. In the previous code, we created the Start Scene using the current layout.

Before we start modifying the layout through code, we call the `beginDelayedTransition()` method of `TransitionManager` with the transition type. The `TransitionManager` will track the changes for the ending scene. When we call the `go()` method, the `TransitionManager` automatically animates the change.

See also

- Refer to the Animation resources web page at https://developer.android.com/guide/topics/resources/animation-resource.html

Creating a Compass using sensor data and RotateAnimation

In the previous chapter, we demonstrated reading sensor data from the physical device sensors. In that recipe, we used the Light Sensor since the data from Environment Sensors generally don't require any extra processing. Although it's easy to get the magnetic field strength data, the numbers themselves don't have much meaning and certainly don't create an appealing display.

In this recipe, we'll demonstrate getting the magnetic field data along with the accelerometer data to calculate magnetic north. We'll use the `SensorManager.getRotationMatrix` to animate the compass while responding to the device movement. Here's a screenshot of our compass application on a physical device:

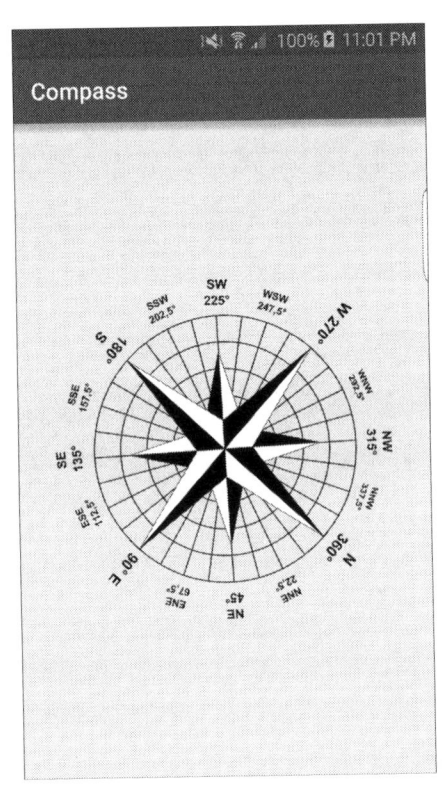

Graphics and Animation

Getting ready

Create a new project in Android Studio and call it: Compass. Use the default **Phone & Tablet** options and select **Empty Activity** when prompted for the **Activity Type**.

We will need an image for the compass indicator. Again, we can turn to www.Pixabay.Com for an image. We used the following image:

https://pixabay.com/en/geography-map-compass-rose-plot-42608/

Though not required, this image has a transparent background, which looks better when rotating the image.

How to do it...

As mentioned in the previous *Getting ready* section, we'll need an image for the compass. You can download the one previously linked, or use any image you prefer, then follow these steps:

1. Copy your image to the res/drawable folder and name it compass.png.
2. Open activity_main.xml and replace the existing TextView with the following ImageView:

   ```xml
   <ImageView
       android:id="@+id/imageViewCompass"
       android:layout_width="wrap_content"
       android:layout_height="wrap_content"
       android:layout_centerInParent="true"
       android:src="@drawable/compass"/>
   ```

3. Now open MainActivity.java and add the following global variable declarations:

   ```java
   private SensorManager mSensorManager;
   private Sensor mMagnetometer;
   private Sensor mAccelerometer;
   private ImageView mImageViewCompass;
   private float[] mGravityValues=new float[3];
   private float[] mAccelerationValues=new float[3];
   private float[] mRotationMatrix=new float[9];
   private float mLastDirectionInDegrees = 0f;
   ```

4. Add the following SensorEventListener class to the MainActivity class:

   ```java
   private SensorEventListener mSensorListener = new
       SensorEventListener() {
       @Override
       public void onSensorChanged(SensorEvent event) {
           calculateCompassDirection(event);
   ```

```
        }
        @Override
        public void onAccuracyChanged(Sensor sensor, int
            accuracy) {
            //Nothing to do
        }
    };
```

5. Override `onResume()` and `onPause()` as follows:

```
@Override
protected void onResume() {
    super.onResume();
    mSensorManager.registerListener(mSensorListener,
        mMagnetometer, SensorManager.SENSOR_DELAY_FASTEST);
    mSensorManager.registerListener(mSensorListener,
        mAccelerometer, SensorManager
        .SENSOR_DELAY_FASTEST);
}

@Override
protected void onPause() {
    super.onPause();
    mSensorManager.unregisterListener(mSensorListener);
}
```

6. Add the following code to the existing `onCreate()` method:

```
mImageViewCompass=(ImageView)findViewById(
    R.id.imageViewCompass);
mSensorManager = (SensorManager) getSystemService(
    Context.SENSOR_SERVICE);
mMagnetometer = mSensorManager.getDefaultSensor(
    Sensor.TYPE_MAGNETIC_FIELD);
mAccelerometer = mSensorManager.getDefaultSensor(
    Sensor.TYPE_ACCELEROMETER);
```

7. The final code does the actual calculations and animation:

```
private void calculateCompassDirection(SensorEvent event) {
    switch (event.sensor.getType()) {
        case Sensor.TYPE_ACCELEROMETER:
            mAccelerationValues = event.values.clone();
            break;
        case Sensor.TYPE_MAGNETIC_FIELD:
            mGravityValues = event.values.clone();
            break;
    }
```

Graphics and Animation

```
            boolean success = SensorManager.getRotationMatrix(
                mRotationMatrix, null, mAccelerationValues,
                mGravityValues);
            if(success){
                float[] orientationValues = new float[3];
                SensorManager.getOrientation(mRotationMatrix,
                    orientationValues);
                float azimuth = (float)Math.toDegrees(
                    -orientationValues[0]);
                RotateAnimation rotateAnimation = new
                    RotateAnimation(
                        mLastDirectionInDegrees, azimuth,
                        Animation.RELATIVE_TO_SELF, 0.5f,
                        Animation.RELATIVE_TO_SELF, 0.5f);
                rotateAnimation.setDuration(50);
                rotateAnimation.setFillAfter(true);
                mImageViewCompass.startAnimation(rotateAnimation);
                mLastDirectionInDegrees = azimuth;
            }
```

8. You're ready to run the application. Although you can run this application on an emulator, without an accelerometer and magnetometer, you won't see the compass move.

How it works...

Since we've already covered reading sensor data in *Reading sensor data – using the Android Sensor Framework* (from the previous chapter), we won't repeat explaining the sensor framework, and instead jump right to the `calculateCompassDirection()` method.

We call this method directly from the `onSensorChanged()` callback. Since we used the same class to handle the sensor callbacks for both the Magnetometer and Accelerometer, we first check which sensor is being reported in the `SensorEvent`. Then we call `SensorManager.getRotationMatrix()`, passing in the last sensor data. If the calculation is successful, it returns a `RotationMatrix`, which we use to call the `SensorManager.getOrientation()` method. `getOrientation()` will return the following data in the `orientationValues` array:

- **Azimuth**: `value [0]`
- **Pitch**: `value [1]`
- **Roll**: `value [2]`

Chapter 9

The azimuth is reported in radians, in the opposite direction, so we reverse the sign and convert it to degrees using `Math.toDegrees()`. The azimuth represents the direction of North, so we use it in our `RotateAnimation`.

With the math already done by the `SensorManager`, the actual compass animation is very simple. We create a `RotateAnimation` using the previous direction, the new direction. We use the `Animation.RELATIVE_TO_SELF` flag and 0.5f (or 50%) to set the center of the image as the rotation point. Before calling `startAnimation()` to update the compass, we set the animation duration using `setDuration()` and `setFillAfter(true)`. (Using `true` indicates we want the image to be left "as is" after the animation completes, otherwise the image would reset back to the original image.) Finally, we save the azimuth for the next sensor update.

There's more...

It's worth taking some time to experiment with the `RotationAnimation` settings and the sensor update timing. In our call to register the sensor listener, we use `SensorManager.SENSOR_DELAY_FASTEST` along with 50 milliseconds for the `setDuration()` to create a fast animation. You could also try using a slower sensor update and a slower animation, and compare the results.

See also

- *Reading sensor data – using the Android Sensor Framework* in the previous chapter for details on reading the sensor data.
- Refer to the **getRotationMatrix() Developer Document** at `http://developer.android.com/reference/android/hardware/SensorManager.html#getRotationMatrix(float[], float[], float[], float[])`
- Refer to the **getOrientation() Developer Document** at `http://developer.android.com/reference/android/hardware/SensorManager.html#getOrientation(float[], float[])`
- Refer to the **RotateAnimation Developer Document** at `http://developer.android.com/reference/android/view/animation/RotateAnimation.html`

231

Graphics and Animation

Creating a slideshow with ViewPager

This recipe will show you how to create a slideshow using the `ViewPager` class. Here is a screenshot showing a transition from one picture to another:

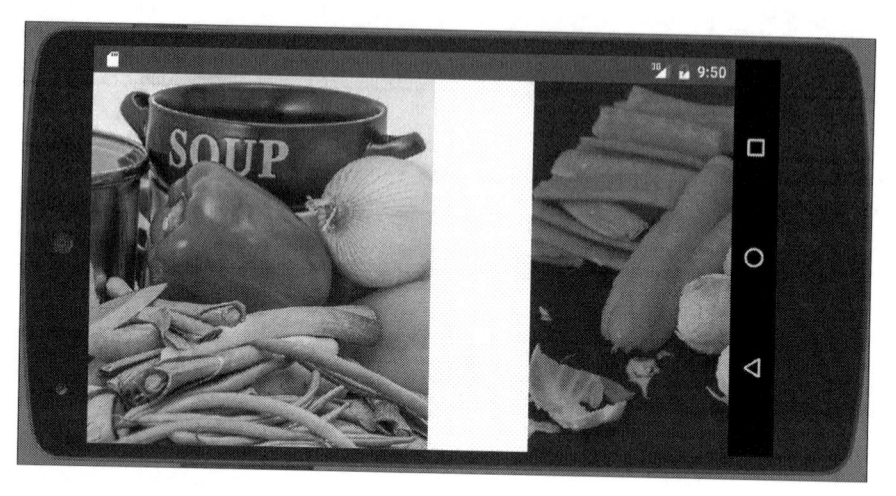

Getting ready

Create a new project in Android Studio and call it: `SlideShow`. Use the default **Phone & Tablet** options and select **Empty Activity** when prompted for the **Activity Type**.

We need several images for the slideshow. For demonstration purposes, we downloaded four images from `www.Pixabay.com` to include in the project source files, but you can use any images.

How to do it...

We'll create a Fragment to display each image for our slideshow, then set up the `ViewPager` in the Main Activity. Here are the steps:

1. Copy four images to the `/res/drawable` folder and name them `slide_0` through `slide_3`, keeping their original file extensions.
2. Create a new layout file called `fragment_slide.xml` using the following XML:

   ```
   <?xml version="1.0" encoding="utf-8"?>
   <LinearLayout xmlns:android="http://schemas.android.com/
       apk/res/android"
       android:orientation="vertical"
       android:layout_width="match_parent"
       android:layout_height="match_parent">
   ```

```
    <ImageView
        android:layout_width="wrap_content"
        android:layout_height="wrap_content"
        android:id="@+id/imageView"
        android:layout_gravity="center_horizontal" />
</LinearLayout>
```

3. Now create a new Java class called `SlideFragment`. It will extend `Fragment` as follows:

   ```
   public class SlideFragment extends Fragment {
   ```

   Use the following import:

   ```
   import android.support.v4.app.Fragment;
   ```

4. Add the following global declaration:

   ```
   private int mImageResourceID;
   ```

5. Add the following empty, default fragment constructor:

   ```
   public SlideFragment() {}
   ```

6. Add the following method to save the image resource ID:

   ```
   public void setImage(int resourceID) {
       mImageResourceID=resourceID;
   }
   ```

7. Override `onCreateView()` as follows:

   ```
   @Override
   public View onCreateView(
           LayoutInflater inflater, ViewGroup container,
           Bundle savedInstanceState) {
       ViewGroup rootView = (ViewGroup) inflater.inflate(
           R.layout.fragment_slide, container, false);
       ImageView imageView = (ImageView)rootView.findViewById(
           R.id.imageView);
       imageView.setImageResource(mImageResourceID);
       return rootView;
   }
   ```

8. Our main activity will display just a `ViewPager`. Open `activity_main.xml` and replace the file contents as follows:

   ```
   <android.support.v4.view.ViewPager
       xmlns:android="http://schemas.android.com/apk/
           res/android"
       android:id="@+id/viewPager"
       android:layout_width="match_parent"
       android:layout_height="match_parent" />
   ```

Graphics and Animation

9. Now open `MainActivity.java` and change `MainActivity` to extend `FragmentActivity` as shown:

    ```
    public class MainActivity extends FragmentActivity {
    ```

    Use the following import:

    ```
    import android.support.v4.app.FragmentActivity;
    ```

10. Add the following global declarations:

    ```
    private final int PAGE_COUNT=4;
    private ViewPager mViewPager;
    private PagerAdapter mPagerAdapter;
    ```

    Use the following imports:

    ```
    import android.support.v4.view.PagerAdapter;
    import android.support.v4.view.ViewPager;
    ```

11. Create the following subclass within `MainActivity`:

    ```
    private class SlideAdapter extends
        FragmentStatePagerAdapter {
        public SlideAdapter(FragmentManager fm) {
            super(fm);
        }
        @Override
        public Fragment getItem(int position) {
            SlideFragment slideFragment = new SlideFragment();
            switch (position) {
                case 0:
                    slideFragment.setImage(R.drawable.slide_0);
                    break;
                case 1:
                    slideFragment.setImage(R.drawable.slide_1);
                    break;
                case 2:
                    slideFragment.setImage(R.drawable.slide_2);
                    break;
                case 3:
                    slideFragment.setImage(R.drawable.slide_3);
                    break;
            }
            return slideFragment;
        }
        @Override
    ```

```
            public int getCount() {
                return PAGE_COUNT;
            }
        }
```

Use the following imports:

```
import android.support.v4.app.Fragment;
import android.support.v4.app.FragmentManager;
import android.support.v4.app.FragmentStatePagerAdapter;
```

12. Override `onBackPressed()` as follows:

    ```
    @Override
    public void onBackPressed() {
        if (mViewPager.getCurrentItem() == 0) {
            super.onBackPressed();
        } else {
            mViewPager.setCurrentItem(
                mViewPager.getCurrentItem() - 1);
        }
    }
    ```

13. Add the following code to the `onCreate()` method:

    ```
    mViewPager = (ViewPager) findViewById(R.id.viewPager);
    mPagerAdapter = new SlideAdapter(getSupportFragmentManager());
    mViewPager.setAdapter(mPagerAdapter);
    ```

14. Run the application on a device or emulator.

How it works...

The first step is to create a fragment. Since we're doing a slideshow, all we need is an `ImageViewer`. We also change `MainActivity` to extend `FragmentActivity` to load the fragments into the `ViewPager`.

The `ViewPager` uses a `FragmentStatePagerAdapter` as the source for the fragments to transition. We create the `SlideAdapter` to handle the two callbacks from the `FragmentStatePagerAdapter` class:

- `getCount()`
- `getItem()`

Graphics and Animation

`getCount()` simply returns the number of pages we have in our slideshow. `getItem()` returns the actual fragment to display. This is where we specify the image we want to display. As you can see, it would be very easy to add or change the slideshow.

Handling the *Back* key isn't a requirement for the `ViewPager`, but it does provide a better user experience. `onBackPressed()` decrements the current page until it reaches the first page, then it sends the *Back* key to the super class, which exits the application.

There's more...

As you can see from the example, the `ViewPager` takes care of most of the work, including handling the transition animations. We can customize the transition if we want, by implementing the `transformPage()` callback on the `ViewPager.PageTransformer` interface. (See the next recipe for a custom animation.)

Creating a Setup Wizard

The `ViewPager` can also be used to create a Setup Wizard. Instead of creating a single fragment to display an image, create a fragment for each step of your wizard and return the appropriate fragment in the `getItem()` callback.

See also

- Refer to the **Android ViewPager Documentation** at http://developer.android.com/reference/android/support/v4/view/ViewPager.html
- Refer to the *Creating a custom Zoom Animation* recipe for an example on creating a custom animation.

Creating a Card Flip Animation with Fragments

The card flip is a common animation that we will demonstrate using fragment transitions. We'll use two different images—one for the front and one for the back, to create the card flip effect. We'll need four animation resources: two for the front and two for the back transitions, which we will define in XML using `objectAnimator`.

Chapter 9

Here's a screenshot of the application we'll build showing the Card Flip Animation in action:

Getting ready

Create a new project in Android Studio and call it: `CardFlip`. Use the default **Phone & Tablet** options and select **Empty Activity** when prompted for the **Activity Type**.

For the front and back images of the playing card, we found the following images on `www.Pixabay.com`:

- `https://pixabay.com/en/ace-hearts-playing-cards-poker-28357/`
- `https://pixabay.com/en/card-game-deck-of-cards-card-game-48978/`

237

Graphics and Animation

How to do it...

We'll need two fragments—one for the front of the card and the other for the back. Each fragment will define the image for the card. Then we'll need four animation files for the full card flip effect. Here are the steps to set up the project structure correctly and to create the resources needed:

1. Once you have front and back images for the cards, copy them to the `res/drawable` folder as `card_front.jpg` and `card_back.jpg` (keep the original file extension of your images if different).

2. Create an animator resource directory: `res/animator`. (In Android Studio, go to **File | New | Android resource directory**. When the **New Android Resource** dialog displays, choose `animator` in the **Resource Type** dropdown.)

3. Create `card_flip_left_enter.xml` in `res/animator` using the following XML:

   ```
   <set xmlns:android="http://schemas.android.com/apk/
           res/android">
       <objectAnimator
           android:valueFrom="1.0"
           android:valueTo="0.0"
           android:propertyName="alpha"
           android:duration="0" />
       <objectAnimator
           android:valueFrom="-180"
           android:valueTo="0"
           android:propertyName="rotationY"
           android:interpolator="@android:interpolator/
               accelerate_decelerate"
           android:duration="@integer/
               card_flip_duration_full"/>
       <objectAnimator
           android:valueFrom="0.0"
           android:valueTo="1.0"
           android:propertyName="alpha"
           android:startOffset="@integer/
               card_flip_duration_half"
           android:duration="1" />
   </set>
   ```

4. Create `card_flip_left_exit.xml` in `res/animator` using the following XML:

   ```
   <set xmlns:android="http://schemas.android.com/apk/res/android">
       <objectAnimator
           android:valueFrom="0"
           android:valueTo="180"
   ```

```xml
        android:propertyName="rotationY"
        android:interpolator="@android:interpolator/
            accelerate_decelerate"
        android:duration="@integer/
            card_flip_duration_full"/>
    <objectAnimator
        android:valueFrom="1.0"
        android:valueTo="0.0"
        android:propertyName="alpha"
        android:startOffset="@integer/
    card_flip_duration_half"
        android:duration="1" />
</set>
```

5. Create `card_flip_right_enter.xml` in res/animator using the following XML:

```xml
<set xmlns:android="http://schemas.android.com/apk/
    res/android">
    <objectAnimator
        android:valueFrom="1.0"
        android:valueTo="0.0"
        android:propertyName="alpha"
        android:duration="0" />
    <objectAnimator
        android:valueFrom="180"
        android:valueTo="0"
        android:propertyName="rotationY"
        android:interpolator="@android:interpolator/
            accelerate_decelerate"
        android:duration="@integer/
            card_flip_duration_full" />
    <objectAnimator
        android:valueFrom="0.0"
        android:valueTo="1.0"
        android:propertyName="alpha"
        android:startOffset="@integer/
            card_flip_duration_half"
        android:duration="1" />
</set>
```

6. Create `card_flip_right_exit.xml` in res/animator using the following XML:

```xml
<set xmlns:android="http://schemas.android.com/apk/
    res/android">
    <objectAnimator
        android:valueFrom="0"
        android:valueTo="-180"
```

Graphics and Animation

```xml
            android:propertyName="rotationY"
            android:interpolator="@android:interpolator/
                accelerate_decelerate"
            android:duration="@integer/
                card_flip_duration_full" />
    <objectAnimator
            android:valueFrom="1.0"
            android:valueTo="0.0"
            android:propertyName="alpha"
            android:startOffset="@integer/
                card_flip_duration_half"
            android:duration="1" />
</set>
```

7. Create a new resource file in `res/values` called `timing.xml` using the following XML:

```xml
<?xml version="1.0" encoding="utf-8"?>
<resources>
    <integer name="card_flip_duration_full">1000</integer>
    <integer name="card_flip_duration_half">500</integer>
</resources>
```

8. Create a new file in `res/layout` called `fragment_card_front.xml` using the following XML:

```xml
<?xml version="1.0" encoding="utf-8"?>
<ImageView xmlns:android="http://schemas.android.com/apk/res/android"
    android:layout_width="match_parent"
    android:layout_height="match_parent"
    android:src="@drawable/card_front"
    android:scaleType="centerCrop" />
```

9. Create a new file in `res/layout` called `fragment_card_back.xml` using the following XML:

```xml
<?xml version="1.0" encoding="utf-8"?>
<ImageView xmlns:android="http://schemas.android.com/apk/res/android"
    android:layout_width="match_parent"
    android:layout_height="match_parent"
    android:src="@drawable/card_back"
    android:scaleType="centerCrop" />
```

Chapter 9

10. Create a new Java class called `CardFrontFragment` using the following code:

    ```
    public class CardFrontFragment extends Fragment {
        @Override
        public View onCreateView(LayoutInflater inflater,
            ViewGroup container, Bundle savedInstanceState) {
            return inflater.inflate(
                R.layout.fragment_card_front, container,
                false);
        }
    }
    ```

11. Create a new Java class called `CardBackFragment` using the following code:

    ```
    public class CardBackFragment extends Fragment {
        @Override
        public View onCreateView(LayoutInflater inflater,
            ViewGroup container, Bundle savedInstanceState) {
            return inflater.inflate(
                R.layout.fragment_card_back, container, false);
        }
    }
    ```

12. Replace the existing `activity_main.xml` file with the following XML:

    ```
    <FrameLayout
        xmlns:android="http://schemas.android.com/apk/
            res/android"
        android:id="@+id/container"
        android:layout_width="match_parent"
        android:layout_height="match_parent" />
    ```

13. Open `MainActivity.java` and add the following global declaration:

    ```
    boolean mShowingBack = false;
    ```

14. Add the following code to the existing `onCreate()` method:

    ```
    FrameLayout frameLayout = (FrameLayout)findViewById(
        R.id.frameLayout);
    frameLayout.setOnClickListener(new View.OnClickListener() {
        @Override
        public void onClick(View v) {
            flipCard();
        }
    });

    if (savedInstanceState == null) {
    ```

Graphics and Animation

```
        getFragmentManager()
            .beginTransaction()
            .add(R.id.frameLayout, new CardFrontFragment())
            .commit();
}
```

15. Add the following method, which handles the actual fragment transition:

```
private void flipCard() {
    if (mShowingBack) {
        mShowingBack = false;
        getFragmentManager().popBackStack();
    } else {
        mShowingBack = true;
        getFragmentManager()
            .beginTransaction()
            .setCustomAnimations(
                R.animator.card_flip_right_enter,
                R.animator.card_flip_right_exit,
                R.animator.card_flip_left_enter,
                R.animator.card_flip_left_exit)
            .replace(R.id.frameLayout, new
                CardBackFragment())
            .addToBackStack(null)
            .commit();
    }
}
```

16. You're ready to run the application on a device or emulator.

How it works...

Most of the effort to create the card flip is in setting up the resources. Since we want a front and back view of the card, we create two fragments with the appropriate images. We call the `flipCard()` method when the card is pressed. The actual animation is handled by the `setCustomAnimations()`. This is where we pass in the four animation resources we defined in XML. As you can see, Android makes it very easy.

It's important to note that we did not use the Support Library Fragment Manager, as the support library does not support the `objectAnimator`. If you want support preAndroid 3.0, you'll need to include the old `anim` resources and check the OS version at runtime, or create the animation resources in code. (See the next recipe.)

See also

- See the next recipe, *Creating a Zoom Animation with a Custom Transition*, for an example of animation resources created in code
- Refer to the **Integer Resource Type** web page at `https://developer.android.com/guide/topics/resources/more-resources.html#Integer`

Creating a Zoom Animation with a Custom Transition

The previous recipe, *Creating a Card Flip Animation with Fragments*, demonstrated a transition animation using animation resource files. In this recipe, we will create a zoom effect using animation resources created in code. The application shows a thumbnail image then expands to an enlarged image when pressed.

The following image contains three screenshots showing the zoom animation in action:

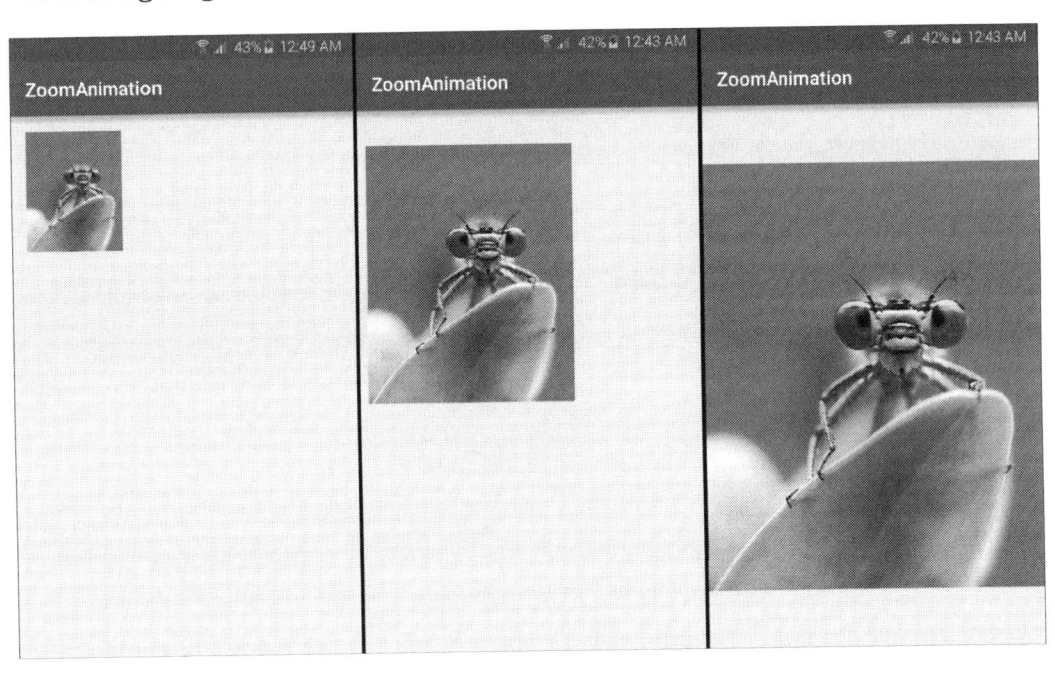

Graphics and Animation

Getting ready

Create a new project in Android Studio and call it: `<project name>`. Use the default **Phone & Tablet** options and select **Empty Activity** when prompted for the **Activity Type**.

For the image needed for this recipe, we downloaded a picture from `www.Pixabay.com` to include in the project source files, but you can use any image.

How to do it...

Once you have your image ready as stated previously, follow these steps:

1. Copy your image to the `res/drawable` folder and name it `image.jpg` (if not a jpeg image, keep the original file extension).

2. Now open `activity_main.xml` and replace the existing XML with the following:

    ```xml
    <?xml version="1.0" encoding="utf-8"?>
    <FrameLayout xmlns:android="http://schemas.android.com/apk/res/android"
        android:id="@+id/frameLayout"
        android:layout_width="match_parent"
        android:layout_height="match_parent">
        <LinearLayout
            android:layout_width="match_parent"
            android:layout_height="wrap_content"
            android:orientation="vertical"
            android:padding="16dp">
            <ImageButton
                android:id="@+id/imageViewThumbnail"
                android:layout_width="wrap_content"
                android:layout_height="wrap_content"
                android:scaleType="centerCrop"
                android:background="@android:color/transparent"/>
        </LinearLayout>
        <ImageView
            android:id="@+id/imageViewExpanded"
            android:layout_width="match_parent"
            android:layout_height="match_parent"
            android:visibility="invisible" />
    </FrameLayout>
    ```

3. Now open `MainActivity.java` and declare the following global variables:

    ```java
    private Animator mCurrentAnimator;
    private ImageView mImageViewExpanded;
    ```

4. Add the `loadSampledResource()` method we created in the *Scaling down large images to avoid Out of Memory exceptions* recipe to scale the image:

```
public Bitmap loadSampledResource(int imageID, int targetHeight,
int targetWidth) {
    final BitmapFactory.Options options = new
        BitmapFactory.Options();
    options.inJustDecodeBounds = true;
    BitmapFactory.decodeResource(getResources(), imageID,
        options);
    final int originalHeight = options.outHeight;
    final int originalWidth = options.outWidth;
    int inSampleSize = 1;
    while ((originalHeight / (inSampleSize *2)) >
        targetHeight && (originalWidth / (inSampleSize *2))
            > targetWidth) {
        inSampleSize *= 2;
    }
    options.inSampleSize =inSampleSize;
    options.inJustDecodeBounds = false;
    return (BitmapFactory.decodeResource(getResources(),
        imageID, options));
}
```

5. Add the following code to the `onCreate()` method:

```
final ImageView imageViewThumbnail = (ImageView)
    findViewById(R.id.imageViewThumbnail);
imageViewThumbnail.setImageBitmap(loadSampledResource(
    R.drawable.image, 100, 100));
imageViewThumbnail.setOnClickListener(new
    View.OnClickListener() {
    @Override
    public void onClick(View view) {
        zoomFromThumbnail((ImageView) view);
    }
});
mImageViewExpanded = (ImageView)
    findViewById(R.id.imageViewExpanded);
mImageViewExpanded.setOnClickListener(new
    View.OnClickListener() {
    @Override
    public void onClick(View v) {
        mImageViewExpanded.setVisibility(View.GONE);
        mImageViewExpanded.setImageBitmap(null);
        imageViewThumbnail.setVisibility(View.VISIBLE);
    }
});
```

Graphics and Animation

6. Add the following `zoomFromThumbnail()` method, which handles the actual animation and is explained later on:

```java
private void zoomFromThumbnail(final ImageView imageViewThumb) {
    if (mCurrentAnimator != null) {
        mCurrentAnimator.cancel();
    }

    final Rect startBounds = new Rect();
    final Rect finalBounds = new Rect();
    final Point globalOffset = new Point();

    imageViewThumb.getGlobalVisibleRect(startBounds);
    findViewById(R.id.frameLayout).getGlobalVisibleRect(
        finalBounds, globalOffset);
    mImageViewExpanded.setImageBitmap(loadSampledResource(
        R.drawable.image, finalBounds.height(),
            finalBounds.width()));

    startBounds.offset(-globalOffset.x, -globalOffset.y);
    finalBounds.offset(-globalOffset.x, -globalOffset.y);

    float startScale;
    if ((float) finalBounds.width() / finalBounds.height()
            > (float) startBounds.width() /
                startBounds.height()) {
        startScale = (float) startBounds.height() /
            finalBounds.height();
        float startWidth = startScale *
            finalBounds.width();
        float deltaWidth = (startWidth -
            startBounds.width()) / 2;
        startBounds.left -= deltaWidth;
        startBounds.right += deltaWidth;
    } else {
        startScale = (float) startBounds.width() /
            finalBounds.width();
        float startHeight = startScale *
            finalBounds.height();
        float deltaHeight = (startHeight -
            startBounds.height()) / 2;
        startBounds.top -= deltaHeight;
        startBounds.bottom += deltaHeight;
    }
}
```

Chapter 9

```
        imageViewThumb.setVisibility(View.GONE);
        mImageViewExpanded.setVisibility(View.VISIBLE);
        mImageViewExpanded.setPivotX(0f);
        mImageViewExpanded.setPivotY(0f);

        AnimatorSet animatorSet = new AnimatorSet();
        animatorSet.play(ObjectAnimator.ofFloat(
            mImageViewExpanded, View.X,startBounds.left,
                finalBounds.left))
                    .with(ObjectAnimator.ofFloat(
                        mImageViewExpanded,
                        View.Y,startBounds.top,
                        finalBounds.top))
                    .with(ObjectAnimator.ofFloat(
                        mImageViewExpanded,
                        View.SCALE_X, startScale, 1f))
                    .with(ObjectAnimator.ofFloat(
                        mImageViewExpanded, View.SCALE_Y,
                        startScale, 1f));
        animatorSet.setDuration(1000);
        animatorSet.setInterpolator(
            new DecelerateInterpolator());
        animatorSet.addListener(new AnimatorListenerAdapter() {
            @Override
            public void onAnimationEnd(Animator animation) {
                mCurrentAnimator = null;
            }
            @Override
            public void onAnimationCancel(Animator animation) {
                mCurrentAnimator = null;
            }
        });
        animatorSet.start();
        mCurrentAnimator = animatorSet;
    }
```

7. Run the application on a device or emulator.

How it works...

First, take a look at the layout file we used. There are two parts—the `LinearLayout` with the thumbnail `ImageView`, and the expanded `ImageView`. We control the visibility of both views as the images are clicked. We set the starting thumbnail image using the same `loadSampledResource()` as discussed in the *Scaling down large images to avoid Out of Memory exceptions* recipe.

Graphics and Animation

The `zoomFromThumbnail()` is where the real work is being done for this demonstration. There's a lot of code, which breaks down as follows.

First, we store the current animation in `mCurrentAnimator`, so we can cancel if the animation is currently running.

Next, we get the starting position of the image using the `getGlobalVisibleRect()` method. This returns the screen position of the view. When we get the visible bounds of the expanded `ImageView`, we also get the `GlobalOffset` of the view to offset the coordinates from app coordinates to screen coordinates.

With the starting bounds set, the next step is to calculate the ending bounds. We want to keep the same aspect ratio for the final image to prevent it from being skewed. We need to calculate how the bounds need to be adjusted to keep the aspect ratio within the expanded `ImageView`. The screenshot shown in the introduction shows how this image was sized, but this will vary by image and device.

With the starting and ending bounds calculated, we can now create the animation—actually, four animations in this case. One animation for each point of the rectangle, as shown in this code:

```
animatorSet.play(ObjectAnimator.ofFloat(mImageViewExpanded,
    View.X,startBounds.left, finalBounds.left))
        .with(ObjectAnimator.ofFloat(mImageViewExpanded,
            View.Y,startBounds.top, finalBounds.top))
        .with(ObjectAnimator.ofFloat(mImageViewExpanded,
            View.SCALE_X,startScale, 1f))
        .with(ObjectAnimator.ofFloat(mImageViewExpanded,
            View.SCALE_Y, startScale, 1f));
```

These two lines of code control how the animation appears:

```
animatorSet.setDuration(1000);
animatorSet.setInterpolator(new AccelerateInterpolator());
```

The `setDuration()` method tells the animator object how long it should take to animate the translations set previously. `setInterpolator()` governs how the translation is made. (The Interpolator was mentioned in the *Introduction*, and a link is provided further on.) After starting the animation with the `start()` method, we save the current animation to the `mCurrentAnimator` variable, so the animation can be cancelled, if needed. We create an `AnimatorListenerAdapter` to respond to the animation events, to clear the `mCurrentAnimator` variable.

Chapter 9

There's more...

When the user presses the Expanded Image, the application just hides the expanded `ImageView` and sets the thumbnail as `visible`. We could create a reverse zoom animation in the `mImageViewExpanded` click event using the expanded bounds as the starting point returning to the thumbnail bounds. (It would probably be easier to create the `mImageViewExpanded` event in the `zoomFromThumbnail()` to avoid having to duplicate calculating the start and stop bounds again.)

Getting the default animation duration

Our code used 1000 milliseconds when setting the duration with `setDuration()`. We purposely used a long duration to make it easier to view the animation. We can get the default Android animation duration using the following code:

```
getResources().getInteger(android.R.integer.config_shortAnimTime)
```

See also

- The first recipe, *Scaling down large images to avoid Out of Memory exceptions*, for a detailed explanation of the `loadSampledResource()` method.
- Refer to the **Interpolator Developer Document** at http://developer.android.com/reference/android/view/animation/Interpolator.html

10
A First Look at OpenGL ES

In this chapter, we will cover the following topics:

- Setting up the OpenGL ES environment
- Drawing shapes on GLSurfaceView
- Applying projection and camera view while drawing
- Moving the triangle with rotation
- Rotating the triangle with user input

Introduction

As we saw in the previous chapter, Android offers many tools for handling graphics and animations. Though the canvas and drawable objects are designed for custom drawing, when you need high performance graphics, especially 3D gaming graphics, Android also supports OpenGL ES. **Open Graphics Library for Embedded Systems** (**OpenGL ES**), is targeted for embedded system. (Embedded systems include consoles and phones.)

This chapter is meant to serve as an introduction to using OpenGL ES on Android. As usual, we'll provide the steps and explain how things work, but we aren't going to be digging into the math or technical details of OpenGL. If you are already familiar with OpenGL ES from other platforms, such as iOS, this chapter should get you up and running quickly. If you are new to OpenGL, hopefully, these recipes will help you decide whether this is an area you want to pursue.

A First Look at OpenGL ES

Android supports the following versions of OpenGL:

- **OpenGL ES 1.0**: Android 1.0
- **OpenGL ES 2.0**: Introduced in Android 2.2 (API 8)
- **OpenGL ES 3.0**: Introduced in Android 4.3 (API 18)
- **OpenGL ES 3.1**: Introduced in Android 5.0 (API 21)

The recipes for this chapter are of an introductory nature and target OpenGL ES 2.0 and higher. OpenGL ES 2.0 is available for nearly all devices currently available. Unlike OpenGL ES 2.0 and lower, OpenGL 3.0 and higher require driver implementation from the hardware manufacturer. This means, even if your application is running on Android 5.0, OpenGL 3.0 and higher may not be available. Therefore, it's a good programming practice to check the available OpenGL versions at runtime. Alternatively, if your application requires 3.0 and higher features, you can add a `<uses-feature/>` element to your Android manifest. (We'll discuss this in the first recipe that follows.)

Unlike the other chapters in this book, this chapter is written more as a tutorial with each recipe building on lessons learned from the previous recipe. The *Getting ready* section of each recipe will clarify the prerequisites.

Set up the OpenGL ES environment

Our first recipe will start by showing the steps to set up an activity to use an OpenGL `GLSurfaceView`. Similar to the Canvas, the `GLSurfaceView` is where your will perform your OpenGL drawing. As this is the starting point, the other recipes will refer to this recipe as the base step when they need a `GLSurfaceView` created.

Getting ready

Create a new project in Android Studio and call it: `SetupOpenGL`. Use the default **Phone & Tablet** options and select **Empty Activity** when prompted for **Activity Type**.

How to do it...

We'll start by indicating the application's use of OpenGL in the Android Manifest, and then we'll add the OpenGL classes to the activity. Here are the steps:

1. Open the Android Manifest and add the following XML:

    ```xml
    <uses-feature android:glEsVersion="0x00020000"
        android:required="true" />
    ```

2. Open `MainActivity.java` and add the following global variables:
   ```
   private GLSurfaceView mGLSurfaceView;
   ```

3. Add the following inner class to the `MainActivity` class:
   ```
   class CustomGLSurfaceView extends GLSurfaceView {

       private final GLRenderer mGLRenderer;

       public CustomGLSurfaceView(Context context){
           super(context);
           setEGLContextClientVersion(2);
           mGLRenderer = new GLRenderer();
           setRenderer(mGLRenderer);
       }
   }
   ```

4. Add another inner class to the `MainActivity` class:
   ```
   class GLRenderer implements GLSurfaceView.Renderer {
       public void onSurfaceCreated(GL10 unused, EGLConfig config) {
           GLES20.glClearColor(0.5f, 0.5f, 0.5f, 1.0f);
       }
       public void onDrawFrame(GL10 unused) {
           GLES20.glClear(GLES20.GL_COLOR_BUFFER_BIT);
       }
       public void onSurfaceChanged(GL10 unused, int width, int height) {
           GLES20.glViewport(0, 0, width, height);
       }
   }
   ```

5. Add the following code to the existing `onCreate()` method:
   ```
   mGLSurfaceView = new CustomGLSurfaceView(this);
   setContentView(mGLSurfaceView);
   ```

6. You're ready to run the application on a device or emulator.

How it works...

If you ran the preceding application, you saw the activity created and the background set to gray. Since these are the basic steps to setting up OpenGL, you'll be reusing this code for the other recipes in this chapter as well. Here is the process explained in detail:

Declaring OpenGL in the Android Manifest

We start by declaring our requirement to use OpenGL ES version 2.0 in the Android Manifest with this line:

```
<uses-feature android:glEsVersion="0x00020000" android:required="true"
/>
```

If we were using Version 3.0, we would use this:

```
<uses-feature android:glEsVersion="0x00030000" android:required="true"
/>
```

For Version 3.1, use this:

```
<uses-feature android:glEsVersion="0x00030001" android:required="true"
/>
```

Extending the GLSurfaceView class

Create a custom OpenGL `SurfaceView` class by extending `GLSurfaceView`, as we do in this code:

```
class CustomGLSurfaceView extends GLSurfaceView {

    private final GLRenderer mGLRenderer;

    public CustomGLSurfaceView(Context context){
        super(context);
        setEGLContextClientVersion(2);
        mGLRenderer = new GLRenderer();
        setRenderer(mGLRenderer);
    }
}
```

Here, we instantiate an OpenGL rendered class and pass it to the `GLSurfaceView` class with the `setRenderer()` method. The OpenGL `SurfaceView` provides a surface for our OpenGL drawing, similar to the `Canvas` and `SurfaceView` objects. The actual drawing is done in the `Renderer`, which we'll create next:

Chapter 10

Creating an OpenGL rendered class

The last step is to create the `GLSurfaceView.Renderer` class and implement the following three callbacks:

- `onSurfaceCreated()`
- `onDrawFrame()`
- `onSurfaceChanged()`

Here is the code:

```
class GLRenderer implements GLSurfaceView.Renderer {
    public void onSurfaceCreated(GL10 unused, EGLConfig config) {
        GLES20.glClearColor(0.5f, 0.5f, 0.5f, 1.0f);
    }
    public void onDrawFrame(GL10 unused) {
        GLES20.glClear(GLES20.GL_COLOR_BUFFER_BIT);
    }
    public void onSurfaceChanged(GL10 unused, int width, int height) {
        GLES20.glViewport(0, 0, width, height);
    }
}
```

Right now, all we're doing with this class is setting up the callbacks and clearing the screen using the color we specify with `glClearColor()` (gray in this case).

There's more...

With the OpenGL environment set up, we'll continue to the next recipe where we'll actually draw on the view.

Drawing shapes on GLSurfaceView

The previous recipe set up the activity to use OpenGL. This recipe will continue by showing how to draw on `OpenGLSurfaceView`.

First, we need to define the shape. With OpenGL, it is important to realize the order in which the vertices of a shape are defined are very important, as they determine the front (face) and back of the shape. It's customary (and the default behavior) to define the vertices counter clockwise. (Though this behavior can be changed, it requires additional code and is not standard practice.)

A First Look at OpenGL ES

It's also important to understand the OpenGL screen coordinate system, as it differs from the Android canvas. The default coordinate system defines (0,0,0) as the center of the screen. The four edge points are as follows:

- **Top left**: (-1.0, 1.0, 0)
- **Top right**: (1.0, 1.0, 0)
- **Bottom left**: (-1.0, -1.0, 0)
- **Bottom right**: (1.0, -1.0, 0)

The Z axis comes straight out of the screen or straight behind.

Here is an illustration showing the X, Y, and Z axes:

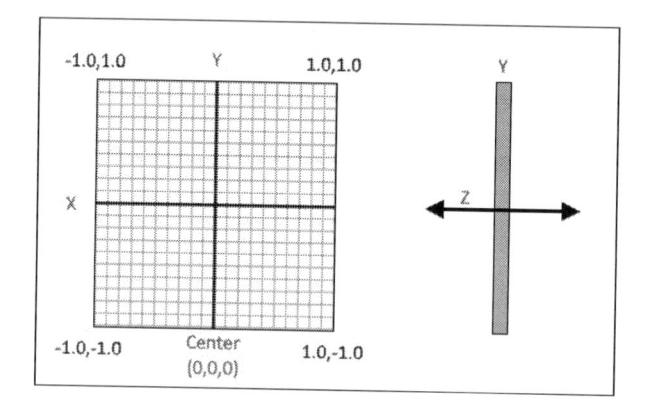

We're going to create a `Triangle` class since it is the base shape. In OpenGL, you generally use a collection of triangles to create objects. To draw a shape with OpenGL, we need to define the following:

- **Vertex shader**: This is to draw the shape
- **Fragment shader**: This is to color the shape
- **Program**: This is an OpenGL ES object for the preceding shaders

The shaders are defined using **OpenGL Shading Language (GLSL)**, and then compiled and added to the OpenGL program object.

Here are two screenshots showing the triangle in both portrait and landscape orientation:

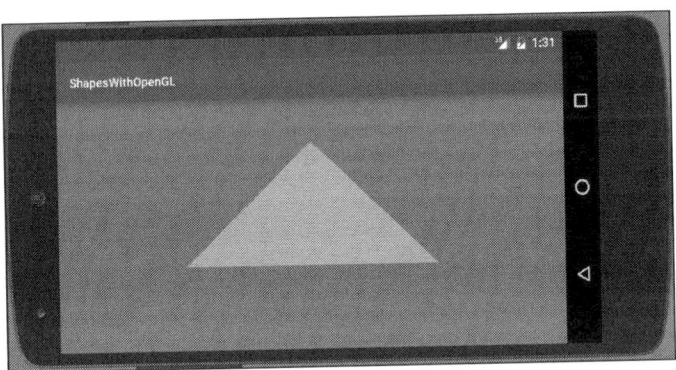

Getting ready

Create a new project in Android Studio and call it: `ShapesWithOpenGL`. Use the default **Phone & Tablet** options and select **Empty Activity** when prompted for **Activity Type**.

This recipe uses the OpenGL environment created in the previous recipe *Set up the Open GL environment*. Refer to the previous recipe if you have not already completed those steps.

A First Look at OpenGL ES

How to do it...

As indicated previously, we'll be using the OpenGL environment created in the previous recipe. The steps that follow will walk you through creating a class for the triangle shape and drawing it on the GLSurfaceView:

1. Create a new Java class called `Triangle`.
2. Add the following global declarations to the `Triangle` class:

   ```
   private final String vertexShaderCode =
           "attribute vec4 vPosition;" +
                   "void main() {" +
           "  gl_Position = vPosition;" +
           "}";

   private final String fragmentShaderCode =
           "precision mediump float;" +
                   "uniform vec4 vColor;" +
                   "void main() {" +
           "  gl_FragColor = vColor;" +
           "}";

   final int COORDS_PER_VERTEX = 3;
   float triangleCoords[] = {
           0.0f,  0.66f, 0.0f,
           -0.5f, -0.33f, 0.0f,
           0.5f, -0.33f, 0.0f
   };

   float color[] = { 0.63f, 0.76f, 0.22f, 1.0f };

   private final int mProgram;
   private FloatBuffer vertexBuffer;
   private int mPositionHandle;
   private int mColorHandle;
   private final int vertexCount = triangleCoords.length / COORDS_PER_VERTEX;
   private final int vertexStride = COORDS_PER_VERTEX * 4;
   ```

3. Add the following `loadShader()` method to the `Triangle` class:

   ```
   public int loadShader(int type, String shaderCode){
       int shader = GLES20.glCreateShader(type);
       GLES20.glShaderSource(shader, shaderCode);
       GLES20.glCompileShader(shader);
       return shader;
   }
   ```

Chapter 10

4. Add the `Triangle` constructor, as shown:

   ```
   public Triangle() {
       int vertexShader = loadShader(
               GLES20.GL_VERTEX_SHADER,
               vertexShaderCode);
       int fragmentShader = loadShader(
               GLES20.GL_FRAGMENT_SHADER,
               fragmentShaderCode);
       mProgram = GLES20.glCreateProgram();
       GLES20.glAttachShader(mProgram, vertexShader);
       GLES20.glAttachShader(mProgram, fragmentShader);
       GLES20.glLinkProgram(mProgram);

       ByteBuffer bb = ByteBuffer.allocateDirect(
               triangleCoords.length * 4);
       bb.order(ByteOrder.nativeOrder());

       vertexBuffer = bb.asFloatBuffer();
       vertexBuffer.put(triangleCoords);
       vertexBuffer.position(0);
   }
   ```

5. Add the `draw()` method, as follows:

   ```
   public void draw() {
       GLES20.glUseProgram(mProgram);
       mPositionHandle = GLES20.glGetAttribLocation(mProgram,
   "vPosition");
       GLES20.glEnableVertexAttribArray(mPositionHandle);
       GLES20.glVertexAttribPointer(mPositionHandle,
               COORDS_PER_VERTEX,
               GLES20.GL_FLOAT, false,
               vertexStride, vertexBuffer);
       mColorHandle = GLES20.glGetUniformLocation(mProgram,
   "vColor");
       GLES20.glUniform4fv(mColorHandle, 1, color, 0);
       GLES20.glDrawArrays(GLES20.GL_TRIANGLES, 0, vertexCount);
       GLES20.glDisableVertexAttribArray(mPositionHandle);
   }
   ```

6. Now open `MainActivity.java` and add a `Triangle` variable to the `GLRenderer` class as follows:

   ```
   private Triangle mTriangle;
   ```

7. Initialize the `Triangle` variable in the `onSurfaceCreated()` callback, as follows:

   ```
   mTriangle = new Triangle();
   ```

A First Look at OpenGL ES

8. Call the `draw()` method in the `onDrawFrame()` callback:

   `mTriangle.draw();`

9. You're ready to run the application on a device or emulator.

How it works...

As mentioned in the introduction, to draw with OpenGL, we first have to define the shaders, which we do with the following code:

```
private final String vertexShaderCode =
        "attribute vec4 vPosition;" +
            "void main() {" +
            "  gl_Position = vPosition;" +
            "}";

private final String fragmentShaderCode =
        "precision mediump float;" +
            "uniform vec4 vColor;" +
            "void main() {" +
            "  gl_FragColor = vColor;" +
            "}";
```

Since this is uncompiled **OpenGL Shading Language (OpenGLSL)**, the next step is to compile and attach it to our OpenGL object, which we do with the following two OpenGL ES methods:

- `glAttachShader()`
- `glLinkProgram()`

After setting up the shaders, we create `ByteBuffer` to store the triangle vertices, which are defined in `triangleCoords`. The `draw()` method is where the actual drawing occurs using the GLES20 library calls, which is called from the `onDrawFrame()` callback.

There's more...

You may have noticed, from the screenshots in the introduction, that the triangles in the Portrait and Landscape do look identical. As you can see from the code, we make no distinction in the orientation when drawing. We'll explain why this is happening and show how to correct this issue in the next recipe.

See also

For more information on the OpenGL Shading Language, refer the following link:

https://www.opengl.org/documentation/glsl/

Applying Projection and Camera View while drawing

As we saw in the previous recipe, when we draw our shape to the screen, the shape is skewed by the screen orientation. The reason for this is because, by default, OpenGL assumes a perfectly square screen. We mentioned before, the default screen coordinates for the top right is (1,1,0) and bottom left is (-1,-1,0).

Since most device screens are not perfectly square, we need to map the display coordinates to match our physical device. In OpenGL, we do this with *Projection*. This recipe will show how to use Projection to match the GLSurfaceView coordinates with the device coordinates. Along with the Projection, we'll also show how to set the Camera View. Here's a screenshot showing the final result:

Getting ready

Create a new project in Android Studio and call it: `ProjectionAndCamera`. Use the default **Phone & Tablet** options and select **Empty Activity** when prompted for **Activity Type**.

This recipe builds on the previous recipe *Drawing shapes on the GLSurfaceView*. If you have not already typed in the previous recipe, do so before starting these steps.

A First Look at OpenGL ES

How to do it...

As stated previously, this recipe will build on the previous recipe, so complete those steps before starting. We will be modifying the previous code to add projection and camera view to the drawing calculations. Here are the steps:

1. Open the `Triangle` class and add the following global declaration to the existing declarations:

   ```
   private int mMVPMatrixHandle;
   ```

2. Add a matrix variable to `vertexShaderCode` and use it in the position calculation. Here is the final result:

   ```
   private final String vertexShaderCode =
           "attribute vec4 vPosition;" +
           "uniform mat4 uMVPMatrix;" +
           "void main() {" +
           "  gl_Position = uMVPMatrix * vPosition;" +
           "}";
   ```

3. Change the `draw()` method to pass in a matrix parameter as follows:

   ```
   public void draw(float[] mvpMatrix) {
   ```

4. To use the transformation matrix, add the following code to the `draw()` method just before the `GLES20.glDrawArrays()` method:

   ```
   mMVPMatrixHandle = GLES20.glGetUniformLocation(mProgram,
   "uMVPMatrix");
   GLES20.glUniformMatrix4fv(mMVPMatrixHandle, 1, false, mvpMatrix,
   0);
   ```

5. Open `MainActivity.java` and add the following class variables to the `GLRenderer` class:

   ```
   private final float[] mMVPMatrix = new float[16];
   private final float[] mProjectionMatrix = new float[16];
   private final float[] mViewMatrix = new float[16];
   ```

6. Modify the `onSurfaceChanged()` callback to calculate the position matrix as follows:

   ```
   public void onSurfaceChanged(GL10 unused, int width, int height) {
       GLES20.glViewport(0, 0, width, height);
       float ratio = (float) width / height;
       Matrix.frustumM(mProjectionMatrix, 0, -ratio, ratio, -1, 1, 3, 7);
   }
   ```

7. Modify the `onDrawFrame()` callback to calculate the Camera View as follows:
   ```
   public void onDrawFrame(GL10 unused) {
       Matrix.setLookAtM(mViewMatrix, 0, 0, 0, -3, 0f, 0f, 0f, 0f,
           1.0f, 0.0f);
       Matrix.multiplyMM(mMVPMatrix, 0, mProjectionMatrix, 0,
           mViewMatrix, 0);
       GLES20.glClear(GLES20.GL_COLOR_BUFFER_BIT);
       mTriangle.draw(mMVPMatrix);
   }
   ```

8. You're ready to run the application on a device or emulator.

How it works...

First, we modify the `vertexShaderCode` to include a matrix variable. We calculate the matrix in the `onSurfaceChanged()` callback using the height and width, which are passed in as parameters. We pass the transformation matrix to the `draw()` method to use it when calculating the position to draw.

Before we call the `draw()` method, we calculate the camera view. These two lines of code calculate the camera view:

```
Matrix.setLookAtM(mViewMatrix, 0, 0, 0, -3, 0f, 0f, 0f, 0f, 1.0f,
    0.0f);
Matrix.multiplyMM(mMVPMatrix, 0, mProjectionMatrix, 0, mViewMatrix,
    0);
```

Without this code, there would actually be no triangle drawn as the camera perspective would not "see" our vertices. (This goes back to our discussion on how the order of the vertices dictate the front and back of the image.)

When you run the program now, you'll see the output shown in the *Introduction*. Notice we have a uniform triangle now, even when the display is rotated.

There's more...

In the next recipe, we will start showing the power of OpenGL by rotating the triangle.

Moving the triangle with rotation

What we've demonstrated so far with OpenGL would probably be easier using the traditional canvas or drawable objects. This recipe will show a bit of the power of OpenGL by rotating the triangle. Not that we can't create movement with the other drawing methods, but how easily we can do this with OpenGL!

A First Look at OpenGL ES

This recipe will demonstrate how to rotate the triangle, as this screenshot shows:

Getting ready

Create a new project in Android Studio and call it: `CreatingMovement`. Use the default **Phone & Tablet** options and select **Empty Activity** when prompted for **Activity Type**.

This recipe builds on the previous recipe *Applying Projection and Camera View While Drawing*. If you have not already typed in the previous recipe, do so before continuing.

How to do it...

Since we are continuing from the previous recipe, we have very little work to do. Open `MainActivity.java` and follow these steps:

1. Add a Matrix to the `GLRendered` class:

   ```
   private float[] mRotationMatrix = new float[16];
   ```

2. In the `onDrawFrame()` callback, replace the existing `mTriangle.draw(mMVPMatrix);` statement with the following code:

   ```
   float[] tempMatrix = new float[16];
   long time = SystemClock.uptimeMillis() % 4000L;
   ```

```
    float angle = 0.090f * ((int) time);
    Matrix.setRotateM(mRotationMatrix, 0, angle, 0, 0, -1.0f);
    Matrix.multiplyMM(tempMatrix, 0, mMVPMatrix, 0, mRotationMatrix,
    0);
    mTriangle.draw(tempMatrix);
```

3. You're ready to run the application on a device or emulator.

How it works...

We're using the `Matrix.setRotateM()` method to calculate a new rotation matrix based on the angle we pass in. For this example, we're using the system uptime to calculate an angle. We can use whatever method we want to derive an angle, such as a sensor reading or touch events.

There's more...

Using the system clock provides the added benefit of creating continuous movement, which certainly looks better for demonstration purposes. The next recipe will demonstrate how to use user input to derivate an angle for rotating the triangle.

The render mode

OpenGL offers a `setRenderMode()` option to draw only when the view is dirty. This can be enabled by adding the following code to the `CustomGLSurfaceView()` constructor just below the `setRenderer()` call:

```
    setRenderMode(GLSurfaceView.RENDERMODE_WHEN_DIRTY);
```

This will cause the display to update once, then wait until we request an update with `requestRender()`.

Rotating the triangle with user input

The previous example demonstrated rotating the triangle based on the system clock. This created a continuously rotating triangle, depending on the render mode we used. But what if you wanted to respond to the input from the user?

In this recipe, we'll show how to respond to user input by overriding the `onTouchEvent()` callback from `GLSurfaceView`. We'll still rotate the triangle using the `Matrix.setRotateM()` method, but instead of deriving an angle from the system time, we'll calculate an angle based on the touch location.

A First Look at OpenGL ES

Here's a screenshot showing this recipe running on a physical device (to highlight the touch, the **Show touches** developer option is enabled):

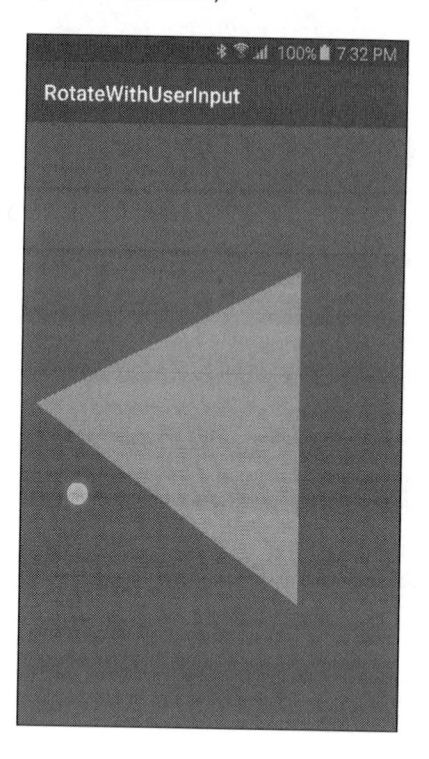

Getting ready

Create a new project in Android Studio and call it: `RotateWithUserInput`. Use the default **Phone & Tablet** options and select **Empty Activity** when prompted for **Activity Type**.

This recipe demonstrates an alternative approach to the previous recipe and therefore will be based on *Applying projection and camera view while drawing* (the same starting point as the previous recipe.)

How to do it...

As stated previously, we will continue, not from the previous recipe, but from the *Applying projection and camera view while drawing* recipe. Open `MainActivity.java` and follow these steps:

1. Add the following global variables to the `MainActivity` class:
   ```
   private float mCenterX=0;
   private float mCenterY=0;
   ```

2. Add the following code the `GLRendered` class:

   ```
   private float[] mRotationMatrix = new float[16];
   public volatile float mAngle;
   public void setAngle(float angle) {
       mAngle = angle;
   }
   ```

3. In the same class, modify the `onDrawFrame()` method by replacing the existing `mTriangle.draw(mMVPMatrix);` statement with the following code:

   ```
   float[] tempMatrix = new float[16];
   Matrix.setRotateM(mRotationMatrix, 0, mAngle, 0, 0, -1.0f);
   Matrix.multiplyMM(tempMatrix, 0, mMVPMatrix, 0, mRotationMatrix, 0);
   mTriangle.draw(tempMatrix);
   ```

4. Add the following code to the `onSurfaceChanged()` callback:

   ```
   mCenterX=width/2;
   mCenterY=height/2;
   ```

5. Add the following code to the `CustomGLSurfaceView` constructor, which is below `setRenderer()`:

   ```
   setRenderMode(GLSurfaceView.RENDERMODE_WHEN_DIRTY);
   ```

6. Add the following `onTouchEvent()` to the `CustomGLSurfaceView` class:

   ```
   @Override
   public boolean onTouchEvent(MotionEvent e) {
     float x = e.getX();
     float y = e.getY();
     switch (e.getAction()) {
         case MotionEvent.ACTION_MOVE:
             double angleRadians = Math.atan2(y-mCenterY,x-mCenterX);
             mGLRenderer.setAngle((float)Math.toDegrees
                (-angleRadians));
             requestRender();
     }
     return true;
   }
   ```

7. You're ready to run the application on a device or emulator.

A First Look at OpenGL ES

How it works...

The obvious difference between this example and the previous recipe is how we derive the angle to pass to the `Matrix.setRotateM()` call. We also changed the `GLSurfaceView` render mode using `setRenderMode()` to only draw on request. We made the request using `requestRender()` after calculating a new angle in the `onTouchEvent()` callback.

We also demonstrated the importance of deriving our own `GLSurfaceView` class. Without our `CustomGLSurfaceView` class, we would not have a way to override the `onTouchEvent` callback, or any other callbacks from `GLSurfaceView`.

There's more...

This concludes the OpenGL ES recipes but we've only just touched upon the power of OpenGL. If you're serious about learning OpenGL, see the links in the next section and check out one of the many books written on OpenGL.

It's also worth checking out one of the many frameworks available, such as the Unreal Engine:

> Unreal Engine 4 is a complete suite of game development tools made by game developers, for game developers.
> https://www.unrealengine.com/what-is-unreal-engine-4

See also

- **OpenGL:** The Industry Standard for High Performance Graphics

    https://www.opengl.org/

- **OpenGL ES:** The Standard for Embedded Accelerated 3D Graphics

    https://www.khronos.org/opengles/

- **Unreal Engine:** Android Quick Start

    https://docs.unrealengine.com/latest/INT/Platforms/Android/GettingStarted/index.html

11
Multimedia

In this chapter, we will cover the following topics:

- Playing sound effects with SoundPool
- Playing audio with MediaPlayer
- Responding to hardware media controls in your app
- Taking a photo with the default camera app
- Taking a photo using the (old) Camera API
- Taking a photo using the Camera2 (the new) API

Introduction

Now that we've explored graphics and animations in the previous chapters, it's time to look at the sound options available in Android. The two most popular options to play sound include:

- **SoundPool**: This is for short sound clips
- **MediaPlayer**: This is designed for larger sound files (like music) and video files

The first two recipes will look at using these libraries. We'll also look at how to use hardware related to sound, such as the volume controls and media playback controls (play, pause, and so on often found on headphones).

The rest of the chapter will focus on using the camera, both indirectly through Intents (to pass the camera request to the default camera application) and directly using the camera APIs. We'll examine the new Camera2 APIs released with Android 5.0 Lollipop (API 21), but we'll also look at the original Camera API since roughly 75 percent of the market doesn't have Lollipop yet. (To help you take advantage of the new features offered in the Camera2 API, we'll show a newer method for using the old Camera APIs to make it easier to use both Camera APIs in your own application.)

Multimedia

Playing sound effects with SoundPool

When you need sound effects in your application, SoundPool is usually a good starting point.

SoundPool is interesting in that it allows us to create special effects with our sounds by changing the play rate and by allowing multiple sounds to play simultaneously.

Popular audio file types supported include:

- 3GPP (.3gp)
- 3GPP (.3gp)
- FLAC (.flac)
- MP3 (.mp3)
- MIDI Type 0 and 1 (.mid, .xmf, and .mxmf)
- Ogg (.ogg)
- WAVE (.wav)

See the *Supported Media Formats* link for a complete list, including network protocols.

As is common in Android, new releases to the OS bring changes to the APIs. The `SoundPool` is no exception and the original `SoundPool` constructor was deprecated in Lollipop (API 21). Rather than setting our minimum API to 21 or relying on deprecated code (that may stop working at some point), we'll implement both the old and the new approach and check the OS version at runtime to use the appropriate method.

This recipe will demonstrate how to play sound effects using the Android `SoundPool` library. To demonstrate playing sounds simultaneously, we'll create two buttons, and each will play a sound when pressed.

Getting ready

Create a new project in Android Studio and call it: SoundPool. Use the default **Phone & Tablet** options, and select **Empty Activity** when prompted for **Activity Type**.

To demonstrate playing sounds simultaneously, we need at least two audio files in the project. We went to SoundBible.com (http://soundbible.com/royalty-free-sounds-5.html) and found two royalty-free public domain sounds to include in the download project files:

The first sound is a longer playing sound:

http://soundbible.com/2032-Water.html

The second sound is shorter:

http://soundbible.com/1615-Metal-Drop.html

How to do it...

As explained previously, we'll need two audio files to include in the project. Once you have your sound files ready, follow these steps:

1. Create a new raw folder (**File | New | Android resource directory**) and chose `raw` in the **Resource type** dropdown.
2. Copy your sound files to `res/raw` as `sound_1` and `sound_2`. (Keep their original extensions.)
3. Open `activity_main.xml` and replace the existing `TextView` with the following Buttons:

   ```
   <Button
       android:layout_width="wrap_content"
       android:layout_height="wrap_content"
       android:text="Play Sound 1"
       android:id="@+id/button1"
       android:layout_centerInParent="true"
       android:onClick="playSound1"/>
   <Button
       android:layout_width="wrap_content"
       android:layout_height="wrap_content"
       android:text="Play Sound 2"
       android:id="@+id/button2"
       android:layout_below="@+id/button1"
       android:layout_centerHorizontal="true"
       android:onClick="playSound2"/>
   ```

4. Now open `ActivityMain.java` and add the following global variables:

   ```
   HashMap<Integer, Integer> mHashMap= null;
   SoundPool mSoundPool;
   ```

5. Modify the existing `onCreate()` method, as follows:

   ```
   final Button button1=(Button)findViewById(R.id.button1);
   button1.setEnabled(false);
   final Button button2=(Button)findViewById(R.id.button2);
   button2.setEnabled(false);

   if (Build.VERSION.SDK_INT >= Build.VERSION_CODES.LOLLIPOP)
   {
       createSoundPoolNew();
   }else{
       createSoundPooolOld();
   }
   ```

Multimedia

```java
    mSoundPool.setOnLoadCompleteListener(new
        SoundPool.OnLoadCompleteListener() {
        @Override
        public void onLoadComplete(SoundPool soundPool, int
            sampleId, int status) {
            button1.setEnabled(true);
            button2.setEnabled(true);
        }
    });
    mHashMap = new HashMap<>();
    mHashMap.put(1, mSoundPool.load(this, R.raw.sound_1, 1));
    mHashMap.put(2, mSoundPool.load(this, R.raw.sound_2, 1));
```

6. Add the `createSoundPoolNew()` method:

```java
@TargetApi(Build.VERSION_CODES.LOLLIPOP)
private void createSoundPoolNew() {
    AudioAttributes audioAttributes = new
        AudioAttributes.Builder()
        .setUsage(AudioAttributes.USAGE_MEDIA)
        .setContentType(
            AudioAttributes.CONTENT_TYPE_SONIFICATION)
        .build();
    mSoundPool = new SoundPool.Builder()
            .setAudioAttributes(audioAttributes)
            .setMaxStreams(2)
            .build();
}
```

7. Add the `createSoundPooolOld()` method:

```java
@SuppressWarnings("deprecation")
private void createSoundPooolOld(){
    mSoundPool = new SoundPool(2, AudioManager.STREAM_MUSIC, 0);
}
```

8. Add the button `onClick()` methods:

```java
public void playSound1(View view){
    mSoundPool.play(mHashMap.get(1), 0.1f, 0.1f, 1, 0,
        1.0f);
}

public void playSound2(View view){
    mSoundPool.play(mHashMap.get(2), 0.9f, 0.9f, 1, 1,
        1.0f);
}
```

9. Override the `onStop()` callback as follows:

   ```
   protected void onStop() {
       super.onStop();
       mSoundPool.release();
   }
   ```

10. Run the application on a device or emulator.

How it works...

The first detail to notice is how we construct the object itself. As we mentioned in the introduction, the SoundPool constructor was changed in Lollipop (API 21). The old constructor was deprecated in favor of using `SoundPool.Builder()`. With a constantly changing environment like Android, changes in the API are very common, so it's a good idea to learn how to work with the changes. As you can see, it's not difficult in this case. We just check the current OS version and call the appropriate method. It is worth noting the method annotations:

   `@TargetApi(Build.VERSION_CODES.LOLLIPOP)`

And:

   `@SuppressWarnings("deprecation")`

After creating SoundPool, we set an `setOnLoadCompleteListener()` listener. Enabling the buttons is mostly for demonstration purposes to illustrate that SoundPool needs to load the sound resources before they are available.

The final point to make on using SoundPool is the call to `play()`. We need to pass in the soundID, which was returned when we loaded the sound using `load()`. The `Play()` gives us a few options, including sound volume (left and right), loop count, and playback rate. To demonstrate the flexibility, we play the first sound (which is longer) at a lower volume to create more of a background effect with the running water. The second sound plays at a higher volume and we play it twice.

There's more...

If you only need a basic sound effect, such as a click, you can use the AudioManager `playSoundEffect()` method. Here's an example:

   ```
   AudioManager audioManager = (AudioManager)
   this.getSystemService(Context.AUDIO_SERVICE);
   audioManager.playSoundEffect(SoundEffectConstants.CLICK);
   ```

You can only specify a sound from the `SoundEffectConstants`; you cannot use your own sound files.

Multimedia

See also

- **Developer Docs: SoundPool**

    `https://developer.android.com/reference/android/media/SoundPool.html`

- **Developer Docs: AudioManager**

    `https://developer.android.com/reference/android/media/AudioManager.html`

Playing audio with MediaPlayer

MediaPlayer is probably one of the most important classes for adding multimedia capability to your applications. It supports the following media sources:

- Project resources
- Local files
- External resources (such as URLs, including streaming)

MediaPlayer supports the following popular audio files:

- 3GPP (`.3gp`)
- 3GPP (`.3gp`)
- FLAC (`.flac`)
- MP3 (`.mp3`)
- MIDI Type 0 and 1 (`.mid`, `.xmf`, and `.mxmf`)
- Ogg (`.ogg`)
- WAVE (`.wav`)

And these popular file types:

- 3GPP (`.3gp`)
- Matroska (`.mkv`)
- WebM (`.webm`)
- MPEG-4 (`.mp4`, `.m4a`)

See the *Supported Media Formats* link for a complete list, including network protocols.

This recipe will demonstrate how to set up MediaPlayer in your app to play a sound included with your project. (For a complete review of the full capability offered by MediaPlayer, see the Developer Docs link at the end of this recipe.)

Getting ready

Create a new project in Android Studio and call it: `MediaPlayer`. Use the default **Phone & Tablet** options and select **Empty Activity** when prompted for **Activity Type**.

We will also need a sound for this recipe and will use the same longer playing "water" sound used in the previous recipe.

The first sound is a longer playing sound:

`http://soundbible.com/2032-Water.html`

How to do it...

As explained previously, we'll need a sound file to include in the project. Once you have your sound file ready, follow these steps:

1. Create a new raw folder (**File | New | Android resource directory**) and chose `raw` in the **resource type** dropdown
2. Copy your sound file to `res/raw` as `sound_1`. (Keep the original extension.)
3. Open `activity_main.xml` and replace the existing `TextView` with the following buttons:

    ```
    <Button
        android:layout_width="100dp"
        android:layout_height="wrap_content"
        android:text="Play"
        android:id="@+id/buttonPlay"
        android:layout_above="@+id/buttonPause"
        android:layout_centerHorizontal="true"
        android:onClick="buttonPlay" />
    <Button
        android:layout_width="100dp"
        android:layout_height="wrap_content"
        android:text="Pause"
        android:id="@+id/buttonPause"
        android:layout_centerInParent="true"
        android:onClick="buttonPause"/>
    <Button
        android:layout_width="100dp"
        android:layout_height="wrap_content"
        android:text="Stop"
        android:id="@+id/buttonStop"
    ```

Multimedia

```
            android:layout_below="@+id/buttonPause"
            android:layout_centerHorizontal="true"
            android:onClick="buttonStop"/>
```

4. Now open `ActivityMain.java` and add the following global variable:

   ```
   MediaPlayer mMediaPlayer;
   ```

5. Add the `buttonPlay()` method:

   ```
   public void buttonPlay(View view) {
       if (mMediaPlayer==null) {
           mMediaPlayer = MediaPlayer.create(this, R.raw.sound_1);
           mMediaPlayer.setLooping(true);
           mMediaPlayer.start();
       } else {
           mMediaPlayer.start();
       }
   }
   ```

6. Add the `buttonPause()` method:

   ```
   public void buttonPause(View view) {
       if (mMediaPlayer!=null && mMediaPlayer.isPlaying()) {
           mMediaPlayer.pause();
       }
   }
   ```

7. Add the `buttonStop()` method:

   ```
   public void buttonStop(View view) {
       if (mMediaPlayer!=null) {
           mMediaPlayer.stop();
           mMediaPlayer.release();
           mMediaPlayer = null;
       }
   }
   ```

8. Finally, override the `onStop()` callback with the following code:

   ```
   protected void onStop() {
       super.onStop();
       if (mMediaPlayer!=null) {
           mMediaPlayer.release();
           mMediaPlayer = null;
       }
   }
   ```

9. You're ready to run the application on a device or emulator.

How it works...

The code here is pretty straightforward. We create MediaPlayer with our sound and start playing the sound. The buttons will replay, pause, and stop accordingly.

Even this basic example illustrates one very important concept regarding MediaPlayer, and that is the *state*. If you're making serious use of MediaPlayer, review the link provided below for detailed information.

There's more...

To make our demonstration easier to follow, we use the UI thread for all our operations. For this example, using a short audio file included with the project, we aren't likely going to experience any UI delays. In general, it's a good idea to use a background thread when preparing MediaPlayer. To make this common task easier, MediaPlayer already includes an asynchronous prepare method called `prepareAsync()`. The following code will create an `OnPreparedListener()` listener and use the `prepareAsync()` method:

```java
mMediaPlayer = new MediaPlayer();
mMediaPlayer.setOnPreparedListener(new MediaPlayer.
OnPreparedListener() {
    @Override
    public void onPrepared(MediaPlayer mp) {
        mMediaPlayer.start();
    }
});
try {
    mMediaPlayer.setDataSource(*//*URI, URL or path here*//*));
} catch (IOException e) {
    e.printStackTrace();
}
mMediaPlayer.prepareAsync();
```

Playing music in the background

Our example is meant to play audio when the application is in the foreground, and will release the MediaPlayer resources in the `onStop()` callback. What if you are creating a music player and want to play music in the background, even when the user is using another application? In that scenario, you'll want to use MediaPlayer in a service, instead of an Activity. You'll use the MediaPlayer library the same way; you'll just need to pass information (such as sound selection) from the UI to your service.

> Note that since a service runs in the same UI thread as the activities, you still do not want to perform potentially blocking operations in a service. MediaPlayer does handle background threads to prevent blocking your UI Thread, otherwise, you would want to perform threading yourself. (See Chapter 14, *Getting Your App Ready for the Play Store* for more information on threading and options.)

Using hardware volume keys to control your app's audio volume

If you want the volume controls to control the volume in your app, use the `setVolumeControlStream()` method to specify your application's audio stream, as follows:

```
setVolumeControlStream(AudioManager.STREAM_MUSIC);
```

See the following `AudioManager` link for the other stream options.

See also

- **Supported Media Formats:** https://developer.android.com/guide/appendix/media-formats.html
- **Developer Docs: MediaPlayer** http://developer.android.com/reference/android/media/MediaPlayer.html
- **Developer Docs: AudioManager:** https://developer.android.com/reference/android/media/AudioManager.html

Responding to hardware media controls in your app

Having your app respond to media controls, such as Play, Pause, Skip, and so on, is a nice touch your users will appreciate.

Android makes this possible through the media library. As with the *Playing sound effects with SoundPool* recipe earlier, the Lollipop release changed how this is done. Unlike the `SoundPool` example, this recipe is able to take advantage of another approach—the compatibility library.

This recipe will show you how to set up `MediaSession` to respond to the hardware buttons, which will work on Lollipop and later, as well as previous `Lollilop` versions using the `MediaSessionCompat` library. (The Compatibility Library will take care of checking the OS version and using the correct API calls automatically.)

Getting ready

Create a new project in Android Studio and call it: `HardwareMediaControls`. Use the default **Phone & Tablet** options and select **Empty Activity** when prompted for the **Activity Type**.

How to do it...

We'll just be using Toasts messages to respond to the hardware events and therefore will not need to make any changes to the activity layout. To get started, open `ActivityMain.java` and follow these steps:

1. Create the following `mMediaSessionCallback` to respond to the media buttons:

    ```
    MediaSessionCompat.Callback mMediaSessionCallback = new
    MediaSessionCompat.Callback() {
        @Override
        public void onPlay() {
            super.onPlay();
            Toast.makeText(MainActivity.this, "onPlay()",
                Toast.LENGTH_SHORT).show();
        }
        @Override
        public void onPause() {
            super.onPause();
            Toast.makeText(MainActivity.this, "onPause()",
                Toast.LENGTH_SHORT).show();
        }
        @Override
        public void onSkipToNext() {
            super.onSkipToNext();
            Toast.makeText(MainActivity.this, "onSkipToNext()",
                Toast.LENGTH_SHORT).show();
        }
        @Override
        public void onSkipToPrevious() {
            super.onSkipToPrevious();
            Toast.makeText(MainActivity.this,
                "onSkipToPrevious()", Toast.LENGTH_SHORT).show();
        }
    };
    ```

Multimedia

2. Add the following code to the existing `onCreate()` callback:

```
MediaSessionCompat mediaSession =
  new MediaSessionCompat(this,
    getApplication().getPackageName());
mediaSession.setCallback(mMediaSessionCallback);
mediaSession.setFlags(MediaSessionCompat.
  FLAG_HANDLES_MEDIA_BUTTONS);
mediaSession.setActive(true);
PlaybackStateCompat state = new
  PlaybackStateCompat.Builder()
  .setActions(
    PlaybackStateCompat.ACTION_PLAY |
    PlaybackStateCompat.ACTION_PLAY_PAUSE |
    PlaybackStateCompat.ACTION_PAUSE |
    PlaybackStateCompat.ACTION_SKIP_TO_NEXT |
    PlaybackStateCompat.ACTION_SKIP_TO_PREVIOUS).build();
mediaSession.setPlaybackState(state);
```

3. Run the application on a device or emulator with media controls (such as headphones) to see the Toast messages.

How it works...

There are four steps to setting this up:

1. Create a `MediaSession.Callback` and attach it to MediaSession
2. Set the MediaSession flags to indicate we want the media buttons
3. Set `SessionState` to `active`
4. Set `PlayBackState` with the actions we're going to handle

Steps 4 and 1 work together as the Callback will only get the events set in the `PlayBackState`.

Since we're not actually controlling any playback in this recipe, we just demonstrate how to respond to the hardware events. You'll want to implement actual functionality in `PlayBackState` and include a call to `setState()` after the `setActions()` call.

This is a very nice example of how the changes to the API can make things easier. And since new `MediaSession` and `PlaybackState` were rolled in to the Compatibility Library, we can take advantage of these new APIs on older versions of the OS.

There's more...

Checking the hardware being used

If you want your app to respond differently based on the current output hardware, you can use `AudioManager` to check. Here's an example:

```
AudioManager audioManager =(AudioManager) this.
getSystemService(Context.AUDIO_SERVICE);
if (audioManager.isBluetoothA2dpOn()) {
    // Adjust output for Bluetooth.
} else if (audioManager.isSpeakerphoneOn()) {
    // Adjust output for Speakerphone.
} else if (audioManager.isWiredHeadsetOn()) {
    //Only checks if a wired headset is plugged in
    //May not be the audio output
} else {
    // Regular speakers?
}
```

See also

- **Developer Docs: MediaSession**

   https://developer.android.com/reference/android/media/session/MediaSession.html

- **Developer Docs: MediaSessionCompat**

   https://developer.android.com/reference/android/support/v4/media/session/MediaSessionCompat.html

- **Developer Docs: PlaybackState**

   https://developer.android.com/reference/android/support/v4/media/session/PlaybackStateCompat.html

- **Developer Docs: PlaybackStateCompat**

   https://developer.android.com/reference/android/support/v4/media/session/PlaybackStateCompat.html

Multimedia

Taking a photo with the default camera app

If your application needs an image from the camera, but is not a camera replacement app, it may be better to allow the "default" camera app to take the picture. This also respects your user's choice of a preferred camera application.

When you take a photo, unless it is specific to just your application, it's considered good practice to make the photo publicly available. (This allows it to be included in the user's photo gallery.) This recipe will demonstrate using the default photo application to click a picture, save it to the public folder, and display the image.

Getting ready

Create a new project in Android Studio and call it: `UsingTheDefaultCameraApp`. Use the default **Phone & Tablet** options and select **Empty Activity** when prompted for **Activity Type**.

How to do it...

We're going to create a layout with an ImageView and button. The button will create an Intent to launch the default Camera app. When the camera app is done, our app will get a callback. Start by opening the Android Manifest and follow these steps:

1. Add the following permission:

    ```xml
    <uses-permission
    android:name="android.permission.READ_EXTERNAL_STORAGE" />
    ```

2. Open the `activity_main.xml` file and replace the existing `TextView` with the following views:

    ```xml
    <ImageView
        android:layout_width="wrap_content"
        android:layout_height="wrap_content"
        android:id="@+id/imageView"
        android:src="@mipmap/ic_launcher"
        android:layout_centerInParent="true"/>

    <Button
        android:layout_width="wrap_content"
        android:layout_height="wrap_content"
        android:text="Take Picture"
        android:id="@+id/button"
        android:layout_alignParentBottom="true"
        android:layout_centerHorizontal="true"
        android:onClick="takePicture"/>
    ```

3. Open `MainActivity.java` and add the following global variables to the `MainActivity` class:

   ```
   final int PHOTO_RESULT=1;
   private Uri mLastPhotoURI=null;
   ```

4. Add the following method to create the URI for the photo:

   ```
   private Uri createFileURI() {
       String timeStamp = new SimpleDateFormat("yyyyMMdd_HHmmss").
           format(System.currentTimeMillis());
       String fileName = "PHOTO_" + timeStamp + ".jpg";
       return Uri.fromFile(new File(Environment.
           getExternalStoragePublicDirectory(
               Environment.DIRECTORY_PICTURES),fileName));
   }
   ```

5. Add the following method to handle the button click:

   ```
   public void takePicture(View view) {
       Intent takePictureIntent = new Intent(
           MediaStore.ACTION_IMAGE_ CAPTURE);
       if (takePictureIntent.resolveActivity(getPackageManager()) !=
           null) {
           mLastPhotoURI = createFileURI();
           takePictureIntent.putExtra(MediaStore.EXTRA_OUTPUT,
               mLastPhotoURI);
           startActivityForResult(takePictureIntent, PHOTO_RESULT);
       }
   }
   ```

6. Add a new method to override `onActivityResult()`, as follows:

   ```
   @Override
   protected void onActivityResult(int requestCode, int resultCode,
   Intent data) {
       if (requestCode == PHOTO_RESULT && resultCode == RESULT_OK ) {
           mImageView.setImageBitmap(BitmapFactory.
               decodeFile(mLastPhotoURI.getPath()));
       }
   }
   ```

7. You're ready to run the application on a device or emulator.

Multimedia

How it works...

There are two parts to working with the default camera app. The first is to set up the intent to launch the app. We create the Intent using `MediaStore.ACTION_IMAGE_CAPTURE` to indicate we want a photo app. We verify a default app exists by checking the results from `resolveActivity()`. As long as it's not null, we know an application is available to handle the intent. (Otherwise, our app will crash.) We create a filename and add it to the intent with: `putExtra(MediaStore.EXTRA_OUTPUT, mLastPhotoURI)`.

When we get the callback in `onActivityResult()`, we first make sure it's the `PHOTO_RESULT` and `RESULT_OK` (the user could have cancelled), then we load the photo in `ImageView`.

There's more...

If you don't care where the picture is stored, you can call the intent without using the `MediaStore.EXTRA_OUTPUT` extra. If you don't specify the output file, the `onActivityResult()` will include a thumbnail of the image in data Intent. Here is how you can display the thumbnail:

```
if (data != null) {
    imageView
 .setImageBitmap((Bitmap) data.getExtras().get("data"));
}
```

Here's the code to load the full resolution image, using the URI returned in `data Intent`:

```
if (data != null) {
    try {
        imageView.setImageBitmap(
            MediaStore.Images.Media. getBitmap(getContentResolver(),
            Uri.parse(data.toUri(Intent.URI_ALLOW_UNSAFE))));
    } catch (IOException e) {
        e.printStackTrace();
    }
}
```

Calling the default video app

It's the same process if you want to call the default video capture application. Just change the intent in Step 5, as follows:

```
Intent takeVideoIntent = new
    Intent(MediaStore.ACTION_VIDEO_CAPTURE);
```

You can get the URI to the video in the `onActivityResult()`, as follows:

    Uri videoUri = intent.getData();

See also

- The *Scaling down large images to avoid Out of Memory exceptions* recipe in *Chapter 9, Graphics and Animation*.

Taking a picture using the (old) Camera API

The previous recipe demonstrated how to use an intent to call the default photo application. If you only need a quick photo, the intent is probably the ideal solution. If not, and you need more control of the camera, this recipe will show you how to use the camera directly with the Camera API.

There are actually two recipes for using the Camera API—one for the original Camera API released in Android 1.0 (API 1) and Camera2 API, released in Android 5.0 (API 21). We'll cover both the new and the old APIs. Ideally, you will want to write your application to the latest and greatest APIs available, but at the time of this writing, Android 5.0 (API 21) only has about a 23 percent market share. If you only use the Camera2 API, you exclude over 75 percent of the market.

Write your app to use Camera2 API to take advantage of the new features available, but still have a functional application using the original Camera API for the rest of your users. To help facilitate using both, this recipe is going to take advantage of newer features in Android, specifically the `TextureView`, introduced in Android 4.0 (API 14). We'll use the `TextureView`, in place of the more traditional `SurfaceView`, for displaying the camera preview. This will allow you to use the same layout with the newer Camera2 API as it uses the `TextureView` as well. (Setting the minimum API to Android 4.0 (API 14) and above, which has over 96 percent market share, isn't limiting your user base much.)

Getting ready

Create a new project in Android Studio and call it `CameraAPI`. \On the **Target Android Devices** dialog, select the **Phone & Tablet** option and chose API 14 (or above) for the **Minimum SDK**. Select **Empty Activity** when prompted for **Activity Type**.

Multimedia

How to do it...

Start by opening the Android Manifest and following these steps:

1. Add the following two permissions:

   ```
   <uses-permission android:name="android.permission.CAMERA"/>
   <uses-permission
   android:name="android.permission.WRITE_EXTERNAL_STORAGE" />
   ```

2. Now open `activity_main.xml` and replace the existing TextView with the following views:

   ```
   <TextureView
       android:layout_width="match_parent"
       android:layout_height="match_parent"
       android:id="@+id/textureView"
       android:layout_alignParentTop="true"
       android:layout_centerHorizontal="true" />

   <Button
       android:layout_width="wrap_content"
       android:layout_height="wrap_content"
       android:text="Take Picture"
       android:id="@+id/button"
       android:layout_alignParentBottom="true"
       android:layout_centerHorizontal="true"
       android:onClick="takePicture"/>
   ```

3. Open `MainActivity.java` and modify the `MainActivity` class declaration to implement the `SurfaceTextureListener`, as follows:

   ```
   public class MainActivity extends AppCompatActivity
           implements TextureView.SurfaceTextureListener {
   ```

4. Add the following global declarations to `MainActivity`:

   ```
   @Deprecated
   private Camera mCamera;
   private TextureView mTextureView;
   ```

5. Create the following `PictureCallback` to handle saving the photo:

   ```
   Camera.PictureCallback pictureCallback = new
     Camera.PictureCallback() {
       @Override
       public void onPictureTaken(byte[] data, Camera camera) {
           try {
   ```

286

```
                String timeStamp = new SimpleDateFormat(
                    "yyyyMMdd_HHmmss").format(
                      System.currentTimeMillis());
                String fileName = "PHOTO_" + timeStamp +
                    ".jpg";
                File pictureFile = new File(Environment.
                    getExternalStoragePublicDirectory(
                      Environment.DIRECTORY_PICTURES),fileName);

                FileOutputStream fileOutputStream =new
                    FileOutputStream(pictureFile.getPath());
                fileOutputStream.write(data);
                fileOutputStream.close();
                Toast.makeText(MainActivity.this, "Picture
                    Taken", Toast.LENGTH_SHORT).show();
            } catch (Exception e) {
                e.printStackTrace();
            }
        }
    };
```

6. Add the following code to the existing `onCreate()` callback:

```
mTextureView = (TextureView)findViewById(R.id.textureView);
mTextureView.setSurfaceTextureListener(this);
```

7. Add the following methods to implement the `SurfaceTextureListener` interface:

```
public void onSurfaceTextureAvailable(SurfaceTexture surface, int
width, int height) {
    mCamera = Camera.open();
    if (mCamera!=null) {
        try {
            mCamera.setPreviewTexture(surface);
            mCamera.startPreview();
        } catch (IOException e) {
            e.printStackTrace();
        }
    }
}
public boolean onSurfaceTextureDestroyed(SurfaceTexture
  surface) {
    if (mCamera!=null) {
        mCamera.stopPreview();
        mCamera.release();
    }
    return true;
}
```

Multimedia

```
      public void onSurfaceTextureSizeChanged(SurfaceTexture
        surface, int width, int height) {
          // Unused
      }
      public void onSurfaceTextureUpdated(SurfaceTexture surface)
      {
          // Unused
      }
```

8. Add the following method to handle the button click:

   ```
   public void takePicture(View view) {
       if (mCamera!=null) {
           mCamera.takePicture(null, null, pictureCallback);
       }
   }
   ```

9. Run the application on a device or emulator with a camera.

How it works...

The first thing to note is, when you're looking at this code in Android Studio, you're going to see a lot of strikethrough code with the following warning:

   `'android.hardware.Camera' is deprecated`

As mentioned in the introduction, the `android.hardware.camera2` API was introduced in Android 5.0 (API 19) and replaces the `android.hardware.camera` APIs.

> You can add the following annotation to suppress the Deprecation warning:
> `@SuppressWarnings("deprecation")`

There are two main steps when using the Camera API:

- Set up the preview
- Capture the image

We get the `TextureView` from our layout, then assign our activity (which implements `SurfaceTextureListener`) as the listener using this code:

   `mTextureView.setSurfaceTextureListener(this);`

When the `TextureView` surface is ready, we get the `onSurfaceTextureAvailable` callback, where we set the preview surface with the following code:

```
mCamera.setPreviewTexture(surface);
mCamera.startPreview();
```

The next step is to take the picture when the button is pressed. We do that with this code:

```
mCamera.takePicture(null, null, pictureCallback);
```

When the picture is ready, we get the `onPictureTaken()` callback in the `Camera.PictureCallback` class we created.

There's more...

Keep in mind, this code is meant to show you how it works, not to create a full commercial application. As most developers know, the real challenge in coding is to handle all the problem cases. Some areas to improve include adding the ability to switch cameras, as the app currently uses the default camera. Also, take a look at the device orientation for both the preview and when saving a picture. A more sophisticated app would handle some of the work on a background thread to avoid delays on the UI thread. (Take a look at the next recipe to see how we do some of the camera processing on a background thread.)

Setting the camera parameters

The Camera API includes parameters, which allow us to adjust the camera settings. With this example, we can change the size of the preview:

```
Camera.Parameters parameters = mCamera.getParameters();
parameters.setPreviewSize(mPreviewSize.width,
mPreviewSize.height);
mCamera.setParameters(parameters);
```

Keep in mind, the hardware must also support the setting we want. In this example, we'd want to query the hardware first to get all available preview modes, then set the one that matches our requirements. (See an example of this in the next recipe when we set the picture resolution.) See `getParameters()` in the Camera documentation link.

See also

- The next recipe: *Taking a picture using the Camera2 (the new) API*
- The *Reading device orientation* recipe in *Chapter 8, Using the Touchscreen and Sensors* for examples on detecting the current device orientation
- **Developer Docs: Building a Camera App** at: https://developer.android.com/guide/topics/media/camera.html#custom-camera
- **Developer Docs: Camera API** at: https://developer.android.com/reference/android/hardware/Camera.html

Multimedia

Taking a picture using the Camera2 (the new) API

Now that we've looked at the old Camera API, it's time to learn about the new Camera2 API. Unfortunately, it's a bit more complicated due to the asynchronous nature of the APIs. Fortunately, the overall concept is the same as the previous Camera API.

Getting ready

Create a new project in Android Studio and call it `Camera2API`. On the **Target Android Devices** dialog, select the **Phone & Tablet** option and chose API 21 (or higher) for the **Minimum SDK**. Select **Empty Activity** when prompted for **Activity Type**.

How to do it...

As you'll see, there's a lot of code for this recipe. Start by opening the Android Manifest and following these steps:

1. Add the following two permissions:

    ```xml
    <uses-permission android:name="android.permission.CAMERA" />
    <uses-permission android:name="android.permission.WRITE_EXTERNAL_STORAGE" />
    ```

2. Now open `activity_main.xml` and replace the existing TextView with the following views:

    ```xml
    <TextureView
        android:layout_width="match_parent"
        android:layout_height="match_parent"
        android:id="@+id/textureView"
        android:layout_alignParentTop="true"
        android:layout_centerHorizontal="true" />

    <Button
        android:layout_width="wrap_content"
        android:layout_height="wrap_content"
        android:text="Take Picture"
        android:id="@+id/button"
        android:layout_alignParentBottom="true"
        android:layout_centerHorizontal="true"
        android:onClick="takePicture"/>
    ```

3. Now open the `MainActivity.java` file and add the following global variables to the `MainActivity` class:

   ```
   private CameraDevice mCameraDevice = null;
   private CaptureRequest.Builder mCaptureRequestBuilder = null;
   private CameraCaptureSession mCameraCaptureSession = null;
   private TextureView mTextureView = null;
   private Size mPreviewSize = null;
   ```

4. Add the following `Comparator` class:

   ```
   static class CompareSizesByArea implements Comparator<Size> {
       @Override
       public int compare(Size lhs, Size rhs) {
           return Long.signum((long) lhs.getWidth() * lhs.getHeight()
   - (long) rhs.getWidth() * rhs.getHeight());
       }
   }
   ```

5. Add the following `CameraDevice.StateCallback`:

   ```
   private CameraDevice.StateCallback mStateCallback = new CameraDevice.StateCallback() {
       @Override
       public void onOpened(CameraDevice camera) {
           mCameraDevice = camera;
           SurfaceTexture texture = mTextureView.getSurfaceTexture();
           if (texture == null) {
               return;
           }
           texture.setDefaultBufferSize(
               mPreviewSize.getWidth(), mPreviewSize.getHeight());
           Surface surface = new Surface(texture);
           try {
               mCaptureRequestBuilder = mCameraDevice.
                   createCaptureRequest(CameraDevice.
                   TEMPLATE_PREVIEW);
           } catch (CameraAccessException e){
               e.printStackTrace();
           }
           mCaptureRequestBuilder.addTarget(surface);
           try {
               mCameraDevice.createCaptureSession(Arrays.
                   asList(surface), mPreviewStateCallback, null);
           } catch (CameraAccessException e) {
               e.printStackTrace();
           }
       }
       @Override
   ```

Multimedia

```
        public void onError(CameraDevice camera, int error) {}
        @Override
        public void onDisconnected(CameraDevice camera) {}
};
```

6. Add the following `SurfaceTextureListener`:

    ```
    private TextureView.SurfaceTextureListener mSurfaceTextureListener =
            new TextureView.SurfaceTextureListener() {
        @Override
        public void onSurfaceTextureUpdated(SurfaceTexture surface) {}
        @Override
        public void onSurfaceTextureSizeChanged(
                SurfaceTexture surface, int width, int height) {}
        @Override
        public boolean onSurfaceTextureDestroyed(
                SurfaceTexture surface) {
            return false;
        }
        @Override
        public void onSurfaceTextureAvailable(
                SurfaceTexture surface, int width, int height) {
            openCamera();
        }
    };
    ```

7. Add the following `CameraCaptureSession.StateCallback`:

    ```
    private CameraCaptureSession.StateCallback mPreviewStateCallback =
    new CameraCaptureSession.StateCallback() {
        @Override
        public void onConfigured(CameraCaptureSession session) {
            startPreview(session);
        }

        @Override
        public void onConfigureFailed(CameraCaptureSession session) {}
    };
    ```

8. Add the following code to the existing `onCreate()` callback:

    ```
    mTextureView = (TextureView) findViewById(R.id.textureView);
    mTextureView.setSurfaceTextureListener(mSurfaceTextureListener);
    ```

9. Add the following methods to override `onPause()` and `onResume()`:

    ```
    @Override
    protected void onPause() {
        super.onPause();
    ```

```java
        if (mCameraDevice != null) {
            mCameraDevice.close();
            mCameraDevice = null;
        }
    }
    @Override
    public void onResume() {
        super.onResume();
        if (mTextureView.isAvailable()) {
            openCamera();
        } else {
            mTextureView.setSurfaceTextureListener(
                mSurfaceTextureListener);
        }
    }
```

10. Add the `openCamera()` method:

```java
    private void openCamera() {
        CameraManager manager = (CameraManager) getSystemService(
            CAMERA_SERVICE);
        try{
            String cameraId = manager.getCameraIdList()[0];
            CameraCharacteristics characteristics =
                manager.getCameraCharacteristics(cameraId);
            StreamConfigurationMap map = characteristics.get(
                CameraCharacteristics.SCALER_STREAM_CONFIGURATION_MAP);
            mPreviewSize = map.getOutputSizes(SurfaceTexture.class)[0];
            manager.openCamera(cameraId, mStateCallback, null);
        } catch(CameraAccessException e) {
            e.printStackTrace();
        } catch (SecurityException e) {
            e.printStackTrace();
        }
    }
```

11. Add the `startPreview()` method:

```java
    private void startPreview(CameraCaptureSession session) {
        mCameraCaptureSession = session;
        mCaptureRequestBuilder.set(
            CaptureRequest.CONTROL_MODE,
            CameraMetadata.CONTROL_MODE_AUTO);
        HandlerThread backgroundThread = new HandlerThread(
            "CameraPreview");
        backgroundThread.start();
```

Multimedia

```java
        Handler backgroundHandler = new Handler(
            backgroundThread.getLooper());
        try {
            mCameraCaptureSession.setRepeatingRequest(
                mCaptureRequestBuilder.build(), null,
                    backgroundHandler);
        } catch (CameraAccessException e) {
            e.printStackTrace();
        }
    }
}
```

12. Add the `getPictureFile()` method:

```java
private File getPictureFile() {
    String timeStamp = new SimpleDateFormat(
        "yyyyMMdd_HHmmss").format(System.currentTimeMillis());
    String fileName = "PHOTO_" + timeStamp + ".jpg";
    return new File(Environment.getExternalStoragePublicDirectory(
        Environment.DIRECTORY_PICTURES),fileName);
}
```

13. Add the `takePicture()` method that saves the image file:

```java
protected void takePicture(View view) {
    if (null == mCameraDevice) {
        return;
    }
    CameraManager manager = (CameraManager)
        getSystemService(Context.CAMERA_SERVICE);
    try {
        CameraCharacteristics characteristics =
            manager.getCameraCharacteristics(
                mCameraDevice.getId());
        StreamConfigurationMap configurationMap =
            characteristics.get(CameraCharacteristics.
                SCALER_STREAM_CONFIGURATION_MAP);
        if (configurationMap == null) return;
        Size largest = Collections.max(
            Arrays.asList(configurationMap.getOutputSizes(
                ImageFormat.JPEG)),
            new CompareSizesByArea());
        ImageReader reader = ImageReader.newInstance(
            largest.getWidth(), largest.getHeight(),
                ImageFormat.JPEG, 1);
        List < Surface > outputSurfaces =
            new ArrayList < Surface > (2);
        outputSurfaces.add(reader.getSurface());
```

```java
outputSurfaces.add(new Surface(
    mTextureView.getSurfaceTexture()));
final CaptureRequest.Builder captureBuilder =
    mCameraDevice.createCaptureRequest(CameraDevice.
        TEMPLATE_STILL_ CAPTURE);
captureBuilder.addTarget(reader.getSurface());
captureBuilder.set(CaptureRequest.CONTROL_MODE,
    CameraMetadata.CONTROL_MODE_AUTO);
ImageReader.OnImageAvailableListener readerListener =
    new ImageReader.OnImageAvailableListener() {
        @Override
        public void onImageAvailable(ImageReader reader) {
            Image image = null;
            try {
                image = reader.acquireLatestImage();
                ByteBuffer buffer = image.getPlanes()[0].
                    getBuffer();
                byte[] bytes = new byte[buffer.capacity()];
                buffer.get(bytes);
                OutputStream output = new FileOutputStream(
                    get PictureFile());
                output.write(bytes);
                output.close();
            } catch (FileNotFoundException e) {
                e.printStackTrace();
            } catch (IOException e) {
                e.printStackTrace();
            } finally {
                if (image != null) {
                    image.close();
                }
            }
        }
    };
HandlerThread thread = new HandlerThread("CameraPicture");
thread.start();
final Handler backgroudHandler = new Handler(
    thread.getLooper());
reader.setOnImageAvailableListener(readerListener,
    backgroudHandler);
final CameraCaptureSession.CaptureCallback captureCallback
    = new CameraCaptureSession.CaptureCallback() {
        @Override
        public void onCaptureCompleted(
```

Multimedia

```
                CameraCaptureSession session, CaptureRequest request,
            TotalCaptureResult result) {
                    super.onCaptureCompleted(session, request,
                        result);
                    Toast.makeText(MainActivity.this, "Picture
                        Saved", Toast.LENGTH_SHORT).show();
                    startPreview(session);
                }
            };
            mCameraDevice.createCaptureSession(outputSurfaces, new
                CameraCaptureSession.StateCallback() {
                @Override
                public vod onConfigured(CameraCaptureSession session) {
                    try {
                        session.capture(captureBuilder.build(),
                            captureCallback, backgroudHandler);
                    } catch (CameraAccessException e) {
                        e.printStackTrace();
                    }
                }
                @Override
                public void onConfigureFailed(CameraCaptureSession
                    session) { }
            }, backgroudHandler);
        } catch (CameraAccessException e) {
            e.printStackTrace();
        }
    }
}
```

14. Run the application on a device or emulator with a camera.

How it works...

Since we learned about the TextureView in the previous recipe, we can jump to the new Camera2 API information.

Though there are more classes involved, just like the older Camera API, there are two basic steps:

- Setting up the preview
- Capturing the image

Setting up the preview

Here's a rundown on how the code sets up the preview:

1. First, we set up the `TextureView.SurfaceTextureListener` with the `setSurfaceTextureListener()` method in `onCreate()`.
2. When we get the `onSurfaceTextureAvailable()` callback, we open the camera.
3. We pass our `CameraDevice.StateCallback` class to the `openCamera()` method, which eventually calls the `onOpened()` callback.
4. `onOpened()` gets the surface for the preview by calling `getSurfaceTexture()` and passes it to the CameraDevice by calling `createCaptureSession()`.
5. Finally, when `CameraCaptureSession.StateCallback onConfigured()` is called, we start the preview with the `setRepeatingRequest()` method.

Capturing the image

Even though the `takePicture()` method may appear to be procedural, capturing an image also involves several classes and relies on callbacks. Here's a breakdown on how the code takes a picture:

1. The user clicks the **Take Picture** button.
2. Then queries the camera to find the largest available image size.
3. Then creates an `ImageReader`.
4. Next, he/she sets up `OnImageAvailableListener`, and saves the image in the `onImageAvailable()` callback.
5. Then, creates `CaptureRequest.Builder` and includes the `ImageReader` surface.
6. Next, creates `CameraCaptureSession.CaptureCallback`, which defines the `onCaptureCompleted()` callback. When the capture is complete, it restarts the preview.
7. Then, calls the `createCaptureSession()` method, creating a `CameraCaptureSession.StateCallback`. This is where the `capture()` method is called, passing in the `CameraCaptureSession.CaptureCallback` created earlier.

There's more...

As with the previous Camera example, we've just created the base code to demonstrate a working Camera application. Again, there are areas for improvement. First, you should handle the device orientation, for both the preview and when saving the images. (See the previous recipe for the link.) Also, with Android 6.0 (API 23) now available, it would be a good time to start using the new permission model. Instead of just checking for an exception as we do in the `openCamera()` method, it would be better to check for the required permission.

Multimedia

See also

- The previous recipe: *Taking a picture using the (old) Camera API*
- *The new Android 6.0 Run-Time permission model* in *Chapter 14, Getting Your App Ready for the Play Store*
- Developer Docs: Camera2 API
- `https://developer.android.com/reference/android/hardware/camera2/package-summary.html`

12
Telephony, Networks, and the Web

In this chapter, we will cover the following topics:

- How to make a phone call
- Monitoring phone call events
- How to send SMS (text) messages
- Receiving SMS messages
- Displaying a web page in your application
- Checking online status and connection type
- Getting started with Volley for Internet requests
- Canceling a Volley request
- Using Volley to request a JSON response
- Using Volley to request an image
- Using Volley's NetworkImageView and ImageLoader

Introduction

We'll start this chapter by looking at Telephony functionality with *How to make a phone call*. After exploring how to make a call, we'll look at how to monitor a phone call with *Monitoring phone call events*. We'll then move on to SMS messaging with *How to send SMS Messages*, and then we'll cover receiving SMS Messages with *Receiving SMS Messages*.

Telephony, Networks, and the Web

We'll then explore the `WebView` for adding browser functionality to your app. At its basic level, the `WebView` is a basic HTML viewer. We'll show how you can extend a `WebViewClient` class and modify the settings through `WebSettings` to create full browser functionality, including JavaScript and Zoom features.

The remaining chapter will cover Volley, a new library made available through AOSP. The *Getting started with Volley for Internet requests* introduction will give some background information on the online libraries available on Android and talk about why Volley was created. It also offers a complete walk-through of adding Volley to your Android Studio project.

How to make a phone call

As we've seen in previous recipes, we can call the default applications simply by using an Intent. To make a phone call, use `Intent.ACTION_DIAL` when creating an Intent. You can include a phone number with the `setData()` method. Here is sample code that will call up the Dialer app with the phone number specified:

```
Intent intent = new Intent(Intent.ACTION_DIAL);
intent.setData(Uri.parse("tel:" + number));
startActivity(intent);
```

Since your application is not doing the dialing and the user must press the **Dial** button, you do not need any dialing permissions in your app. The following recipe will show you how to place a call directly, bypassing the `Dial` activity. (For this, you will need to add a permission.)

Getting ready

Create a new project in Android Studio and call it `DialPhone`. Use the default **Phone & Tablet** option and select **Empty Activity** when prompted for **Activity Type**.

How to do it...

First, we need to add the appropriate permission to make the call. Then, we need to add a button to call our `Dial` method. Start by opening the Android Manifest and follow these steps:

1. Add the following permission:

    ```
    <uses-permission android:name=
        "android.permission.CALL_PHONE"></uses-permission>
    ```

2. Open `activity_main.xml` and replace the existing `TextView` with the following button:

    ```
    <Button
        android:id="@+id/button"
        android:layout_width="wrap_content"
    ```

```
            android:layout_height="wrap_content"
            android:text="Dial"
            android:layout_centerInParent="true"
            android:onClick="dialPhone"/>
```

3. Add this method that will check whether your app has been granted the CALL_PHONE permission:

```
private boolean checkPermission(String permission) {
    int permissionCheck =
        ContextCompat.checkSelfPermission(
            this, permission);
    return (permissionCheck ==
        PackageManager.PERMISSION_GRANTED);
}
```

4. Add the code to dial the number:

```
public void dialPhone(View view){
    if (checkPermission("android.permission.CALL_PHONE")) {
        Intent intent = new Intent(Intent.ACTION_CALL);
        intent.setData(Uri.parse("tel:0123456789"));
        startActivity(intent);
    }
}
```

5. Before running this on your device, be sure to replace 0123456789 with a valid number.

How it works...

As we saw from the code in the introduction, we don't need any permissions when calling the default Dialer application. But if we want to dial a number directly, we need to add the CALL_PHONE permission. Starting with Android 6.0 Marshmallow (API 23), permissions are no longer granted during installation, therefore, we check whether the application has permission before attempting to dial.

See also

- For more information, refer to the *The new Runtime permission model* recipe in *Chapter 14, Your App Ready for the Play Store*.

Telephony, Networks, and the Web

Monitoring phone call events

In the previous recipe, we demonstrated how to make a phone call, both with an Intent to call the default application as well as by directly dialing the number with no UI.

What if you want to be notified when the calls ends? This is where it gets a bit more complicated as you'll need to monitor the Telephony events and track the phone state. In this recipe, we'll demonstrate how to create a `PhoneStateListener` to read the phone state events.

Getting ready

Create a new project in Android Studio and call it `PhoneStateListener`. Use the default **Phone & Tablet** option and select **Empty Activity** when prompted for **Activity Type**.

Although it's not required, you can use the previous recipe to initiate a phone call to view the events. Otherwise, use the default dialer and/or watch the events from an incoming call. (The example code provided in the download files includes the previous recipe to make it easier to view the events.)

How to do it...

We only need a single `TextView` on the layout to display the event information. If you are continuing from the previous recipe or starting a new recipe, open the `activity_main.xml` file and follow these steps:

1. Add or modify the `TextView` as follows:

   ```
   <TextView
       android:id="@+id/textView"
       android:layout_width="wrap_content"
       android:layout_height="wrap_content" />
   ```

2. Add the following permission to the Android Manifest:

   ```
   <uses-permission android:name=
       "android.permission.READ_PHONE_STATE">
   </uses-permission>
   ```

3. Open `MainActivity.java` and add the following `PhoneStateListener` class to the `MainActivity` class:

   ```
   PhoneStateListener mPhoneStateListener = new
       PhoneStateListener() {
       @Override
       public void onCallStateChanged(int state,
           String number) {
           String phoneState = number;
   ```

```
            switch (state) {
                case TelephonyManager.CALL_STATE_IDLE:
                    phoneState += "CALL_STATE_IDLE\n";
                case TelephonyManager.CALL_STATE_RINGING:
                    phoneState += "CALL_STATE_RINGING\n";
                case TelephonyManager.CALL_STATE_OFFHOOK:
                    phoneState += "CALL_STATE_OFFHOOK\n";
            }
            TextView textView = (TextView)findViewById(
                R.id.textView);
            textView.append(phoneState);
        }
    };
```

4. Modify `onCreate()` to set up the listener:

   ```
   final TelephonyManager telephonyManager =
       (TelephonyManager)
           getSystemService(Context.TELEPHONY_SERVICE);
   telephonyManager.listen(mPhoneStateListener,
       PhoneStateListener.LISTEN_CALL_STATE);
   ```

5. Run the application on a device and initiate and/or receive phone calls to view the events.

How it works...

To demonstrate using the listener, we create the Telephony listener in the `onCreate()` with these two lines of code:

```
final TelephonyManager telephonyManager = (TelephonyManager)
    getSystemService(Context.TELEPHONY_SERVICE);
telephonyManager.listen(mPhoneStateListener,
    PhoneStateListener.LISTEN_CALL_STATE);
```

When a `PhoneState` event occurs, it is sent to our `PhoneStateListener` class.

There's more...

In this recipe, we are monitoring the Call State events, as indicated with this constant: `LISTEN_CALL_STATE`. The other interesting options include the following:

- `LISTEN_CALL_FORWARDING_INDICATOR`
- `LISTEN_DATA_CONNECTION_STATE`
- `LISTEN_SIGNAL_STRENGTHS`

Telephony, Networks, and the Web

Take a look at the following `PhoneStateListener` link for a complete list.

When we're done listening for events, call the `listen()` method and pass `LISTEN_NONE`, as shown here:

```
telephonyManager.listen(mPhoneStateListener,PhoneStateListener.LISTEN_NONE);
```

See also

- **Developer Docs: PhoneStateListener** at https://developer.android.com/reference/android/telephony/PhoneStateListener.html

How to send SMS (text) messages

Since you're probably already familiar with SMS (or text) messages, we won't spend time explaining what they are or why they are important. (If you're not familiar with SMS or want more information, see the link provided in the *See also* section of this recipe.) This recipe will demonstrate how to send an SMS Message. (The next recipe will demonstrate how to receive notifications of new messages and how to read existing messages.)

Getting ready

Create a new project in Android Studio and call it `SendSMS`. Use the default **Phone & Tablet** option and select **Empty Activity** when prompted for **Activity Type**.

How to do it...

First, we'll add the necessary permissions for sending an SMS. Then, we'll create a layout with a **Phone Number** and **Message** fields and a **Send** button. When the Send button is clicked on, we'll create and send the SMS. Here are the steps:

1. Open the Android Manifest and add the following permission:

    ```
    <uses-permission android:name=
        "android.permission.SEND_SMS"/>
    ```

2. Open `activity_main.xml` and replace the existing `TextView` with the following XML:

    ```
    <EditText
        android:id="@+id/editTextNumber"
        android:layout_width="match_parent"
        android:layout_height="wrap_content"
        android:inputType="number"
        android:ems="10"
    ```

```
            android:layout_alignParentTop="true"
            android:layout_centerHorizontal="true"
            android:hint="Number"/>
    <EditText
            android:id="@+id/editTextMsg"
            android:layout_width="match_parent"
            android:layout_height="wrap_content"
            android:layout_below="@+id/editTextNumber"
            android:layout_centerHorizontal="true"
            android:hint="Message"/>
    <Button
            android:id="@+id/buttonSend"
            android:layout_width="wrap_content"
            android:layout_height="wrap_content"
            android:text="Send"
            android:layout_below="@+id/editTextMsg"
            android:layout_centerHorizontal="true"
            android:onClick="send"/>
```

3. Open `MainActivity.java` and add the following global variables:

```
final int SEND_SMS_PERMISSION_REQUEST_CODE=1;
Button mButtonSend;
```

4. Add the following code to the existing `onCreate()` callback:

```
mButtonSend = (Button)findViewById(R.id.buttonSend);
mButtonSend.setEnabled(false);

if (checkCallPermission(Manifest.permission.SEND_SMS)) {
    mButtonSend.setEnabled(true);
} else {
    ActivityCompat.requestPermissions(this,
            new String[]{Manifest.permission.SEND_SMS},
            SEND_SMS_PERMISSION_REQUEST_CODE);
}
```

5. Add the following method to check the permission:

```
private boolean checkPermission(String permission) {
    int permissionCheck =
        ContextCompat.checkSelfPermission(this,permission);
    return (permissionCheck ==
        PackageManager.PERMISSION_GRANTED);
}
```

Telephony, Networks, and the Web

6. Override `onRequestPermissionsResult()` to handle the permission request response:

    ```
    @Override
    public void onRequestPermissionsResult(int requestCode,
            String permissions[], int[] grantResults) {
        switch (requestCode) {
            case SEND_SMS_PERMISSION_REQUEST_CODE: {
                if (grantResults.length > 0
                    && grantResults[0] ==
                        PackageManager.PERMISSION_GRANTED) {
                    mButtonSend.setEnabled(true);
                }
                return;
            }
        }
    }
    ```

7. And finally, add the method to actually send the SMS:

    ```
    public void send(View view) {
        String phoneNumber = ((EditText)findViewById(
            R.id.editTextNumber)).getText().toString();
        String msg = ((EditText)findViewById(
            R.id.editTextMsg)).getText().toString();

        if (phoneNumber==null || phoneNumber.
            length()==0 || msg==null || msg.length()==0 ) {
            return;
        }

        if (checkPermission(Manifest.permission.SEND_SMS)) {
            SmsManager smsManager = SmsManager.getDefault();
            smsManager.sendTextMessage(phoneNumber, null, msg,
                null, null);
        } else {
            Toast.makeText(MainActivity.this, "No Permission",
                Toast.LENGTH_SHORT).show();
        }
    }
    ```

8. You're ready to run the application on a device or emulator. (Use the emulator device number, such as 5556, when sending to another emulator.)

How it works...

The code for sending an SMS is only two lines, as shown here:

```
SmsManager smsManager = SmsManager.getDefault();
smsManager.sendTextMessage(phoneNumber, null, msg, null, null);
```

The `sendTextMessage()` method does the actual sending. Most of the code for this recipe is to set up the permissions since the permission model was changed in Android 6.0 Marshmallow (API 23).

There's more...

As simple as it is to send SMS messages, we still have a few more options.

Multipart messages

Though it can vary depending on the carrier, 160 is typically the maximum characters allowed per text message. You could modify the preceding code to check whether the message exceeds 160 characters and if so, you can call the SMSManager `divideMessage()` method. The method returns an `ArrayList`, which you can send to `sendMultipartTextMessage()`. Here's an example:

```
ArrayList<String> messages=smsManager.divideMessage(msg);
smsManager.sendMultipartTextMessage(
    phoneNumber, null, messages, null, null);
```

> Note that messages sent with `sendMultipartTextMessage()` may not work correctly when using an emulator, so be sure to test on a real device.

Delivery status notification

If you'd like to be notified of the status of the messages, there are two optional fields you can use. Here's the `sendTextMessage()` method as defined in the **SMSManager** documentation:

```
sendTextMessage(String destinationAddress, String scAddress,
    String text, PendingIntent sentIntent, PendingIntent
        deliveryIntent)
```

Telephony, Networks, and the Web

You can include a pending Intent to be notified of the send status and/or delivery status. Upon receipt of your pending Intent, it will include a result code with either `Activity.RESULT_OK`, if it sent successfully, or an error code as defined in the **SMSManager** documentation (link mentioned in the following See also section):

- RESULT_ERROR_GENERIC_FAILURE: Generic failure cause
- RESULT_ERROR_NO_SERVICE: Failed because service is currently unavailable
- RESULT_ERROR_NULL_PDU: Failed because no PDU was provided
- RESULT_ERROR_RADIO_OFF: Failed because radio was explicitly turned off

See also

- Short Message Service on Wikipedia at `https://en.wikipedia.org/wiki/Short_Message_Service`
- **Developer Docs: SMSManager** at `https://developer.android.com/reference/android/telephony/SmsManager.html`

Receiving SMS messages

This recipe will demonstrate how to set up a Broadcast Receiver to notify you of new SMS messages. It's useful to note that your app does not need to be running to receive the SMS Intent. Android will start your service to process the SMS.

Getting ready

Create a new project in Android Studio and call it `ReceiveSMS`. Use the default **Phone & Tablet** option and select **Empty Activity** when prompted for **Activity Type**.

How to do it...

We won't be using a layout in this demonstration as all the work will be in the Broadcast Receiver. We'll use Toasts to display incoming SMS messages. Open the Android Manifest and follow these steps:

1. Add the following permission:

    ```
    <uses-permission android:name=
        "android.permission.RECEIVE_SMS" />
    ```

2. Add the following declaration for the broadcast receiver to the `<application>` element:

   ```xml
   <receiver android:name=".SMSBroadcastReceiver">
       <intent-filter>
           <action android:name=
               "android.provider.Telephony.SMS_RECEIVED">
           </action>
       </intent-filter>
   </receiver>
   ```

3. Open `MainActivity.java` and add the following method:

   ```java
   private boolean checkPermission(String permission) {
       int permissionCheck =
           ContextCompat.checkSelfPermission(
               this, permission);
       return (permissionCheck ==
           PackageManager.PERMISSION_GRANTED);
   }
   ```

4. Modify the existing `onCreate()` callback to check the permission:

   ```java
   if (!checkPermission(Manifest.permission.RECEIVE_SMS)) {
       ActivityCompat.requestPermissions(this,
           new String[]{Manifest.permission.RECEIVE_SMS}, 0);
   }
   ```

5. Add a new Java class to the project called `SMSBroadcastReceiver` using the following code:

   ```java
   public class SMSBroadcastReceiver extends BroadcastReceiver {
       final String SMS_RECEIVED =
           "android.provider.Telephony.SMS_RECEIVED";

       @Override
       public void onReceive(Context context, Intent intent) {
           if (SMS_RECEIVED.equals(intent.getAction())) {
               Bundle bundle = intent.getExtras();
               if (bundle != null) {
                   Object[] pdus = (Object[]) bundle.get(
                       "pdus");
                   String format = bundle.getString("format");
                   final SmsMessage[] messages = new
                       SmsMessage[pdus.length];
                   for (int i = 0; i < pdus.length; i++) {
                       if (Build.VERSION.SDK_INT >=
                           Build.VERSION_CODES.M) {
   ```

```
                        messages[i] = SmsMessage.
                            createFromPdu((byte[]) pdus[i],
                                format);
                    } else {
                        messages[i] =
                            SmsMessage.createFromPdu(
                                (byte[]) pdus[i]);
                    }
                    Toast.makeText(context,
                        messages[0].getMessageBody(),
                            Toast.LENGTH_SHORT).show();
                }
            }
        }
    }
}
```

6. You're ready to run the application on a device or emulator.

How it works...

Just like in the previous recipe on sending SMS messages, we first need to check whether the app has permission. (On pre-Android 6.0 devices, the manifest declaration will automatically provide the permission, but for Marshmallow and later, we'll need to prompt the user as we do here.)

As you can see, Broadcast receiver receives the notification of new SMS messages. We tell the system we want to receive the new SMS Received Broadcasts using this code in the Android Manifest:

```
<receiver android:name=".SMSBroadcastReceiver">
    <intent-filter>
        <action android:name=
            "android.provider.Telephony.SMS_RECEIVED"></action>
    </intent-filter>
</receiver>
```

The notification comes in through the standard `onRecieve()` callback so we check the action using this code:

```
if (SMS_RECEIVED.equals(intent.getAction())) {}
```

This is probably the most complicated line of code in this demonstration:

```
messages[i] = SmsMessage.createFromPdu((byte[]) pdus[i]);
```

Basically, it calls the `SmsMessage` library to create an SMSMessage object from the PDU. (The PDU, short for Protocol Data Unit, is the binary data format for SMS messages.) If you're not familiar with the PDU formation, you don't need to be. The `SmsMessage` library will take care of it for you and return an SMSMessage object.

> If your app is not receiving SMS broadcast messages, an existing application may be blocking your app. You can try increasing the priority value in `intent-filter` as shown here, or disabling/uninstalling the other app(s):
>
> ```
> <intent-filter android:priority="100">
>     <action android:name=
>         "android.provider.Telephony.SMS_RECEIVED" />
> </intent-filter>
> ```

There's more...

This recipe demonstrates displaying SMS messages as they are received, but what about reading existing messages?

Reading existing SMS messages

First, to read the existing messages, you'll need the following permission:

```
<uses-permission android:name="android.permission.READ_SMS" />
```

Here's an example of getting a cursor using the SMS content provider:

```
Cursor cursor = getContentResolver().query(
    Uri.parse("content://sms/"), null, null, null, null);
while (cursor.moveToNext()) {
    textView.append("From :" + cursor.getString(1) + " : " +
        cursor.getString(11)+"\n");
}
```

Telephony, Networks, and the Web

At the time of writing, the SMS content provider has over 30 columns. Here are the first 12, which are the most useful (remember, the column count starts at zero):

0. `_id`
1. `thread_id`
2. `address`
3. `person`
4. `date`
5. `protocol`
6. `read`
7. `status`
8. `type`
9. `reply_path_present`
10. `subject`
11. `body`

Keep in mind, the content provider is not part of the public API and can change without notification.

See also

- **Developer Docs: SmsManager** at https://developer.android.com/reference/android/telephony/SmsManager.html
- **PDU (Protocol Data Unit)** at https://en.wikipedia.org/wiki/Protocol_data_unit
- **Developer Docs: Telephony.Sms.Intents** at https://developer.android.com/reference/android/provider/Telephony.Sms.Intents.html

Displaying a web page in your application

When you want to display HTML content on a web page, you have two choices: call the default browser or display them within your app. If you just want to call the default browser, use an Intent as follows:

```
Uri uri = Uri.parse("https://www.packtpub.com/");
Intent intent = new Intent(Intent.ACTION_VIEW, uri);
startActivity(intent);
```

If you need to display the content within your own application, you can use the `WebView`. This recipe will show how to display a web page in your application, as can be seen in this screenshot:

Getting ready

Create a new project in Android Studio and call it `WebView`. Use the default **Phone & Tablet** option and select **Empty Activity** when prompted for **Activity Type**.

Telephony, Networks, and the Web

How to do it...

We're going to create the `WebView` through code so we won't be modifying the layout. We'll start by opening the Android Manifest and following these steps:

1. Add the following permission:

   ```
   <uses-permission android:name=
       "android.permission.INTERNET"/>
   ```

2. Modify the existing `onCreate()` to include the following code:

   ```
   WebView webview = new WebView(this);
   setContentView(webview);
   webview.loadUrl("https://www.packtpub.com/");
   ```

3. You're ready to run the application on a device or emulator.

How it works...

We create a `WebView` to use as our layout and load our webpage with `loadUrl()`. The preceding code works, but at this level, it is very basic and only displays the first page. If you click on any links, the default browser will handle the request.

There's more...

What if you want full web browsing functionality so any link they click on still loads in your `WebView`? Create a `WebViewClient` as shown in this code:

```
webview.setWebViewClient(new WebViewClient());
```

Controlling page navigation

If you want more control over the page navigation, such as only allowing links within your own website, you can create your own `WebViewClient` class and override the `shouldOverrideUrlLoading()` callback, as shown here:

```
private class mWebViewClient extends WebViewClient {
    @Override
    public boolean shouldOverrideUrlLoading(WebView view,
        String url) {
        if (Uri.parse(url).getHost().equals("www.packtpub.com")) {
            return false;   //Don't override since it's the same
                            //host
        } else {
```

```
            return true;  //Stop the navigation since it's a
                          //different site
        }
    }
}
```

How to enable JavaScript

There are many other changes we can customize through `WebSettings` of `WebView`. If you want to enable JavaScript, get `WebSettings` of `WebView` and call `setJavaScriptEnabled()`, as shown:

```
WebSettings webSettings = webview.getSettings();
webSettings.setJavaScriptEnabled(true);
```

Enable built-in zoom

Another `webSetting` option is `setBuiltInZoomControls()`. Continuing from the preceding code, just add:

```
webSettings.setBuiltInZoomControls(true);
```

Check the `webSetting` link in the next section for a large list of additional options.

See also

- **Developer Docs: WebView** at https://developer.android.com/reference/android/webkit/WebView.html
- **Developer Docs: WebSettings** at https://developer.android.com/reference/android/webkit/WebSettings.html
- **Developer Docs: android.webkit** at https://developer.android.com/reference/android/webkit/package-summary.html

Checking online status and connection type

This is a simple recipe, but one that is very common and will probably be included in every Internet application you build: checking online status. While checking online status, we can also check the connection type: WIFI or MOBILE.

Getting ready

Create a new project in Android Studio and call it `isOnline`. Use the default **Phone & Tablet** option and select **Empty Activity** when prompted for **Activity Type**.

Telephony, Networks, and the Web

How to do it...

First, we need to add the necessary permissions to access the network. Then, we'll create a simple layout with a `Button` and `TextView`. To get started, open the Android Manifest and follow these steps:

1. Add the following permissions:

    ```
    <uses-permission android:name=
        "android.permission.INTERNET"/>
    <uses-permission android:name=
        "android.permission.ACCESS_NETWORK_STATE" />
    ```

2. Open the `activity_main.xml` file and replace the existing `TextView` with the following views:

    ```
    <TextView
        android:id="@+id/textView"
        android:layout_width="wrap_content"
        android:layout_height="wrap_content"
        android:text="" />
    <Button
        android:layout_width="wrap_content"
        android:layout_height="wrap_content"
        android:text="Check"
        android:layout_centerInParent="true"
        android:onClick="checkStatus"/>
    ```

3. Add this method to report if connected:

    ```
    private boolean isOnline() {
        ConnectivityManager connectivityManager =
            (ConnectivityManager)
                getSystemService(Context.CONNECTIVITY_SERVICE);
        NetworkInfo networkInfo =
            connectivityManager.getActiveNetworkInfo();
        return (networkInfo != null &&
            networkInfo.isConnected());
    }
    ```

4. Add the following method to handle the button click:

    ```
    public void checkStatus(View view) {
        TextView textView = (TextView)
            findViewById(R.id.textView);
        if (isOnline()) {
            ConnectivityManager connectivityManager = (
                ConnectivityManager)
                    getSystemService(
    ```

```
            Context.CONNECTIVITY_SERVICE);
        NetworkInfo networkInfo =
            connectivityManager.getActiveNetworkInfo();
        textView.setText(networkInfo.getTypeName());
    } else {
        textView.setText("Offline");
    }
}
```

5. You're ready to run the application on a device or emulator.

How it works...

We created the `isOnline()` method to make it easy to reuse this code.

To check the status, we get an instance of `ConnectivityManager` to read the `NetworkInfo` state. If it reports we are connected, we get the name of the active network by calling `getType()`, which returns one of the following constants:

- TYPE_MOBILE
- TYPE_WIFI
- TYPE_WIMAX
- TYPE_ETHERNET
- TYPE_BLUETOOTH

Also, see the `ConnectivityManager` link later for additional constants. For display purposes, we call `getTypeName()`. We could call `getType()` to get a numeric constant instead.

There's more...

Let's look at some additional constants of `ConnectivityManager`.

Monitoring network state changes

If your application needs to respond to changes in the network status, take a look at the `CONNECTIVITY_ACTION` in `ConnectivityManager`. You need to create a broadcast receiver, and then register for the event. Here's an example of how to include the action in the receiver's intent filter through the Android Manifest:

```
<receiver android:name="com.vcs.timetrac.VCSBroadcastReceiver">
    <intent-filter>
        <action android:name=
            "android.net.conn.CONNECTIVITY_CHANGE" />
    </intent-filter>
</receiver>
```

Telephony, Networks, and the Web

Be careful using the Android manifest as it will notify your app every time the network state changes, even if your app isn't being used. This can cause unnecessary drain on the battery. If your app only needs to respond to network changes while the user is actually using your app, create the listeners in the code instead.

See also

- **Developer Docs: ConnectivityManager** at `https://developer.android.com/reference/android/net/ConnectivityManager.html`
- **Developer Docs: NetworkInfo** at `https://developer.android.com/reference/android/net/NetworkInfo.html`

Getting started with Volley for Internet requests

Android includes multiple libraries for Internet queries, including the Apache `HttpClient` and `HttpURLConnection`. The Apache `HttpClient` was the recommended library before Android 2.3 Gingerbread (API 9). Android 2.3 Gingerbread (API 9) saw many improvements to the `HttpURLConnection` library and it became the recommended library, and still remains so today. With the release of Android 6.0, the Apache `HttpClient` has been removed completely from the SDK, leaving the `HttpURLConnection` library as the recommended replacement.

Though the `HttpURLConnection` library still works and has its uses, there are drawbacks: it's not the easiest library to use if you are new to writing web requests and it requires a lot of repetitive overhead code. Fortunately, we have a new option from *Ficus Kirkpatrick*, a Google Developer from the Google Play group. He released a library called Volley, which provides a simplified wrapper. (It uses the `HttpURLConnection` library, by default, and can also be used with other libraries.)

> You can see his Google I/O presentation here:
> `https://www.youtube.com/watch?v=yhv8l9F44qo`

Several reasons to use Volley over `HttpURLConnection` include the following:

- Thread pool (defaults to four threads)
- Transparent disk cache
- Queue priority settings

Chapter 12

There are additional benefits, but these three alone make it worth learning about Volley. A fourth benefit, which if you've ever used `HttpURLConnection` will become apparent, is the lack of boilerplate code. Instead of having to write a bunch of standard `try/catch` code around many of your calls, the library will handle the checks internally, allowing you to focus more on the specific task at hand.

Volley has built-in support for the following request types:

- String
- JSON
- Image
- Custom

While Volley excels at multiple small request calls (such as when scrolling through a `ListView`), it is not good at large file downloads as the returned objects are parsed in memory. For larger file downloads, take a look at the `DownloadManager` (see the link at the end of the recipe). Also, for the same reason, it's not a solution for streaming content; for that, refer to `HttpURLConnection`.

Since Volley is currently not in the Android SDK, we need to download the code and add it to our project. This recipe will walk you through the steps of adding Volley to your application project and making a simple request.

Getting ready

Before creating your new project, download the Volley project files hosted on the **Android Open Source Project** (**AOSP**) website using the following Git command:

```
git clone https://android.googlesource.com/platform/frameworks/volley
```

If you are unfamiliar with Git, see the Git (software) link at the end of this recipe for additional information and help finding a Git client for your platform. Git is a **Version Control Software** (**VCS**) used on many platforms. (Once installed, you can also integrate Git VCS in Android Studio.)

Create a new project in Android Studio and call it `SetupVolley`. Use the default **Phone & Tablet** option and select **Empty Activity** when prompted for **Activity Type**.

Telephony, Networks, and the Web

How to do it...

Before starting these steps, make sure you've downloaded the Volley project as described previously. We'll start the steps below by adding Volley to our project to make a simple Internet call. We'll use a single button in our layout to initiate the request and a `TextView` to display the results. Here are the steps:

1. Open the Android Manifest and add the following permission:

   ```
   <uses-permission android:name=
       "android.permission.INTERNET"/>
   ```

2. Import the `Volley` module by going to **File | New | Import Module** (see the following screenshot) and follow the wizard.

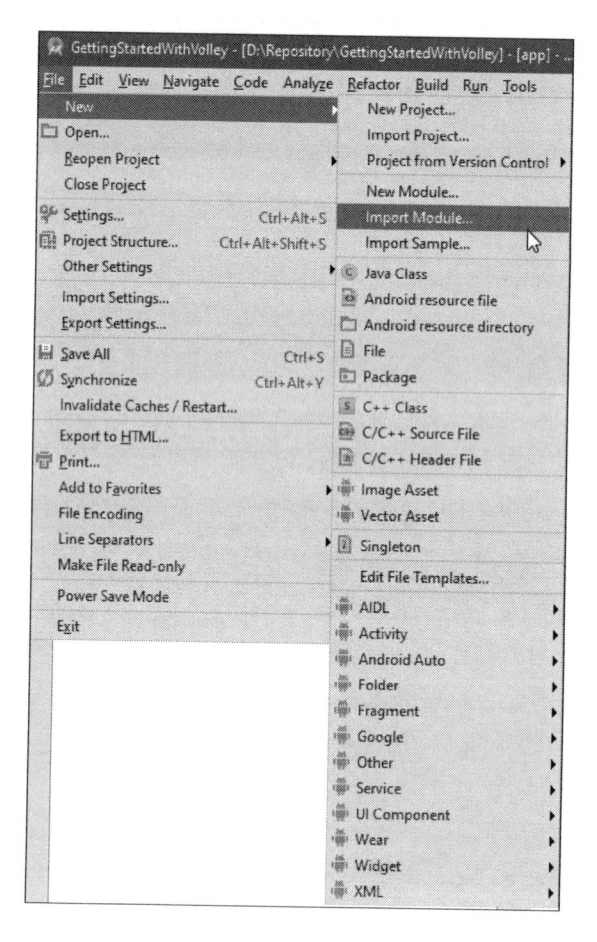

3. On the second page of the **New Module** Import Wizard (see the following screenshot), you need to specify the location of the Volley files and assign the **Module name**. This is the name we'll need in the next step:

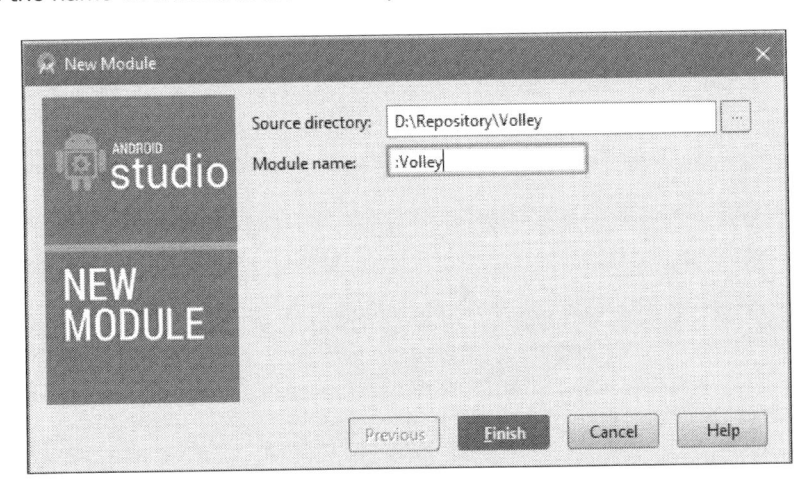

4. Under the `Gradle Scripts` section, open the `build.gradle` (Module: app) file. See the following screenshot:

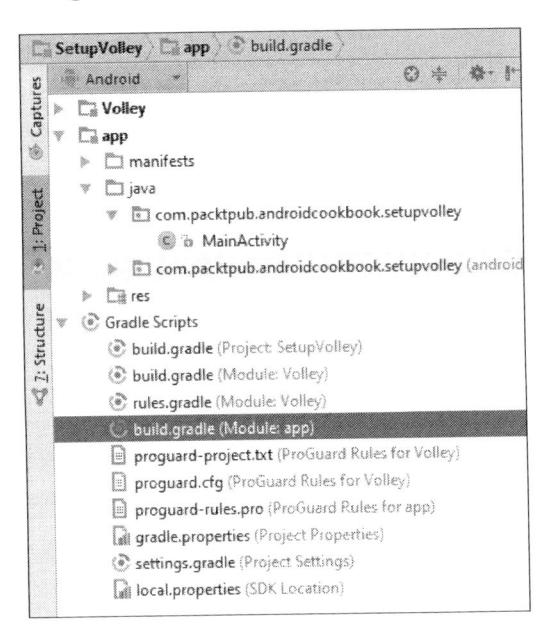

Telephony, Networks, and the Web

5. Add/verify the following statement in the `dependencies` section:

   ```
   compile project(":Volley")
   ```

   > The value in parenthesis needs to match the Module name you specified in the previous step.

6. Under `Gradle Scripts`, open the `settings.gradle` file and verify the contents as follows:

   ```
   include ':app', ':Volley'
   ```

7. Open the `activity_main.xml` file and replace the existing `TextView` with the following `TextView` and `Button` elements:

   ```xml
   <TextView
       android:id="@+id/textView"
       android:layout_width="wrap_content"
       android:layout_height="wrap_content"
       android:layout_alignParentTop="true"
       android:layout_alignParentLeft="true"
       android:layout_above="@+id/button" />
   <Button
       android:id="@+id/button"
       android:layout_width="wrap_content"
       android:layout_height="wrap_content"
       android:text="Request"
       android:layout_alignParentBottom="true"
       android:layout_centerHorizontal="true"
       android:onClick="sendRequest"/>
   ```

8. Add the `sendRequest()` method called by the button click:

   ```java
   public void sendRequest(View view) {
       final TextView textView = (TextView)
           findViewById(R.id.textView);
       RequestQueue queue = Volley.newRequestQueue(this);
       String url ="https://www.packtpub.com/";
       StringRequest stringRequest = new StringRequest(
           Request.Method.GET, url,
               new Response.Listener<String>() {
           @Override
           public void onResponse(String response) {
               textView.setText(
                   response.substring(0,500));
           }
   ```

```
            }, new Response.ErrorListener() {
                @Override
                public void onErrorResponse(VolleyError error) {
                    textView.setText("onErrorResponse(): "+
                        error.getMessage());
                }
            });
            queue.add(stringRequest);
    }
```

9. You're ready to run the application on a device or emulator.

How it works...

It's probably helpful to understand that in Volley, Internet transactions are called *requests*. To execute a request, add it to the queue. To make this happen, we first create an instance of a Volley `RequestQueue`, and then create a `StringRequest` and add it to the queue. A `StringRequest` is just what it sounds like; we are requesting a string response.

For this recipe, we just call the Packt Publishing website and get the page as a string response. Since this is just for illustration, we only display the first 500 characters.

There's more...

Now that you have Volley properly set up and making Internet requests, this recipe will be the building block for the Volley recipes that follow.

See also

- **Volley**: Git at Google at `https://android.googlesource.com/platform/frameworks/volley`
- **Git** (software): Wikipedia, the free encyclopedia at `https://en.wikipedia.org/wiki/Git_(software)`
- **Developer Docs: DownloadManager** at `http://developer.android.com/reference/android/app/DownloadManager.html`
- **Developer Docs: HttpURLConnection** at `https://developer.android.com/reference/java/net/HttpURLConnection.html`

Telephony, Networks, and the Web

Canceling a Volley request

In the previous recipe, we demonstrated how to add a request to the Volley queue. What happens if you no longer need the response? This could happen if the user is scrolling through a `ListView` and you're updating the `ListItems` by fetching information from the Web. It would be wasteful of bandwidth, power, and CPU cycles to allow the requests to complete knowing you are just going to discard the response.

If you were using the `HTTPURLConnection` library, you would need to track all requests and cancel them manually. This recipe will show you how easy it is to cancel the request in Volley.

Getting ready

If you have not already completed the previous recipe, *Getting started with Volley for Internet requests*, you will need to follow steps 1-5 to add the Volley module to your application.

Create a new project in Android Studio and call it `CancelVolleyRequest`. Use the default **Phone & Tablet** option and select **Empty Activity** when prompted for **Activity Type**.

How to do it...

If you have not already added the Volley module to your application, review the previous section. With Volley added to your project, follow these steps:

1. Open `activity_main.xml` and replace the existing `TextView` with the following XML:

   ```
   <TextView
       android:id="@+id/textView"
       android:layout_width="wrap_content"
       android:layout_height="wrap_content"
       android:layout_alignParentTop="true"
       android:layout_alignParentLeft="true"
       android:layout_above="@+id/button" />
   <Button
       android:id="@+id/button"
       android:layout_width="100dp"
       android:layout_height="wrap_content"
       android:text="Request"
       android:layout_centerInParent="true"
       android:onClick="sendRequest"/>
   <Button
       android:id="@+id/buttonClose"
       android:layout_width="100dp"
   ```

```
            android:layout_height="wrap_content"
            android:layout_below="@+id/button"
            android:layout_centerHorizontal="true"
            android:text="Close"
            android:onClick="close"/>
```

2. Open `MainActivity.java` and add the following global variable:

   ```
   RequestQueue mRequestQueue;
   ```

3. Edit the existing `onCreate()` to initialize the `RequestQueue`:

   ```
   mRequestQueue = Volley.newRequestQueue(this);
   ```

4. Add the following `sendRequest()` method (note that this is similar to the `sendRequest()` method from the previous recipe with several changes):

   ```
   public void sendRequest(View view) {
       final TextView textView = (TextView)
           findViewById(R.id.textView);

       String url ="https://www.packtpub.com/";
       StringRequest stringRequest = new StringRequest(
           Request.Method.GET, url,
               new Response.Listener<String>() {
           @Override
           public void onResponse(String response) {
               textView.setText(
                   response.substring(0,500));
           }
       }, new Response.ErrorListener() {
           @Override
           public void onErrorResponse(VolleyError error) {
               textView.setText("onErrorResponse(): "+
                   error.getMessage());
           }
       });
       stringRequest.setTag(this);
       mRequestQueue.add(stringRequest);
       finish();
   }
   ```

5. Add the **Close** button's `onClick` method:

   ```
   public void close(View view){
       finish();
   }
   ```

Telephony, Networks, and the Web

6. Create the following override for the `onStop()` callback:
   ```
   @Override
   protected void onStop() {
       super.onStop();
       mRequestQueue.cancelAll(this);
   }
   ```
7. You're ready to run the application on a device or emulator.

How it works...

To cancel the requests, we can call the `RequestQueue cancelAll()` method and pass in our tag. In this example, we used the activity, `this`, as our tag, but we could use any object as our tag. This allows you to create whatever grouping you might need for your requests.

There's more...

We're not just demonstrating how easy it is to cancel requests, we're also demonstrating a defensive programming tactic. By ensuring all our requests are canceled, we won't have to add code to check for a null activity in our responses, since Volley guarantees that we will not receive *any* responses from a request after it has been canceled.

Using Volley to request a JSON response

Since JavaScript Object Notation (JSON) is probably the most common data-interchange format, you'll likely find yourself needing to call a JSON web service. (If you are unfamiliar with JSON, review the link at the end of this recipe.) This recipe will demonstrate how to make a JSON Request using Volley.

Getting ready

Create a new project in Android Studio and call it `JSONRequest`. Use the default **Phone & Tablet** option and select **Empty Activity** when prompted for **Activity Type**.

This recipe will be using the Volley setup as described in *Getting started with Volley for Internet requests*. Follow steps 1-5 to add Volley to your new project.

Chapter 12

How to do it...

With Volley added to your project as described previously, follow these steps:

1. Open `activity_main.xml` and replace the existing `TextView` with the following XML:

```xml
<TextView
    android:id="@+id/textView"
    android:layout_width="wrap_content"
    android:layout_height="wrap_content"
    android:layout_alignParentTop="true"
    android:layout_alignParentLeft="true"
    android:layout_above="@+id/button" />
<Button
    android:id="@+id/button"
    android:layout_width="wrap_content"
    android:layout_height="wrap_content"
    android:text="Request"
    android:layout_alignParentBottom="true"
    android:layout_centerHorizontal="true"
    android:onClick="sendRequest"/>
```

2. Add the following `sendRequest()` method:

```java
public void sendRequest(View view) {
    final TextView textView = (TextView)
        findViewById(R.id.textView);
    RequestQueue queue = Volley.newRequestQueue(this);
    String url ="<json service>";
    //"http://ip.jsontest.com/"

    JsonObjectRequest jsonObjectRequest = new
        JsonObjectRequest(Request.Method.GET, url, null,
            new Response.Listener<JSONObject>() {
        @Override
        public void onResponse(JSONObject response) {
            textView.setText(response.toString());
        }
    }, new Response.ErrorListener() {
        @Override
        public void onErrorResponse(VolleyError error) {
            textView.setText("onErrorResponse(): "+
                error.getMessage());
```

327

```
            }
        });
        queue.add(jsonObjectRequest);
}
```

3. Replace the `url` string in the code before you run this application.

How it works...

Requesting a JSON response using `JsonObjectRequest()` basically works the same as the `StringRequest()`. The difference is the response, which is returned as a `JSONObject`.

To run this code, you will need to replace the `url` parameter with your web service URL. If you don't have a web service to test against, you can try a link from the JSON Test website (http://www.jsontest.com/).

There's more...

In the preceding example, we requested a `JSONObject` with `JsonObjectRequest`. We can also request a `JSONARray` with `JsonArrayRequest`.

See also

- Visit the JSON web page at http://json.org/
- **Developer Docs: org.json (JSON Libraries)** at http://developer.android.com/reference/org/json/package-summary.html

Using Volley to request an image

Once you make your JSON Requests as demonstrated in the previous recipe, the next most likely call you'll be making is to get an image. This recipe will demonstrate how to request an image to update an `ImageView`.

Getting ready

Create a new project in Android Studio and call it `ImageRequest`. Use the default **Phone & Tablet** option and select **Empty Activity** when prompted for **Activity Type**.

This recipe will be using the setup described in the *Getting started with Volley for Internet requests* recipe. Follow steps 1-5 to add Volley to your new project.

How to do it...

With Volley added to your project, as described previously, follow these steps:

1. Open `activity_main.xml` and replace the existing `TextView` with the following XML:

    ```xml
    <ImageView
        android:id="@+id/imageView"
        android:layout_width="wrap_content"
        android:layout_height="wrap_content"
        android:layout_centerInParent="true" />
    <Button
        android:id="@+id/button"
        android:layout_width="wrap_content"
        android:layout_height="wrap_content"
        android:text="Request"
        android:layout_alignParentBottom="true"
        android:layout_centerHorizontal="true"
        android:onClick="sendRequest"/>
    ```

2. Add the following `sendRequest()` method:

    ```java
    public void sendRequest(View view) {
        final ImageView imageView =
            (ImageView)findViewById(R.id.imageView);
        RequestQueue queue = Volley.newRequestQueue(this);
        String url ="http://www.android.com/static/img/
            logos-2x/android-wordmark-8EC047.png";
        ImageRequest imageRequest = new ImageRequest(url,
            new Response.Listener<Bitmap>() {
                @Override
                public void onResponse(Bitmap bitmap) {
                    imageView.setImageBitmap(bitmap);
                }
            }, 0, 0, ImageView.ScaleType.CENTER, null,
            new Response.ErrorListener() {
                @Override
                public void onErrorResponse(VolleyError error) {
                    error.printStackTrace();
                }
            });
        queue.add(imageRequest);
    }
    ```

3. Run the application on a device or emulator.

Telephony, Networks, and the Web

How it works...

This recipe, basically, works in the same way as the previous two Volley requests. In this recipe, we pass a URL to an image and load the `ImageView` in the response.

We've now covered the three basic request types: String, JSON, and Image.

There's more...

Though the basic types will probably cover most of your needs, Volley is extensible and you can also implement a custom response by extending `Request<T>`.

This recipe demonstrates a problem with our example code. If you change the orientation of the device, you'll see the image flicker as the activity is recreated.

Creating a Volley singleton

It's recommended to instantiate Volley as a singleton. (An alternative approach would be to create the queue in the application class.) To create a singleton class in Android Studio, go to **New | File | Singleton** and give it a class name, such as `VolleySingleton`.

Move the code to create the request queue to the singleton class. If you create a method as follows:

```
public <T> void addToRequestQueue(Request<T> req) {
    mRequestQueue.add(req);
}
```

Then, you can add to your queue from anywhere using the following code:

```
VolleySingleton.getInstance(this).addToRequestQueue(stringRequest);
```

The key to making this work properly is to always use the Application Context (not an Activity or Broadcast Receiver Context) by calling `getApplicationContext()` on the context passed in.

See also

- **Developer Docs: Application (class)** at https://developer.android.com/reference/android/app/Application.html

Using Volley's NetworkImageView and ImageLoader

Our last recipe on Volley will not be a request per se, but a replacement for the `ImageView`. Requesting an image to populate an `ImageView` is such a common task; Volley combines the functionality to a new view called `NetworkImageView`. This recipe will demonstrate how to use a `NetworkImageView`.

Getting ready

Create a new project in Android Studio and call it `NetworkImageView`. Use the default **Phone & Tablet** option and select **Empty Activity** when prompted for **Activity Type**.

This recipe will be using the setup described in the *Getting started with Volley for Internet requests* recipe. Follow Steps 1-5 to add Volley to your new project.

How to do it...

With Volley added to your project as described previously, follow these steps:

1. Open `activity_main.xml` and replace the existing `TextView` with the following XML:

    ```xml
    <com.android.volley.toolbox.NetworkImageView
        android:id="@+id/networkImageView"
        android:layout_width="wrap_content"
        android:layout_height="wrap_content"
        android:layout_centerInParent="true" />
    ```

2. Add the following code to the existing `onCreate()` callback:

    ```
    NetworkImageView networkImageView = (NetworkImageView)
        findViewById(R.id.networkImageView);
    String url="http://www.android.com/static/img/
        logos-2x/android-wordmark-8EC047.png";
    RequestQueue queue = Volley.newRequestQueue(this);
    ImageLoader imageLoader = new ImageLoader(queue,
        new ImageLoader.ImageCache() {
            private final LruCache<String, Bitmap>
                cache = new LruCache<String, Bitmap>(20);

            @Override
            public Bitmap getBitmap(String url) {
                return cache.get(url);
            }
    ```

Telephony, Networks, and the Web

```
        @Override
        public void putBitmap(String url, Bitmap bitmap) {
            cache.put(url, bitmap);
        }
    });
    networkImageView.setImageUrl(url,imageLoader);
```

3. You're ready to run the application on a device or emulator.

How it works...

This example is very different from the previous Volley examples. Instead of creating a request object, we create an `ImageLoader`. The `ImageLoader` class allows us to override the default caching behavior, such as the number of bitmaps or how the size is calculated. (We could change the cache to be based on total memory instead of image count.) See the `LruCache` link later for more information.

With the `ImageLoader` created, you can assign the image URL to the `NetworkImageView` and pass the `ImageLoader` as the second parameter.

There's more...

As we mentioned in the previous recipe, the problem with our Volley example is that we create the queue in the activity. This is most noticeable with images, but regardless, it's recommended to create a Volley singleton. See the *Create a Volley singleton* section in the previous recipe for more information.

If you create a singleton as described in the previous recipe, you can also move the `ImageLoader` code to the singleton and expose the `ImageLoader` like this:

```
public ImageLoader getImageLoader() {
    return mImageLoader;
}
```

With the singleton created, this recipe could be coded as follows:

```
NetworkImageView networkImageView =
    (NetworkImageView)findViewById(R.id.networkImageView);
String url="http://www.android.com/static/img/logos-2x/
    android-wordmark-8EC047.png";
networkImageView.setImageUrl(url,
    VolleySingleton.getInstance(this).getImageLoader());
```

See also

- **Developer Docs: LruCache** at https://developer.android.com/reference/android/util/LruCache.html

13
Getting Location and Using Geofencing

In this chapter, we will cover the following topics:

- How to get the last location
- Resolving problems reported with the GoogleApiClient OnConnectionFailedListener
- How to receive location updates
- Create and monitor a Geofence

Introduction

Location awareness offers many benefits to an app, so many in fact that even desktop apps now attempt to get the user's location. Location uses ranges from turn-by-turn directions, "find the nearest" applications, alerts based on location, and there are now even location-based games that get you out exploring with your device.

The Google APIs offer many rich features for creating location-aware applications and mapping features. Our first recipe *How to get the last location* will look at obtaining the last known location as stored on the device. If your app is not location intensive, this may provide an ideal way to get the user's location without a large resource overhead. If you need constant updates, then turn to the *How to receive location updates* recipe. Though constant location updates requires more resources, users are likely to understand when you're giving them turn-by-turn directions. If you are requesting location updates for a proximity location, take a look at using the Geofence option instead, in the *Create and monitor a Geofence* recipe.

All the recipes in this chapter use the Google Libraries. If you have not already downloaded the SDK Packages, follow the instructions from Google.

Getting Location and Using Geofencing

> Add SDK Packages from `http://developer.android.com/sdk/installing/adding-packages.html`.

Now that you have the location, there's a good chance you'll want to map it as well. This is another area where Google makes this very easy on Android using the Google Maps API. To get started with Google Maps, take a look at the **Google Maps Activity** option when creating a new project in Android Studio. Instead of selecting **Blank Activity**, as we normally do for these recipes, choose **Google Maps Activity**, as shown in this screenshot:

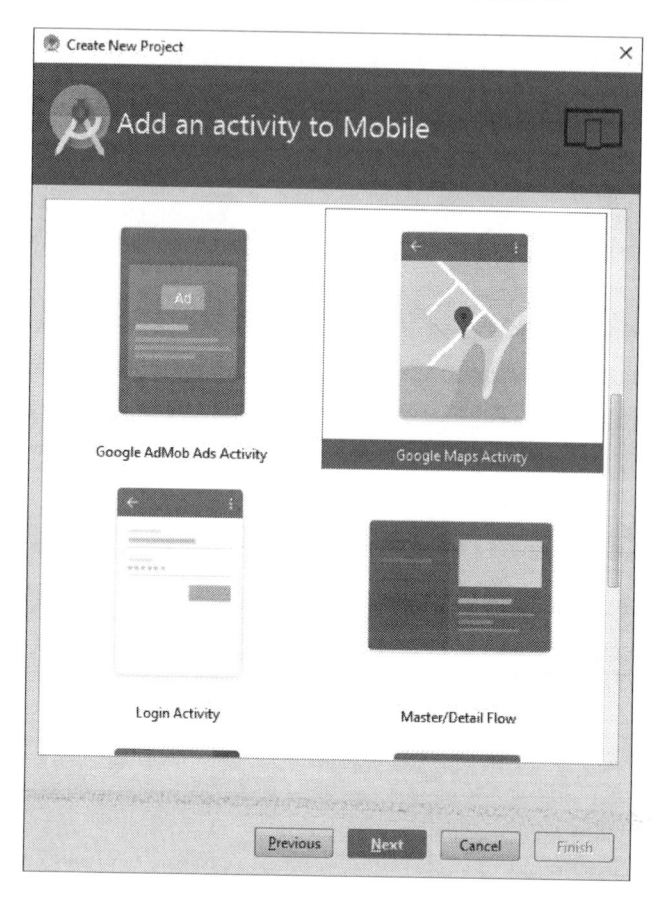

How to get the last location

We'll start this chapter with a simple recipe that is commonly needed: how to get the last known location. This is an easy way to use APIs with very little overhead resource drain. (This means, your app won't be responsible for killing the battery.)

This recipe also provides a good introduction to setting up the Google Location APIs.

Getting ready

Create a new project in Android Studio and call it: `GetLastLocation`. Use the default **Phone & Tablet** options, and select **Empty Activity** when prompted for **Activity Type**.

How to do it...

First, we'll add the necessary permissions to the Android Manifest, then we'll create a layout with a `Button` and a `TextView` element. Finally, we'll create a `GoogleAPIClient` API to access the last location. Open the Android Manifest and follow these steps:

1. Add the following permission:

    ```
    <uses-permission android:name=
    "android.permission.ACCESS_COARSE_LOCATION"/>
    ```

2. Under the **Gradle Scripts** section, open the **build.gradle (Module: app)** file, as shown in this screenshot:

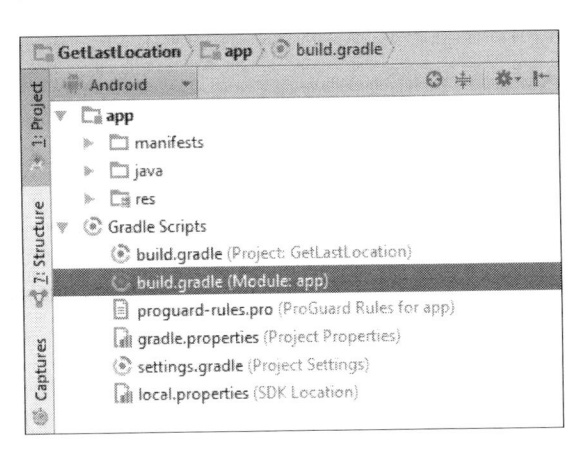

3. Add the following statement to the `dependencies` section:

    ```
    compile 'com.google.android.gms:play-services:8.4.0'
    ```

335

Getting Location and Using Geofencing

4. Open `activity_main.xml` and replace the existing `TextView` with the following XML:

   ```xml
   <TextView
       android:id="@+id/textView"
       android:layout_width="wrap_content"
       android:layout_height="wrap_content" />
   <Button
       android:id="@+id/button"
       android:layout_width="wrap_content"
       android:layout_height="wrap_content"
       android:text="Get Location"
       android:layout_centerInParent="true"
       android:onClick="getLocation"/>
   ```

5. Open `MainActivity.java` and add the following global variables:

   ```java
   GoogleApiClient mGoogleApiClient;
   TextView mTextView;
   Button mButton;
   ```

6. Add the class for `ConnectionCallbacks`:

   ```java
   GoogleApiClient.ConnectionCallbacks mConnectionCallbacks =
       new GoogleApiClient.ConnectionCallbacks() {
           @Override
           public void onConnected(Bundle bundle) {
               mButton.setEnabled(true);
           }
           @Override
           public void onConnectionSuspended(int i) {}
   };
   ```

7. Add the class to handle the `OnConnectionFailedListener` callback:

   ```java
   GoogleApiClient.OnConnectionFailedListener
       mOnConnectionFailedListener = new
           GoogleApiClient.OnConnectionFailedListener() {
           @Override
           public void onConnectionFailed(ConnectionResult
               connectionResult) {
               Toast.makeText(MainActivity.this,
                   connectionResult.toString(),
                     Toast.LENGTH_LONG).show();
           }
   };
   ```

8. Add the following code to the existing `onCreate()` method:

```
mTextView = (TextView) findViewById(R.id.textView);
mButton = (Button) findViewById(R.id.button);
mButton.setEnabled(false);
setupGoogleApiClient();
```

9. Add the method to set up `GoogleAPIClient`:

```
protected synchronized void setupGoogleApiClient() {
    mGoogleApiClient = new GoogleApiClient.Builder(this)
        .addConnectionCallbacks(mConnectionCallbacks)
        .addOnConnectionFailedListener(
            mOnConnectionFailedListener)
        .addApi(LocationServices.API)
        .build();
    mGoogleApiClient.connect();
}
```

10. Add the following method for the button click:

```
public void getLocation(View view) {
    try {
        Location lastLocation =
            LocationServices.FusedLocationApi.
                getLastLocation(
                mGoogleApiClient);
        if (lastLocation != null) {
            mTextView.setText(
                DateFormat.getTimeInstance().format(
                    lastLocation.getTime()) + "\n" +
                    "Latitude="+lastLocation.getLatitude() +
                    "\n" + "Longitude=" +
                        lastLocation.getLongitude());
        } else {
            Toast.makeText(MainActivity.this, "null",
                Toast.LENGTH_LONG).show();
        }
    }
    catch (SecurityException e) {e.printStackTrace();}
}
```

11. You're ready to run the application on a device or emulator.

Getting Location and Using Geofencing

How it works...

Before we can call the `getLastLocation()` method, we need to set up `GoogleApiClient`. We call the `GoogleApiClient.Builder` method in our `setupGoogleApiClient()` method, then connect to the library. When the library is ready, it calls our `ConnectionCallbacks.onConnected()` method. For demonstration purposes, this is where we enable the button. (We'll use this callback in later recipes to start additional features.)

We used a button to show we can call `getLastLocation()` on demand; it's not a one-time call. The system is responsible for updating the location and may return the same last location on repeated calls. (This can be seen in the timestamp—it's the location timestamp, not the timestamp when the button is pressed.)

This approach of calling the location on demand can be useful in situations where you only need the location when something happens in your app (such as geocoding an object). Since the system is responsible for the location updates, your app will not be responsible for a battery drain from location updates.

The accuracy of the location object we receive is based on our permission setting. We used `ACCESS_COARSE_LOCATION`, but if we want higher accuracy, we can request `ACCESS_FINE_LOCATION` instead, with the following permission:

```
<uses-permission android:name=
"android.permission.ACCESS_FINE_LOCATION"/>
```

Lastly, to keep the code focused on `GoogleApiClient`, we just wrap the `getLastLocation()` with `SecurityException`. In a production application, you should check and request the permission as shown in the previous chapter. (See *The new run-time permission model*.)

There's more...

If a problem occurs when connecting to the `GoogleApiClient`, the `OnConnectionFailedListener` is called. In this example, we display a Toast. The next recipe, *Resolving problems reported with the GoogleApiClient OnConnectionFailedListener*, will show a more robust way to handle this situation.

Testing the location can be a challenge since it's difficult to actually move the device when testing and debugging. Fortunately, we have the ability to simulate GPS data with the emulator. (It is possible to create mock locations on a physical device as well, but it's not as easy.)

Mock locations

There are three ways to simulate locations with the emulator:

- Android Studio
- DDMS
- The `Geo` command through Telnet

To set a mock location in Android Studio, follow these steps:

1. Navigate to **Tools** | **Android** | **Android Device Monitor**.
2. Select the **Emulator Control** tab in the device window.
3. Enter GPS coordinates under **Location Controls**.

Here's a screenshot showing the **Location Controls**:

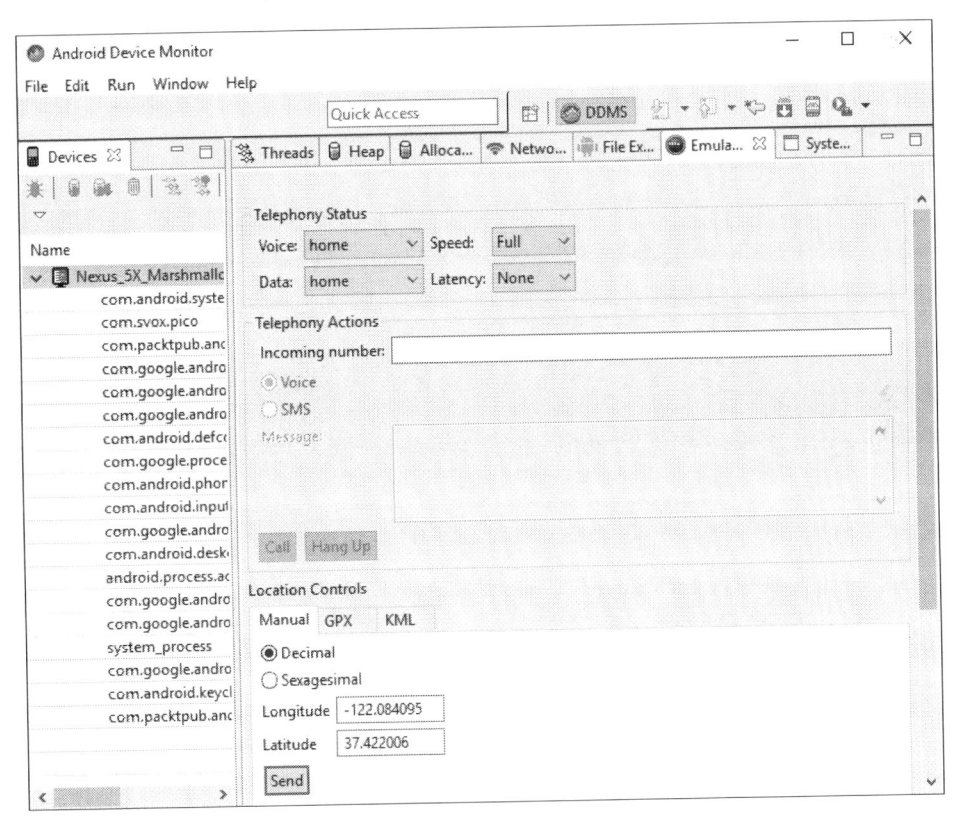

> Not that simulating the location works by sending GPS data. Therefore, for your app to receive the mock location, it will need to be receiving GPS data. Testing `lastLocation()` may not send the mock GPS data since it doesn't rely solely on the GPS for determining the device location. Try the mock location with the recipe *How to receive Location Updates* where we can request the priority. (We can't force the system to use any specific location sensor, we can only make a request. The system will choose the optimum solution to deliver the results.)

See also

- The *The new Android 6.0 run-time permission model* recipe in *Chapter 14, Getting Your App Ready for the Play Store*
- Setting up Google Play Services: https://developers.google.com/android/guides/setup
- The **FusedLocationProviderApi** interface: https://developers.google.com/android/reference/com/google/android/gms/location/FusedLocationProviderApi

Resolving problems reported with the GoogleApiClient OnConnectionFailedListener

With the constantly changing nature of Google APIs, your users are likely to attempt to use your application, but not be able to because their files are out of date. In the previous example, we just show a Toast, but we can do better. We can use the `GoogleApiAvailability` library to display a dialog to help the user resolve the problem.

We'll continue with the previous recipe and add code to the `onConnectionFailed()` callback. We'll use the error result to display additional information to the user to resolve their problem.

Getting ready

This recipe will continue from the previous recipe, *How to get the last location*. If you are loading the project from the downloaded source files, it is called `HandleGoogleAPIError`.

How to do it...

Since we are continuing from the previous recipe, we'll only cover the steps necessary to update the previous code. Open `ActivityMain.java` and follow these steps:

1. Add the following lines to the global class variables:

   ```
   private final int REQUEST_RESOLVE_GOOGLE_CLIENT_ERROR=1;
   boolean mResolvingError;
   ```

2. Add the following method to show the Google API error dialog:

   ```
   private void showGoogleAPIErrorDialog(int errorCode) {
     GoogleApiAvailability googleApiAvailability =
       GoogleApiAvailability.getInstance();
     Dialog errorDialog = googleApiAvailability.getErrorDialog(
       this, errorCode, REQUEST_RESOLVE_GOOGLE_CLIENT_ERROR);
     errorDialog.show();
   }
   ```

3. Add the following code to override `onActivityResult()`:

   ```
   @Override
   protected void onActivityResult(int requestCode, int
     resultCode, Intent data) {
     if (requestCode == REQUEST_RESOLVE_GOOGLE_CLIENT_ERROR) {
       mResolvingError = false;
       if (resultCode == RESULT_OK &&
         !mGoogleApiClient.isConnecting() &&
         !mGoogleApiClient.isConnected()) {
         mGoogleApiClient.connect();
       }
     }
   }
   ```

4. In `onConnectionFailed()`, replace the existing line of code calling Toast, using the following code:

   ```
   if (mResolvingError) {
     return;
   } else if (connectionResult.hasResolution()) {
     mResolvingError = true;
     try {
       connectionResult.startResolutionForResult(
         MainActivity.this, REQUEST_RESOLVE_GOOGLE_CLIENT_ERROR);
     } catch (IntentSender.SendIntentException e) {
       mGoogleApiClient.connect();
     }
   ```

Getting Location and Using Geofencing

```
    } else {
      showGoogleAPIErrorDialog(
        connectionResult.getErrorCode());
    }
```

5. You're ready to run the application on a device or emulator.

How it works...

Instead of displaying the error message with a Toast as we did before, we now check `connectionResult` to see what we can do. The `GoogleAPIClient` uses the `connectionResult` to indicate possible courses of action. We can call the `hasResolution()` method, as follows:

```
connectionResult.hasResolution()
```

If the response is `true`, then it's something the user can resolve, such as enabling the location service. If the response is `false`, we get an instance of the `GoogleApiAvailability` and call the `getErrorDialog()` method. When finished, our `onActivityResult()` callback is called, where we reset `mResolvingError` and, if successful, attempt to reconnect.

> If you do not have a device with an older Google API for testing, you can try testing on an emulator with an older Google API version.

There's more...

If your application is using fragments, you can get a dialog fragment instead, using this code:

```
ErrorDialogFragment errorFragment = new ErrorDialogFragment();
Bundle args = new Bundle();
args.putInt("dialog_error", errorCode);
errorFragment.setArguments(args);
errorFragment.show(getSupportFragmentManager(), "errordialog");
```

See also

- Accessing Google APIs: https://developers.google.com/android/guides/api-client

How to receive location updates

If your application needs frequent location updates, your application can request periodic updates. This recipe will demonstrate this using the `requestLocationUpdates()` method from `GoogleApiClient`.

Getting ready

Create a new project in Android Studio and call it: `LocationUpdates`. Use the default **Phone & Tablet** options and select **Empty Activity** when prompted for **Activity Type**.

How to do it...

Since we are receiving updates from the system, we won't need a button for this recipe. Our layout will consist of just the `TextView` to see the location data. Open the Android Manifest and follow these steps:

1. Add the following permission:

    ```
    <uses-permission android:name="android.permission.ACCESS_FINE_LOCATION"/>
    ```

2. Open the file `build.gradle (Module: app)` and add the following statement to the `dependencies` section:

    ```
    compile 'com.google.android.gms:play-services:8.4.0'
    ```

3. Open `activity_main.xml` and replace the existing `TextView` with the following XML:

    ```
    <TextView
        android:id="@+id/textView"
        android:layout_width="wrap_content"
        android:layout_height="wrap_content" />
    ```

4. Open `MainActivity.java` and add the following global variables:

    ```
    GoogleApiClient mGoogleApiClient;
    LocationRequest mLocationRequest;
    TextView mTextView;
    ```

5. Create the following `LocationListener` class:

    ```
    LocationListener mLocationListener = new LocationListener() {
        @Override
        public void onLocationChanged(Location location) {
            if (location != null) {
                mTextView.setText(
    ```

```java
                DateFormat.getTimeInstance().format(
                location.getTime()) + "\n" +
                "Latitude="+location.getLatitude()+"\n" +
                "Longitude="+location.getLongitude());
        }
    }
};
```

6. Create a `ConnectionCallbacks` class to receive the location updates:

```java
GoogleApiClient.ConnectionCallbacks mConnectionCallbacks =
    new GoogleApiClient.ConnectionCallbacks() {
        @Override
        public void onConnected(Bundle bundle) {
            Log.i("onConnected()", "start");
            try {
                LocationServices.FusedLocationApi.
                    requestLocationUpdates(
                        mGoogleApiClient, mLocationRequest,
                        mLocationListener);
            } catch (SecurityException e) {
                Log.i("onConnected()","SecurityException:
                    "+e.getMessage());
            }
        }
        @Override
        public void onConnectionSuspended(int i) {}
};
```

7. Create an `OnConnectionFailedListener` class:

```java
GoogleApiClient.OnConnectionFailedListener
mOnConnectionFailedListener = new GoogleApiClient.
OnConnectionFailedListener() {
        @Override
        public void onConnectionFailed(
            ConnectionResult connectionResult) {
            Toast.makeText(MainActivity.this,
                connectionResult.toString(),
                Toast.LENGTH_LONG).show();
            Log.i("onConnected()", "SecurityException: "
                +connectionResult.toString());
        }
};
```

8. Add the following code to the existing `onCreate()` callback:

```java
mTextView = (TextView) findViewById(R.id.textView);
setupLocationRequest();
```

9. Create the `setupLocationRequest()` method:

   ```
   protected synchronized void setupLocationRequest() {
       mLocationRequest = new LocationRequest();
       mLocationRequest.setInterval(10000);
       mLocationRequest.setFastestInterval(10000);
       mLocationRequest.setPriority(
          LocationRequest.PRIORITY_HIGH_ACCURACY);
       mGoogleApiClient = new GoogleApiClient.Builder(this)
               .addConnectionCallbacks(mConnectionCallbacks)
               .addOnConnectionFailedListener(
                   mOnConnectionFailedListener)
               .addApi(LocationServices.API)
               .build();
       mGoogleApiClient.connect();
   }
   ```

10. You're ready to run the application on a device or emulator.

How it works...

This recipe is similar to the *How to get the last location* recipe, as we need to set up the `GoogleApiClient` as we did before. But, instead of calling the `lastLocation()` method on demand, we call the `requestLocationUpdates()` method to receive periodic location updates through the `LocationListener` class.

The `requestLocationUpdates()` method requires three parameters:

- `GoogleApiClient`
- `LocationRequest`
- `LocationListener`

We create the `GoogleApiClient` as we did before. This is the code to create our `LocationRequest`:

```
mLocationRequest = new LocationRequest();
mLocationRequest.setInterval(10000);
mLocationRequest.setFastestInterval(10000);
mLocationRequest.setPriority(LocationRequest.
   PRIORITY_HIGH_ACCURACY)
```

When calling `setInterval()`, it's generally best to use the slowest delay that works for your purposes, as it requires less device resources. The same idea applies when calling `setPriority()`. The third parameter, the `LocationListener`, is where we define the callback method `onLocationChanged()`. Here we just display the location data along with the location timestamp.

Getting Location and Using Geofencing

There's more...

Unlike the previous Android APIs, the `GoogleApiClient` API does not allow the selection of specific sensors for the location updates. As mentioned in the *Mock Locations* section of *How to get the last Location*, using `LocationRequest.PRIORITY_HIGH_ACCURACY` along with the `ACCESS_FINE_LOCATION` permission should use the GPS sensor. Refer to the *Mock Locations* section for instructions on simulating your location.

Stop receiving location updates

When your application no longer needs location updates, call the `removeLocationUpdates()` method, as shown here:

```
LocationServices.FusedLocationApi.removeLocationUpdates(
    mGoogleApiClient, mLocationListener);
```

Generally, you would want to disable updates when your application is no longer in the foreground, but this depends on your specific application requirements. If your application needs constant updates, it may be more desirable to create a background service to handle the callbacks.

See also

- **Developer Docs: onLocationChanged** at https://developer.android.com/reference/com/google/android/gms/location/LocationRequest.html

Create and monitor a Geofence

If your application needs to know when the user enters a certain location, there's an alternative to having to continuously check the user location: Geofencing. A Geofence is a location (latitude and longitude) along with a radius. You can create a Geofence and let the system notify you when the user enters the location proximity you specified. (Android currently allows up to 100 Geofences per user.)

Geofence properties include:

- **Location**: The longitude and latitude
- **Radius**: The size of the circle (in meters)
- **Loitering delay** : How long the user may remain within the radius before sending notifications
- **Expiration**: How long until the Geofence automatically expires

- **Transition type**: These are listed as follows:
    - GEOFENCE_TRANSITION_ENTER
    - GEOFENCE_TRANSITION_EXIT
    - INITIAL_TRIGGER_DWELL

This recipe will show you how to create a Geofence object and use it to create an instance of `GeofencingRequest`.

Getting ready

Create a new project in Android Studio and call it: Geofence. Use the default **Phone & Tablet** options and select **Empty Activity** when prompted for **Activity Type**.

How to do it...

We won't need a layout for this recipe as we'll use Toasts and Notifications for the user interaction. We will need to create an additional Java class for `IntentService`, which handles the Geofence alerts. Open the Android Manifest and follow these steps:

1. Add the following permission:

    ```
    <uses-permission android:name=
    "android.permission.ACCESS_FINE_LOCATION"/>
    ```

2. Open the file `build.gradle` (Module: app) and add the following statement to the `dependencies` section:

    ```
    compile 'com.google.android.gms:play-services:8.4.0'
    ```

3. Create a new Java class called `GeofenceIntentService` and extend the `IntentService` class. The declaration will look as follows:

    ```
    public class GeofenceIntentService extends IntentService {
    ```

4. Add the following constructor:

    ```
    public GeofenceIntentService() {
        super("GeofenceIntentService");
    }
    ```

5. Add `onHandleIntent()` to receive the Geofence alert:

    ```
    protected void onHandleIntent(Intent intent) {
        GeofencingEvent geofencingEvent =
            GeofencingEvent.fromIntent(intent);
        if (geofencingEvent.hasError()) {
    ```

347

```
            Toast.makeText(getApplicationContext(), "Geofence
              error code= " + geofencingEvent.getErrorCode(),
                Toast.LENGTH_SHORT).show();
            return;
        }
        int geofenceTransition =
          geofencingEvent.getGeofenceTransition();
        if (geofenceTransition ==
          Geofence.GEOFENCE_TRANSITION_DWELL) {
            sendNotification();
        }
    }
```

6. Add the `sendNotification()` method to display the message to the user:

```
    private void sendNotification() {
        Log.i("GeofenceIntentService", "sendNotification()");
        Uri notificationSoundUri =
          RingtoneManager.getDefaultUri(
            RingtoneManager.TYPE_NOTIFICATION);
        NotificationCompat.Builder notificationBuilder = new
          NotificationCompat.Builder(this)
                .setSmallIcon(R.mipmap.ic_launcher)
                .setContentTitle("Geofence Alert")
                .setContentText("GEOFENCE_TRANSITION_DWELL")
                .setSound(notificationSoundUri)
                .setLights(Color.BLUE, 500, 500);
        NotificationManager notificationManager =
          (NotificationManager)
            getApplicationContext().getSystemService(
              Context.NOTIFICATION_SERVICE);
        notificationManager.notify(0,
          notificationBuilder.build());
    }
```

7. Open the Android manifest and add the following within the `<application>` element, at the same level as the `<activity>` element:

```
    <service android:name=".GeofenceIntentService"/>
```

8. Open `MainActivity.java` and add the following global variables:

```
    private final int MINIMUM_RECOMENDED_RADIUS=100;
    GoogleApiClient mGoogleApiClient;
    PendingIntent mGeofencePendingIntent;
```

9. Create the following `ResultCallback` class:

```
ResultCallback mResultCallback = new ResultCallback() {
    @Override
    public void onResult(Result result) {
        Log.i("onResult()", "result: " +
            result.getStatus().toString());
    }
};
```

10. Create a `ConnectionCallbacks` class:

```
GoogleApiClient.ConnectionCallbacks mConnectionCallbacks = new
GoogleApiClient.ConnectionCallbacks() {
    @Override
    public void onConnected(Bundle bundle) {
        try {
          LocationServices.GeofencingApi.addGeofences(
              mGoogleApiClient,
              createGeofencingRequest(),
              getGeofencePendingIntent()
          ).setResultCallback(mResultCallback);
        } catch (SecurityException e) {
            Log.i("onConnected()", "SecurityException: " +
              e.getMessage());
        }
    }
    @Override
    public void onConnectionSuspended(int i) {}
};
```

11. Create an `OnConnectionFailedListener` class:

```
GoogleApiClient.OnConnectionFailedListener
mOnConnectionFailedListener = new GoogleApiClient.
OnConnectionFailedListener() {
    @Override
    public void onConnectionFailed(ConnectionResult
      connectionResult) {
        Log.i("onConnectionFailed()", "connectionResult: "
          +connectionResult.toString());
    }
};
```

12. Add the following code to the existing `onCreate()` callback:

```
setupGoogleApiClient();
```

Getting Location and Using Geofencing

13. Add the method to setup the `GoogleAPIClient`:

    ```
    protected synchronized void setupGoogleApiClient() {
        mGoogleApiClient = new GoogleApiClient.Builder(this)
            .addConnectionCallbacks(mConnectionCallbacks)
            .addOnConnectionFailedListener(
              mOnConnectionFailedListener)
            .addApi(LocationServices.API)
            .build();
        mGoogleApiClient.connect();
    }
    ```

14. Create the `setupGoogleApiClient()` method:

    ```
    protected synchronized void setupGoogleApiClient() {
        mGoogleApiClient = new GoogleApiClient.Builder(this)
            .addConnectionCallbacks(mConnectionCallbacks)
            .addOnConnectionFailedListener(
              mOnConnectionFailedListener)
            .addApi(LocationServices.API)
            .build();
        mGoogleApiClient.connect();
    }
    ```

15. Create a pending intent with the following method:

    ```
    private PendingIntent getGeofencePendingIntent() {
        if (mGeofencePendingIntent != null) {
            return mGeofencePendingIntent;
        }
        Intent intent = new Intent(this,
          GeofenceIntentService.class);
        return PendingIntent.getService(this, 0, intent,
          PendingIntent.FLAG_UPDATE_CURRENT);
    }
    ```

16. Create the `geofence` object and add it to a list for the request:

    ```
    private List createGeofenceList() {
        List<Geofence> geofenceList = new ArrayList<Geofence>();
        geofenceList.add(new Geofence.Builder()
                .setRequestId("GeofenceLocation")
                .setCircularRegion(
                    37.422006, //Latitude
                    -122.084095, //Longitude
                    MINIMUM_RECOMENDED_RADIUS)
                .setLoiteringDelay(30000)
                .setExpirationDuration(Geofence.NEVER_EXPIRE)
                .setTransitionTypes(
                  Geofence.GEOFENCE_TRANSITION_DWELL)
    ```

```
            .build());
        return geofenceList;
    }
```

17. Create the `createGeofencingRequest()` method as follows:

```
    private GeofencingRequest createGeofencingRequest() {
        GeofencingRequest.Builder builder = new
            GeofencingRequest.Builder();
        builder.setInitialTrigger(
            GeofencingRequest.INITIAL_TRIGGER_DWELL);
        builder.addGeofences(createGeofenceList());
        return builder.build();
    }
```

18. You're ready to run the application on a device or emulator.

How it works...

First, we add the `ACCESS_FINE_LOCATION` permission as this is required for Geofencing. We set up the `GoogleApiClient` as we've done in previous recipes and wait until `onConnected()` is called to set up the `GeofencingApi`.

Before we can call the `GeofencingApi.addGeofences()` method, we have to prepare three objects:

- `GoogleApiClient`
- Geofence Request
- Pending Intent

We already created the `GoogleApiClient`, which we saved in the `mGoogleApiClient`.

To create the Geofence Request, we use the `GeofencingRequest.Builder`. The builder requires the list of Geofence objects, which are created in the `createGeofenceList()` method. (Even though we are only creating a single Geofence object, the builder requires a list, so we just add our single Geofence to an `ArrayList`.) Here is where we set the Geofence properties:

```
    .setRequestId("GeofenceLocation")
    .setCircularRegion(
            37.422006, //Latitude
            -122.084095, //Longitude
            MINIMUM_RECOMENDED_RADIUS)
    .setLoiteringDelay(30000)
    .setExpirationDuration(Geofence.NEVER_EXPIRE)
    .setTransitionTypes(Geofence.GEOFENCE_TRANSITION_DWELL)
```

Getting Location and Using Geofencing

Only the Loitering delay is optional, but we need it since we are using the `DWELL` transition. When calling `setTransitionTypes()`, we can combine multiple transition types using the OR operator, shown with the pipe. Here's an example using `ENTER` and `EXIT` instead:

```
.setTransitionTypes(Geofence.GEOFENCE_TRANSITION_ENTER |
    Geofence.GEOFENCE_TRANSITION_EXIT)
```

For this example, we used the same default latitude and longitude as the emulator. Change these values as needed.

Our call to `Geofence.Builder()` creates the Geofence object. With the Geofence list ready, we call the `GeofencingRequest.Builder` and set our initial trigger to `INITIAL_TRIGGER_DWELL`. (If you change the preceding transition types, you may want to change the initial trigger as well.)

The last object we need is a Pending Intent, which is how the system will notify our app when the Geofence criteria are met. We created the `GeofenceIntentService` to handle the Geofence intent by sending a notification to the user. (For more information on notifications, refer to the *Lights, Action, and Sound Redux using Notifications* recipe in *Chapter 7, Alerts and Notifications*.)

With all three objects created, we just call `LocationServices.GeofencingApi.addGeofences()` and wait for the notification to arrive.

There's more...

To stop receiving Geofence notifications, you can call the `removeGeofences()` method with either the `RequestID` parameter or `PendingIntent`. The following example uses the same `PendingIntent` method we used for the notification:

```
LocationServices.GeofencingApi.removeGeofences(
    mGoogleApiClient,
    getGeofencePendingIntent()
).setResultCallback(mResultCallback);
```

See also

- The `Geofence.Builder` class at: https://developers.google.com/android/reference/com/google/android/gms/location/Geofence.Builder.html
- The `GeofencingRequest.Builder` class at: https://developers.google.com/android/reference/com/google/android/gms/location/GeofencingRequest.Builder

14
Getting your app ready for the Play Store

In this chapter, we will cover the following topics:

- The new Android 6.0 Run-Time permission model
- How to schedule an alarm
- Receive notification of device boot
- Using AsyncTask for background work
- Adding speech recognition to your app
- Push Notification using Google Cloud Messaging
- How to add Google sign-in to your app

Introduction

As we approach the end of this book, it's time to add the finishing touches to your application before releasing it to the Play Store. The recipes in this chapter cover the topics that can make a difference between users keeping your app or removing it.

Our first recipe, *The new Android 6.0 Run-Time permission model*, is certainly an important topic, possibly being the primary reason Android went from version 5.x to version 6! Changes to the Android permission model have been requested for some time, so this new model is a welcome change, at least for users.

Next, we'll take a look at using alarms in Android. One of the primary benefits of alarms is that the OS is responsible for maintaining the alarm, even when your application is not running. Since alarms do not persist after rebooting the device, we'll also look at how to detect a device reboot so you can recreate your alarms in *Receive notification of device boot*.

Getting your app ready for the Play Store

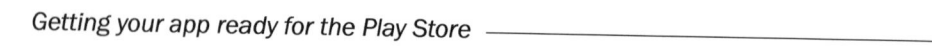

Almost any serious Android application will need a way to perform potentially blocking tasks off the main thread. Otherwise, your app runs the risk of being perceived as sluggish, or worse, completely nonresponsive. `AsyncTask` was designed to make it easier to create a background worker task as we'll demonstrate in the *Using the AsyncTask for background work* recipe.

If you want your app to benefit from hands-free typing or voice recognition, take a look at the *Adding Speech Recognition to your app* recipe in which we'll explore the Google Speech API.

Possibly one of the most interesting features for communicating with your users is Push Notification or **Google Cloud Messaging (GCM)** as Google calls it. The *Push Notification using Google Cloud Messaging* recipe will walk you through the adding of GCM to your application as well as explain the bigger picture.

Finally, we'll end the chapter with a recipe showing how to make your app more comfortable and encourage users to log in with the *How to add Google Sign-In to your app* recipe

The new Android 6.0 Run-Time permission model

The old security model was a sore point for many in Android. It's common to see reviews commenting on the permissions an app requires. Sometimes, permissions were out of the line (like a Flashlight app requiring internet permission), but other times, the developer had good reasons to request certain permissions. The main problem was that it was an all-or-nothing prospect.

This finally changed with the Android 6 Marshmallow (API 23) release. The new permission model still declares permissions in the manifest as before, but users have the option of selectively accepting or denying each permission. Users can even revoke a previously granted permission.

Although this is a welcome change for many; however, for a developer, it has the potential to break the code that was working before. We've talked about this permission change in the previous recipes, as it has far reaching implications. This recipe will put it all together to serve as a single point of reference when implementing this change in your own apps.

One important point to remember is that this change only affects users of Android 6.0 (API 23) and above.

Getting ready

Create a new project in Android Studio and call it `RuntimePermission`. Use the default **Phone & Tablet** option and select **Empty Activity** when prompted for **Activity Type**.

The sample source code sets the minimum API to 23, but this is not required. If your `compileSdkVersion` is API 23 or above, the compiler will flag your code for the new security model.

How to do it...

We need to start by adding our required permission to the manifest, then we'll add a button to call our check permission code. Open the Android Manifest and follow these steps:

1. Add the following permission:

   ```
   <uses-permission android:name=
       "android.permission.SEND_SMS"/>
   ```

2. Open `activity_main.xml` and replace the existing `TextView` with this button:

   ```
   <Button
       android:id="@+id/button"
       android:layout_width="wrap_content"
       android:layout_height="wrap_content"
       android:text="Do Something"
       android:layout_centerInParent="true"
       android:onClick="doSomething"/>
   ```

3. Open `MainActivity.java` and add the following constant to the class:

   ```
   private final int REQUEST_PERMISSION_SEND_SMS=1;
   ```

4. Add this method for permission check:

   ```
   private boolean checkPermission(String permission) {
       int permissionCheck =
           ContextCompat.checkSelfPermission(
               this, permission);
       return (permissionCheck ==
           PackageManager.PERMISSION_GRANTED);
   }
   ```

5. Add this method to show the explanation dialog:

   ```
   private void showExplanation(String title,
       String message, final String permission,
           final int permissionRequestCode) {
       AlertDialog.Builder builder = new
           AlertDialog.Builder(this);
   ```

Getting your app ready for the Play Store

```
        builder.setTitle(title)
                .setMessage(message)
                .setPositiveButton(android.R.string.ok,
                    new DialogInterface.OnClickListener() {
            public void onClick(DialogInterface dialog, int id) {
                requestPermission(permission,
                    permissionRequestCode);
            }
        });
        builder.create().show();
    }
```

6. Add this method to request the permission:

```
private void requestPermission(String permissionName,
    int permissionRequestCode) {
    ActivityCompat.requestPermissions(this,
        new String[]{permissionName},
            permissionRequestCode);
}
```

7. Add the method for button click:

```
public void doSomething(View view) {
    if (!checkPermission(Manifest.permission.SEND_SMS)) {
        if (ActivityCompat.
            shouldShowRequestPermissionRationale(this,
                Manifest.permission.SEND_SMS)) {
            showExplanation("Permission Needed",
                "Rationale", Manifest.permission.SEND_SMS,
                    REQUEST_PERMISSION_SEND_SMS);
        } else {
            requestPermission(Manifest.permission.SEND_SMS,
                REQUEST_PERMISSION_SEND_SMS);
        }
    } else {
        Toast.makeText(MainActivity.this, "Permission
            (already) Granted!",
                Toast.LENGTH_SHORT).show();
    }
}
```

8. Override onRequestPermissionsResult() as follows:

```
@Override
public void onRequestPermissionsResult(
    int requestCode,
    String permissions[],
    int[] grantResults) {
```

```
        switch (requestCode) {
            case REQUEST_PERMISSION_SEND_SMS: {
                if (grantResults.length > 0 &&
                    grantResults[0] ==
                        PackageManager.PERMISSION_GRANTED) {
                    Toast.makeText(MainActivity.this,
                        "Permission Granted!",
                            Toast.LENGTH_SHORT).show();
                } else {
                    Toast.makeText(MainActivity.this,
                        "Permission Denied!",
                            Toast.LENGTH_SHORT).show();
                }
                return;
            }
        }
    }
```

9. Now, you're ready to run the application on a device or emulator.

How it works...

Using the new runtime permission model involves the following:

1. Check to see whether you have the desired permissions.
2. If not, check whether we should display the rationale (meaning, the request was previously denied).
3. Request the permission; only the OS can display the permission request.
4. Handle the request response.

Here are the corresponding methods:

- `ContextCompat.checkSelfPermission`
- `ActivityCompat.requestPermissions`
- `ActivityCompat.shouldShowRequestPermissionRationale`
- `onRequestPermissionsResult`

> Even though you are requesting permissions at runtime, the desired permission must be listed in the Android Manifest. If the permission is not specified, the OS will automatically deny the request.

There's more...

You can grant/revoke permissions through the ADB with the following:

```
adb shell pm [grant|revoke] <package> <permission-name>
```

Here's an example to grant the SEND_SMS permission for our test app:

```
adb shell pm grant com.packtpub.androidcookbook.runtimepermissions android.permission.SEND_SMS
```

See also

- **Developer Docs: System Permissions** at https://developer.android.com/guide/topics/security/permissions.html

How to schedule an alarm

Android provides `AlarmManager` to create and schedule alarms. Alarms offer the following features:

- Schedule alarms for a set time or interval
- Maintained by the OS, not your application, so alarms are triggered even if your application is not running, or the device is asleep
- Can be used to trigger periodic tasks (such as an hourly news update), even if your application is not running
- Your app does not use resources (such as timers or background services), since the OS manages the scheduling

Alarms are not the best solution if you need a simple delay while your application is running, for example, a short delay for a UI event. For short delays, it's easier and more efficient to use a Handler, as we've done in several previous recipes.

When using alarms, keep these best practices in mind:

- Use as infrequent alarm timing as possible
- Avoid waking up the device
- Use as imprecise timing as possible—the more precise the timing, the more resources required
- Avoid setting alarm times based on clock time (such as 12:00); add random adjustments if possible to avoid congestion on servers (especially important when checking for new content, such as weather or news)

Alarms have three properties, as follows:

- Alarm type (see in the following list)
- Trigger time (if the time has already passed, the alarm is triggered immediately)
- Pending Intent

A repeating alarm has the same three properties, plus an Interval:

- Alarm type (see in the following list)
- Trigger time (if the time has already passed, it triggers immediately)
- Interval
- Pending Intent

There are four alarm types:

- `RTC` (**Real Time Clock**): This is based on the wall clock time. This does not wake the device.
- `RTC_WAKEUP`: This is based on the wall clock time. This wakes the device if it is sleeping.
- `ELAPSED_REALTIME`: This is based on the time elapsed since the device boot. This does not wake the device.
- `ELAPSED_REALTIME_WAKEUP`: This is based on the time elapsed since the device boot. This wakes the device if it is sleeping.

Elapsed Real Time is better for time interval alarms—such as every 30 minutes.

> Alarms do not persist after device reboots. All alarms are cancelled when a device shuts down, so it is your app's responsibility to reset the alarms on device boot. (See *Receive notification of device boot* for more information.)

The following recipe will demonstrate how to create alarms with `AlarmManager`.

Getting ready

Create a new project in Android Studio and call it: `Alarms`. Use the default **Phone & Tablet** option and select **Empty Activity** when prompted for **Activity Type**.

Getting your app ready for the Play Store

How to do it...

Setting an alarm requires a Pending Intent, which Android sends when the alarm is triggered. Therefore, we need to set up a Broadcast Receiving to capture the alarm intent. Our UI will consist of just a simple button to set the alarm. To start, open the Android Manifest and follow these steps:

1. Add the following `<receiver>` to the `<application>` element at the same level as the existing `<activity>` element:

    ```xml
    <receiver android:name=".AlarmBroadcastReceiver">
        <intent-filter>
            <action android:name="com.packtpub.androidcookbook.
                alarms.ACTION_ALARM" />
        </intent-filter>
    </receiver>
    ```

2. Open `activity_main.xml` and replace the existing TextView with the following button:

    ```xml
    <Button
        android:id="@+id/button"
        android:layout_width="wrap_content"
        android:layout_height="wrap_content"
        android:text="Set Alarm"
        android:layout_centerInParent="true"
        android:onClick="setAlarm"/>
    ```

3. Create a new Java class called `AlarmBroadcastReceiver` using the following code:

    ```java
    public class AlarmBroadcastReceiver extends
            BroadcastReceiver {

        public static final String ACTION_ALARM=
            "com.packtpub.androidcookbook.alarms.ACTION_ALARM";

        @Override
        public void onReceive(Context context, Intent intent) {
            if (ACTION_ALARM.equals(intent.getAction())) {
                Toast.makeText(context, ACTION_ALARM,
                    Toast.LENGTH_SHORT).show();
            }
        }
    }
    ```

4. Open `ActivityMain.java` and add the method for the button click:
   ```
   public void setAlarm(View view) {
       Intent intentToFire = new Intent(
           getApplicationContext(),
               AlarmBroadcastReceiver.class);
       intentToFire.setAction(
           AlarmBroadcastReceiver.ACTION_ALARM);
       PendingIntent alarmIntent = PendingIntent.getBroadcast(
           getApplicationContext(), 0, intentToFire, 0);
       AlarmManager alarmManager =
           (AlarmManager)getApplicationContext().
               getSystemService(Context.ALARM_SERVICE);
       long thirtyMinutes=SystemClock.elapsedRealtime() + 30 *
           60 * 1000;
       alarmManager.set(AlarmManager.ELAPSED_REALTIME,
           thirtyMinutes, alarmIntent);
   }
   ```

5. You're ready to run the application on a device or emulator.

How it works...

Creating the alarm is done with this line of code:

```
alarmManager.set(AlarmManager.ELAPSED_REALTIME, thirtyMinutes,
    alarmIntent);
```

Here's the method signature:

```
set(AlarmType, Time, PendingIntent);
```

> Prior to Android 4.4 KitKat (API 19), this was the method to request an exact time. Android 4.4 and later will consider this as an inexact time for efficiency, but will not deliver the intent prior to the requested time. (See `setExact()` as follows if you need an exact time.)

To set the alarm, we create a Pending Intent with our previously defined alarm action:

```
public static final String ACTION_ALARM=
    "com.packtpub.androidcookbook.alarms.ACTION_ALARM";
```

(This is an arbitrary string and could be anything we want, but it needs to be unique, so we prepend our package name.) We check for this action in the Broadcast Receiver's `onReceive()` callback.

There's more...

If you click the **Set Alarm** button and wait for thirty minutes, you will see the Toast when the alarm triggers. If you are too impatient to wait and click the **Set Alarm** button again before the first alarm is triggered, you wouldn't get two alarms. Instead, the OS will replace the first alarm with the new alarm, since they both use the same Pending Intent. (If you need multiple alarms, you need to create different Pending Intents, such as using different Actions.)

Cancel the alarm

If you want to cancel the alarm, call the `cancel()` method by passing the same Pending Intent you have used to create the alarm. If we continue with our recipe, this is how it would look:

```
alarmManager.cancel(alarmIntent);
```

Repeating alarm

If you want to create a repeating alarm, use the `setRepeating()` method. The Signature is similar to the `set()` method, but with an interval. This is shown as follows:

```
setRepeating(AlarmType, Time (in milliseconds), Interval,
    PendingIntent);
```

For the Interval, you can specify the interval time in milliseconds or use one of the predefined `AlarmManager` constants:

- INTERVAL_DAY
- INTERVAL_FIFTEEN_MINUTES
- INTERVAL_HALF_DAY
- INTERVAL_HALF_HOUR
- INTERVAL_HOUR

See also

- **Developer Docs: AlarmManager** at https://developer.android.com/reference/android/app/AlarmManager.html

Receive notification of device boot

Android sends out many intents during its lifetime. One of the first intents sent is ACTION_BOOT_COMPLETED. If your application needs to know when the device boots, you need to capture this intent.

This recipe will walk you through the steps required to be notified when the device boots.

Getting ready

Create a new project in Android Studio and call it `DeviceBoot`. Use the default **Phone & Tablet** option and select **Empty Activity** when prompted for **Activity Type**.

How to do it...

To start, open the Android Manifest and follow these steps:

1. Add the following permission:

    ```
    <uses-permission android:name=
        "android.permission.RECEIVE_BOOT_COMPLETED"/>
    ```

2. Add the following `<receiver>` to the `<application>` element, at the same level as the existing `<activity>` element:

    ```
    <receiver android:name=".BootBroadcastReceiver">
        <intent-filter>
            <action android:name="android.intent.action.
                BOOT_COMPLETED"/>
        </intent-filter>
    </receiver>
    ```

3. Create a new Java class called `BootBroadcastReceiver` using the following code:

    ```
    public class BootBroadcastReceiver extends
        BroadcastReceiver {
        @Override
        public void onReceive(Context context, Intent intent) {
            if (intent.getAction().equals(
                "android.intent.action.BOOT_COMPLETED")) {
                Toast.makeText(context, "BOOT_COMPLETED",
                    Toast.LENGTH_SHORT).show();
            }
        }
    }
    ```

4. Reboot the device to see the Toast.

How it works...

When the device boots, Android will send the `BOOT_COMPLETED` intent. As long as our application has the permission to receive the intent, we will receive notifications in our Broadcast Receiver.

Getting your app ready for the Play Store

There are three aspects to make this work:

- A permission for `RECEIVE_BOOT_COMPLETED`
- Adding `BOOT_COMPLETED` to the receiver intent filter
- Checking for the `BOOT_COMPLETED` action in the Broadcast Receiver

Obviously, you'll want to replace the Toast message with your own code, such as for recreating any alarms you might need.

There's more...

If you followed the previous recipe, then you already have a Broadcast Receiver. You don't need a separate `BroadcastReceiver` for each action, just check for each action as needed. Here's an example if we need to handle another action:

```java
public void onReceive(Context context, Intent intent) {
    if (intent.getAction().equals(
        "android.intent.action.BOOT_COMPLETED")) {
        Toast.makeText(context, "BOOT_COMPLETED",
            Toast.LENGTH_SHORT).show();
    } else if (intent.getAction().equals("<another_action>")) {
        //handle another action
    }
}
```

See also

- **Developer Docs: Intent** at https://developer.android.com/reference/android/content/Intent.html

Using the AsyncTask for background work

Throughout this book, we have mentioned the importance of not blocking the main thread. Performing long running operations on the main thread can cause your application to appear sluggish, or worse, hang. If your application doesn't respond within about 5 seconds, the system will likely display the **Application Not Responding** (**ANR**) dialog with the option to terminate your app. (This is something you will want to avoid as it's a good way to get your app uninstalled.)

Android applications use a single thread model with two simple rules, as follows:

- Don't block the main thread
- Perform all UI operations *on* the main thread

When Android starts your application, it automatically creates the main (or UI) thread. This is the thread from which all UI operations must be called. The first rule is "Don't block the main thread". This means that you need to create a background, or a worker, thread for any long-running or potentially-blocking task. This is why all network based tasks should be performed off the main thread.

Android offers the following options when working with background threads:

- `Activity.runOnUiThread()`
- `View.post()`
- `View.postDelayed()`
- `Handler`
- `AsyncTask`

This recipe will explore the `AsyncTask` class; since it was created previously, you wouldn't have to use the Handler or post methods directly.

Getting ready

Create a new project in Android Studio and call it: `AsyncTask`. Use the default **Phone & Tablet** option and select **Empty Activity** when prompted for **Activity Type**.

How to do it...

We only need a single button for this example. Open `activity_main.xml` and follow these steps:

1. Replace the existing TextView with the following button:

    ```xml
    <Button
        android:id="@+id/buttonStart"
        android:layout_width="wrap_content"
        android:layout_height="wrap_content"
        android:text="Start"
        android:layout_centerInParent="true"
        android:onClick="start" />
    ```

2. Open `MainActivity.java` and add the following global variable:

    ```java
    Button mButtonStart;
    ```

Getting your app ready for the Play Store

3. Add the `AsyncTask` class:

```java
private class CountingTask extends AsyncTask<Integer, Integer, Integer> {
    @Override
    protected Integer doInBackground(Integer... params) {
        int count = params[0];
        for (int x=0;x<=count; x++){
            //Nothing to do
        }
        return count;
    }
    @Override
    protected void onPostExecute(Integer integer) {
        super.onPostExecute(integer);
        mButtonStart.setEnabled(true);
    }
}
```

4. Add the following code to the `onCreate()` to initialize the button:

```java
mButtonStart=(Button)findViewById(R.id.buttonStart);
```

5. Add the method for the button click:

```java
public void start(View view){
    mButtonStart.setEnabled(false);
    new CountingTask().execute(10000000);
}
```

6. You're ready to run the application on a device or emulator.

How it works...

This is a very simple example of the `AsyncTask` just to get it working. Technically, only `doInBackground()` is required, but usually, you may want to receive notifications via `onPostExecute()` when it finishes.

The `AsyncTask` works by creating a worker thread for the `doInBackground()` method, then responds back on the UI thread in the `onPostExecute()` callback.

Notice how we have waited until `onPostExecute()` is called before we do any UI actions such as enabling the button. If we attempt to modify the UI in the worker thread, it would either not compile or throw a runtime exception. You should also note how we instantiated a new `CountingTask` object on each button click. This is because an `AsyncTask` can only execute once. Attempting to call execute again will also throw an exception.

Chapter 14

There's more...

At its minimum, the `AsyncTask` can be very simple but it is still very flexible with more options available if you need them. When using an `AsyncTask` with an Activity, it's important to understand whether the Activity is destroyed and recreated (such as during an orientation change), or the `AsyncTask` continues to run. This can leave your `AsyncTask` orphaned and it might respond back to the now destroyed activity (causing a `NullPointer` exception). For this reason, it's common to use the `AysncTask` with a Fragment (which is not destroyed on screen rotation), or use a Loader instead. (See the link for Loaders in the following section.)

Parameter types

For many people, the most confusing aspect of the `AsyncTask` is the parameters when creating their own class. If you look at our class declaration, there are three parameters for the `AsyncTask`; they are defined as follows:

```
AsyncTask<Params, Progress, Result >
```

The parameters are generic types and used as follows:

- **Params**: This is the parameter type to call `doInBackground()`
- **Progress**: This is the parameter type to post updates
- **Result**: This is the parameter type to post results

When you declare your own class, substitute the parameters with the variable type you need.

Here's the process flow for the `AsyncTask` and how the preceding parameters are used:

- `onPreExecute()`: This is called before `doInBackground()` begins
- `doInBackground(Params)`: This executes in a background thread
- `onProgressUpdate(Progress)`: This is called (on the UI thread) in response to the calling `publishProgress(Progress)` in the worker thread
- `onPostExecute(Result)`: This is called (on the UI thread) when the worker thread finishes

Cancel the task

To cancel the task, call the cancel method on the object as follows:

```
< AsyncTask>.cancel(true);
```

You will need to have the object instance to access the `cancel()` method. (We did not save the object in our previous example.) After setting `cancel(true)`, the calling `isCancelled()` in `doInBackground()` will return `true`, allowing you to exit a loop. If cancelled, `onCancelled()` will be called instead of `onPostExecute()`.

See also

- Refer to the *Access data in the background using a Loader* recipe, in *Chapter 6, Working with Data*
- **Developer Docs: AsyncTask** at http://developer.android.com/reference/android/os/AsyncTask.html

Adding speech recognition to your app

Android 2.2 (API 8) introduced speech recognition in Android, and it continues to improve with almost every new major Android release. This recipe will demonstrate how to add speech recognition to your app using the Google Speech service.

Getting ready

Create a new project in Android Studio and call it `SpeechRecognition`. Use the default **Phone & Tablet** option and select **Empty Activity** when prompted for **Activity Type**.

How to do it...

We'll start by adding a Speak Now (or microphone) button to the layout, then we'll add the necessary code to call the speech recognizer. Open `activity_main.xml` and follow these steps:

1. Replace the existing `TextView` with the following XML:

    ```xml
    <TextView
        android:id="@+id/textView"
        android:layout_width="wrap_content"
        android:layout_height="wrap_content"
        android:layout_alignParentTop="true"
        android:layout_alignParentLeft="true"
        android:layout_alignParentStart="true" />
    <ImageButton
        android:id="@+id/imageButton"
        android:layout_width="wrap_content"
        android:layout_height="wrap_content"
        android:layout_alignParentBottom="true"
        android:layout_centerHorizontal="true"
        android:src="@android:drawable/ic_btn_speak_now"
        android:onClick="speakNow"/>
    ```

2. Define the `REQUEST_SPEECH` constant:

   ```
   private final int REQUEST_SPEECH=1;
   ```

3. Add the following code to the existing `onCreate()` callback:

   ```
   PackageManager pm = getPackageManager();
   List<ResolveInfo> activities = pm.queryIntentActivities(
       new Intent(RecognizerIntent.
           ACTION_RECOGNIZE_SPEECH), 0);
   if (activities.size() == 0) {
       findViewById(R.id.imageButton).setEnabled(false);
       Toast.makeText(this, "Speech Recognition Not
           Supported", Toast.LENGTH_LONG).show();
   }
   ```

4. Add the button click method:

   ```
   public void speakNow(View view) {
       Intent intent = new Intent(RecognizerIntent.
           ACTION_RECOGNIZE_SPEECH);
       intent.putExtra(RecognizerIntent.EXTRA_LANGUAGE_MODEL,
           RecognizerIntent.LANGUAGE_MODEL_FREE_FORM);
       startActivityForResult(intent, REQUEST_SPEECH);
   }
   ```

5. Add the following code to override the `onActivityResult()` callback:

   ```
   @Override
   protected void onActivityResult(int requestCode, int
       resultCode, Intent data) {
       super.onActivityResult(requestCode, resultCode, data);
       if (requestCode==REQUEST_SPEECH && resultCode ==
           RESULT_OK && data!=null) {
           ArrayList<String> result = data
               .getStringArrayListExtra(
                   RecognizerIntent.EXTRA_RESULTS);
           TextView textView = (TextView)findViewById(
               R.id.textView);
           if (result.size()>0){
               textView.setText("");
               for (String item : result ) {
                   textView.append(item+"\n");
               }
           }
       }
   }
   ```

6. You're ready to run the application on a device or emulator.

Getting your app ready for the Play Store

How it works...

The work here is done by the Google Speech Recognizer included in Android. To make sure the service is available on the device, we call `PackageManager` in `onCreate()`. If at least one activity is registered to handle the `RecognizerIntent.ACTION_RECOGNIZE_SPEECH` intent, then we know it's available. If no activities are available, we display a Toast indicating speech recognition is not available and disable the mic button.

The button click starts the recognition process by calling an intent created with `RecognizerIntent.ACTION_RECOGNIZE_SPEECH`.

The `EXTRA_LANGUAGE_MODEL` parameter is required and has the following two choices:

- `LANGUAGE_MODEL_FREE_FORM`
- `LANGUAGE_MODEL_WEB_SEARCH`

We get the result back in the `onActivityResult()` callback. If we get back `RESULT_OK`, then we should have a list of words recognized, which we can retrieve using `getStringArrayListExtra()`. The array list will be ordered starting with the highest recognition confidence.

If you want to retrieve the confidence rating, retrieve the float array using `EXTRA_CONFIDENCE_SCORES`. Here's an example:

```
float[] confidence = data.getFloatArrayExtra(
    RecognizerIntent.EXTRA_CONFIDENCE_SCORES);
```

The confidence rating is optional and may not be present. A score of 1.0 indicates highest confidence, while 0.0 indicates lowest confidence.

There's more...

Using the intent is a quick and easy way to get speech recognition; however, if you would prefer not to use the default Google activity, you can call the `SpeechRecognizer` class directly. Here's an example of how to instantiate the class:

```
SpeechRecognizer speechRecognizer =
    SpeechRecognizer.createSpeechRecognizer(this);
```

You will need to add the `RECORD_AUDIO` permission and implement the `RecognitionListener` class to handle the speech events. (See the following links for more information.)

See also

- **Developer Docs: RecognizerIntent** at `http://developer.android.com/reference/android/speech/RecognizerIntent.html`
- **Developer Docs: SpeechRecognizer** at `http://developer.android.com/reference/android/speech/SpeechRecognizer.html`
- **Developer Docs: RecognitionListener** at `http://developer.android.com/reference/android/speech/RecognitionListener.html`

Push Notification using GCM

GCM, Google's version of Push Notification, allows your application to receive messages. The idea is similar to SMS messages, but much more flexible. There are three components to GCM:

- Your server (this is where you initiate the message)
- Google's GCM server
- Android device (although GCM is also available on other platforms)

When the user starts your application, your code needs to connect to the GCM server and obtain a device token, then send that token to your server. Your server is responsible for initiating the message and passing it to the GCM server. Your server needs to track the device tokens that have to be sent when initiating the message. (Your server tells the GCM server which device tokens needs to be sent.)

You can implement your own server or choose to use one of many services available. The next chapter, *Backend Service Options*, will look at several BaaS options, many of which also offer Push Notification. (The *Simple Testing Option* section offers an option to verify that your code is working.)

This recipe will walk you through the steps to add GCM using the current (Version 8.3) Google Services library. Before getting to the steps, it's worth noting that GCM is supported all the way back to API 8, as long as the user has a Google account. A Google account is not required after Android 4.0.4.

Getting ready

Create a new project in Android Studio and call it GCM. Use the default **Phone & Tablet** option and select **Empty Activity** when prompted for **Activity Type**.

Getting your app ready for the Play Store

GCM uses the Google Services plugin, which requires a Google Services configuration file available from the Google Developer Console. To create the configuration file, you will need the following information:

- Your application package name
- When you have the information, log in to this Google link and follow the wizard to enable GCM for your app: `https://developers.google.com/mobile/add`

> If you download the source files, you will need to create a new package name when following the preceding steps, as the existing package name has already been registered.

How to do it...

After completing the preceding Getting Ready section, follow these steps:

1. Copy the `google-services.json` file, which you downloaded in the *Getting Ready* section, to your app folder (`<project folder>\GCM\app`).

2. Open the project Gradle build file: `build.gradle (Project: GCM)`, and add the following to the `buildscript dependencies` sections:

   ```
   classpath 'com.google.gms:google-services:1.5.0-beta2'
   ```

3. Open the app module Gradle build file: `build.gradle (Module: app)`, and add the following statement to the beginning of the file (above the `android` section):

   ```
   apply plugin: 'com.google.gms.google-services'
   ```

4. In the same module build file as step 3, add the following statement to the dependencies section:

   ```
   compile 'com.google.android.gms:play-services-auth:8.3.0'
   ```

5. Open the Android Manifest and add the following permissions:

   ```
   <uses-permission android:name=
       "android.permission.WAKE_LOCK" />
   <permission android:name="< packageName >
       .permission.C2D_MESSAGE"
       android:protectionLevel="signature" />
   <uses-permission android:name="< packageName >
       .permission.C2D_MESSAGE" />
   ```

6. Within the `<application>` element, add the following `<receiver>` and `<service>` declarations (these should be at the same level as the `<activity>`):

   ```
   <receiver
       android:name="com.google.android.gms.gcm.GcmReceiver"
       android:exported="true"
   ```

```xml
            android:permission="com.google.android.c2dm.
                permission.SEND" >
            <intent-filter>
                <action android:name="com.google.android.c2dm.
                    intent.RECEIVE" />
                <category android:name="<packageName>" />
                <action android:name="com.google.android.
                    c2dm.intent.REGISTRATION" />
            </intent-filter>
        </receiver>
        <service
            android:name=".GCMService"
            android:exported="false" >
            <intent-filter>
                <action android:name="com.google.android.c2dm.
                    intent.GCM_RECEIVED_ACTION"/>
                <action android:name="com.google.android.c2dm.
                    intent.RECEIVE" />
            </intent-filter>
        </service>
        <service
            android:name=".GCMInstanceService"
            android:exported="false">
            <intent-filter>
                <action android:name="com.google.android.gms.
                    iid.InstanceID" />
            </intent-filter>
        </service>
        <service
            android:name=".GCMRegistrationService"
            android:exported="false">
        </service>
```

7. Create a new Java class called `GCMRegistrationService` that extends `IntentService`, as follows:

```java
public class GCMRegistrationService extends IntentService {

    private final String SENT_TOKEN="SENT_TOKEN";

    public GCMRegistrationService() {
        super("GCMRegistrationService");
    }
```

```java
        @Override
        protected void onHandleIntent(Intent intent) {
            super.onCreate();
            SharedPreferences sharedPreferences =
                PreferenceManager.
                    getDefaultSharedPreferences(this);
            try {
                InstanceID instanceID = InstanceID.
                    getInstance(this);
                String token = instanceID.getToken(
                    getString(R.string.gcm_defaultSenderId),
                        GoogleCloudMessaging.INSTANCE_ID_SCOPE,
                            null);
                Log.i("GCMRegistrationService", "GCM
                    Registration Token: " + token);
                //sendTokenToServer(token);
                sharedPreferences.edit().putBoolean(SENT_TOKEN,
                    true).apply();
            } catch (Exception e) {
                sharedPreferences.edit().putBoolean(SENT_TOKEN,
                    false).apply();
            }
        }
    }
```

8. Create a new Java class called `GCMInstanceService` that extends `InstanceIDListenerService`, as follows:

```java
public class GCMInstanceService extends
    InstanceIDListenerService {
    @Override
        public void onTokenRefresh() {
        Intent intent = new Intent(this,
            GCMRegistrationService.class);
        startService(intent);
    }
}
```

9. Create a new Java class called `GCMService` that extends `GcmListenerService`, as follows:

```java
public class GCMService extends GcmListenerService {

    @Override
    public void onMessageReceived(String from, Bundle data) {
        super.onMessageReceived(from, data);
```

```
            Log.i("GCMService", "onMessageReceived(): " +
                data.toString());
        }
    }
```

10. Add the following code to the existing `onCreate()` callback:

    ```
    Intent intent = new Intent(this,
        GCMRegistrationService.class);
    startService(intent);
    ```

11. You're ready to run the application on a device or emulator.

How it works...

Most of the actual GCM code is encapsulated within the Google APIs, simplifying the implementation. We just have to set up the project to include Google Services, and give our app the required permissions.

> **Important!** When adding the permissions in Steps 5 and 6, replace the `<packageName>` placeholder with your application's package name.

The most complicated aspect of GCM is probably the multiple services required. Even though the code in each service is minimal, each service has a specific task. There are two main aspects of GCM:

- Registering the app with the GCM server
- Receiving messages

This is the code to register with the GCM server:

```
String token = instanceID.getToken(getString(
    R.string.gcm_defaultSenderId),
        GoogleCloudMessaging.INSTANCE_ID_SCOPE, null);
```

We don't call `getToken()` in the Activity, because it could block the UI thread. Instead, we call the `GCMRegistrationService`, which handles the call in a background thread. After you receive the device token, you need to send it to your server, as it is needed when initiating a message.

The process of receiving a GCM message is handled in `GCMService`, which extends `GcmListenerService`. Since the Google API already handles most of the work, all we have to do is respond to the `onMessageReceived()` callback.

Getting your app ready for the Play Store

There's more...

To make it easier to type, we left out an important Google Services API verification that should be included in any production application. Instead of calling `GCMRegistrationService` directly, as we did in `onCreate()` in the preceding section, first check whether the Google API Service is available. Here's an example showing how to call the `isGooglePlayServicesAvailable()` method:

```java
    private boolean isGooglePlayServicesAvailable() {
        GoogleApiAvailability googleApiAvailability =
            GoogleApiAvailability.getInstance();
        int resultCode = googleApiAvailability.
            isGooglePlayServicesAvailable(this);
        if (resultCode != ConnectionResult.SUCCESS) {
            if (googleApiAvailability.
                isUserResolvableError(resultCode)) {
                googleApiAvailability.getErrorDialog(this, resultCode,
                    PLAY_SERVICES_RESOLUTION_REQUEST).show();
            } else {
                Toast.makeText(MainActivity.this, "Unsupported
                    Device", Toast.LENGTH_SHORT).show();
                finish();
            }
            return false;
        }
        return true;
    }
```

Then, change the `onCreate()` code to call this method first:

```java
    if (isGooglePlayServicesAvailable()) {
        Intent intent = new Intent(this,
            GCMRegistrationService.class);
        startService(intent);
    }
```

Simple testing option

To help to verify that your code is working correctly, a testing application was created and posted on Google Play. This app will run on both a physical device and an emulator. The Google Play listing also includes a link to download the source code and run the project directly, making it easier to enter the required fields.

> **GCM (Push Notification) Tester**: Refer to the following link for more information:
> `https://play.google.com/store/apps/details?id=com.eboyer.gcmtester`

See also

- Refer to the Google Cloud Messaging web page at `https://developers.google.com/android/reference/com/google/android/gms/gcm/GoogleCloudMessaging`
- Refer to the About the GCM Connection server web page at `https://developers.google.com/cloud-messaging/server`

How to add Google sign-in to your app

A Google sign-in allows your users to sign in to your application using their Google credentials. This recipe will walk you through the process of adding a Google sign-in to your application. Here's a screenshot showing the Google sign-in button in the application that we'll create in the recipe:

Getting your app ready for the Play Store

Getting ready

Create a new project in Android Studio and call it `GoogleSignIn`. Use the default **Phone & Tablet** option and select **Empty Activity** when prompted for **Activity Type**.

The Google sign-in uses the Google Services plugin, which requires a Google Services Configuration file, which is available from the Google Developer Console. To create the configuration file, you will need the following information:

- Your application package name
- Your signing certificate's SHA-1 hash code (see the *Authenticating Your Client* link at the end of the recipe for more information)

When you have the information, log in to this Google link and follow the wizard to enable sign-in:

`https://developers.google.com/mobile/add`

> If you are downloading the source files, you will need to create a new package name when following the preceding steps, as the existing package name has already been registered.

How to do it...

After completing the preceding *Getting Ready* section, follow these steps:

1. Copy the `google-services.json` file you downloaded in the *Getting Ready* section to your app folder (`<project folder>\GoogleSignIn\app`)

2. Open the project Gradle build file: `build.gradle (Project: GoogleSignIn)`, and add the following to the `buildscript dependencies` section:

   `classpath 'com.google.gms:google-services:1.5.0-beta2'`

3. Open the app module Gradle build file: `build.gradle (Module: app)`, and add the following statement to the beginning of the file (above the `android` section):

   `apply plugin: 'com.google.gms.google-services'`

4. In the same module build file as Step 3, add the following statement to the dependencies section:

   `compile 'com.google.android.gms:play-services-auth:8.3.0'`

5. Open `activity_main.xml` and replace the existing `TextView` with the following XML:

   ```xml
   <TextView
       android:id="@+id/textView"
       android:layout_width="wrap_content"
       android:layout_height="wrap_content"
       android:layout_alignParentTop="true" />

   <com.google.android.gms.common.SignInButton
       android:id="@+id/signInButton"
       android:layout_width="wrap_content"
       android:layout_height="wrap_content"
       android:layout_centerInParent="true" />
   ```

6. Open `MainActivity.java` and add the following global declarations:

   ```java
   private final int REQUEST_SIGN_IN=1;
   GoogleApiClient mGoogleApiClient;
   ```

7. Add the following `OnConnectionFailedListener`:

   ```java
   GoogleApiClient.OnConnectionFailedListener
       mOnConnectionFailedListener = new
           GoogleApiClient.OnConnectionFailedListener() {
       @Override
       public void onConnectionFailed(ConnectionResult
           connectionResult) {
           Toast.makeText(MainActivity.this,
           "connectionResult="+connectionResult.
           getErrorMessage(),
           Toast.LENGTH_SHORT).show();
       }
   };
   ```

8. Add the following code to the existing `onCreate()`:

   ```java
   GoogleSignInOptions googleSignInOptions = new
       GoogleSignInOptions.Builder(
           GoogleSignInOptions.DEFAULT_SIGN_IN)
       .requestEmail()
       .build();
   mGoogleApiClient = new GoogleApiClient.Builder(this)
       .addOnConnectionFailedListener(
           mOnConnectionFailedListener)
       .addConnectionCallbacks(mConnectionCallbacks)
       .addApi(Auth.GOOGLE_SIGN_IN_API, googleSignInOptions)
       .build();
   ```

Getting your app ready for the Play Store

```java
    findViewById(R.id.signInButton).setOnClickListener(
        new View.OnClickListener() {
        @Override
        public void onClick(View v) {
            signIn();
        }
    });
```

9. Create an override for the `onActivityResult()` callback as follows:

```java
@Override
public void onActivityResult(int requestCode, int
        resultCode, Intent data) {
    super.onActivityResult(requestCode, resultCode, data);
    if (requestCode == REQUEST_SIGN_IN) {
        GoogleSignInResult googleSignInResult =
            Auth.GoogleSignInApi.
                getSignInResultFromIntent(data);
        if (googleSignInResult.isSuccess()) {
            GoogleSignInAccount googleSignInAccount =
                googleSignInResult.getSignInAccount();
            TextView textView =
                (TextView)findViewById(R.id.textView);
            textView.setText("Signed in: " +
                googleSignInAccount.getDisplayName());
            findViewById(R.id.signInButton).
                setVisibility(View.GONE);
        }
    }
}
```

10. You're ready to run the application on a device or emulator.

How it works...

Google has made it relatively simple to add a Google sign-in with their `GoogleApiClient` and `GoogleSignInOptions` APIs. First, we create a `GoogleSignInOptions` object with the builder. This is where we specify the sign-in options we want, such as requesting e-mail ID. Then, we pass it to the `GoogleApiClient` builder.

When the user clicks on the Google sign-in button (created with the `com.google.android.gms.common.SignInButton` class), we send an Intent for `GoogleSignInApi` to the handle. We process the result in `onActivityResult()`. If the sign-in was successful, we can get the account details. In our example, we just get the e-mail, but additional information is available such as the following:

- `getDisplayName()`: This is the display name
- `getEmail()`: The e-mail address
- `getId()`: The unique ID for the Google account
- `getPhotoUrl()`: The display photo
- `getIdToken()`: This is for the backend authentication

See the *GoogleSignInAccount* link in the *See also* section for a complete list.

There's more...

If you want your application to be available to a wider audience, you'll want to think about localization.

Localization resources

Google provides many localized strings in the SDK, located at this link: `<SDK install folder>/sdk/extras/google/google_play_services/libproject/google-play-services_lib/res/`.

See also

- Refer to the web page talking about authenticating your client at `https://developers.google.com/android/guides/client-auth`
- Visit GoogleSignInAccount at `https://developers.google.com/android/reference/com/google/android/gms/auth/api/signin/GoogleSignInAccount`

15
The Backend as a Service Options

In this chapter, we will cover the following topics:

- App42
- Backendless
- Buddy
- Firebase
- Kinvey

Introduction

As your application and user base grow, it's likely you'll want to connect your app across devices and even users, such as a high score leaderboard. You have two choices:

- Create and maintain your own server
- Use a **Backend as a Service** (**BaaS**) provider

As a mobile developer, creating and maintaining a web server is a time consuming prospect that could likely divert you from your development efforts.

> Here's some background information if you are unfamiliar with BaaS providers:
> Wikipedia – Mobile backend as a service:
> `https://en.wikipedia.org/wiki/Mobile_backend_as_a_service`

The Backend as a Service Options

We're going to take a look at several BaaS providers with features specifically targeting Android developers. Only the providers offering native Android support and free subscription are included. (Providers offering only a free trial or paid-only plans were not included.) As your application outgrows the free tier, all these providers offer higher tier services with varying monthly fees.

The following table provides quick comparison of the monthly free service offered by each provider:

Provider	Monthly Users	API Calls	Push Notification	File Storage
Firebase	Unlimited	100 SC	N/A	1 GB
Buddy	*	20/sec	5 Million	10 GB
App42	*	1 Million / month	1 Million	1 GB
Kinvey	1000	*	*	30 GB
Backendless	100	50/sec	1 Million	20 GB

* = not posted on their website

N/A = feature Not Available

SC = Simultaneous Connections

> **Disclaimer**: The information for the preceding table and following recipes was obtained from their public websites, and is subject to change at their discretion. As you know, the mobile industry is constantly changing; expect prices and services to change. Use this information as a starting point only.

Lastly, this is not meant to be an exhaustive list of BaaS providers. Hopefully, this chapter will provide a good introduction to what a BaaS can do and how you can make use of one for your app. The recipes that follow will look at each provider and take you through the steps of adding their library to your project. This will give you a direct comparison between the services. As you will see, some services are easier to use than others, and this may be a deciding factor.

App42

App42 is the BaaS API product of ShepHertz, a cloud provider of multiple services, including gaming platforms, Platform as a Service, and Marketing Analytics. They have a very rich feature set, including many services especially useful for games.

The App42 Android SDK supports the following:

- User service
- Storage service
- Custom code service
- Push notification service
- Event service
- Gift management service
- Timer service
- Social service
- A/B test service
- Buddy service
- Avatar service
- Achievement service
- Leaderboard service
- Reward service
- Upload service
- Gallery service
- Geo service
- Session service
- Review service
- Cart service
- Catalogue service
- Message service
- Recommender service
- Email service
- Logging service

To register for App42/ShepHertz, visit the following link: https://apphq.shephertz.com/register

The Backend as a Service Options

Here's a screenshot of the App4 sign up screen:

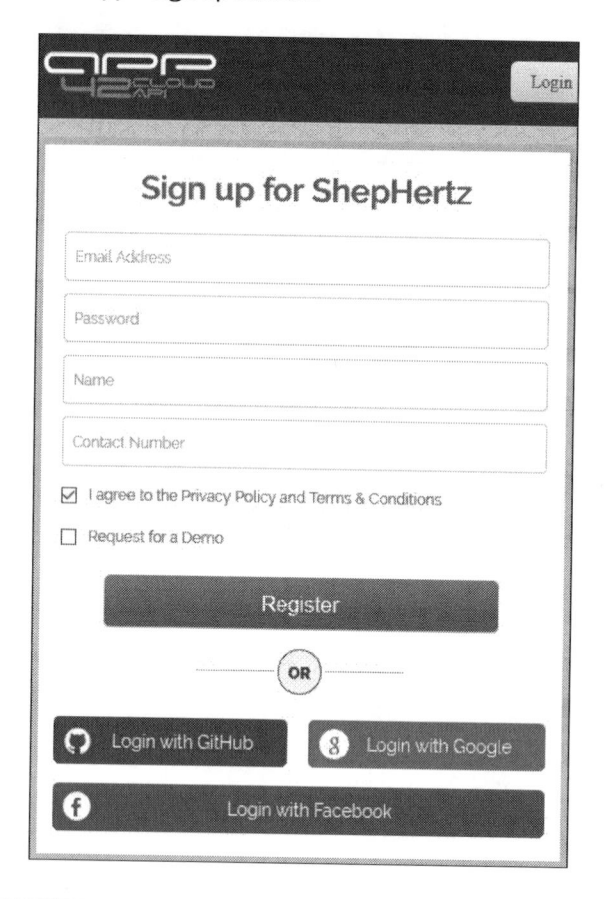

Getting ready

Create a new project in Android Studio and call it `App42`. Use the default **Phone & Tablet** option and select **Empty Activity** when prompted for **Activity Type**.

Download and extract the App42 SDK from the following link:

`https://github.com/shephertz/App42_ANDROID_SDK/archive/master.zip`

After creating your App42 account (see the preceding link), log in to the AppHQ Management Console, and register your app. You will need the ApiKey and SecretKey.

How to do it...

To add support for App42 to your project, start by opening the Android Manifest and following these steps:

1. Add the following permissions:

   ```
   <uses-permission android:name=
       "android.permission.INTERNET"/>
   <uses-permission android:name=
       "android.permission.ACCESS_NETWORK_STATE" />
   ```

2. Open the following folder in your file browser: `<project folder>\App42\app\libs` (if the `libs` folder does not exist, create it) and copy the `App42_ANDROID-CAMPAIGN_x.x.jar` file to the `app\libs` folder.

3. Open the app module's Gradle build file: `build.gradle (Module: app)` and add the following to the `dependencies` section:

   ```
   compile files('libs/App42_ANDROID-CAMPAIGN_x.x.jar')
   ```

4. Open `ActivityMain.java` and add the following import:

   ```
   import com.shephertz.app42.paas.sdk.android.App42API;
   ```

5. Add the following code to the `onCreate()` callback:

   ```
   App42API.initialize(this, "YOUR_API_KEY",
       "YOUR_SECRET_KEY");
   ```

6. You're ready to run the application on a device or emulator.

How it works...

Unfortunately, App42 does not support the Gradle build format, so you need to download the JAR file and copy it to the `\libs` folder manually.

In Step 3, replace `x.x` in `App42_ANDROID-CAMPAIGN_x.x.jar` with the current version number from the file you downloaded.

Replace the `YOUR_API_KEY` and `YOUR_SECRET_KEY` in step 5 with the credentials you received when you registered your application with App42.

The Backend as a Service Options

There's more...

Here's an example of registering a user with the App42 API:

```
UserService userService = App42API.buildUserService();
userService.createUser("userName", "password", "email",
    new App42CallBack() {
    public void onSuccess(Object response) {
        User user = (User)response;
        Log.i("UserService","userName is " + user.getUserName());
        Log.i("UserService", "emailId is " + user.getEmail());
    }
    public void onException(Exception ex) {
        System.out.println("Exception Message"+ex.getMessage());
    }
});
```

See also

- For more information, refer to the App42 web page at http://api.shephertz.com/

Backendless

Besides **MBaaS** (**Mobile Backend as a Service**, as they call it), Backendless offers several other services such as Hosting, API Services, and Marketplace. Their MBaaS features include:

- User management
- Data persistence
- Geolocation
- Media streaming
- Publish/Subscribe messaging
- Push notifications
- Custom business logic
- Analytics
- Mobile code generation

> To sign up for Backendless, follow this link:
> `https://develop.backendless.com/#registration`

Here's a screenshot of the Backendless sign up window:

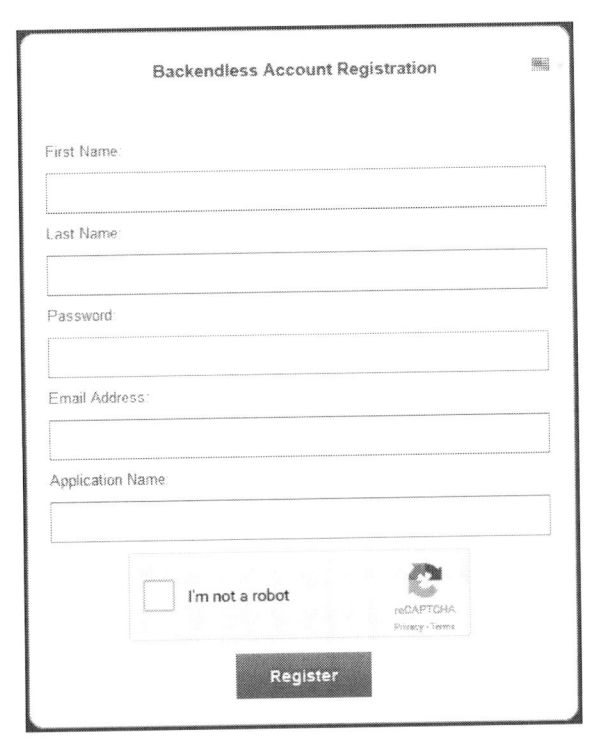

Getting ready

Create a new project in Android Studio and call it `Backendless`. Use the default **Phone & Tablet** options, and select **Empty Activity** when prompted for **Activity Type**.

You will need a **Backendless** account (see the preceding link) and to register your application through their **Backendless** Console. Once you have your App ID and Secret Key, begin the following steps.

The Backend as a Service Options

How to do it...

To add `Backendless` to your project, open the Android Manifest and follow these steps:

1. Add the following permissions:

   ```
   <uses-permission android:name=
        "android.permission.INTERNET"/>
   <uses-permission android:name=
        "android.permission.ACCESS_NETWORK_STATE" />
   ```

2. Open the app module Gradle build file: `build.gradle (Module: app)` and add the following to the `dependencies` section:

   ```
   compile 'com.backendless:android:3.0.3'
   ```

3. Open `ActivityMain.java` and add the following import:

   ```
   import com.backendless.Backendless;
   ```

4. Add the following code to the `onCreate()` callback:

   ```
   String appVersion = "v1";
   Backendless.initApp(
        this, YOUR_APP_ID, YOUR_SECRET_KEY, appVersion);
   ```

5. You're ready to run the application on a device or emulator.

How it works...

Replace `YOUR_APP_ID` and `YOUR_SECRET_KEY` in Step 4 with the credentials you received from the **Backendless** Console.

If you prefer to download the SDK directly instead of using the Maven dependency, it is available here: `https://backendless.com/sdk/java/3.0.0/backendless-sdk-android.zip`.

There's more...

Here's an example of registering a user with the `BackendlessUser` object:

```
BackendlessUser user = new BackendlessUser();
user.setEmail("<user@email>");
user.setPassword("<password>");
Backendless.UserService.register(user, new
     BackendlessCallback<BackendlessUser>() {
     @Override
```

```
public void handleResponse(BackendlessUser backendlessUser) {
    Log.d("Registration", backendlessUser.getEmail() + "
        successfully registered");
}
} );
```

See also

- For more information, refer to the Backendless web page at `https://backendless.com/`

Buddy

Buddy is a bit different than the other BaaS providers in this list as they are heavily focused on connecting devices and sensors. To help maintain privacy regulations, Buddy lets you chose to host your data in the US or EU.

Buddy supports common scenarios like:

- Recording metrics events
- Sending push notifications
- Receiving and securely storing telemetry data
- Storing and managing binary files
- Deep mobile analytics about how customers are using the application
- Integrate device or application data with your company BI systems
- Sandboxed, private data in the geographical location of your choice.

If you'd like to review or contribute to the Buddy SDK, the source is available with the following Git command:

```
git clone https://github.com/BuddyPlatform/Buddy-Android-SDK.git
```

> To sign up for Buddy, follow this link:
> `https://www.buddyplatform.com/Signup`

The Backend as a Service Options

Here's a screenshot of the Buddy sign up:

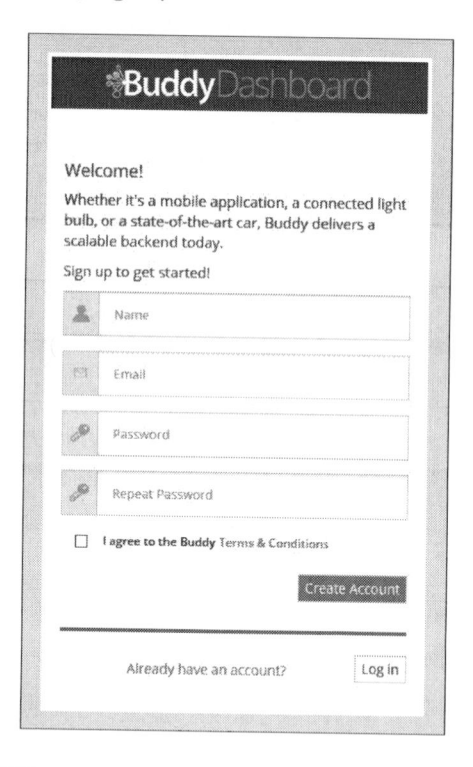

Getting ready

Create a new project in Android Studio and call it `Buddy`. Use the default **Phone & Tablet** options and select **Empty Activity** when prompted for **Activity Type**.

You will need a Buddy account (see the preceding link), and will have to register your application through their Dashboard. Once you have your App ID and App Key, begin the following steps.

How to do it...

To add Buddy to your project, open the Android Manifest and follow these steps:

1. Add the following permissions:

    ```
    <uses-permission android:name=
        "android.permission.INTERNET"/>
    <uses-permission android:name=
        "android.permission.ACCESS_NETWORK_STATE" />
    ```

2. Open the app module Gradle build file: `build.gradle (Module: app)` and add the following to the `dependencies` section:

   ```
   compile 'com.buddy:androidsdk:+'
   ```

3. Open `ActivityMain.java` and add the following import:

   ```
   import com.buddy.sdk.Buddy;
   ```

4. Add the following code to the `onCreate()` callback:

   ```
   Buddy.init(myContext, "appId", "appKey");
   ```

5. You're ready to run the application on a device or emulator.

How it works...

Replace `appId` and `appKey` in Step 4 with the credentials you received from the Buddy Dashboard.

Similar to most of the other BaaS providers, we simply add a reference to the Maven repository to our Gradle build. Then, we add an import and start calling the Buddy APIs.

There's more...

Here's an example of registering a user with Buddy:

```
Buddy.createUser("someUser", "somePassword", null, null, null,
    null, null, null, new BuddyCallback<User>(User.class) {
    @Override
    public void completed(BuddyResult<User> result) {
        if (result.getIsSuccess()) {
            Log.w(APP_LOG, "User created: " +
                result.getResult().userName);
        }
    }
});
```

See also

- For more information, refer to the Buddy web page: https://buddy.com/

The Backend as a Service Options

Firebase

Firebase is a BaaS provider primarily focused on database functionality. While they are not as fully featured as most of the other BaaS providers, they do databases well. They are the only provider on this list with autosyncing database functionality.

Firebase services include:

- Firebase real-time database
- Firebase authentication
- Firebase hosting
- User authentication—e-mail and password, Facebook, Twitter, GitHub, and Google

Since they were recently acquired by Google, you can expect further integration with Google Cloud solutions, as you can see on this link:

`https://cloud.google.com/solutions/mobile/firebase-app-engine-android-studio`

> To sign up with Firebase, visit this link:
> `https://www.firebase.com/login/`

Here's a screenshot of the Firebase sign up window:

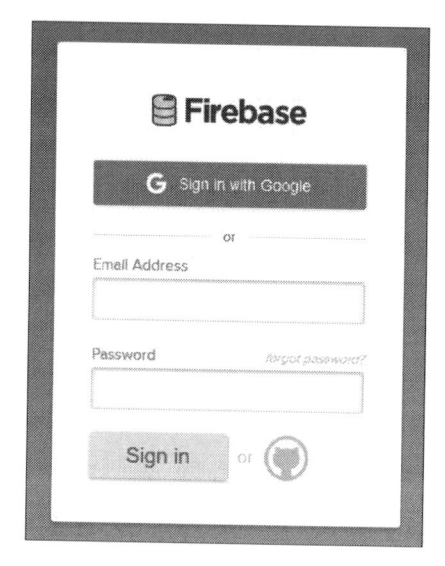

Getting ready

Create a new project in Android Studio and call it `Firebase`. Use the default **Phone & Tablet** options and select **Empty Activity** when prompted for **Activity Type**.

You will need the Firebase URL that is provided when you register your application with Firebase.

How to do it...

To add Firebase to your project, start by opening the Android Manifest and following these steps:

1. Add the following permissions:

   ```
   <uses-permission android:name=
       "android.permission.INTERNET"/>
   ```

2. Open the app module Gradle build file: `build.gradle (Module: app)` and add the following to the `dependencies` section:

   ```
   compile 'com.firebase:firebase-client-android:2.5.0+'
   ```

3. Open `ActivityMain.java` and add the following import:

   ```
   import com.firebase.client.Firebase;
   ```

4. Add the following code to the `onCreate()` callback:

   ```
   Firebase.setAndroidContext(this);
   Firebase firebase = new Firebase("https://<YOUR-FIREBASE-APP>.firebaseio.com/");
   ```

5. You're ready to run the application on a device or emulator.

How it works...

Adding support for Firebase to your application is rather straight forward. Replace the `<YOUR-FIREBASE-APP>` placeholder with the link provided by Firebase when you registered your app.

There's more...

Here's an example of registering a user with Firebase:

```
firebase.createUser("bobtony@firebase.com",
    "correcthorsebatterystaple", new
        Firebase.ValueResultHandler<Map<String, Object>>() {
    @Override
```

The Backend as a Service Options

```
public void onSuccess(Map<String, Object> result) {
    Log.i("Firebase", "Successfully created user account with
        uid: " + result.get("uid"));
}
@Override
public void onError(FirebaseError firebaseError) {
    // there was an error
}
});
```

See also

- For more information, refer to the Firebase web page at `https://www.firebase.com/`

Kinvey

Kinvey is one of the earliest providers to begin offering mobile backend services. Their features include:

- User management
- Data storage
- File storage
- Push notifications
- Social network integration
- Location services
- Lifecycle management
- Versioning

> Sign up for Kinvey at `https://console.kinvey.com/sign-up`.

Here's a screenshot of the Kinvey sign up window:

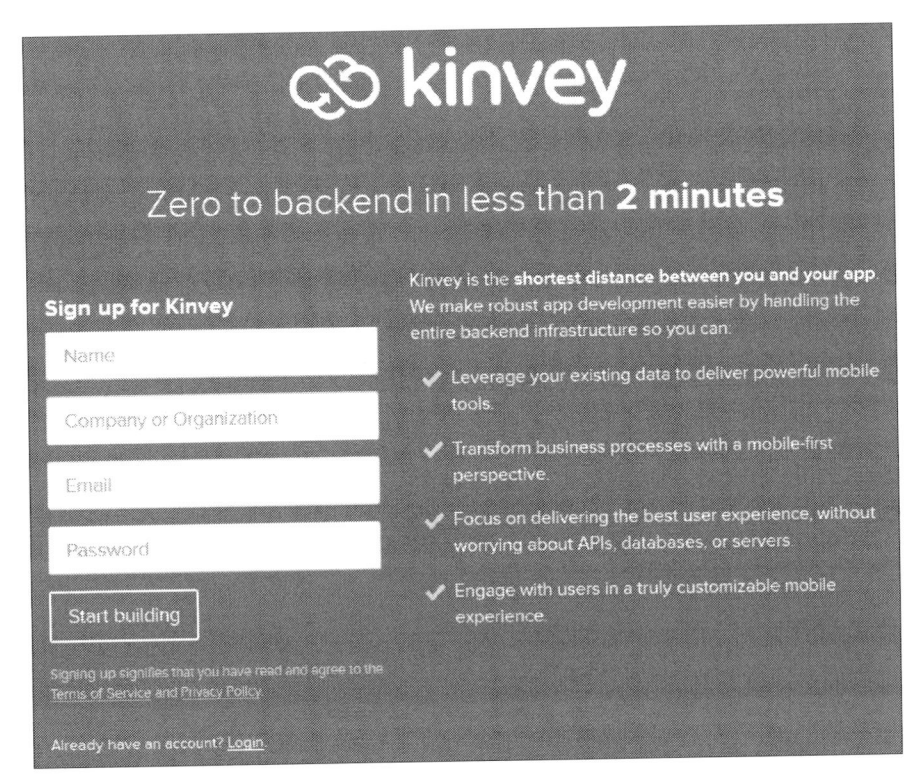

Getting ready

Create a new project in Android Studio and call it `Kinvey`. Use the default **Phone & Tablet** options and select **Empty Activity** when prompted for **Activity Type**.

Download and extract the Kinvey SDK from the following link: `download.kinvey.com/Android/kinvey-android-2.10.5.zip`

You will need a Kinvey account (see the preceding link), and will have to register your application through their developer console. Once you have your App Key and App Secret, begin the following steps.

The Backend as a Service Options

How to do it...

To add Kinvey to your project, follow these steps:

1. Add the following permission to the Android Manifest:

    ```
    <uses-permission android:name=
        "android.permission.INTERNET"/>
    ```

2. Open the following folder in your file browser: `<project folder>\Kinvey\app\libs` (if the `libs` folder does not exist, create it) and copy all the files from the SDK `lib` and `libJar` folders to the `app\libs` folder.

3. Open the app module Gradle build file: `build.gradle (Module: app)` and add the following `repositories` and `dependencies` (leave any existing entries in place):

    ```
    repositories {
        flatDir {
            dirs 'libs'
        }
    }

    dependencies {
        compile fileTree(dir: 'libs', include: ['*.jar'])
        compile(name:'kinvey-android-*', ext:'aar')
    }
    ```

4. Open `MainActivity.java` and add the following import:

    ```
    import com.kinvey.android.Client;
    ```

5. Add the following to the class declarations:

    ```
    final Client mKinveyClient = new mKinveyClient(
        "your_app_key", "your_app_secret",
            this.getApplicationContext()).build();
    ```

6. You're ready to run the application on a device or emulator.

How it works...

Kinvey isn't the easiest of the BaaS to set up as it doesn't offer a simple Gradle dependency. Instead, you need to add their libraries directly to the project libraries as we did in Step 2.

These steps will have the Kinvey client set up and ready to begin adding additional functionality to your application. Just make sure to replace the placeholders in the Kinvey Client Builder with your application credentials.

There's more...

To verify your setup is working correctly, call the following code in the `onCreate()` method or on a button click:

```
mKinveyClient.ping(new KinveyPingCallback() {
    public void onFailure(Throwable t) {
        Log.d("KinveyPingCallback", "Kinvey Ping Failed", t);
    }

    public void onSuccess(Boolean b) {
        Log.d("KinveyPingCallback", "Kinvey Ping Success");
    }
});
```

See also

- For more information, refer to the Kinvey web page at http://www.kinvey.com/

Index

A

About the GCM Connection server web page
  reference link 377
AccelerateInterpolator function 217
action 162
Action Bar
  about 69
  Search, adding to 118-123
  setting, as Overlay 127
activity
  about 1
  data, passing to 10-12
  declaring 2, 3
  launching, menu item used 73
  lifecycle 19-21
  result, returning from 12, 13
  shutting down 23
  starting, with intent object 4-6
  state, saving 14-17
  switching between 6-10
  lifecycle 19-21
activity lifecycle, states
  active 22
  destroyed 22
  paused 22
  stopped 22
Adapters
  using 38-41
ADB
  permissions, granting/revoking through 358
addAction()
  button, adding to notification 179

alarm
  best practices 358
  canceling 362
  features 358
  repeating 362
  scheduling 359-361
  types 359
Alert Dialog
  creating 170-172
  custom layout, creating 173
  icon, adding 172
  list, using 172, 173
Android 6.0 Run-Time permission model 354-357
Android Design Support Library
  reference link 62
Android Developer Menu Resources site
  reference link 74
Android Developer Sensor
  reference link 206
Android Framework
  Drawable Animation 215
  Property Animation 215
  View Animation 215
Android Manifest
  about 3
  OpenGL, declaring in 254
Android Notification Design Guidelines
  reference link 162
Android Open Source Project (AOSP) 319
Android SDK 43, 48
Android SDK bundle
  URL 2

Android Sensor Framework
  events, using 206-208
  using 202-205
Android Studio
  mock location, setting in 339
Android Universal Image Loader 221
Android Universal Image Loader page
  reference link 221
Android ViewPager Documentation
  reference link 236
android.webkit
  reference link 315
Animation resources web page
  reference link 226
animations 215
app
  Google sign-in, adding to 377-380
  speech recognition, adding to 368-370
App42
  about 384
  adding, to project 387
  reference link 388
  reference link, for registration 385
  sign up screen 386
  working 387
App42 Android SDK
  supported services 385
App42 API
  user, registering with 388
app full screen
  displaying 123-125
application
  web page, displaying in 312-314
  attributes, reference link 3
Application Not Responding (ANR) 221, 364
AppWidgetProvider class
  methods 111
app widgets 47
asset files 142
AsyncTask
  parameters 367
  process flow 367
  using, for background work 364-366

attributes, Home screen widget 111
attributes, RelativeLayout 29
audio
  playing, with MediaPlayer 274-277
AudioManager
  URL 274, 278
available space
  checking 141

B

Backend as a Service (BaaS) 383, 384
Backendless
  adding, to project 390
  reference link 391
  reference link, for registration 388
  sign up window 389
  working 390
BackendlessUser object
  user, registering with 390
background
  music, playing in 277
background work
  AsyncTask, using for 364-366
back stack 9
Buddy
  about 391
  adding, to project 392
  reference link 393
  reference link, for registration 391
  sign up page 392
  supported common scenarios 391
  user, registering with 393
  working 393
built-in zoom
  enabling 315
button state
  displaying, graphics used 52-54

C

cache files 137
Call State events
  monitoring 303
Camera2 (new) API
  picture, taking with 290-296

Camera API
  camera parameters, setting 289
  image, capturing 297
  preview, setting up 297
Camera API (old)
  picture, taking with 285-288
camera view
  applying, while drawing 261-263
canvas 58
Card Flip Animation
  creating, with Fragments 236-242
click events
  listening for 192-194
client authentication
  reference link 381
common gestures
  recognizing 194-196
Compass
  creating, RotateAnimation used 227-231
  creating, sensor data used 227-231
compound control 59
Configuration Developer Link
  reference link 213
connection type
  checking 315-317
ConnectivityManager
  network state changes, monitoring 317, 318
  reference link 318
content provider
  reference link 159
Contextual Action Bar (CAB) 78
Contextual Action Mode
  about 69
  enabling, for view 78-81
Contextual Batch Mode
  using, with ListView 82-85
Current Device Rotation
  obtaining 212
custom component
  creating 57, 58
custom layout
  used, for creating Toast 166-170
Custom Transition
  Zoom Animation, creating with 243-248

D

data
  accessing, in background 154-159
  passing, between Fragments 98-107
  passing, to activities 10-12
database
  upgrading 154
default animation duration
  obtaining 249
default camera app
  photo, taking with 282, 283
default video app
  calling 284
designated folders
  using, for screen-specific resources 54
device boot
  notification, receiving of 362-364
device orientation
  reading 210-212
directories
  working with 141
Display Developer Link
  reference link 213
DownloadManager
  reference link 323
drawable 54
Drawable Animation 215

E

Eclipse ADT solution 2
emulator
  locations, simulating with 339
environment sensors 208
expanded notifications 180
external storage
  about 130
  text file, reading from 137-140
  text file, writing to 137-140

F

file
  deleting 141
  preventing, from being included in
      galleries 141

Firebase
  about 394
  adding, to project 395
  reference link 396
  reference link, for registration 394
  services 394
  sign up window 395
  user, registering with 395
  working 395

Flashlight
  making, with Heads-Up Notification 186-190

Floating Context Menu
  creating 78

Fragment
  adding, during runtime 94-97
  Card Flip Animation, creating with 236-242
  creating 92-94
  data, passing between 98-107
  main callbacks 92
  removing, during runtime 94-97
  using 92-94

Fragment classes
  DialogFragment 92
  ListFragment 92
  PreferenceFragment 92

fragment shader 256

FusedLocationProviderApi interface
  reference link 340

G

GCM
  components 371

Geofence
  creating 347-352
  monitoring 347-352
  properties 346

Geofence.Builder class
  reference link 352

GeofencingRequest.Builder class
  reference link 352

getOrientation() Developer Document
  reference link 231

GLSurfaceView class
  extending 254
  shapes, drawing on 255-260

Google APIs
  about 333
  reference link 342

Google Cloud Messaging (GCM) 354

Google Cloud solutions
  reference link 394

Google Play Services
  reference link 340

Google sign-in
  adding, to app 377-380

graphics
  used, for displaying button state 52-54

GridLayout
  using 33-36

GridView
  using 38-41

H

hardware media controls
  responding to 278-280

hardware volume keys
  used, for controlling app's audio volume 278

Heads-Up Notification
  Flashlight, making with 186-190

Hierarchy Viewer
  about 43
  layout, optimizing with 42-46

Home screen widget
  attributes 111
  creating 110-116
  shortcut, creating on 108-110

HttpURLConnection
  reference link 323

I

image
  requesting, Volley used 328-330

ImageLoader, Volley
  using 331

ImageView 79

Immersive Mode 123, 124

inheritance 61

Integer Resource Type web page
  reference link 243

intent object
  about 2
  activities, starting with 4-6
internal storage
  about 130
  text file, reading from 134-136
  text file, writing to 134-136
Interpolator Developer Document
  reference link 249
Interpolators 217

J

JavaScript
  enabling 315
JSON
  URL 328
JSON response
  requesting, Volley used 326-328

K

Kinvey
  about 396
  adding, to project 398
  features 396
  reference link 399
  reference link, for registration 396
  sign up window 397
  working 398
Kinvey SDK
  download link 397

L

large images
  scaling down, to avoid Out of Memory exceptions 217-220
last location
  obtaining 335-338
layout
  about 25
  defining 26, 27
  differences 37
  inflating 26, 27
  optimizing, with Hierarchy Viewer 42-46
  similarities 37
  widgets, inserting into 49-51

layout, inflating
  draw 42
  layout 42
  measure 42
layout properties
  modifying, during runtime 41, 42
lights 162
LinearLayout
  example 30
  using 30, 32
ListView
  Contextual Batch Mode, using with 82-85
  using 38-41
Loader
  data, accessing in background 154-159
Localization Resources 381
locations
  simulating, with emulator 339
  updates, receiving 343-345
  updates, stop receiving 346
lock screen notifications 181
long-press events
  listening for 192-194
LruCache
  reference link 332

M

main callbacks, Fragment
  onActivityCreated() 92
  onAttach() 92
  onCreate() 92
  onCreateView() 92
  onDestroyView() 92
  onDetach() 92
  onPause() 92
  onResume() 92
  onStart() 92
  onStop() 92
MediaPlayer
  about 269
  audio, playing with 274-277
  notification, creating 182-184
  supported audio files 274
  supported file types 274
  supported media sources 274
  URL 278

media scanner 141
MediaSession
  reference link 185
  URL 281
MediaSessionCompat
  URL 281
Menu API 69
menu item
  grouping 74
  modifying, during runtime 75-77
  used, for launching activity 73
menus
  modifying, during runtime 75-77
methods, AppWidgetProvider class
  onAppWidgetOptionsChanged() 111
  onDeleted() 111
  onDisabled() 112
  onEnabled() 112
  onReceive() 112
  onUpdate() 111
Mobile Backend as a Service (MBaaS)
  about 388
  features 388
mock location
  setting, in Android Studio 339
motion sensors 209
multipart messages 307
multiple preference file
  using 19
music
  playing, in background 277

N

NetworkImageView, Volley
  using 331
NetworkInfo
  reference link 318
notification
  receiving, of device boot 362-364

O

onDraw() 57
online status
  checking 315-317
onLocationChanged
  reference link 346

onMeasure() 57
onRestoreInstanceState() callback 17
OpenGL
  declaring, in Android Manifest 254
  reference link 268
  rendered class, creating 255
  versions 252
OpenGL Shading Language
    (OpenGLSL) 256, 260
Open Graphics Library for Embedded Systems.
    (OpenGL ES)
  about 251
  environment, setting up 252, 253
  reference link 268
Options menu
  creating 70-72
Overlay
  Action Bar, setting as 127

P

page navigation
  controlling 314
PDU (Protocol Data Unit)
  reference link 312
permissions
  granting, through ADB 358
  revoking, through ADB 358
persistent activity data
  storing 18
phone call
  making 300, 301
phone call events
  monitoring 302, 303
PhoneStateListener
  reference link 304
photo
  taking, with default camera app 282, 283
Picasso
  about 221
  reference link 221
picture
  taking, with Camera2 (new) API 290-296
  taking, with (old) Camera API 285-288
pinch-to-zoom, with multi-touch
    gestures 197, 198

PlaybackState
　URL 281
pop-up menu
　about 69
　creating 86-89
pop-up message 14
position sensors 209
problems
　resolving, reported with GoogleApiClient OnConnectionFailedListener 340-342
progress dialog
　displaying 173-176
ProgressDialog
　about 173
　settings 176
projection
　applying, while drawing 261-263
properties, Geofence
　expiration 346
　location 346
　loitering delay 346
　radius 346
　transition type 347
Property Animation 215
Property Animation system 216
public folders
　obtaining 141
Push Notification, with GCM 371-376

R

raw files 142
RelativeLayout
　attributes 29
　using 28, 29
Request Code 14
resource files
　using 142-146
resource identifiers
　reference link 55
resource selection 63
result
　returning, from activities 12, 13
RotateAnimation
　used, for creating Compass 227-231

RotateAnimation Developer Document
　reference link 231
rotation
　triangle, moving with 263-265
runtime
　widgets, creating at 55, 56

S

screen-specific resources
　designated folders, using for 54
SDK Packages, Android
　reference link 334
Search
　adding, to Action Bar 118-122
sensor data
　reading 206-208
　used, for creating Compass 227-231
services 2
Setup Wizard
　creating, ViewPager used 236
shapes
　drawing, on GLSurfaceView 255-260
ShepHertz
　reference link, for registration 385
shortcut
　creating, on Home screen 108-110
　removing 110
Short Message Service
　reference link 308
simple data
　storing 130-133
slideshow
　creating, with ViewPager 232-236
SmsManager
　reference link 312
SMS messages
　delivery status notification 307
　reading 311, 312
　receiving 308-311
　sending 304-306
sound effects
　playing, with SoundPool 270-273
SoundPool
　about 269
　sound effects, playing with 270-273
　URL 274

speech recognition
  adding, to app 368-370
SQLite database
  creating 147-153
  using 147-153
state selector 52
static Fragment 94
Sticky Immersion 126
style
  about 59
  applying, to view 59, 61
  turning, into theme 62
sub menus
  creating 73
Swipe-to-Refresh functionality
  adding 200-202
System UI
  dimming 126

T

TableLayout
  using 33-36
tables
  creating 33-36
tap gestures
  recognizing 194-196
task
  canceling 367
text file
  reading, from external storage 137-140
  reading, from internal storage 134-136
  writing, to external storage 137-140
  writing, to internal storage 134-136
textViewStyle item 61
theme
  about 48
  selecting, based on Android version 63-66
  style, turning into 62
Toast
  about 51
  creating, custom layout used 166-170
Toast object 14
transition animation
  applying 223-225
  built-in animations 222
  ending scene, defining 225

group-level animations 222
lifecycle callbacks 222
resource file support 222
starting scene, creating 222-225
transition-based animation 222
transition, creating 222-225
transition, starting 222-225
Transition Framework
  about 222
  limitations 222
transitions
  AutoTransition (default transition) 222
  ChangeBounds 222
  Fade 222
translucent system bars 127
triangle
  moving, with rotation 263-265
  rotating, with user input 265-268

U

Unreal Engine
  reference link 268
Unreal Engine 4
  about 268
  reference link 268
user
  attention, obtaining 163-166
  registering, with App42 API 388
  registering, with BackendlessUser object 390
  registering, with Buddy 393
  registering, with Firebase 395
  triangle, rotating with 265-268

V

Version Control Software (VCS) 319
vertex shader 256
vibrate option
  using 176-178
view
  Contextual Action Mode, enabling for 78-81
  style, applying to 59-61
View Animation
  about 215
  demonstrating 216
  drawbacks 216

View object
  reference link 59
ViewPager
  slideshow, creating with 232-236
  used, for creating Setup Wizard 236
Volley
  about 221
  for Internet requests 318-323
  reference link 323
  request types 319
  used, for requesting image 328, 329
  used, for requesting JSON response 326-328
Volley Request
  creating 324-326
Volley Singleton
  creating 330

W

web page
  displaying, in application 312-314
WebSettings
  reference link 315
WebView
  reference link 315
widgets
  about 47
  creating, at runtime 55, 56
  inserting, into layout 49-51

Z

Zoom Animation
  creating, with Custom Transition 243-248

Made in the USA
Lexington, KY
14 April 2016